D1103813

Development Theory and the Economics of Growth

Development and Inequality in the Market Economy

The purpose of this series is to encourage and foster analytical and policy-oriented work on market-based reform in developing and postsocialist countries. Special attention will be devoted in the series to exploring the effects of free market policies on social inequality and sustainable growth and development.

Editor:
Andrés Solimano

Editorial Board:
Alice Amsden
François Bourguignon
William Easterly
Patricio Meller
Vito Tanzi
Lance Taylor

Titles in the Series:

Andrés Solimano, Editor. *Road Maps to Prosperity: Essays on Growth and Development*

Andrés Solimano, Editor. *Social Inequality: Values, Growth, and the State*

Lance Taylor, Editor. *After Neoliberalism: What Next for Latin America?*

Andrés Solimano, Eduardo Aninat, and Nancy Birdsall, Editors. *Distributive Justice and Economic Development: The Case of Chile and Developing Countries*

Jaime Ros. *Development Theory and the Economics of Growth*

Felipe Larraín B., Editor. *Capital Flows, Capital Controls, and Currency Crises: Latin America in the 1990s*

Development Theory and the Economics of Growth

Jaime Ros

Ann Arbor

THE UNIVERSITY OF MICHIGAN PRESS

2003   2002   2001   2000   4   3   2   1

*A CIP catalog record for this book is available
from the British Library.*

Library of Congress Cataloging-in-Publication Data

Ros, Jaime.
    Development theory and the economics of growth / Jaime Ros.
        p. cm. — (Development and inequality in the market economy)
    Includes bibliographical references and index.
    ISBN 0-472-11141-8 (cloth : alk. paper)
        1. Development economics.   2. Economic development.   I. Title.
    II. Series

    HD75 .R67 2000
    338.9 — dc21   00-037741

To Adriana

Contents

Figures

Tables

Preface

If modern technology has shown the potential to raise living standards to first-world levels, why is it that the vast majority of the world's population lives in poverty in underdeveloped countries? The contemporary economics of growth is far from having convincing answers to this and other central questions about underdevelopment and growth. The views that emerge from current growth theory on the nature of underdevelopment — as a dearth of physical capital, a lack of human capital, or technological backwardness — are unsatisfactory and at best incomplete. This book argues that classical development theory, which grew out of a reflection on underdevelopment as a paradoxical situation involving low wages together with low rates of return to capital, has much to contribute to overcoming the shortcomings of contemporary approaches. Those early theoretical insights and contributions relied on a paradigm of increasing returns to scale, imperfect competition, and elastic labor supplies that was later abandoned, without good analytical reasons, in the mainstream of the economics profession.

The situation described motivates this book, which blends recent developments in growth theory with earlier seminal contributions to development economics. The professional economist and researcher will find in it an original thesis concerning the contribution that classical development theory can make to the research program of modern growth economics. Graduate and advanced undergraduate students in economics will find a balanced theoretical treatment and an empirical assessment of new and earlier approaches to economic growth and development.

The book is at the intersection of my teaching activity and research interests over the past decade. It grew out of lecture notes from my graduate courses on development economics and macroeconomic theory at the University of Notre Dame and a longtime interest in classical development economics and the growth performance of developing countries in the postwar period. While the book has had a rather long gestation period, it is only over the past three years that this old project took its present shape. In particular, in 1997 a Residential Fellowship from the Helen Kellogg Institute at Notre Dame and a sabbatical leave

from the Economics Department allowed me to make substantial progress toward the completion of this project.

I am grateful to the many graduate students who provided feedback
on my courses. Special thanks are due to two former students. Maiju
Perala provided excellent and enthusiastic research assistance, and
Katarina Keller acted as a critical potential consumer of the book, giving
valuable editing advice on all of its chapters.

Peter Skott provided thoughtful and constructive comments on every aspect of the book, and several other colleagues commented on all
or parts of it. I am indebted to Ernie Bartell, Amitava Dutt, Carlos
Ibarra, Julio López, Nora Lustig, José Molinas, Jorn Rattso, and Lance
Taylor for their comments and the many suggestions for improvement
that were provided. The book also benefited from comments by partici-
pants in seminars and lecture series at Notre Dame, the Centro de
Investigación y Docencia Económicas (CIDE) in Mexico City, the 1997
meeting of the Latin American and Caribbean Economics Association
(LACEA) in Mexico City, the Universidad Católica del Perú in Lima,
the Universidad de Montevideo, and the Economic Commission for
Latin America and the Caribbean in Santiago de Chile. I am grateful to
Ernie Bartell and Guillermo O'Donnell as former directors of the
Kellogg Institute and to Scott Mainwaring as its present director for
their encouragement and support. My thanks go also to the staff of the
Kellogg Institute for a supportive environment that made the conclusion
of this project possible.

Introduction

One way to describe this book is as a collection of essays "trespassing" between two disciplines: development economics and growth theory. This way of stating it immediately raises a puzzle that motivates the book. For, as most external observers would probably agree, these two fields should be one and the same, with no need for trespassing at all. At least, they should be interacting closely. The trouble is, of course, that they are not. Growth theory and development economics have for a long time been distant cousins, and occasionally they are even hostile. Most of this introduction is about why this is so. The rest of the book is an effort to show why they should be interacting more closely: many insights of development economics are not only very valuable but can be made perfectly intelligible to researchers working on the economics of growth, and some of the formal contributions of orthodox growth theory can be put to good use in clarifying unsettled (and sometimes obscurely formulated) issues in development theory.

In recent years, after two decades of quasi-inactivity in the field, the economics of growth has again become the subject of intense theoretical and empirical research. This renewed effort has taken two directions. Some have adapted and extended the neoclassical growth model as formalized by Robert Solow (1956) and others in the mid-1950s, while retaining the assumptions of constant returns to scale and exogenous technical progress. Others have taken more radical departures from the neoclassical model by bringing in increasing returns to scale and attempting to model technological change. This last is the new brand of endogenous growth theory. In both cases, and this is perhaps the most novel feature of the reawakened field, these efforts try to explain the process of economic growth in developed and developing countries alike within a unified analytical framework. Important questions such as why some nations are poorer than others and why the economies of some countries grow so much faster than others are now at the center of the research agenda of mainstream growth theory.

This contemporary revival of growth economics, or at least most of it, has proceeded on the rather astonishing premise that before the mid-1980s the only answers to those questions were to be found in the neoclassical growth model. The premise is astonishing for at least two reasons. First, some 50 years ago a then new field of economic theory emerged aiming to answer similar questions, address issues about the persistence of underdevelopment, and search for the means with which to overcome poverty. The nature of the issues addressed by the pioneers of development economics — Rosenstein-Rodan, Nurkse, Prebisch, Hirschman, and Leibenstein among others — forced the new field to rely on a paradigm built upon notions of imperfect competition, increasing returns, and labor surpluses, which today are used extensively but were then poorly integrated, or altogether alien, to the established body of economic theory.

Second, and somewhat ironically, the Solow model was not primarily meant to answer such questions but rather to provide a solution to some difficulties in growth theory at the time (the adjustment of the warranted to the natural rate of growth in the Harrod-Domar model). Having the neoclassical growth model explain differences in income levels and growth rates across countries requires a number of additional assumptions that Solow himself probably did not have in mind: in a nutshell, that countries differ only (in ways relevant to growth) in their capital-labor ratios, savings rates, and population growth rates.

This is perhaps one reason why development economics had taken a distinctive approach a decade before the rise to dominance of the neoclassical growth theory. Whether one could make fruitful empirical generalizations about the economic experience of developing countries or not, it was clear that the stylized facts on which traditional growth theory focused — with its emphasis on the stability of the capital-output ratio, savings rates, and income shares — had little relevance to the experience of developing countries. Lewis (1954), for example, had tried to account for the trend increase, rather than the stability, of saving and investment rates in the course of economic development. Given its purposes, growth theory tended to adopt a very high level of aggregation, often an economy with one sector producing one good. The striking and persistent presence of dualism (technological and organizational) in underdeveloped countries led development economics to operate at a lower level of aggregation, with at least two sectors using different technologies.

Growth theory soon became concentrated on the analysis of steady states in which most or all economic variables expand at the same rate. Because this analysis did not fit well the experience of developing countries, development theory had to focus instead on disequilibrium states and the process of transition from one steady state to the other. As Rosenstein-Rodan (1984, 207–8) argued: ". . . an analysis of the disequilibrium growth process is what is essential for understanding economic development problems. The *Economic Journal* article of 1943 attempted to study the dynamic path towards equilibrium, not merely the conditions which must be satisfied at the point of equilibrium."

This does not mean that development theory was uninterested in steady states. It became concerned, however, with a particular kind of steady state quite alien to conventional growth theory: low-level equilibrium traps, which are, as the name suggests, equilibria that are locally stable (small departures from it generate forces that bring the economy back to the equilibrium state) but globally unstable, so that large shocks can cause a cumulative departure from the original equilibrium. Leibenstein (1957, 187), for example, stated: "The crucial aspects of our theory has to do with an explanation of why the subsistence equilibrium state should possess stability in the small but not in the large."

This leads us finally to an important aspect. To the pioneers of development theory, underdevelopment appeared to be a situation characterized by a lack of capital — which was consistent with labor receiving lower wages than in developed countries — but also by a low rate of return to capital. For Nurkse (1953, 1), for example, the scarcity of capital was "at the very centre of the problem of development in economically backward countries. The so-called 'underdeveloped' areas, as compared with the advanced, are underequipped with capital in relation to their population and natural resources." This lack of capital resulted from a low capacity to save, given the low level of real income, but also from the "weakness of investment incentives" that had its source in a low rate of return to capital (chap. 1). The paradox of both capital and labor receiving lower returns, and the surprising conclusion that the lack of capital may have to be attributed to a low profit rate, understandably led to the search for a novel analytical framework, as anyone familiar with the modern controversies over neoclassical growth theory would probably agree.

This approach generated a model, or rather a set of economic growth models, that departs in two ways from the early neoclassical approach to growth theory.[1] The first difference refers to increasing returns to scale and the associated technological and pecuniary externalities. In his 1943 article on the problem of industrialization in Eastern and Southeastern Europe, and in later contributions, Rosenstein-Rodan was probably the economist who departed most radically from traditional theory in this respect. Nurkse, drawing on Adam Smith and Allyn Young, stressed in turn the role of income effects associated with increasing returns.

The second departure refers to an elastic labor supply arising from the presence of a labor surplus. Early views on underdevelopment as a situation characterized by a small capital endowment in relation to available labor supplies led to the conclusion that the elasticity of the labor supply under these conditions was likely to be higher than in developed economies that have much higher capital endowments per worker. With a low aggregate capital-labor ratio, the marginal product of labor at full employment in the capital-using sector would be so low that a fraction of the labor force would remain employed in a noncapitalist or subsistence sector, using technologies with negligible capital intensity. Lewis was the economist who developed and emphasized the labor surplus assumption.

These two ingredients — increasing returns and labor surplus — were present from the "beginning" in Rosenstein-Rodan (1943), as he rightly claimed (Rosenstein-Rodan 1984).[2] A moderate dose of increasing returns and an elastic labor supply can together generate multiple equilibria so that, depending on initial conditions, the economy can get stuck in a development trap. This was not the only development trap model in the early literature, but it is, as this book will argue, the most interesting and relevant one for the present state of growth theory.

Aim and Scope

Modern Growth Theory and Classical Development Economics

The book develops four major themes. The first is the relation between modern growth theory and classical development economics (chaps. 2 through 6). Just as development theory did several decades ago, recent endogenous growth theory has departed from the old neoclassical theory in various ways. Yet, as indicated, the recent wave of theoretical and empirical research on economic growth has generally ignored the earlier contributions of development theory.[3] I shall argue that this neglect is one reason why the lively controversies on convergence, technical progress, and increasing returns that have developed between followers of the Solow model and endogenous growth theorists appear at times to be in a dead end, confused by an all-or-nothing situation involving the assumptions of constant returns to scale and the dramatically increasing returns to scale involved in the assumption of constant (or increasing) returns to capital.

This debate appears to have missed a simple implication of early development theory: that a moderate dose of increasing returns to scale combined with the presence of a labor surplus can make a dramatic difference in the neoclassical model, a difference that modifies its transitional dynamics in a way that can overcome the long recognized empirical shortcomings of the Solow model[4] while at the same time being free from some of the theoretical and empirical objections that have been raised against the new brand of endogenous growth models. As a result, I shall argue, the key contributions of classical development economics provide an approach to the problem of economic development that is more general and more promising empirically than those adopted in either old or new growth theory.

The corollary of this argument is that it may be essential to draw much more heavily on the very rich past of development theory if the ongoing research effort is to tackle satisfactorily the formidable task that it has set for itself. At the same time, new growth theory yields other insights, such as the importance of human capital accumulation and endogenous technological change to growth as well as the adverse effects of inequality on growth, areas from which development economics can benefit. I shall explore the possibility of cross-fertilization and attempt to combine the contributions of development theory with these recent developments.

In doing so, we shall neglect neo-Schumpeterian growth models.[5] While extremely interesting, this line of research appears to be less relevant to the development problems of developing countries than to those of advanced industrial economies. In the context of developing economies, the neoclassical assumption of exogenous technical progress — in the sense of an external increase in the stock of knowledge — is less disturbing than when the objective is to explain the growth process in developed economies. This is partly because the interactions between growth and technical progress are greater in advanced economies, where most technological innovations take place and are first introduced. Moreover, one can safely assume that developing countries are generally off their long-run steady state position. As a result, a lot more remains to be explained in the case of developing countries once we have set aside the interactions between growth and technical progress. Even then, and even if we can appropriately take the growth in the "stock of knowledge" as exogenous in the case of developing countries, the rate of adoption of new knowledge is not exogenous and many of the intervening factors will often be neglected in our analysis. The development model with skill acquisition presented in chapter 6 contributes to filling this gap, but much remains to be done in the future.

The Scope of Classical Development Economics

A second theme refers to the scope of early writing on development theory. I shall argue that this analytical framework can help us think about a much wider variety of development problems than those to which it was originally applied. Development traps can arise under a broad set of circumstances involving increasing returns, demand elasticities, and factor supply elasticities. These circumstances are not confined to low levels of economic development. Because the slow rate of accumulation in the trap is due to a low rate of return to capital, the approach has greater generality than other poverty trap models, which rely, for example, on vicious circles between income and savings or population growth. The framework can be fruitfully applied to any situation in which a combination of demand and factor supply elasticities together with a dose of increasing returns in new industries interact to hold back the "inducement to invest."

Moreover, these circumstances are not confined to a closed system. Although sometimes formulated or illustrated with a closed economy, the argument survives the extension to the case of an open economy. Interestingly, opening the economy to trade and capital movements introduces important differences and modifies policy implications but does not make the underlying coordination problems less important. Coordination failures are likely to emerge, in particular, in the transition from old to new patterns of production and trade specialization. Arguably, this situation is characteristic of a number of semi-industrial "sandwich economies" in which old comparative advantages in labor-intensive industries are being eroded and the new ones in capital- and technology-intensive activities are only slowly emerging. Thus, in contrast to the counterrevolution[6] in development theory, which denied the usefulness of the approach for the small open economy of a "typical" developing country, we shall argue that it can be fruitfully applied to the development problems of open economies (chaps. 7 through 10).[7]

In fact, it is when it is applied to the interpretation of postwar development experience that the approach taken by early development theory shows its greatest strengths and most useful insights. From this perspective, we can view the staggering success stories of East Asia's industrialization (and, to a lesser extent, of a few Latin American countries for some time before the 1980s) as a succession of policy interventions that accelerated the transition between different patterns of production and trade specialization. It is difficult to see how a primarily market-driven development model that inspires many of today's policy recommendations to developing countries could have "traversed" those transitions so successfully. This is not because market-based successes have been entirely absent (this is very debatable). It is hard to see simply because sound theory suggests exactly the opposite: that market forces are unlikely to address effectively (or at least efficiently) the coordination problems of the transition. Chapter 9 provides the theoretical basis as well as empirical support for this assertion.

The extension of the analysis to open economy issues addresses also the role of some neglected factors in cross-country growth analysis, such

as the pattern of trade specialization, as determined by industrial policies and natural resource endowments, and that of uneven development
in the world economy. Again, special attention is given to how earlier
contributions — such as Graham's model of trade protection under increasing returns, Lewis's model of "tropical trade," or Prebisch's insights on uneven development in the international economy — can illumi-
nate frequently addressed questions.

Development Economics and the Economics of Development Theory

A third theme is the relationship of early development theory to development economics as it evolved after the neoclassical resurgence of the
1960s. The reaction of many second and third generations of development economists to the counterrevolution was to emphasize demand
rigidities, inelastic supplies determined by technological rigidities or
nonoptimizing agents, and effective demand failures, all of which were
supposedly pervasive in developing countries. Yet these were not the
departures that, in my view, make the development models of early
development theory an alternative approach to current growth theory.
Nor were these the aspects emphasized by the pioneers.[8] Development
economics was "born macro," as Taylor and Arida (1988) phrased it in
their survey of development theories, but it was not born Keynesian or
structuralist. In Lewis's view, "from the point of view of countries with
surplus labor, Keynesianism is only a footnote to neo-classicism — albeit
a long, important and fascinating footnote" (1954, 140). Nurkse was
more blunt:

> We are here in the classical world of Say's law. In underdeveloped
> areas there is generally no "deflationary gap" through excessive sav-
> ings. Production creates its own demand, and the size of the market
> depends on the volume of production. In the last analysis, the market
> can be enlarged only through an all-round increase in productivity.
> Capacity to buy means capacity to produce. (1953, 8–9)

We need not take these warnings against the "Keynesian temptation"
of development economics too literally to recognize that, no matter how
valid Keynes's insights and later contributions to development
macroeconomics based on them were, the development problems on
which Rosenstein-Rodan, Nurkse, and Lewis focused would remain even
if Keynesian problems were successfully overcome. Increasing returns to
scale are essential to the development problem and irrelevant to the
Keynesian argument. Despite some similarities — such as the presence of

an elastic labor supply, which, however, need not arise, as in Keynes, from a low level of resource utilization—we should not confuse these development problems with the effective demand problems on which Keynes focused. Not much is lost, for example, by assuming Say's law when looking at income differences across countries: as briefly discussed in chapter 1, differences in resource utilization account for a very small fraction of the large gaps in income per capita across the world.

In the case of differences in growth performance, which approach to take depends on the particular questions one is seeking to answer. Keynesian economics seems to have little to say about why Europe and Japan grew faster than the United States in the postwar period or why the East Asian newly industrializing countries (NICs) grew faster than the Latin American countries during the 1960s and 1970s. Yet economies depart from the factor accumulation path, sometimes for prolonged periods of time, and Keynesian problems and structural constraints are not always successfully overcome. Abandoning Say's law seems essential, I shall argue, in understanding why Latin America grew so little in the 1980s compared to its long-run performance, just as it is essential to understanding the poor performance of the U.S. economy during the interwar period or that of the Japanese economy in the 1990s.

There are thus a number of situations (in developing and developed countries alike) in which medium- or even long-term growth performance cannot be properly explained if one remains strictly within the framework of the early development theorists. This was well recognized by the later structuralist contributions to development economics. The neglect of effective demand failures and structural constraints, while in the spirit of early development theory, can therefore be an important limitation under some circumstances, and the last two chapters are devoted to remedying this neglect. These chapters focus on Kalecki's dual economy model and the contributions of two- and three-gap models to the analysis of the growth performance of economies operating under foreign exchange and fiscal constraints.

Resource Reallocation, Factor Accumulation, and Growth

A fourth theme runs through the whole book and refers to the links between resource reallocation, factor accumulation, and technological change. The traditional division between the "static" analysis of resource allocation and the "dynamic" analysis of growth, as well as the analysis of growth as the outcome of two separate forces, factor accumulation and technical progress, become too artificial in the presence of increasing returns. A reallocation of resources (toward or away from the activities affected by increasing returns) may then have long-lasting effects on growth, and growth itself has to be seen as a process of resource reallocation rather than of mere factor accumulation-cum-technical change.

Moreover, as Kaldor and others argued, the distinction between movements along a production function and technical progress (shifts of the production function) becomes blurred under increasing returns to scale. With the expansion of output, more capital-intensive (or "roundabout") methods of production become profitable and are adopted. This is so whether these techniques were already known, and not used because they were unprofitable at a lower scale of output, or are truly new and become part of the stock of knowledge as the incentives for their invention appear with the expansion of the market. In developing economies, unlike those of developed countries, these technical changes mostly result from the adoption of technologies that were known elsewhere. From this perspective, they constitute a movement along a production function. Yet their adoption, unlike the typical movement along a production function, is not the consequence of a change in factor prices leading to the substitution of capital for labor but rather the result of these more capital-intensive techniques becoming profitable as the scale of output increases.

The links among resource reallocation, factor accumulation, and technological change are evident in the process of economic growth over the last two centuries. This process has been marked by industrialization, understood as the expansion of the range of goods produced under increasing returns, and the simultaneous sharp increase in the capital-labor ratio. These two aspects, which chapter 1 highlights in the context of the postwar experience, are intimately connected. Paraphrasing Allyn Young (1928), the division of a group of complex processes into a succession of simpler processes, which is made economical by the expansion of output in the presence of increasing returns, lends itself to the use of "roundabout" methods of production that imply the use of more capital in relation to labor.[9]

This approach to growth as resource reallocation was present in classical development economics.[10] The approach faded away, at least in the more theoretically oriented literature, with the triumph of the counterrevolution in development theory that has dominated the field since the mid-1960s. The neoclassical resurgence brought back the assumption of constant returns to scale and perfect competition and restored the traditional distinction between resource allocation and factor accumulation. The move coincided with, and perhaps contributed to, a declining interest in the analysis of growth during the 1970s. Endogenous growth theory has revived the interest in growth and has even brought increasing returns to scale back into the analysis. But it has remained largely within the frame-work of one-sector or quasi-one-sector models, thus missing the links between growth and resource reallocation.[11]

Interacting with the development of these four themes is an empirical analysis of a number of questions raised by the postwar development experience as well as theoretical explanations. How extensively can savings rates and demographic factors account for the vast differences in incomes across the world? How much of these differences should be attributed instead to human capital gaps or differences in technologies? Or are those differences perhaps the path-dependent outcome of vicious and virtuous circles of development and underdevelopment in otherwise structurally similar economies? The empirical evidence on these and other issues is presented in such a way as to justify the need to relax restrictive assumptions and motivate extensions of, or departures from, simpler theoretical models. Almost every chapter refers to relevant empirical findings in the literature. Most chapters either present original findings or make new use of past research results — for instance, the literature on the Verdoorn law or research on cross-country growth regressions — to address the empirical questions.

Overall, a case for the approach of classical development economics emerges from this empirical analysis. This case is based largely on: (1) its consistency with the cross-country pattern of growth rates at low-, middle-, and high-income levels (chaps. 4 and 6); (2) its ability to accommodate the role of generally omitted factors such as industrial policy and natural resources in explaining the links between growth and international trade (chaps. 8 and 9); and (3) the links between income distribution and growth at different levels of economic development (chap. 10). At the same time, remaining within the original limits and motivations of this approach would imply taking too narrow a view of the development process. This view of "underdevelopment" and its implications for the process of economic growth needs to be broadened to cover a fuller range of development traps that can arise as a result of interactions between capital accumulation and skill acquisition or between growth and economic inequality.

Is this theoretical and empirical vindication of development theory also a policy rehabilitation? The answer is not clear-cut. Classical development economics focused on some coordination problems that would remain in an otherwise well-functioning market economy. One may criticize the associated policy prescriptions for having neglected other sources of malfunctioning and for its overoptimistic attitude toward government policy interventions. Yet such criticisms do not make these problems disappear. The aim of economic reforms in developing countries over the past 15 years has been to alleviate the malfunctioning of the market economy arising from policy distortions. Rather than reducing it, these reform processes may have enhanced the relevance of classical development economics; precisely because these other (policy) sources of malfunctioning are being removed, the focus may now have to shift again to the kind of market failures with which early development theory was concerned.

In any case, the scope of the book is largely confined to the positive, rather than the normative, implications of the approach taken by early development theory. In this sense, it is closer to Kaldor's later writing on economic growth and development, with its concern over why growth rates differ among countries (1966, 1967), than to the normative concerns that inspired the pioneers of development economics.

Overview

Chapter 1 discusses some relevant features of current international differences in incomes and growth trends since the mid-1960s. I then turn to an analytical review of possible explanations of these stylized facts. I begin, in chapter 2, with the neoclassical paradigm in growth theory, which, in its simplest version, is captured by the standard Solow model. Its key assumptions imply a distribution of income according to marginal productivity and a long-run rate of growth determined by labor force growth and exogenous technical progress. The chapter contrasts the implications of the model, including its behavior off its steady state, with the observed international differences in per capita incomes and growth rates. I then consider some extensions. These include cross-country differences in production functions; human capital accumulation à la Mankiw, Romer, and Weil (1992); and endogenous investment shares. I examine their implications for the model's properties.

Solow's is the most parsimonious of models. I refer to it as a model of a "mature capitalist economy" and highlight five assumptions: (1) the absence of labor surplus, (2) a technology with constant returns to scale, (3) perfect competition in goods and factor markets, (4) absence of international relations, and (5) Say's law. The rest of the book drops these assumptions one by one.

Thus, chapter 3 brings in, along with the capitalist sector of the Solow model, a noncapitalist sector using "subsistence technologies." The simplest case refers to a two-sector, one-good economy with constant returns to scale in both sectors. This case has identical properties to Lewis's (1954) classic model: a long off-steady-state transition period in which the capitalist sector faces a perfectly elastic labor supply, leading to a Solow-type steady state in which the noncapitalist sector has disappeared. Along with an empirical evaluation of Lewis's views on the determinants of the saving rate throughout the development process, I address two major themes: (1) the conditions under which the two sectors coexist and (2) those under which this coexistence generates a more or less elastic labor supply for the capitalist sector. The assimilation of these two issues has been a source of confusion in the past. I compare Lewis's type of labor surplus to other related notions and examine the factors affecting the elasticity of labor supply. This analysis highlights the role of returns to labor in the subsistence sector, the elasticity of substitution in consumption between subsistence and capitalist sector goods, and the existence of underemployment due to efficiency wage considerations in the capitalist sector.

Chapter 4 introduces increasing returns to scale. I recall first the main sources of aggregate increasing returns to scale in the early development literature (external and internal to the firm). I then focus on the case of technological external economies arising from workers' training or learning by doing. Combined with a labor surplus, the presence of external effects raises the possibility of multiple equilibria, one of which is a Solow-type mature economy equilibrium and another a critical level of investments below which there is a poverty trap. The role of increasing returns and elastic labor supplies in the process of capital accumulation is assessed empirically by looking at the evidence on returns to scale and the pattern of growth rates at low-, middle-, and high-income levels.

Chapter 5 brings in internal economies of scale and abandons the assumption of perfect competition. Combined with elastic factor supplies, economies of scale are a source of pecuniary external economies again yielding the possibility of multiple equilibria. The associated coordination problems are illustrated with two cases: (1) "horizontal" external economies involving demand spillovers across producers of final goods, as in the formalization of the "big push" argument by Murphy et al. (1989b); and (2) "vertical" external effects or dynamic pecuniary externalities among producers of intermediate and final goods, in the spirit of Hirschman's "forward and backward linkages." I also discuss a model with increasing returns to specialization in the spirit of Allyn Young (1928) in which the interaction between economies of specialization and demand elasticities can lead to a poverty trap à la Nurkse (1953).

Chapter 6 extends the analysis of old and new models of growth under conditions of increasing returns. I first review the contributions of endogenous growth theory, focusing on models with nondiminishing returns to capital and those based on human capital accumulation à la Lucas (1988). The empirical implications of these models are assessed and contrasted with those of classical development economics. While I find the latter more convincing, a shortcoming is the absence of off-the-job processes of skill acquisition and of external effects of this type of human capital accumulation that appear to have played an important role in the growth experiences of the postwar period. I attempt to remedy these limitations by bringing these processes and external effects into the analytical framework of early development theory. The resulting model is one in which physical capital accumulation remains an engine of growth but its interaction with processes of skill acquisition also play a major role in affecting the speed of the transition to the steady state.

Chapter 7 turns to open economy development problems. After reviewing some implications of openness for the neoclassical growth model and discussing the gains from trade in a small open economy setting, I look at the conditions under which the argument for infant industry protection applies. I highlight the role of increasing returns in a model with technological externalities due to learning by doing. I then look at the case of different rates of technical progress across sectors and countries. Finally, I abandon the small open economy assumption and examine the determination of the terms of trade between a North and a South that differ in the productivity of food production and their capital endowments per worker. Drawing on the insights of Lewis (1969) and Prebisch (United Nations 1950), I examine the conditions under which growth in each region may have asymmetrical effects on the terms of trade and income levels in the other region.

Chapter 8 looks at the role of natural resources in the process of industrialization. I discuss the very different views that have been advanced on this issue. These include the view that specialization in resource-intensive goods can be harmful to industrialization and growth — as argued by Graham (1923), the Prebisch-Singer thesis on the terms of trade for primary commodities, and the modern literature on the "Dutch disease" — and the opposite view, present in Hla Myint's (1958) "vent for surplus" approach to trade and development and the "staples thesis" of Canadian economic historians, for which exports of resource-intensive goods can turn into an engine of growth and transformation. I analyze the key assumptions made in each of these contrasting arguments, focusing on the role of returns to scale, international factor mobility, and the domestic linkages of resource-intensive sectors.

Chapter 9 continues the analysis of the links between the pattern of trade specialization and growth. The analytical framework is a model with multiple short-run equilibria in which the pattern of specialization affects the steady state level of income and the rate of convergence to the steady state. The analysis draws on a number of recent contributions on "vertical" pecuniary externalities arising from internal economies of scale in the provision of nontraded intermediate inputs. This, and other examples of multiple equilibria in previous chapters, provides the framework for a discussion of development traps in the open economy and the scope and limitations of industrial policy in increasing the rate of capital accumulation. The chapter also presents an empirical analysis of the relationship between growth and the pattern of international specialization, as conditioned by policy and resource endowment, that proves useful in clarifying some puzzles in the recent literature on cross-country growth regressions.

Chapter 10 examines the links between income distribution and growth. The aim of the chapter is to explore the role of inequality in explaining the economic setbacks suffered at low- and middle-income levels. I examine first some salient features of income distribution in developed and developing countries and review alternative views on the relationships between income distribution, income level, and the rate of income growth. I then examine, in a formal model, the conditions under which Kuznets's observed relationship between inequality and income per capita may hold and look at the effects of technical progress, population growth, and skill formation in shaping the relationship between income level and inequality as well as the effects of growth on inequality. The chapter also discusses the recent literature on the reverse links between inequality and growth, focusing on the specific channels through which inequality may be harmful to growth. I then bring together the different strands of the literature to show how this integration can help explain the emergence of "inequality traps" at low- and medium-income levels.

Chapter 11 turns to effective demand problems. The types of effective demand failures on which I focus are, however, different from the typically Keynesian situations for which monetary and/or fiscal policies are an effective remedy. Kalecki's analysis of unemployment and excess capacity in manufacturing arising from the inelasticity of food production in the countryside provides a prototype model. I then look at two-gap and inflation models of developing open economies in which foreign exchange constraints, rather than agricultural or wage-goods constraints, can generate a similar type of effective demand failure. Finally, I consider situations in which foreign exchange constraints operate directly on the domestic supply of goods through the rationing of imports and where the interactions between domestic supply of manufactures and agricultural exports can give rise to vicious circles of economic decline. Arguably, such processes appear to be behind the collapse or stagnation of a number of sub-Saharan African economies in recent decades.

Chapter 12 extends the (largely) short-run analysis of demand constraints in chapter 11 to examine the growth path of a demand-constrained open economy. I begin with a Harrod-Domar model of growth in a small open economy and then move on to the contributions of the literature on three-gap models in which, besides foreign exchange shortages, fiscal or investment constraints originating in an overindebtedness trap may prevent the economy from achieving a full capacity growth path. I then compare the demand-constrained growth trajectories to the factor accumulation paths of neoclassical and development theory examined in previous chapters and consider the implications of Keynesian and structuralist models for the controversies over the long-run convergence of per capita incomes. The chapter concludes by illustrating the relevance of the models for the analysis of the stabilization and adjustment problems of highly indebted countries in Latin America during the 1980s and 1990s.

The last chapter begins by summarizing the empirical findings of the book. It then turns to a theoretical defense of classical development economics, arguing that, with the exception of "horizontal" pecuniary externalities in perfectly tradable goods, the analysis of development traps remains largely intact in an open economy. This motivates a discussion of some common misinterpretations of "big push" arguments, including their assimilation in Smithian circular relationships between the division of labor and the size of the market and in Keynesian effective demand arguments in economies with underutilization of resources. The chapter includes a brief discussion of the "balanced versus unbalanced growth" debate, highlighting how it revolves around different ways of dealing with the same development problems. The chapter concludes by making the case for a unified research agenda that will bring the contributions of early development theory together with those of the contemporary economics of growth.

CHAPTER 1

Some Stylized Facts

Why are some countries richer than others? Why do some economies grow faster than others? One can answer these questions at different levels, involving varying degrees of understanding. In this chapter, I begin at the more observable level by looking at what Abramovitz (1952) called the "immediate determinants" of output levels and growth rates. Immediately, a word of warning is necessary. These proximate determinants need not be independent of each other. They may not even be independent of per capita income levels and growth rates themselves. Much of this book will be precisely about how the factors highlighted here are determined and how they interact. The main purpose of this chapter is simply to present some stylized facts in the form of robust statistical relationships. Explanations thereof begin in the next chapter.

Incomes per Capita around the World

At our initial level, we look at differences in per capita incomes within a simple and widely used framework.[1] Income per capita is equal to income per worker times the ratio of workers to the total population (the activity rate). Higher incomes per capita thus may result from either a higher level of output per worker or a higher ratio of workers to the total population. Demographic and social factors largely explain differences in activity rates. Output per worker can be related to the amount of resources, human and nonhuman, per worker and to the efficiency with which these resources are used and allocated. Resources include the stock of capital; the skills, knowledge, and energy level of the labor force; and the natural resources available. Higher efficiency may result from a better allocation of given resources, through, for example, specialization in international trade, productivity gains arising from the expansion of the scale of economic activity, or movements toward the production frontier (adoption of best-practice techniques or reductions in X-inefficiencies).

Table 1 presents information on 62 countries, aggregated into six groups according to their 1997 income per capita adjusted for differences

16

in purchasing power across countries.[2] The first two groups include, broadly speaking, the high-income economies in the Organization for Economic Cooperation and Development (OECD). Group 3 is a diverse collection of upper-middle-income countries in Southern Europe, Latin America, and East Asia. The bulk of the developing economies in the sample is concentrated in groups 4, 5, and 6. The information in the table refers to different variables reflecting or influencing the availability of resources and the efficiency in their use. The appendix to this chapter gives a full definition of these variables together with data sources and a detailed account of the composition of each country group.

Table 1 reproduces a well-known feature of the world economy: its vast heterogeneity in terms of per capita incomes. Income gaps between rich and poor countries are enormous, of the order 20 to one, when we compare groups 1 and 6. Lower activity rates in middle- and low-income countries—determined by sociodemographic factors such as lower participation of women in the labor force and higher dependency ratios than those found in rich countries—account for some of these differences. This is especially the case in groups 4 and 5 since a number of countries in group 6 have not yet begun the demographic transition and still have relatively low dependency ratios.

TABLE 1. Comparative Economic Characteristics in the 1990s[a]

	Averages for Country Groups					
	1	2	3	4	5	6
GDP per capita[b]	100	83.9	52.3	25.0	13.2	4.8
Activity rate (%)	50.3	48.9	45.4	42.7	40.2	43.1
GDP per worker[b]	100	86.0	58.2	29.3	16.7	5.7
Capital per worker[b]	100	83.4	45.8	25.4	12.5	3.4[c]
Education (years)	11.0	10.6	7.8[d]	5.0[e]	4.7	2.1
Arable land (hectares per worker)	0.68[f]	0.95	0.60[d]	0.55	0.56	0.53
Trade share (%)	98.2	67.1	38.5	28.4[g]	24.5[h]	20.1
Frankel-Romer trade share (%)	50.6	20.8	18.7	14.3	20.4	14.6
Market size[b]	100	52.0	19.7[d]	19.5[e]	4.6	14.8
Industrial employment share (%)	30.3	29.5	31.2[d]	20.6[e]	19.6	9.5
Number of countries	10	10	11	11	10	10

Note: See the appendix to this chapter for countries in each group, data sources, and definitions.
[a]1997 or the latest available year.
[b]As a percentage of group 1 average
[c]Average excludes Nepal
[d]Average excludes Taiwan
[e]Average excludes Yugoslavia
[f]Average excludes Belgium and Luxembourg
[g]Average excludes Botswana
[h]Average excludes Swaziland

On the whole, however, income differences are clearly related to wide productivity gaps. What accounts for these large differences in output per worker? Perhaps the most salient feature of table 1 is how closely output per worker correlates with both the stock of capital per worker and the educational level of the labor force. This last is measured by the mean number of years of schooling of the population aged 25 years and above, arguably the best indicator of the stock of human capital per worker that is available for current production.[3] Figures 1 and 2 show these relationships for our sample of countries, and table 2 shows log linear regressions of gross domestic product (GDP) per worker and each of these two variables.

No aggregate measures of natural resources are available. A crude proxy is the amount of a country's arable land. Figure 3 shows the absence of any discernible relationship between arable land per worker and output per worker. High-income countries can be resource rich (Australia, Canada, and the United States) or resource poor (Japan, Hong Kong, and the Netherlands). Similarly, some low-income countries in the sample are land poor (Sri Lanka and Nepal) while others are land rich (Zambia and Paraguay). The correlation coefficient between arable land per capita and output per worker in table 3 and regression 3

TABLE 2.   Cross-Country Regressions

Regression: Independent Variable	1	2	3	4	5
Constant	3.18	7.09	4.53	1.69	1.81
	(8.41)	(40.82)	(7.94)	(2.09)	(1.88)
Log of capital per worker (K/L)	0.71	—	0.45	0.27	0.30
	(17.48)	—	(4.78)	(3.61)	(3.52)
Log of education (EDU)	—	1.49	0.60	0.36	0.43
	—	(16.03)	(3.04)	(2.19)	(2.60)
Log of arable land per capita (LAND)	—	—	−0.02	—	—
	—	—	(−0.29)	—	—
Log of trade share 1 (OPEN1)	—	—	—	0.24	—
	—	—	—	(3.54)	—
Log of trade share 2 (OPEN2)	—	—	—	—	0.17
	—	—	—	—	(2.18)
Log of market size (SIZE)	—	—	—	0.08	0.08
	—	—	—	(2.72)	(2.06)
Log of industrial employment (IND)	—	—	—	0.62	0.61
	—	—	—	(4.92)	(4.35)
N	61	60	58	57	59
Adjusted R^2	0.84	0.82	0.86	0.93	0.91

t-statistics in parentheses
Dependent variable: logarithm (log) of real GDP per worker in 1997 (Y/L)

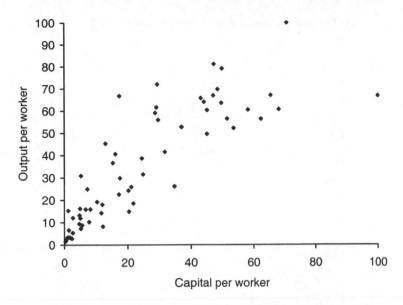

Fig. 1. Output per worker and capital per worker expressed as percentages of maximum value. See the appendix to this chapter for sources and definitions.

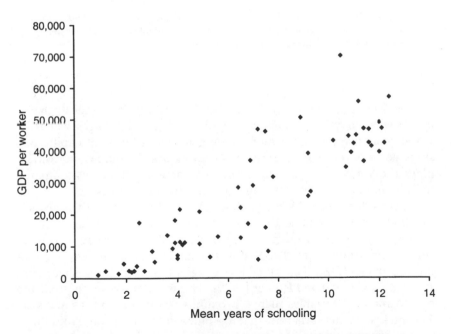

Fig. 2. GDP per worker and education. GDP is measured in 1997 current international dollars. See the appendix to this chapter for sources and definitions.

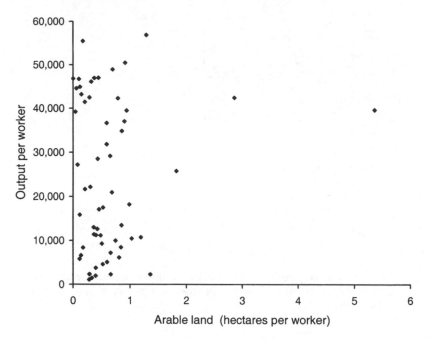

Fig. 3. Output per worker and arable land per worker. Output per worker is measured in 1997 current international dollars. See the appendix to this chapter for sources and definitions.

in table 2 confirm the weakness of the relationship. This suggests that — unlike what may have happened in the preindustrial stages when the world economy was much more homogeneous in terms of capital and skills per worker than it is today[4] — the natural resource endowment plays a very minor role as a determinant of income differences compared to other factor endowments (human and capital resources).

I consider three efficiency variables. The first of these variables is the trade share for allocative and technical efficiency gains resulting from specialization in international trade. (Table 1 presents two measures of the trade share. The first is the standard measure [exports plus imports over GDP]. The other is a geography-based trade share constructed by Frankel and Romer [1999]. This is the trade share predicted by geographical variables such as proximity to other countries and size. The interest of this variable is that it is independent of income or of third factors affecting trade and income [although perhaps not completely independent of these factors].) The second of the three efficiency variables is the economy's size, as measured by total GDP to capture efficiency gains resulting from pure scale effects. The third efficiency variable is the employment share of industrial activities for (gains from resource allocation toward sectors with increasing returns.)

As shown in table 1 and the cross-country correlations in table 3, these efficiency variables are, as expected, positively correlated with output per worker.[5] In the case of the economy's size its close positive correlation with income per capita becomes spoiled only when group 6 (which includes India) is included. On the other hand, the three variables have the expected positive influence in the cross-country regression presented in table 2. The fact that both trade share and size are highly significant is consistent with the observation that small economies (such as those of Hong Kong, Switzerland, and Luxembourg in our sample) have to be very open to achieve high levels of income while large economies need not (United States, Japan). Yet trade may not be a perfect substitute for domestic market size; far from being annihilated by the presence of other variables in the regression equation, including trade share, the coefficient of economic size remains highly significant. Examples that illustrate this influence are a number of poor countries with very open economies and small domestic markets (Zambia, Ivory Coast).

Growth Rates since 1965

I now turn to growth performance during the period 1965–92.[6] Table 4 aggregates countries into seven groups, depending on the growth rate of GDP per worker. As a secondary criterion, I also consider their initial

TABLE 3. Cross-Country Correlations

Variable	Y/L	K/L[a]	EDU[b]	LAND[c]	OPEN1[d]	OPEN2	SIZE[b]	IND[b]
Y/L	1.00	—	—	—	—	—	—	—
K/L[a]	0.84**	1.00	—	—	—	—	—	—
EDU[b]	0.88**	0.86**	1.00	—	—	—	—	—
LAND[c]	0.12	0.17	0.20	1.00	—	—	—	—
OPEN1[d]	0.62**	0.46**	0.46**	−0.12	1.00	—	—	—
OPEN2	0.39**	0.30*	0.17	−0.29*	0.56**	1.00	—	—
SIZE[b]	0.35**	0.26*	0.33**	0.08	−0.11	−0.15	1.00	—
IND[b]	0.71**	0.59**	0.67**	0.01	0.42**	0.15	0.19	1.00

[a]Excludes Nepal
[b]Excludes Taiwan and Yugoslavia
[c]Excludes Belgium, Luxembourg, and Taiwan
[d]Excludes Botswana and Swaziland
*Statistically significant at 5% level   **Statistically significant at 1% level

level of income. Thus, groups 3 and 4 are composed of high-income countries with relatively high and low growth rates, respectively. Groups 5, 6, and 7 include developing countries only. The table presents, for these seven groups, the average growth rates of per capita and per worker GDP along with a number of other performance indicators.

Growth, Factor Accumulation, and Productivity Growth

A well-known observation refers to the wide dispersion of growth rates. Whether measured in per capita or per worker terms, the differences between the extremes of the distribution (groups 1 and 7) in table 4 are staggering. They are such that, while group 1 had a per capita income 25 percent lower than group 7 in 1965, by 1992 incomes in the fastest growing economies were over five times higher than in the stagnant or declining economies of group 7.

Growth rates of GDP per capita and per worker are closely associated. That is, in accounting for differences in the growth of per capita income changes in activity rates—that is, changes in labor input per capita, given by the difference between the two growth rates—play a

TABLE 4.   Growth Performance, 1965–92

	Averages for Country Groups						
	1	2	3	4	5	6	7
Growth rates (% per year)							
GDP per capita[a]	6.7	3.1	2.7	1.9	2.1	1.1	−0.7
GDP per worker[a]	6.1	3.1	2.3	1.0	1.8	0.7	−0.8
Capital per worker[a]	8.0	4.9	3.3	2.9	2.9	2.5	1.9
Industrial employment share	2.8[c]	0.9[d,e]	−0.9	−1.4[g]	0.5	0.5	0.3
Education	2.2[c]	2.1[e]	2.2[f]	1.4	2.7[h]	2.3[i]	2.5[j]
Education 1965 (years)	3.6	4.0	5.7[f]	7.9	2.1[h]	3.3[i]	2.5[j]
GDP per worker[b]	62.0	94.0	201.7	236.8	10.8	26.2	31.5
Industrial employment share							
1965 (%)	24.0[c]	23.4[d]	38.6[f]	39.8[g]	11.7	17.3	17.3
Number of countries	5	9	10	10	10	9	9

Note: See the appendix to this chapter for countries in each group, data sources, and definitions.
[a]Growth rate calculated as a trend over the period
[b]Average over the period of 1965–92 or the closest available. Mean value = 100.
[c]Average excludes Taiwan
[d]Average excludes Swaziland
[e]Average excludes Yugoslavia
[f]Average excludes Luxembourg
[g]Average excludes Iceland
[h]Average excludes Morocco
[i]Average excludes Ivory Coast
[j]Average excludes Nigeria and Madagascar

secondary role compared to that of labor productivity growth. Yet, just as in the case of income levels, cross-country differences in growth rates are narrower in the case of GDP per worker, and changes in activity rates are far from negligible. For example, activity rates in the fastest growing economies show a rising trend at a rate of 0.6 percent per year. Changes in activity rates are also significant in the two groups of advanced industrial economies (groups 3 and 4). In the case of group 4, the rising activity rate accounts for more than one-third of the growth in per capita incomes.

The accumulation of capital per worker appears to have a major systematic influence on the growth of per capita and per worker GDP, showing a close positive correlation with these two indicators across country groups. Indeed, the very fast growth of capital per worker appears as the most distinctive characteristic of the rapidly growing economies in groups 1 and 2. This is not, however, their only attribute. They also feature an initial level of education well above those of the developing economies in groups 5, 6, and 7 along with fairly rapid progress in education. At the other extreme, the stagnant economies of group 7 feature both a slow pace of capital accumulation per worker and a low initial level of education. Regression 2 in table 5 summarizes these observations by showing the growth rate of labor productivity positively correlated with the growth of the capital-labor ratio and the initial level of education.

TABLE 5.   Cross-Country Regressions

Regression: Independent Variable	1	2	3
Constant	−0.01	−0.003	0.02
	(−0.80)	(−0.75)	(6.98)
Growth rate of capital per worker	0.45	0.46	—
	(6.17)	(6.79)	—
Rate of progress in education[a]	0.08	—	—
	(0.46)	—	—
Initial level of education (1965)	0.004	0.003	—
	(1.44)	(1.69)	—
Rate of industrialization[b]	0.22	0.19	0.28
	(2.03)	(2.28)	(2.52)
N	53	53	57
Adjusted R^2	0.53	0.54	0.09

[a]Growth rate per year of mean years of schooling
[b]Growth rate of industrial employment share
t-statistics in parentheses
Dependent variable: trend growth rate of GDP per worker 1965–92

Table 4 also shows that capital per worker grew faster than output per worker across all country groups. There was a general increase in capital-output ratios in the period 1965–90. Regression 2 in table 5 indicates that capital deepening was faster the higher the growth of output per worker and varied inversely with the initial level of educational achievement and the rate of industrialization. This is more clearly seen if we rewrite regression 1 as:[7]

$$g(k/y) = 0.007 + 1.17g(y) - 0.072\log EDU65 - 0.41g_{IND}, \qquad (1')$$

where $g(k/y)$ is the rate of growth of the capital output ratio, $g(y)$ the growth rate of output per worker, and g_{IND} the growth rate of the industrial employment share. Equation 1' shows that an increase of one percentage point in the growth of output per worker is associated with a 1.2 percentage point change in the rate of capital deepening for given values of the other variables. Given this close association between labor productivity growth and capital deepening, it is somewhat paradoxical to find (from table 4) that capital deepening was fastest at the top and bottom of the growth table. In groups 1 and 7, the rate of capital deepening was on the order of 2 percent per year. The explanation lies in the behavior of the other variables and indicates the very different nature of capital deepening between these two country groups. In group 1, the rapidly rising capital-output ratio is indeed largely associated with the rapid growth of output per worker, with the relatively high level of education and rapid industrialization moderating capital deepening. In contrast, in group 7 it is the low level of educational achievement and the slow process of industrialization that accelerate the process of capital deepening despite a falling output per worker.

The relationship between the initial level of education and subsequent growth deserves further attention. Using a data set of 29 countries, Azariadis and Drazen (1990) observed that no country with a low ratio of literacy to GDP was able to grow quickly in the period 1960–80. Moreover, in their sample all countries that grew at fast rates had exceptionally well-qualified labor forces given their starting level of per capita income. This suggested to them that a threshold, that is, a critical level of relative human capital, was necessary to achieve fast growth.

Figure 4 shows the relationship between the rate of growth of per capita GDP in 1965–97 and the (logarithm of) mean years of schooling of the population 25 years and over circa 1965 for 91 countries for which information on education was available. The figure suggests an observation that is similar to, albeit less definitive than, that of Azariadis and Drazen. In the bottom quintile in the distribution according to schooling (17 countries with less than 1.3 years of schooling), only

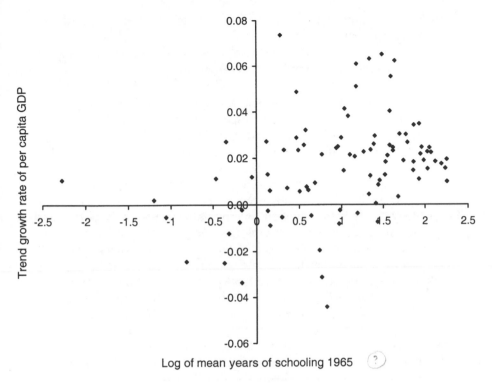

Fig. 4. **Initial level of education (ca. 1965) and per capita GDP growth, 1965–97**

two countries (Pakistan and Syria) grew at above the median growth rate (three countries do so if one includes Botswana, a borderline case). Moreover, only three countries with a level of schooling below the median (Botswana, Indonesia, and Malaysia) were able to grow at rates above 4 percent per year. The most notable case is Botswana (with a remarkable 7.4 percent per capita GDP growth rate despite an initial 1.3 years of schooling).[8]

Figure 4 also indicates that high initial levels of education are not a sufficient condition for the achievement of high growth rates. Nine countries are clearly in the high-education and slow-growth category. This group includes mostly Latin American countries—in particular, Argentina, Uruguay, and Panama, all of which had more than four years of schooling and a per capita GDP growth rate of less than 1.5 percent. In other regions, the most notable cases are New Zealand, South Africa, and the Philippines. The most remarkable of all countries in this category is certainly Argentina, with 5.3 years of schooling in 1965 and a growth rate of 0.34 percent per year.

Absolute Divergence, Conditional Convergence?

The international dispersion of per capita income has been on the rise over the last century and a quarter. Figure 5 shows the world distribution of per capita incomes in 1870 and 1993 and illustrates the process of divergence of per capita GDP that took place between those years. The high-income economies today have six to nine times the GDP per capita than the high-income economies in 1870, and the composition of this group has remained largely unaltered.[9] In contrast, the low-income countries today barely increased their income per capita over the period and continue to be largely the same as the poor countries in 1870. In between, the median economy has around four times the income of 1870. This picture implies that the richest countries in 1870, with (exceptions such as Argentina) are those that have grown at the highest rates over the period 1870–1993, even though they were not the only ones to grow quickly. The poorest countries in 1870 have clearly lagged behind. Thus, according to Pritchett (1995) the ratio of GDP per capita of the richest to the poorest country rose from 8.7 in 1870 to 51.6 in 1985. The standard deviation of log per capita income, which was between 0.513 and 0.636 in 1870, rose to 1.025 in 1985.[10]

The data for our 60 countries over a shorter and more recent period of time show no strong tendencies toward either divergence or convergence of per capita incomes (see table 4). The growth performance of the high-income economies in groups 3 and 4 lagged behind that of the two groups of middle economies (1 and 2, with the fastest growth rates). At the same time, however, those high-income economies clearly grew at faster rates than many other developing countries in the sample (concentrated in groups 5, 6, and 7) and especially more than the poor countries that constitute the bulk of groups 6 and 7. Other (larger) data sets for similar time periods also feature the absence of convergence. The general result has been stated by Barro (1991, 407–8) as follows: "The hypothesis that poor countries tend to grow faster than rich countries seems to be inconsistent with the cross country evidence, which indicates that per capita growth rates have little correlation with the starting level of per capita product."

This lack of "absolute convergence" should not be confused with the absence of "conditional convergence" — the existence of an inverse relationship between the initial level of per capita income and its subsequent growth once one controls for the determinants of the steady state

(a)

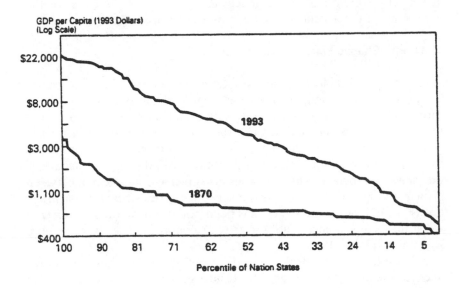

(b)

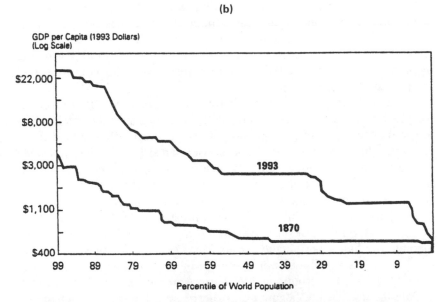

Fig. 5.   International distribution of per capita GDP, 1870–1993. (From
DeLong 1997 [based on the World Bank's *World Development Report* for
1995] and Maddison 1995.)

Development Theory and the Economics of Growth

level of income. The absence of absolute convergence can theoretically accompany conditional convergence; this, in fact, is the claim of the extensions of the neoclassical growth model discussed in chapter 2.

The Hump-Shaped Pattern of Growth Rates

A closer look at table 4 reveals an interesting pattern. Consider groups 2, 3, and 4, with average or above-average incomes per worker. These three groups together come close to today's advanced industrial economies. Within this set of countries, there is a strong tendency toward convergence of productivity levels: group 2 with the lowest incomes is the fastest growing of the three, and group 4 with the highest incomes is the slowest growing. There is thus an inverse relationship between growth and income level across the set of countries with above-average levels of GDP per worker. This has been noted repeatedly and referred to as the "convergence club" of OECD countries (see, in particular, Baumol and Wolff 1988).

Consider now groups 1, 5, 6, and 7, developing countries with below-average incomes per worker. The fastest-growing countries (group 1) have the highest incomes. Here the negative relationship between growth rates and income levels across country groups disappears, and there is a tendency for per capita incomes to diverge. Evidence of the growing dispersion of incomes among developing countries has been noted in other studies; the United Nations Conference on Trade and Development (UNCTAD 1997), for example, has estimated a near doubling of the income ratio between the richest and poorest developing countries over the past four decades.

The lack of strong tendencies toward convergence or divergence for the whole sample is the result of the fact that growth acceleration tends to occur at middle-income levels, as has been noted several times and for other time periods.[11] The consequence is a tendency toward divergence among middle- and low-income countries (and to some extent among high- and low-income countries) and a tendency toward convergence among middle- and high-income countries. The growth acceleration at middle-income levels is illustrated by the performance of groups 1 and 2. Besides Botswana, which still has a rather low income, the first group includes four East Asian economies, which can be classified as middle- or upper-middle-income for the average of the period. The second group includes European and Asian countries with middle incomes at the beginning of the period. Figure 6, which shows growth rates and levels of GDP per capita (average of 1965 and 1990 levels) for the whole sample, illustrates the hump-shaped pattern of

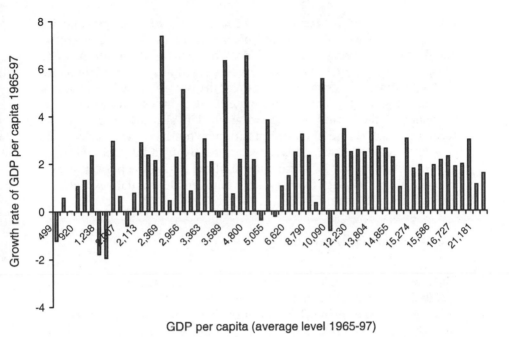

Fig. 6. Growth rates and levels of GDP per capita

growth rates that features the largest incidence of high-growth rates occurring at middle-income levels. This pattern would probably emerge more clearly if the 1980s were excluded from the period of analysis since a number of previously fast-growing middle-income countries in Latin America then plunged into economic stagnation following the debt crisis of the early 1980s.

The acceleration of growth rates at middle-income levels has been given different explanations. These will be examined in later chapters. At this stage, it is worth pointing out that there is some support in the data for the view that high-growth rates at middle-income levels are characteristic of the transition to an industrialized economy, with growth being rather slow before and after the process of industrialization. Regression 3 in table 5 relates overall productivity growth to the pace of industrialization, measured by the difference in the growth rates of industrial and overall employment.[12] This is one of the so-called Kaldor's laws, stating that the faster the rate of industrialization the higher the rate of productivity growth in the economy as a whole.[13] According to

Kaldor (1967, 7): ". . . fast rates of economic growth are almost invariably associated with the fast rate of growth of the secondary sector, mainly, manufacturing, and . . . this is an attribute of an intermediate stage of development; it is a characteristic of the transition from 'immaturity' to 'maturity.'" A common feature of the two groups with the fastest growth rates is indeed an intermediate level of industrialization at the beginning of the period. Moreover, group 1 is also the group that recorded the fastest rate of industrialization by far during the period. The growth of output per worker is slower in the highly industrialized economies of groups 3 and 4, which deindustrialized during the period, as well as in the industrializing (though from a much smaller initial base) economies of groups 5, 6, and 7.

The "Twin-Peaked" Distribution

The fact that the largest incidence of high-growth rates tends to occur in middle-income groups is not the same as all middle-income economies being the fastest growing. The transition from "immaturity to maturity" is much less smooth than a superficial reading of figure 6 would suggest, and some of the major setbacks also appear to take place at middle-income levels. This is part of the explanation why, as Quah (1993) has argued, perhaps pushing the reading of the evidence too far (as we shall see), the variation in the country data is "as rich in the cross-section dimension as it is in the time-series."[14] A number of economic and institutional upheavals, to be discussed in later chapters, can throw rapidly growing economies off the path of economic transformation that leads to high-income levels. In our sample and time period, we have already referred to the stagnation of highly indebted countries during the 1980s. Over a longer time span, the relative decline of Argentina, once among the richest countries in the world, is a remarkable example.

Growth acceleration at middle-income levels, coupled with occasional setbacks, probably constitutes a major reason why the world's distribution of per capita income has evolved toward a persistent bimodal or "twin-peaked" distribution. Using data for 1962–84, Quah (1993) calculated the probability that a country in one income group will move into another group in the following year. The resulting "transition matrix," with countries divided into five income groups (see table 6) depending on their per capita incomes relative to the global average, can then be used to simulate the evolving dispersion of per capita incomes. It is worth noting the very high probabilities that countries in groups 1 and 5, the highest- and lowest-income countries, respectively, will remain within the same group from one year to the next.

Holding these probabilities constant over time, Quah shows that the distribution of incomes eventually stabilizes in a "twin-peaked" distribution similar to that observed in the world economy today, with many poor and rich countries and relatively few in between. As an illustration, figure 7 uses Quah's transition probabilities to simulate the distribution of per capita incomes. Starting from an egalitarian distribution with a zero standard deviation in the log of per capita incomes, income dispersion increases within the first 70 years and then stabilizes with a standard deviation of around 1.5.

Quah's estimated transition matrix implies, with probability one, that any less-developed country will eventually move up through all the stages to become a high-income country and conversely that any developed economy will eventually move down to become underdeveloped. This two-way movement produces the long-run stable distribution. Rowthorn and Kozul-Wright (1998) have observed that the experience of the past 150 years suggests that countries do move downward but only to a limited extent. There is no recorded case, for example, of a country in the high-income or even moderately developed category moving all the way down to the lowest income level. This suggests the presence of ratchet effects that limit downward mobility. By allowing a ratchet effect—so that a country in group N can fall back into group $N + 1$ but having done so cannot fall back further into group $N + 2$—while assuming all other probabilities to be as in Quah, Rowthorn and Kozul-Wright show this limited downward mobility to have a dramatic impact on the evolution of income dispersion. The ratchet effect implies that the initial polarization of incomes is more rapid and acute than with Quah's probabilities, since the limited downward mobility must initially have inegalitarian effects. At the same time, the gap between rich and poor countries eventually

TABLE 6.   Quah's Transition Probabilities

	year $t + 1$				
	Group 1	Group 2	Group 3	Group 4	Group 5
Group 1	0.99	0.01	—	—	—
Group 2	0.02	0.94	0.04	—	—
Group 3	—	0.04	0.92	0.04	—
Group 4	—	—	0.04	0.92	0.05
Group 5	—	—	—	0.03	0.97

Source: Quah 1993; Rowthorn and Kozul-Wright 1998.

Note: Groupings are based on income level relative to the world average in descending order so that group 5 includes countries with one-fourth or less of the world's average income. Row totals may not sum to unity because of rounding errors.

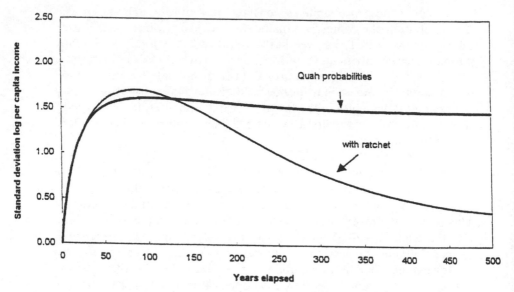

Fig. 7. Global income dispersion. (From Rowthorn and Kozul-Wright 1998, 19.)

narrows as more countries move into the upper-income groups (see fig. 7). The process of convergence is very slow, however, and it takes 330 years from the initial starting point to reach the stage where 95 percent of all countries are in the first two groups.

The bimodal income distribution implied by the transition matrices calculated over recent decades plus the ratchet effects suggested by historical experience thus seem quite consistent with the hump-shaped pattern of growth rates. Both suggest no rapid tendency for low-income countries, as a group, to converge to high-income levels while at the same time some lower-middle-income and upper-middle-income countries occasionally change places between the two modes of the distribution. Both suggest that at some stage and for a prolonged period one should observe the ample and recognizable valley that separates the developed and most of the developing countries and is characteristic of today's world.

This chapter has provided empirical evidence, rather than explanations, of levels of income or growth rates across economies. It gives background information on what will be explained in subsequent chapters.

APPENDIX

Country Groupings

The indicators in this chapter refer to 62 countries without centrally planned economies for which data on capital per worker were available in the Penn World Table. In the first section, these 62 countries were classified according to their real GDP per capita in 1997 (or the closest year for which information was available)[15] and aggregated into the six income groups in table A1.1. Within each group, countries are listed according to income per capita level, and figures are in U.S. dollars at 1997 international prices.

In the second section, the 62 countries were classified according to their trend growth rate of GDP per worker from 1965 to 1992. As a secondary criterion, the classification used the level of GDP per capita in order to separate two groups of developed countries (groups 3 and 4) from the developing economies in groups 5, 6, and 7. Table A1.2 shows the composition of each of the seven groups.

Definitions and Data Sources

Data sources for this chapter are the Penn World Table (PWT) (Mark 5.6); World Bank *World Development Indicators 1999* CD-Rom (*WDI 1999*); OECD *Historical Statistics* 1996; the United Nations Development Program (UNDP) *Human Development Report* (various issues); Barro and Lee 1993a, 1994; and Frankel and Romer 1999. On the methodology for the construction of the Penn World Table, see Summers and Heston 1988, 1991; and Heston and Summers 1996.

A full description of definitions and data sources for the variables used in this chapter follows.

> *Activity rate:* Labor force as a percentage of population in 1997. Source: *WDI 1999*. For Taiwan: Labor force participation rate in 1997. Source: Directorate-General of Budget, Accounting, and Statistics, Executive Yuan, the Republic of China Internet pages.
>
> *Arable land per worker* (LAND): Arable land (hectares per worker) in 1996. Source: *WDI 1999*.
>
> *Capital per worker* (K/L): Nonresidential capital stock per worker in 1990 (1985 international prices). Average for group 1 = 100. Source: PWT (Mark 5.6).
>
> *Capital per worker growth rate:* Trend growth rate of capital per worker from 1965 to 1992 (or the closest year for which statistics are available) calculated by regressing the logarithm of capital per worker on a constant and time. Source: PWT (Mark 5.6).

Education (EDU): Mean years of schooling 1992. Source: *Human Development Report,* 1994. Mean years of schooling 1965, population aged 25 years and above. Source: Barro and Lee 1994.

Frankel-Romer Constructed Trade Share (OPEN 2): Trade share predicted by geographical variables. Source: Frankel and Romer 1999.

GDP per capita: GDP per capita in 1997 at current international dollars. Average for group 1 = 100. Source: *WDI 1999.* For those countries with no or insufficient data in *WDI* (Taiwan 1990; Yugoslavia 1990), latest observation available in PWT 5.6 data on real GDP per capita is used.

GDP per capita growth rate: Trend growth rate of GDP per capita 1965–92 (constant 1995 prices) calculated by regressing the logarithm of the GDP per capita on a constant and time. Source: *WDI 1999.*

GDP per worker (Y/L): GDP per worker in 1997 at current international dollars. Average for group 1 = 100. Source: *WDI 1999.*

GDP per worker growth rate: Trend growth rate of GDP per worker 1965–92 (constant 1995 prices) calculated by regressing the logarithm of the GDP per worker on a constant and time. Source: *WDI 1999.*

Industrial employment share (IND): Percentage of labor force in industry 1965 and 1990. Source: UNDP *Human Development Report,* 1990, 1994; and UNDP *Human Development Database,* 1998.

Market size (SIZE): GDP in 1997 at current international dollars. Source: *WDI 1999.*

Population: Population in 1997. Source: *WDI 1999.* For Taiwan: Population 1997. *Source:* Directorate-General of Budget, Accounting, and Statistics, Executive Yuan, the Republic of China Internet pages.

Rate of progress in education: Logarithmic growth rate of education between 1965 and 1992. Source: *Human Development Report,* 1994; and Barro and Lee 1994.

Rate of industrialization: Logarithmic growth rate of the share of labor force in industry between 1965 and 1990. Source: UNDP *Human Development Report,* 1990, 1994; and UNDP *Human Development Database,* 1998.

Trade share (OPEN 1): Exports plus imports as a percentage of GDP in 1997 or the closest year available. Source: *WDI 1999.* For countries with insufficient or no data in *WDI* (Belgium, Luxembourg, Panama, Taiwan, and Yugoslavia) the latest PWT (Mark 5.6) value is used (except for those with no statistics after 1990, Botswana and Swaziland).

TABLE A1.1. Groupings according to Real GDP per Capita in 1997

	Group					
	1	2	3	4	5	6
Average income	$24,825	$20,825	$12,995	$6,207	$3,267	$1,194
Countries	Luxembourg	France	Israel	Mexico	Guatemala	Honduras
	United States	Iceland	New Zealand	Botswana	Paraguay	Ivory Coast
	Switzerland	Germany	Spain	Panama	Philippines	India
	Norway	Netherlands	Portugal	Colombia	Jamaica	Kenya
	Hong Kong, China	United Kingdom	South Korea, Republic	Thailand	Swaziland	Nepal
	Japan	Ireland	Chile	Turkey	Morocco	Zambia
	Denmark	Italy	Greece	Yugoslavia	Syrian Arab Republic	Madagascar
	Belgium	Australia	Argentina	Iran, Islamic Republic	Bolivia	Nigeria
	Canada	Finland	Taiwan	Ecuador	Sri Lanka	Malawi
	Austria	Sweden	Mauritius	Dominican Republic	Zimbabwe	Sierra Leone
			Venezuela	Peru		
Number of countries	10	10	11	11	10	10

TABLE A1.2. Groupings according to Trend Growth Rate of GDP per Worker

	Group						
	1	2	3	4	5	6	7
Criteria	Fast growth	Medium high growth	Medium growth developed	Slow growth developed	Medium growth developing	Slow growth developing	Slow or no growth developing
Growth rate	$g > 4.0\%$	$4.0\% > g > 2.5\%$	$2.5\% > g > 2.0\%$	$2.0\% > g$	$2.3\% > g > 1.0\%$	$1.0\% > g > 0.3\%$	$0.3\% > g$
Countries	Botswana	Swaziland	Finland	Iceland	Mauritius	Colombia	Nigeria
	Taiwan	Japan	Italy	United Kingdom	Sri Lanka	Mexico	Argentina
	South Korea, Republic	Ireland	Portugal	Denmark	Ecuador	Philippines	Sierra Leone
	Hong Kong, China	Yugoslavia	Luxembourg	Australia	India	Bolivia	Iran
	Thailand	Syrian Arab Republic	Israel	Sweden	Morocco	Guatemala	Peru
		Paraguay	France	Netherlands	Dominican Republic	Chile	Zambia
		Greece	Norway	Canada	Kenya	Honduras	Madagascar
		Austria	Belgium	Switzerland	Nepal	Panama	Jamaica
		Turkey	Spain	United States	Malawi	Ivory Coast	Venezuela
			Germany (West)	New Zealand	Zimbabwe		
Number of countries	5	9	10	10	10	9	9

CHAPTER 2

A Mature Economy: Growth and Factor Accumulation

We now embark on the search for analytical accounts of the differences in income levels and growth performance described in chapter 1. Just as some chess books begin with a basic understanding of "endgames," that is, when the battle is almost over and only a few pieces of the original puzzle remain, I begin with a model of a "mature economy"—a picture of what an economy looks like after the transition to a developed state has been completed. This starting point serves two purposes. First, just as in chess books, the understanding of endgames facilitates a discussion of openings and intermediate situations. In addition, it will help to introduce a simple analytical framework and a number of concepts that will be used in later chapters.

I begin with a standard version of the Solow model and derive its implications for income levels and growth rates across countries. In this version of the model, all countries have access to the same technologies, there are only two factors of production (physical capital and labor), and the savings rate is constant. This crude version does not stand up to the evidence well. I therefore subsequently relax some of its assumptions and extend the model to allow for different technologies across countries, human capital accumulation, and endogenous investment shares.

The Solow Model

The economy considered produces one good, which can be either consumed or invested. Production is undertaken by competitive profit-maximizing firms under conditions of constant returns to scale. Investment is the same as saving so that Say's law prevails and there are no effective demand problems.[1] The labor market clears at full employment through changes in the real wage, but the properties of the model will remain the same if there is a constant rate of unemployment (with a real wage above the market-clearing level). Technical progress is exogenous and labor augmenting (or Harrod-neutral), that is, it increases output per worker without changing the capital-output ratio.

The model is a theory of how the economy converges to a steady state and of the configuration of this steady state. It includes an explanation of why the steady state value of the capital-labor endowment is what it is and of the determination of the economy's rate of growth inside and outside the steady state.[2] There are several ways to present this theory. Along with the standard presentation using a diagram that shows the steady state, capital-labor ratio at the intersection of gross investment and effective depreciation, I also present the model in (capital intensity, real wage) space. The resulting diagram will prove useful in later chapters by facilitating the comparison with alternative growth theories.

The Model

Technology displays constant returns to scale and diminishing returns to variable proportions. We assume a Cobb-Douglas production function:

$$Y = K^a (EL)^{1-a} \quad a < 1,$$

where Y is output, K is the capital stock, L is labor input in natural units, and EL is labor input in effective units. Dividing total output by effective labor (EL), output per effective worker is:

$$y^E = (k^E)^a \quad y^E = Y/(EL) \quad k^E = K/(EL). \tag{1}$$

Figure 8 shows the graph of equation 1 as a curve that begins at the origin and has a positive and diminishing slope as k increases. In the short run, with given factor endowments $(K$ and $L)$ and a given state of technology (E), the ratio k^E is thus given. The value of y^E along the curve shows, then, the full employment level of output per worker corresponding to each given value of the k^E ratio.

Over time, technology and factor endowments change. Technical progress proceeds at a rate β. The labor force grows at an exogenous rate (n). The savings rate (s) is fixed, and thus a constant fraction of total income is devoted to the replacement and expansion of the capital stock period after period. The capital-labor ratio (k^E) will also be changing at a rate equal to the difference between gross investment per effective worker (sy^E) and the effective depreciation of the capital-labor ratio — determined by the depreciation rate (δ) and the growth rate of the effective labor supply $(n + \beta)$:

$$dk^E/dt = sy^E - (n + \beta + \delta)k^E. \tag{2}$$

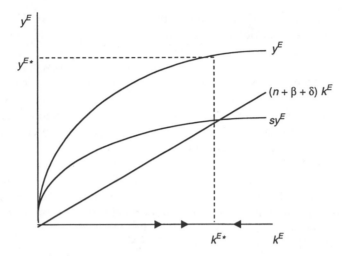

Fig. 8.   The Solow model

The first term in the right-hand side (RHS) of equation 2 is gross investment per effective worker. This term, proportional to output per effective worker, is a function of k^E and is shown in figure 8 as the sy^E curve, which has, like the y^E curve, a positive and diminishing slope. The term $(n + \beta + \delta)$ is the sum of the growth rate of the effective labor supply and the depreciation rate. When multiplied by a given value of k^E, it shows the amount of investment required to keep k^E constant at that given value. In figure 8, this is a line from the origin with positive and constant slope, given our assumptions of positive and constant values for n, β, and δ.

If initially dk^E/dt is positive, will the capital-labor ratio (k^E) keep growing forever or will it converge to a constant value? Substituting from equation 1 into equation 2 and dividing both sides of the equation by k^E, the proportionate rate of growth of k^E is given by:

$$\hat{k}^E = s/(k^E)^{1-a} - (n + \beta + \delta) \quad \text{where } \hat{k}^E = (dk^E/dt)(1/k^E),$$

which shows that the growth rate k^E is a decreasing function of its level provided that $a < 1$ (diminishing returns to capital). In the Cobb-Douglas specification adopted, the growth rate then converges to zero for the value of k^E given by:

$$k^{*E} = [s/(n + \beta + \delta)]^{1/(1-a)}. \tag{3}$$

This is the steady state level of the capital-labor ratio. The steady state value of output per worker is obtained by substituting from equation 3 into equation 1:

$$y^{*E} = [s/(n + \beta + \delta)]^{a/(1-a)}. \tag{4}$$

Figure 8 illustrates the determination of k^{E*} at the intersection of the gross investment curve and the line of effective depreciation. Indeed, k^{E*} is the solution to equation 2 for $dk^E/dt = 0$ and therefore to the equation $sy^E = (n + \beta + \delta)k^E$. The steady state value of output per worker is the value on the y^E curve corresponding to k^{E*}. The figure also illustrates the stability of this steady state. For values of k^E below k^{E*}, the gross investment curve is above the depreciation line and thus actual investment is larger than the amount required to keep k^E constant at that given value. The capital-labor ratio increases toward k^{E*}. Analogous reasoning applies to the case of values where k^E is higher than the steady state level.

An Alternative Presentation: The Real Wage Diagram

Consider the determination of the real wage in this economy. From the first-order conditions for profit maximization, taking as given the capital stock and technology and assuming atomistic competition, we get the labor demand function (in effective units) $(EL)^d = [(1 - a)/w^E]^{1/a}K$, where w^E is the real wage per effective worker. This yields a downward-sloping labor demand curve. Given the exogenous labor supply, the real wage adjusts to clear the labor market. Setting labor demand equal to the exogenous labor supply (EL) and then solving for w^E, we obtain this short-run equilibrium wage (w^E):

$$w^E = (1 - a)(k^E)^a. \tag{5}$$

In $(\log k^E, \log w^E)$ space (where log refers to the natural logarithm, equation 5 is the equation of an upward-sloping line with slope equal to a, the capital share in the production function.

Consider what happens to the market-clearing wage as the capital-labor ratio increases. A higher capital stock increases the demand for labor, and the real wage required to keep labor demand equal to a given labor supply must increase. Alternatively, a higher capital stock (given the labor supply) increases the marginal product of labor at full employment, and, since in competitive equilibrium the real wage is equal to the marginal product of labor at full employment, the real wage must increase with the capital stock. The locus of (k^E, w^E) combinations along

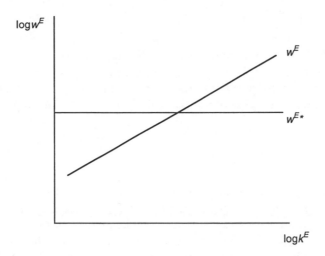

Fig. 9. The Solow model in the real wage diagram

which the labor market clears is shown as the w^E line in figure 9, which
provides an alternative presentation of the Solow model in $(\log k^E, w^E)$
space. The w^E line is thus a schedule of *short-run equilibria* showing the
market-clearing value of the real wage at each level of the capital-labor
ratio. Note that the slope of the w^E line is less than unity under diminishing returns to capital $(a < 1)$, and thus the rate at which the real wage
increases with the capital-labor ratio is decreasing. It is also worth noting
that the real wage is a scale-independent function of capital intensity
only under the present assumption of constant returns to scale.[3]

The w^{E*} line in figure 9 is a schedule of *long-run equilibria* along
which the capital-labor ratio (k^E) remains constant over time. Therefore,
it shows the value of the real wage required to generate the steady state
rate of capital accumulation at each given level of the capital-labor ratio.
This required real wage is obtained as follows. Consider the rate of
capital accumulation (I/K) expressed as:

$$I/K = (s/a)r - \delta, \tag{6}$$

where I is net investment, r is the profit rate on capital, a is the
profit share in competitive equilibrium, and s and δ, as before, are the
saving and the depreciation rates. The profit rate can be expressed, in
turn, as a function of the real wage. Since in competitive equilibrium we
have $r = aY/K = ay^E/k^E$, using equations 1 and 5 we obtain:

$$r = a[(1 - a)/w^E]^{(1-a)/a}. \tag{7}$$

Substituting from equation 7 into equation 6, we can solve for the value of the real wage (w^{*E}) required to generate the steady state rate of accumulation by setting the rate of capital accumulation equal to the growth rate of the effective labor supply $(n + \beta)$. The required real wage is:

$$w^{*E} = (1 - a)[s/(n + \beta + \delta)]^{a/(1-a)}. \tag{8}$$

Equation 8 defines the schedule of long-run equilibria or stationary capital-labor ratios. Under our present assumptions, this is a horizontal line in $(\log k^E, \log w^E)$ space (see fig. 9). Given s, n, β, and δ, there is a unique real wage yielding a profit rate such that the capital stock grows at the rate of effective labor supply growth. Clearly, if there is a steady state, the steady state value of the real wage must be given by equation 8: values off this locus imply that the capital-labor ratio is changing over time and, from equation 5, that the real wage must be changing as well.[4]

Properties

Two well-known results follow from this setup. The first is that the economy described converges to a steady state in which output and the capital stock grow at the same rate, equal to the Harrod-Domar natural rate. This growth rate is the sum of the rate of growth of the labor force (n) and the rate of technical progress (β) and is thus independent of the savings rate. In the steady state, the real wage (w) and output per worker (y) grow at the same rate as the rate of labor-augmenting technical progress (since $w = w^E E$, $y = y^E E$, and w^E and y^E are constant in the steady state).

The second result refers to what happens when the economy is off the equilibrium path. Suppose, for example, that the capital-labor ratio is below its steady state value. Due to the relative abundance of labor, the market-clearing wage is below the wage required to generate the steady state rate of capital accumulation. In this situation, the profit rate is relatively high and the capital stock will be growing faster than the effective labor force (see eq. 6). With the capital stock per effective worker increasing, labor productivity and per capita incomes will be growing at a faster rate than technical progress. Will the capital-labor ratio (k^E) and income per effective worker keep growing forever? It will not because the increasing capital-labor ratio pulls with it the real wage, driving the profit rate down and reducing the rate of capital accumulation. The latter will thus gradually converge toward its steady state value and, when the adjustment is completed, the wage per effective worker (w^E) and the profit rate both remain stationary. During the adjustment, the economy's growth rate is higher than in the steady state, and growth is faster the lower the initial value of the capital endowment per worker is. Thus, and this is the result that I want to emphasize, starting from a relatively low capital-labor ratio, the economy converges to the equilibrium path at a diminishing rate of growth.

In terms of figure 9, this property implies that the excess of the growth rate over its steady state value is a positive function of the gap between the w^E and w^{*E} lines. Indeed, using equation 6, the profit rate in the steady state must be such that:

$$n + \beta = (s/a)r^* - \delta, \tag{9}$$

where r^* is the steady state value of the profit rate, derived from equation 7 under $w^E = w^{*E}$. Subtracting equation 9 from equation 6, and using $\hat{y}^E = a\hat{k}^E$, we can express the growth of output per effective worker as a function of the gap between r and r^*:

$$\hat{y}^E = s(r - r^*). \tag{10}$$

Using equations 7, 8, and 10, as shown in the appendix to this chapter, we have as an approximation:

$$\hat{y}^E = \Omega(\log w^{*E} - \log w^E) = \Omega(\log y^{*E} - \log y^E), \tag{10'}$$

where $\Omega = (1 - a)(n + \beta + \delta)$. Equation 10' shows the growth of output per effective worker as an increasing function of the gap between the actual level of income and its steady state value.

The presence of diminishing returns to capital is critical to these properties of the model. To better understand this role, it will be useful to consider for a moment an economy with a constant population and no technical progress. In such an economy, output will eventually stagnate since its equilibrium path is a stationary state in which the economy generates a gross investment just equal to the depreciation of the capital stock. If, starting from this equilibrium, net investment becomes positive, the larger capital stock will have two consequences. First, output per worker will increase since each worker has a greater capital stock to his or her disposal. Second, at the initial real wage labor demand will be greater; in the face of an inelastic labor supply, the real wage has to be higher to clear the labor market. To say that there are diminishing returns to capital is the same as saying that the positive effect of the larger capital stock on labor productivity is not strong enough to offset the negative effect of the higher equilibrium real wage on the rate of profit. As a result, the market wage rises above the required wage. The rate of return on capital falls below its stationary state value, and the positive level of net investment cannot be sustained. The capital stock contracts and eventually returns to the initial equilibrium value. In this equilibrium state, there is not, and there cannot be, an endogenous process of capital accumulation. This helps us to understand the crucial role played by technological progress and growth of the labor force in this theory; steady state growth is the outcome of these forces simply because there are no other forces capable of neutralizing the influence of diminishing returns to capital.

All this is so, of course, on the equilibrium path. If the capital stock per worker is smaller than in the steady state, there is an additional force that drives growth: the fact that the rate of return on capital is higher than in the steady state (the market wage is lower than the required wage). With diminishing returns to capital, this driving force is strongest the smaller the capital-labor ratio is since the lower real wages more than offset the low labor productivity associated with the small capital-labor ratio. Hence, the second result of the model is that, off the steady state, the economy's growth rate is higher the lower the capital-labor ratio is with respect to its steady state value.

Empirical Shortcomings

The Solow model thus has clear answers to the questions: why are some countries richer than others and why do some economies grow faster than others? Regarding the first question, there are two sources of income differences across countries. First, they may be due to different steady state values of output per worker. Assuming access to the same technology, we know from equation 4 that they arise from differences in savings behavior, population growth, and depreciation rates. The second source refers to disequilibrium differences in capital-labor ratios, that is, to gaps across countries in their position vis-à-vis their steady state. Thus, a large difference in output per worker between two countries, for example, the United States and India, may be the result of the United States having a higher steady state level of income than India does and/or of India being much further away from its steady state than is the United States. Let us then look at the question of how large the differences are in the steady state levels of income implied by the Solow model.

Actual and Steady State Values of Output per Worker

Table 7 shows the actual levels of output per worker in 1997, along with other indicators, in five groups of countries. The information refers to a sample of 73 countries for which the relevant information was available. I aggregated these 73 countries into five income groups selected in such a way as to minimize the dispersion of incomes around the mean and to have approximately 15 countries in each group. Group 1, for example, includes 18 high-income countries (most of them members of the OECD) and group 5 includes 13 low-income countries, mostly in sub-Saharan Africa and South Asia. The appendix presents the data sources used and the detailed composition of the country groups.

The first few rows of the table reveal a well-known result (see Mankiw, Romer, and Weil [MRW] 1992): income levels tend to be positively correlated with investment ratios and negatively correlated with population growth rates. That is, countries with relatively high incomes tend to have higher investment ratios and lower population growth rates. That is why, when using equation 4 to regress incomes against investment ratios and a measure of $(n + \beta + \delta)$, one obtains coefficients that have the signs expected by the Solow model. The estimates for our country sample are:

$$\log y_{97} = -0.69 + 1.27 \log(I/Y) - 4.57 \log(n + \beta + \delta) \text{ (adj.) } R^2 = 0.29.$$
$$\quad\;\; (-0.29) \quad (3.4) \qquad\qquad (-4.99) \qquad\qquad\qquad N = 73$$

TABLE 7.   Actual and Steady State Income Gaps in the Solow Model

	Averages for Country Groups				
	1	2	3	4	5
GDP per worker (1997)[a]	46,693	26,488	11,775	4,995	1,988
Investment share (%)[b]	23.2	21.4	24.9	21.4	19.4
Growth of the labor force (%)[c]	1.4	2.2	3.0	2.7	2.4
GDP per worker (1965)[a]	23,358	17,471	7,378	4,358	1,973
Income as a percentage of group 1 (1997)	100	56.7	25.2	10.7	4.3
Steady state income as a percentage of group 1	100	90.5	92.7	87.6	85
Number of countries	18	14	13	15	13

Note: See the appendix to this chapter for data sources.

[a]Figures are in 1997 international dollars.

[b]Average share 1965–97 (of gross investment in GDP)

[c]Trend growth rate of the labor force (1965–97) (percentage per year)

The t-statistics are in parentheses. Following MRW 1992 $(\beta + \delta)$ is assumed to be .05 $(\beta = .02$ and $\delta = .03)$. I/Y is the investment share (the average for the period 1965–97).

Is it possible to say more? It is if we make some additional assumptions. To begin with, let us use a version of the Solow model that leaves aside differences in technology. Assume therefore the same initial levels of technology (E_0) and uniform rates of technical progress across countries. Equation 4 then allows us to estimate the steady state values of output per worker in any given group as a fraction of that in group 1. More precisely, letting subscript i refer to groups 2 to 5, equation 4 implies that:

$$\log(y_i^*/y_1^*) = a/(1 - a)\{[\log(s_i/s_1)] - \log[(n_i + \beta + \delta)/(n_1 + \beta + \delta)]\}. \quad (4')$$

Further, assume with MRW (1992) that $(\beta + \delta)$ is 0.05, a profit share (a) equal to one-third, and measure s as the investment share (I/Y). Then, using the data in table 7 and plugging it into equation 4', we can obtain the predicted steady state levels of income for groups 2 to 5 (relative to group 1) and compare them with the actual differences in output per worker. We can thus address the question of how much of the income gaps across countries can be explained by differences in their steady state income levels.

The results are shown in rows 5 and 6 of table 7. Differences in the steady state income levels turn out to be very small compared to the actual income gaps in 1997. Consider, for example, the richest and poorest countries: while the actual income gap between them is in the 20 to one range, the steady state income of group 5 is only 15 percent lower than that of group 1. It is worth noting that the assumed value of the profit share (a) of one-third is far from being uniform across countries. The capital share varies significantly, tending to be higher than one-third in many developing countries for which information is available. It is apparent from equation 4' that had we assumed a profit share for groups 2 to 5 higher than the value of one-third that seems appropriate for group 1, the predicted income gaps would have been even narrower. This is because a higher profit share tends to increase the steady state income level in groups 2 through 5.[5]

Differences in Growth Rates

The answer of the Solow model to the second question — why do some economies grow faster than others? — is that differences in growth rates of output per worker should reflect differences in the exogenous rate of labor productivity growth and in the position relative to the steady state (the component of growth due to transitional dynamics). Formally, using $\hat{y} = \beta + \hat{y}^E$, equation 10' implies that:

$$\hat{y} = \beta + \Omega(\log y^{*E} - \log y^E), \tag{11}$$

where Ω, equal to $(1 - a)(n + \beta + \delta)$, is the rate of convergence — the fraction of the gap between the actual and the steady state level of income that is eliminated per unit of time. Equation 11 shows the growth of output per worker as the sum of two components: (1) an exogenous one given by the rate of technical progress (β); and (2) a transitional one, due to capital deepening, which is proportional to the gap between the initial and the steady state values of output per effective worker.

As shown by equation 11, and as emphasized by MRW (1992), the Solow model does not imply that poor countries should systematically grow faster than rich countries, even if one neglects differences in exogenous rates of technical progress across countries (and assumes equal βs). Convergence is conditional on the determinants of the steady state, and the implications of the model are consistent with a poor country (close to its steady state) growing more slowly than a richer country that is further away from the steady state.

For this to happen, however, the implied differences in the steady state levels of income must be very large (similar, or even larger in the example above, than the observed differences in actual levels of output per worker). Yet the picture that emerges from the analysis is that the income gaps implied by the Solow model are largely the result of international differences in the position relative to the steady state rather than of differences in steady state values of output per worker. Poor countries would appear to be poorer than others largely because they are much further away from the steady state than wealthier countries are. As we know, such a view has clear implications for differences in growth rates across countries: poor economies should grow faster than rich ones.

The evidence presented in chapter 1 has already indicated that this implication finds no empirical support. Much of the "convergence controversy" revolves precisely around the fact that the Solow model appears to overstate a tendency toward convergence in the world economy. We can confirm this implication by using equation 11 to estimate the growth rates predicted by the model.[6] The main difficulty here is that we do not have estimates of the initial gap relative to the steady state (y^{*E}/y^E_0). However, we can decompose this term, for each group of countries, as follows:

$$\log(yi^{*E}/yi^E_0) = \log(y^{*E}_i/y^{*\,E}_1) + \log(y^{*\,E}_1/y^E_{1\,0}) + \log(y^E_{1\,0}/y^E_{i\,0}).$$

The first term in the RHS is the gap in steady state incomes between each country group and group 1. This is the gap estimated in table 7 (since according to the assumption of identical technologies the ratios of output per effective worker are the same as the ratios of output per worker). The third term is the initial 1965 gap in actual incomes that can be obtained from table 7. The second term is the gap, within group 1, between the initial level of income and the steady state level of income in 1997. We can obtain an estimate of this term, conditional upon the assumption that the model correctly predicts the growth rate of group 1,[7] by using equation 11 to solve for the value of $\log(y^{*\,E}_1/y^E_{1\,0})$ implied by the model.

Table 8 shows the predicted growth rates (with a capital share equal to one-third in all groups) together with actual growth rates. Given that differences in the steady state levels of income only explain a small part of actual income gaps, the predicted growth rates increase, as expected, as we move down along the income scale. This is not, however, what happens with actual growth performances. Instead of narrowing over time, the evidence suggests widening income gaps across broad groups of countries (in particular, between groups 1, 2, and 3 on one side and groups 4 and 5 on the other). The results in table 8 add something to this well-known picture, for not only is there no tendency toward absolute convergence but there are no strong tendencies toward conditional convergence either. This is evident in the case of group 5. Its growth performance suggests that this group was moving *away* rather than *toward* its steady state level of income, given that its growth rate (0.2 percent growth in GDP per worker) was well below the rate of technical progress, which is in the order of 2 percent per year.

TABLE 8.   Actual and Predicted GDP Growth Rates (1965–97) in the Solow Model

	Averages for Country Groups				
	1	2	3	4	5
Growth rates per year					
GDP (actual)	3.5	3.4	4.5	3.1	2.6
GDP (predicted)	3.5	4.7	7.9	9.1	10.2
GDP per worker (actual)	2.1	1.3	1.5	0.5	0.2
GDP per worker (predicted)	2.1	2.6	4.9	6.5	7.8
Number of countries	18	14	13	15	13

Note: See the appendix to this chapter for data sources.

Extensions: Technology and Human Capital

The differences in growth rates predicted by the Solow model are thus larger than those observed, and they often have the wrong sign. This applies, however, to a very crude version of the neoclassical growth model, one with no technological gaps, no factors of production other than labor and physical capital, and constant savings rates. We have reestablished what has been known for a long time: poor countries are such due to factors other than exclusively their relatively low capital-labor ratios, savings rates, and higher population growth rates.[8] I now turn to the question of what those factors might be and review some popular extensions of the Solow model.

The natural candidates are suggested by equation 10. The growth of output per worker for any given country can be written as $\hat{y} = \beta + s(r - r^*)$. The fact that differences in growth rates are smaller than predicted by the Solow model may be due to one or more of the following reasons. First, the model may overstate the gap between the actual and the steady state profit rate $(r - r^*)$, the more so as we move down the income scale from richer to poorer countries. Second, rates of technical progress (β) may be significantly different across countries and may counteract the effects of diminishing returns to capital. Third, investment rates (s) may change throughout the transition in such a way as to offset the effect of the gap $(r - r^*)$.

Technology Gaps

In a broad interpretation, the variable E in the production function captures any factors affecting the efficiency with which different countries use their capital and labor inputs, including resource endowments, institutions, and access to best practice techniques. In the simple version of the Solow model, cross-country differences in this variable were assumed away. We have thus, in particular, assumed the existence of an internationally accessible production function. Technology gap explanations focus on this assumption and consider it the major source of the empirical shortcomings of the Solow model.

What if different economies, in particular those of developing and developed countries, operated on different production functions? The low productivity of the technologies in use in underdeveloped countries can then generate low incomes independently of differences in savings rates, population growth, or factor endowment. Moreover, the low productivity of the technologies can be the source of both the low incomes and the slow growth of the poorer countries. Formally, we can write the growth rate of output per worker as:[9]

$$g_y = \beta + a[(sE^{1-a}/k^{1-a}) - (n + \beta + \delta)]. \tag{12}$$

Consider now two economies with identical saving rates, population growth rates, and capital-labor ratios but different production functions reflected in different values of E. The economy using the inferior technology necessarily has a lower output per worker (since eq. 1 implies that $y = E^{1-a}k^a$, and k is by assumption the same in the two economies). From equation 12, it also has a lower growth rate, since its profit rate (equal to $a\, E^{1-a}/k^{1-a}$) is smaller as a result of the lower productivity of its technology. Clearly, if differences in E are sufficiently large, there is nothing to prevent countries with low incomes and less productive technologies from having relatively low growth rates.

Islam (1995) followed a panel data approach to estimate an extended version of the Solow model that allows for "country-specific effects." From these estimates, he then constructed country-specific indices of the initial levels of E. Using them to adjust the steady state income gaps implied by the Solow model has a number of shortcomings, including the fact that country-specific effects were estimated on the assumption that the exogenous rate of technical progress (β) is uniform across countries. Nevertheless, these estimates will prove helpful in illustrating the potential and limitations of interpreting these differences as a result of technological gaps.

Table 9 shows Islam's estimates of E for our five groups of countries (as a percentage of group 1). Multiplying these by the steady state income gaps implied by the Solow model yields the steady state income gaps adjusted for country-specific effects. These are shown in the third row of the table. From the information in table 7 and the new values of

TABLE 9.   Steady State Income Gaps and Growth Rates in a Solow Model Adjusted for Country-Specific Effects

	Averages for Country Groups				
	1	2	3	4	5
Country-specific value of E	100	57.5	35.4	18.4[a]	9.9[b]
Income as a percentage of group 1 (1997)	100	56.7	25.2	10.7	4.3
Steady state income (predicted)	100	52.6	32.8	16.1	8.4
GDP growth (actual) (1965–97)	3.5	3.4	4.5	3.1	2.6
GDP growth (predicted)	3.5	3.4	5.2	4.4	4.5
Number of countries	18	14	13	15	13

Note: See the appendix to this chapter for data sources.
[a]Average excludes Indonesia
[b]Average excludes Burkina Faso

steady state income, we can then use equation 11 to estimate the predicted growth rates implied by these new values. These estimates assume a capital share of one-third.

As the table reveals, adjusting the Solow model for country-specific differences in E has the effect of dramatically enlarging the predicted steady state income gaps and thus of bringing them closer to the actual income gaps. The picture that emerges is almost the exact opposite of that seen in the simple Solow model. Economies are now very close to their steady states, and this reduces the differences in growth rates considerably.

That the adjusted model fits the evidence much better than the original should not be surprising: the estimates of E are those that make the adjusted Solow model best fit the data. The question, then, is whether a technology gap interpretation of differences in E provides a satisfactory account of income levels and growth rates.

A number of difficulties arise when one adopts this perspective. First, differences in E are simply too large to be interpreted as technology gaps. It is hard to see why some countries should persistently use technologies that are 10 times less productive than others (as implied by the differences in E between groups 1 and 5).[10] Even a technology gap of five to one implies, as Mankiw (1995, 283) observes, that poor countries are using technologies that are about 80 years out of date (assuming that technological change enhances productivity by 2 percent per year). If their profit rates are so low as a result of the use of inferior technologies, why haven't the many opportunities for technology transfer, in the presence of international capital mobility, narrowed the technology gaps that account for these low profit rates?

The gaps in E are so large that the transitional component of growth rates in the poorer countries (especially groups 4 and 5) turns out to be negative. In other words, these countries appear to have been initially above their steady states and to be converging from above by reducing their capital stocks per effective worker. This raises a troubling question: with such extremely low incomes, how did they get above their steady states? These observations suggest that the good fit of the model is to a large extent illusory. The low income levels and slow growth performance of poor countries have to be attributed to poorer countries operating with very inferior technologies, while the key question of why they do so seems hard to answer.

Even if we were to accept the possible existence of such large technology gaps and assume that countries have operated on vastly different production functions, rates of technological progress should now be different also. Accounting for these differences should be an essential part of a technology gap explanation of why growth rates differ. The natural hypothesis, which goes back to Gershenkron 1962, is that the larger the technological gap the faster the rate of technical progress will be since the profit opportunities and potential technological jumps are larger. In terms of equation 11, this view amounts to reducing the transitory component of the growth in output per worker (due to capital deepening) while at the same time increasing the exogenous component due to technological progress. While reasonable at first sight, this view has implications that are hard to reconcile with the evidence. Depending on the function relating the rate of technical progress to the technology gap, the resulting model may fit the data better or worse than the simple Solow model. However, insofar as technology gaps are proportional to actual income gaps, the model will share with the Solow model the feature that, for countries with similar characteristics (similar steady state income levels), growth rates should increase as we move down the income scale. To the extent that large technology gaps should lead to high growth rates as a result of rapid technical progress, convergence is seen as a process of technological catch-up instead of the result of capital deepening along a production function. But the transitional dynamics remain largely unaffected, and, as we have seen, this feature is the major empirical shortcoming of the Solow model.

Of course the determinants of the steady state level of income need not be the same as in the Solow model (savings rate and population growth). Suppose that the country-specific rate of technological progress is a function of the gap with respect to the best-practice technique and of an index of the country's ability to adopt more advanced technologies (for a simple formulation of this function, see Bernard and Jones 1996). With different abilities to adopt technology, otherwise similar countries will not converge to the same level of technology, and thus to the same steady state level of income, even though their rates of technological progress will converge. Technology gaps will persist in the steady state, these equilibrium gaps being determined by differences across countries in their ability to adopt technological advances. This, then, raises the question of what determines these different abilities. I now turn to this issue, although only insofar as it relates to the differences in human capital.

Adding Human Capital

MRW (1992) extended the Solow model by adding human capital accumulation. In their view, human capital is the key omitted factor in the simple version of the Solow model. Suppose, then, that technology is now described by:

$$Y = K^a H^b (EL)^{1-a-b} \quad a + b < 1,$$

where H is human capital. As before, the production function exhibits constant returns to scale and the inequality $a + b < 1$ ensures the presence of diminishing returns to all capital. Normalizing by effective labor:

$$y^E = (k^E)^a (h^E)^b \tag{13}$$

or

$$y = E^{1-a-b} k^a h^b,$$

where: $h^E = H/(EL)$ and $h = H/L$,

which shows that output per worker (y) depends now on skills per worker (h) in addition to capital per worker (k) and technology (E). MRW treat physical and human capital symmetrically. They assume that both types of capital depreciate at the same rate (δ) and that society invests a fraction, s_H, of its total income in human capital. The accumulation equations for physical and human capital (in terms of their ratios to effective labor) are then:

$$\hat{k}^E = sy^E/k^E - (n + \beta + \delta) \tag{14}$$

$$\hat{h}^E = s_H y^E/h^E - (n + \beta + \delta). \tag{15}$$

From equations 13, 14, and 15, setting $\hat{k}^E = \hat{h}^E = 0$, we obtain the steady state values of k^E and h^E:

$$k^{*E} = [s^{1-b} s_H^{b}/(n + \beta + \delta)]^{1/(1-a-b)} \tag{16}$$

$$h^{*E} = [s^a s_H^{1-a}/(n + \beta + \delta)]^{1/(1-a-b)}. \tag{17}$$

Figure 10 illustrates in ($\log k^E$, $\log h^E$) space the determination of k^{*E} and h^{*E} at the intersection of two schedules, $\hat{k}^E = 0$ and $\hat{h}^E = 0$, along which one of the two capital stocks per effective worker (physical and human, respectively) remains stationary. These two schedules — derived from equations 13 and 14 and 13 and 15, setting $\hat{k}^E = 0$ and $\hat{h}^E = 0$, respectively — are upward sloping due to the positive productivity effects of physical and human capital. For instance, a higher endowment of human capital per worker raises productivity (eq. 13) and stimulates the accumulation of physical capital (eq. 14); to keep k^E constant requires a higher physical capital-labor ratio and thus the positive slope of the $\hat{k}^E = 0$ locus. We can follow similar reasoning to derive the dynamics of the economy off the two loci. To the left of the $\hat{h}^E = 0$ locus, for example, k^E

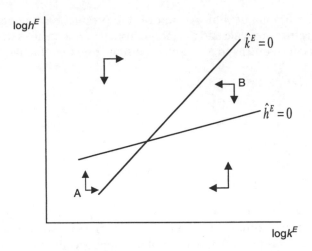

Fig. 10.   The MRW extension of the Solow model

is relatively low at each level of h^E. Output per worker, and thus the accumulation of human capital, must be less than that required to keep h^E stationary, and the stock of human capital per effective worker must then be falling.

Provided that returns to physical and human capital combined diminish $(a + b < 1)$, the two loci intersect at a stable equilibrium.[11] On this equilibrium path, both capital ratios are stationary and the economy, as in the Solow model, grows at the Harrod-Domar natural growth rate. Off the steady state, adjustments will take place in k^E and h^E, and thus the growth rate will be above or below the natural rate. As shown in figure 10, the two schedules divide the ($\log k^E$, $\log h^E$) space into four regions. Two (indicated by points A and B) yield, respectively (and unambiguously), a growth rate above and below the natural rate. In the first case, growth is accompanied by physical and human capital deepening, while in the second a reduction of both physical and human capital per effective worker takes place. The other two regions feature, respectively, physical capital deepening with a reduction of human capital per effective worker (and thus an unambiguously rising k/h ratio) and human capital accumulation with a reduction in the stock of physical capital per effective worker (and therefore a declining k/h ratio).

Substituting now equations 16 and 17 into 13, we can solve for the steady state value of output per worker:

$$y^* = E[s^a s_H^b/(n + \beta + \delta)^{(a+b)}]^{1/(1-a-b)}. \tag{18}$$

Equation 18 shows that, besides E, s, and $(n + \beta + \delta)$ the rate of human capital accumulation (s_H) also affects the steady state value of output per worker. In figure 10, a higher s_H shifts the schedule $\hat{h}^E = 0$ upward and increases the steady state values of h^E and k^E (and thus of output per worker). An alternative way in which MRW express the role of human capital is by combining equations 17 and 18 to derive an equation showing y^* as the product of two terms: (1) the steady state value of output per worker in the Solow model, or $E[s/(n + \beta + \delta)]^{a/(1-a)}$; and (2) a term that is proportional to the steady state level of human capital per effective worker, or $(h^{*E})^{b/(1-a)}$:

$$y^* = E[s/(n + \beta + \delta)]^{a/(1-a)}(h^{*E})^{b/(1-a)}. \tag{19}$$

We can use equation 19, as we did with equation 4, to obtain the steady state income gaps implied by this modification of the Solow model. I now perform the exercise using the data provided by MRW (1992) for their intermediate sample of 75 countries (few data on the proxy for s_H are available after that year). The exercise requires estimates of h^{*E} and thus of s_H and b, which affect the value of h^{*E}. MRW use the percentage of the working-age population in secondary school as a proxy for s_H. Table 10 shows this variable for five income groups into which the 75 countries of MRW's sample were aggregated. I also use the estimate of b (= 0.23) obtained by MRW in their tests of conditional convergence. Using equation 17, we can then estimate the values of h^{*E} implied by the model. The results, presented in table 10, yield very large differences across countries in the steady state values of human capital. It is worth noting, by looking at the second and third rows of the table, that the human capital gaps implied by the model are indeed much larger than the actual ones, as measured by the differences in average years of schooling in the population over age 25.[12]

Multiplying the steady state income gaps implied by the Solow model for 1985 by the factor $(h^{*E})^{b/(1-a)}$, given the estimate of h^{*E} in table 10, yields the steady state income levels implied by the MRW model. As table 10 shows, adding human capital to the Solow model, in the way MRW do it, has the effect of dramatically enlarging the steady state income gaps and bringing them closer to the actual income gaps. The very large equilibrium differences in human capital implied by the model explain this feature. As a comparison with table 9 shows, these differences are of a similar, or even larger, magnitude than those in Islam's (1995) estimates of E. It is not surprising, therefore, that, as in the technology gap explanation, the picture that emerges is almost the exact opposite of that in the simple Solow model. Differences in actual income levels are largely the outcome of differences in the determinants of the steady state that now include the rate of human capital accumulation, savings behavior, and population growth.

These implications are also illustrated by the regression estimate of equation 18, reported by MRW for the intermediate sample of 75 countries:

$$\log y_{85} = 7.81 + 0.70\log(s) + 0.73\log(s_H) - 1.50\log(n + \beta + \delta) \quad \text{(adj.)} \; R^2 = 0.77,$$
$$\quad\quad (1.19) \quad (0.15) \quad\quad\quad (0.10) \quad\quad\quad\quad (0.40)$$

where $(\beta + \delta)$ is assumed to be .05 ($\beta = .02$ and $\delta = .03$), s is the investment share (average for the period 1960–85), and s_H is the percentage of the working-age population in secondary school (average for 1960–85). Standard errors are in parentheses.

In contrast to the Solow model, where low incomes are the result of a scarcity of physical capital relative to labor, with poor economies being well below their steady state, the vision of underdevelopment that

TABLE 10. Steady State Income Gaps and Growth Rates in the Neoclassical Model with Human Capital

	Averages for Country Groups[a]				
	1	2	3	4	5
MRW proxy for s_H[b]	9.5	7.2	6.7	5.0	2.2
Steady state value of h^E	6.0	2.6	2.1	1.1	0.4
	(100)	(43.0)	(36.0)	(18.9)	(5.9)
Education (years)[c]	7.9	4.7	3.3	3.0	1.7
	(100)	(59.9)	(41.8)	(37.7)	(21.1)
Income as a percentage of group					
1 (1985)	100	49.5	27.9	15.6	7.1
Predicted steady state income	100	63.9	37.9	26.4	18.1
Actual GDP growth rate					
(1960–85)	4.2	4.3	5.5	4.6	3.3
Predicted GDP growth rate					
(1960–85)	4.2	5.2	6.6	6.5	6.5
Implied levels of:					
Capital per worker (K/L)[d]	100	26.5	8.7	2.4	0.6
Output per unit of capital					
(Y/K)[d]	100	186.9	320.5	649.4	1176.5
Number of countries	18	16	14	14	13

[a]Figures in parentheses are percentages of group 1.

[b]Percentage of the working-age population in secondary school, average, 1960–85. *Source:* MRW 1992.

[c]Mean years of schooling in the total population over age 25, average, 1960–85. *Source:* Islam 1995.

[d]As percentages of group 1

emerges from the MRW model is one of a dearth of human capital, itself the result of low rates of investment in education. This solution to the shortcomings of the Solow model has been criticized on two grounds. First, if differences in human capital are really so large as to explain much of *actual* income gaps, then the wages of skilled labor and the returns to education in poor countries should be much higher than what we observe. Indeed, allowing for free mobility of physical capital and assuming that the wage for unskilled labor in the poorest countries is one-tenth the wage for unskilled labor in the United States, Romer (1995) shows that the baseline MRW model with exponents of one-third on each of the three factors (K, H, L)—that is, with $a = b = 1/3$—has a number of counterfactual implications: (1) the wage for skilled labor should be 10 times larger in the poorest countries than in the United States, (2) the ratio of the wage for skilled labor to the wage for unskilled labor in the poor country should be 200 (given that this ratio is two in the United States), and (3) the implied rate of return to education in poor countries should be 100 times larger than that in the United States rather than the factor of two or three suggested by the empirical evidence.

The second criticism concerns the importance that MRW attribute to differences in schooling both as a source of differences in output per worker and as a measure of human capital gaps. In his comment to Mankiw (1995), Phelps makes the point that "all or most persons in the labor force could forget everything they learned beyond the ninth grade, say, without putting much of a dent in today's output" (1995, 312). His argument is that most schooling is learning how to learn, which facilitates the adoption and dissemination of technological advances and involves precautionary and thus seemingly redundant knowledge. This is because the young do not know the sequence of jobs that will be most in demand over the course of their working lives. The implication is that international differences in human capital, as understood by MRW, are of little importance, and may even have the wrong sign, in explaining actual differences in productivity levels.[13] The criticism also suggests that those differences that matter—whatever the correct measure of human capital as a factor in the production function is—are likely to be smaller than is implied by the estimates of MRW. In this respect, we may also recall our previous observation that other measures of actual gaps in educational achievement, broader than those of MRW, are significantly smaller than the steady state gaps in human capital implied by the MRW model.

Consider now the implications of the augmented Solow model for international differences in growth rates. We can derive an equation, as we did earlier, to estimate the growth rates predicted by the model. The equation turns out to be the same as equation 11 except that the rate of convergence (Ω) is now equal to $(1 - a - b)(n + \beta + \delta)$ (see MRW 1992). Using this equation, we obtain the predicted growth rates shown in table 10 for the 1960–85 period. It is immediately apparent that the differences in growth rates are smaller than those reported for the Solow model in table 8 and thus closer to actual growth rates, especially in the case of groups 4 and 5. The predicted growth rates are lower since developing country groups are now seen as being much closer to their respective steady states. Moreover, by broadening the notion of capital the MRW model features a larger capital share (twice that of the Solow model), and this slows down the pace of conditional convergence. For these two reasons, the transitional component of growth rates in the developing country groups is now much smaller than in the Solow model.

Although the MRW extension fits the observed differences in growth rates better than the original Solow model, it still overstates the transitional component of growth in developing countries. As shown in table 10, this overestimation becomes larger as we move down the income scale. This suggests again that the very slow growth of the poorest countries (groups 4 and 5) does not seem to reflect a slow rate of conditional convergence. For, no matter how slow this pace is assumed to be, the growth of output per worker should have been at least 2 percent per year (with corresponding GDP growth rates of over 4 or 5 percent per year) as long as these countries are seen to be below their steady state. Thus, the only way in which the model, without further extensions, can generate growth rates below 2 percent for the poorest countries is by enlarging their human capital gaps even more so that initially these countries were *above* their steady state.[14] This interpretation implies that over the period the countries in groups 4 and 5 had been moving toward the steady state from above, that is, that they had been reducing their stocks of human and physical capital per effective worker.

The main problem with this interpretation is that it does not survive as soon as we allow some degree of international capital mobility. The source of the difficulty is ultimately the assumption of international access to a common production function with constant returns to scale. The following exercise illustrates the problem. Consider the MRW estimates of a and b in their tests of conditional convergence ($a = 0.44$, $b = 0.23$) and assume a Cobb-Douglas production function (eq. 13). We can then estimate the gaps in capital per worker and output per unit of capital implied by the actual gaps in human capital *on the assumption of no international differences in technology* (same value of E across countries). The results are shown at the bottom of table 10. They imply very large gaps in capital per worker, which in turn generate very large international differences in the average productivity of capital (*Y*/*K*). These suggest differences in profit rates that, with some degree of capital mobility, should produce strong tendencies toward absolute convergence. This tendency could be prevented by large differentials in the wages of skilled labor in favor of poor countries. Yet, as noted earlier, the observed differentials are far less than would be required. Extended to allow for some capital mobility, the MRW version of the Solow model does not seem to provide a satisfactory solution to the shortcomings of technology gap explanations. Human capital gaps alone, on the assumption that all countries have access to the same technology, do not turn out to be a better explanation of income levels and growth rates than technology gaps are.

Endogeneous Investment Rates

In the Solow model, the investment rate (*s*) is exogenous and remains constant throughout the lengthy transition to the steady state. Would the relaxation of this assumption improve the fit of the Solow model? The investment rate can vary for two reasons when the economy is off the steady state. In the absence of international capital mobility, the investment rate can change along with the domestic savings rate as a result of an increasing level of income and a diminishing marginal product of capital (and thus a falling real interest rate). With international capital mobility, the investment share will also respond to differences in international rates of return and will thus be partially or completely delinked from the domestic savings rate. While this tends to accentuate convergence in a capital model with diminishing returns to capital, the presence of international mobility can also make investment more responsive to international differences in political risk, with novel implications for the determinants of the steady state. We now look at the implications of these different ways of extending the neoclassical growth model.

Endogenous Savings and Poverty Traps

What if the savings rate is endogenous (and determined by intertemporally optimizing households? King and Rebelo (1993) addressed this issue by experimenting with alternative specifications of the households' utility function. In one set of experiments, they used a utility function with constant elasticity of intertemporal substitution. This case leaves the basic convergence properties of the Solow model unchanged, although the pace of convergence depends on the value of elasticity of substitution.

With elasticity equal to one, the simulations show rapid convergence, with falling savings and output growth rates during the transition. The fact that the real interest rate is initially very high and falls during the transition, together with the assumption of relatively high elasticity of intertemporal substitution, accounts for the behavior of the savings rate over time. Because savings are high initially, the rate of convergence is very high (with a half-life of only five years).[15] The relevant conclusion for our purposes here is that with relatively high elasticity of substitution the endogeneity of the savings rate actually exacerbates the counterfactual implications of the neoclassical model. It implies an even faster rate of convergence than that of the neoclassical growth model with a fixed savings rate. In addition, it has the implication that savings rates in poor countries should tend to be higher than in rich countries, rather than lower as observed in the data, to the extent that poor countries can be assumed to be further away from the steady state.

Smaller elasticities of intertemporal substitution have the effect of slowing down the pace of convergence. With elasticity equal to 0.1 (an estimate obtained in Hall 1988), the savings rate increases during the transition period and the growth of output is considerably smaller: instead of five years in the case of elasticity equal to one, the half-life is now 18 years. With less intertemporal substitution in preferences, the savings rate is less elastic and the high interest rates in the initial stages do not offset the tendency to smooth the consumption profile. This is why the savings rate now increases over time. However, because the profit rate is very high in the initial stages, due to low capital-labor ratios, and falls throughout the process, the basic property of a diminishing output growth rate during the transition remains.

In another experiment, King and Rebelo (1993) use a utility function of the Stone-Geary form in which there is a subsistence level of per capita consumption and the elasticity of intertemporal substitution then varies over time. The model features, along with a Solow-type steady state, an unstable steady state at the level of the capital stock compatible with subsistence consumption. The savings rate shows a hump-shaped path. This is because the elasticity of substitution rises as output increases. At low output levels, the model behaves like the one with low elasticity of substitution, and savings rates rise with output. In the latter stages of the transition, the elasticity of substitution is much higher, tending toward its steady state value of one, and thus as output increases the savings rate declines. Interestingly, even though the profit rate falls as output increases, now the growth rate of output does not diminish throughout the transition but has a hump-shaped path similar to that of the savings rate.

The basic insight of the model goes back to the older development literature on poverty traps (Nelson 1956; Leibenstein 1957). We can illustrate it with a consumption function of the following form:

$$c = (\psi - \delta\kappa) + \phi(y - \psi),$$

where c is consumption per worker, ψ is subsistence income per worker, κ is the capital-labor ratio consistent with a subsistence level of income, and ϕ is the propensity to consume out of nonsubsistence income. This consumption function has the property that when income per worker is at the subsistence level savings are just equal to the depreciation of the capital stock (since then $y - c = \delta k$).

The corresponding savings function is:

$$s = \delta\kappa/y + (1 - \phi)(1 - \psi/y), \tag{20}$$

which shows the savings rate as a nonlinear function of the level of income per worker and thus, from equation 1, of the capital-labor ratio. The savings rate rises with income per worker on the condition that the marginal propensity to consume out of nonsubsistence income (ϕ) is less than the average propensity to consume out of subsistence income, that is, less than the ratio of subsistence consumption to subsistence income $(\psi - \delta\kappa)/\psi$. This is equivalent to the condition that the marginal propensity to save $(1 - \phi)$ should be higher than the product of the depreciation rate and the capital-output ratio compatible with a subsistence level of income $(\delta\kappa/\psi)$.[16] Otherwise, the savings rate would tend to fall as income rises above the subsistence level.

Substituting from equations 20 and 1 into equation 4 and using equation 8—leaving aside technical progress and population growth and setting E, for simplicity, equal to 1—yields the following equation for the w^* schedule:

$$w^* = (1 - a)[(\kappa/k^a) + (1 - \phi)(1 - \psi/k^a)/\delta]^{a/(1-a)}. \tag{21}$$

Unlike the Solow model—where there is a unique value of w^*, independent of the capital-labor ratio—the required value of the real wage (w^*) is now a function of the capital-labor ratio. Taking logs in equation 21 and differentiating yields the slope of the w^* locus:

$$\mathrm{dlog}w^*/\mathrm{dlog}k = D/\{\kappa + [(1 - \phi)/\delta](k^a - \psi)\},$$

where $D = (1 - \phi)\psi/(\delta - a\kappa)[a/(1 - a)]$.

The slope of the w^* schedule is positive and falls as k increases, provided that savings are positive and the savings rate rises with income

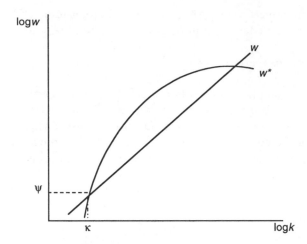

Fig. 11.   A poverty trap model with endogenous savings

per worker.[17] The reason for this upward-sloping w^* schedule is that, as the capital-labor ratio (and thus income per capita) increases, so does the savings rate. The required wage rises, since to maintain a given rate of capital accumulation a lower profit rate is required.

As shown in figure 11, there is now the possibility of multiple equilibria. One of them, at the high-k intersection, is similar to the steady state in the Solow model. The other is a low-k intersection at the subsistence level of income.[18] This intersection is unstable, and below it there is a poverty trap. This trap occurs because at low levels of k income per capita is scarcely sufficient for subsistence and savings fall below depreciation. It is only when the economy has a capital-labor ratio larger than κ, the level consistent with subsistence income, that investment rates can become larger than depreciation and a virtuous circle develops between the expansion of income and a rising savings rate. Eventually, however, the falling profit rate will cause a reduction in the investment rate and thus the hump-shaped pattern of the growth rate.

This hump-shaped path of output growth replicates the similar pattern of growth rates among the developing country groups 2 through 5 and was encountered in chapter 1. The present extension then suggests that the very low growth rates of the poorer countries in groups 4 and 5 arise because their economies are so close to a subsistence level of consumption that their savings rates, and as a result their growth rates, are much lower than those of countries in groups 2 and 3, which have moved further away from the savings trap. This is so even though their capital-labor ratios are lower and their profit rates much higher than in those groups of countries. As King and Rebelo put it: "[D]espite the good investment opportunities, the country does not invest because production is barely enough to attend to subsistence consumption and to the replacement of the depreciated capital stock" (1993, 918).

Such an interpretation of the growth performance of the poorer countries, even though it is appealing at first sight, has a strong counterfactual implication, which is pointed out by King and Rebelo. As their simulations of this case show, the marginal product of capital is very high in the initial stages of development and falls during the transition, just as in the Solow model and the other simulations. With even a small amount of international capital mobility, capital should be rapidly flowing to these countries, alleviating the poverty trap problem and causing the hump-shaped pattern to disappear.

International Capital Mobility and Political Risk

With a large degree of international capital mobility, posttax risk-adjusted rates of return on capital will tend to be equal across countries. This strengthens the process of convergence to the steady state. Moreover, it modifies the nature of steady state, for equilibrium output per worker becomes unrelated to savings and population growth rates. Adjusted for taxes and risk factors, capital-labor ratios, output per worker, and factor prices tend to absolute convergence, even though in the steady state incomes per capita will be higher in countries with high savings rates that will be receiving interest payments from countries with low savings rates. With access to the same technology using physical capital and labor, differences in the steady state values of the capital-labor ratio and the marginal product of capital will fully reflect differences in tax rates and political risk. With immobile human capital in the production function, differences in the capital-labor ratio will also depend on the steady state value of human capital per worker to the extent that returns on human capital are not equalized.

All this suggests that extending the neoclassical growth model to explicitly allow for international capital mobility and political risk can modify the convergence properties of the model considerably. The closed economy determinants of the steady state (investment rates in physical and human capital and population growth) lose importance while political risk becomes an overwhelming influence. More formally, leave aside technical progress and population growth and suppose that the rate of accumulation of capital is a function of the difference between the current profit rate and a risk-adjusted, international profit rate (r^*):

$$I/K = f(r - r^*) \quad f' > 0 \quad f(0) = 0.$$

Setting I/K equal to zero and using the profit function (eq. 7), the schedule of long-run equilibria is now determined by:

$$w^* = (1 - a)(a/r^*)^{(1-a)/a}.$$

Unlike the required wage in the Solow model (see eq. 8), here w^* is independent of the savings rate and population growth and depends on, besides technological parameters, the risk-adjusted profit rate. An increase in political risk, which raises r^* and reduces capital accumulation, has the effect of reducing the steady state value of the real wage. In terms of the real wage diagram, the increase in risk implies a downward shift of the w^* schedule.

Our focus here will be on whether the fact that the low- and lower-middle income countries are not converging to the high-income levels of the rich countries is attributable to the role of political risk factors. It is worth noting that a number of authors have expressed serious doubts about political risk being able to offset the vast differences in rates of return between poor and rich countries implied by the Solow model (see, e.g., Lucas 1988).[19] On the other side, Barro's work (1991, 1997) can largely be seen as an extension of the Solow model that, in addition to the role of human capital, controls for the role of political risk among the determinants of the steady state. The main finding is a positive, although slow, rate of conditional convergence on the order of 2 percent per year that vindicates the neoclassical growth model when extended to include these determinants.

Table 11 shows for the five groups of countries, into which we have aggregated our 73 countries, the growth rates and rule of law index (RLI) used by Barro (1997) as an indicator of political risk. The rule of law index, described in the appendix to this chapter, is available for the years 1982 to 1995, so this is the period for which we can make international comparisons. The average values for the RLI in the first row suggest a close positive correlation between this index and income level and, together with the average growth rates in the second row, they indicate a broadly positive influence of the RLI on growth rates. The last few rows in the table present estimates of the RLI and growth rates separately for the fast- and slow-growing countries in each of the five groups — that is, for countries with growth rates above and below the median growth rate, respectively. The exercise can be seen as a "regression" of growth rates on the RLI that controls for the likely two-way influence (suggested by the first row) between income levels and risk factors (as measured by the RLI).

Differences in RLI values appear to have a significant impact on growth rates at middle-income levels (group 3) where the slowly growing countries have clearly smaller RLI values than fast-growing countries at similar income levels.[20] This is not the case in the high income economies of group 1, where the RLIs are all very high and similar across countries (see appendix). More surprisingly, at low-income levels (groups 4 and 5) growth rates do not appear to be significantly correlated with the RLI values. Differences in RLI values are very small compared to the large differences in growth rates between the fast- and slow-growing countries in these groups and have the wrong sign. Given the similarities in RLIs, the risk-adjusted rates of return on capital should also be rather similar in these two types of countries. Surely, all the countries in groups 4 and 5 have very low RLIs, and this is likely to have been a factor in explaining their generally slow growth. But, if this is the major factor explaining the slow growth of low-income countries, why is it that the same low RLIs did not prevent the fast-growing economies in these groups from growing at faster rates than, say, the slow-growing economies of groups 1 and 2 with their much higher RLIs?

Table 11 and the previous discussion also suggest that the positive relationship between RLIs and growth rates across country groups may be attributable to the existence of a positive relationship between growth and income for the particular time period and country sample for which data on RLIs are available.

In the next two chapters, I turn to approaches, older than the Solow model, that may help to elucidate the solutions to these puzzles.

TABLE 11. Growth and Political Risk, 1982–95

	Averages for Country Groups				
	1	2	3	4	5
Rule of law index	0.92	0.71	0.51	0.48[b]	0.42[c,d]
Growth rate	2.4	1.9	0.9	0.5[b]	−0.7[c,d]
Rule of law index in:					
Fast-growing countries[a]	0.90	0.69	0.56	0.45	0.41[c]
	(3.2)	(3.5)	(2.1)	(2.3)	(0.8)[c]
Slow-growing countries[a]	0.95	0.72	0.44	0.51[b]	0.42[d]
	(1.6)	(0.3)	(−0.5)	(−1.9)[b]	(−1.8)[d]
Number of countries	18	14	13	15	13

Note: See appendix to this chapter for data sources.
[a]Growth rates are in parentheses.
[b]Average excludes Mauritania
[c]Average excludes Benin
[d]Average excludes Burundi and Rwanda

APPENDIX

Derivation of the Rate of Convergence (eq. 10′)

Equation 10 implies: $\hat{y}^E = s(r - r^*) = s(r/r^* - 1)r^*$. From equations 7 and 8, r^* is given by:

$$r^* = (a/s)(n + \beta + \delta). \tag{A.1}$$

Substituting from equation A.1 into equation 10:

$$\hat{y}^E = a(r/r^* - 1)(n + \beta + \delta). \tag{A.2}$$

Taking logs in equation 7 and using this equation to solve for $\log w^{*E} - \log w^E$, we have:

$$\log w^{*E} - \log w^E = [a/(1 - a)](\log r - \log r^*). \tag{A.3}$$

Now, using the approximation $r/r^* - 1 = \log(r/r^*)$, and substituting from equation A.3 into equation A.2:

$$\hat{y}^E = (1 - a)(n + \beta + \delta)(\log w^{*E} - \log w^E). \tag{A.4}$$

Data Sources and the Rule of Law Index

The main source of data is the *World Bank World Development Indicators 1999* CD-Rom. The sample of 73 countries excludes those with centrally planned economies and very small countries with populations of less than a million in 1960 whose real income is likely to be dominated by idiosyncratic factors. I aggregated these 73 countries into five groups according to their real income levels in 1997. The composition of each group is shown in table A2.1 (figures in 1997 international dollars).

The table also shows, in parentheses beside each country, the value of the rule of law index for the period 1982–95 used in the analysis in the section "Endogenous Investment Rates." The scale of the index is between zero and one, with higher values denoting better rule of law maintenance. The index is calculated, following Barro (1997), as a summation of five variables divided by the maximum value. The five variables are:

1. Government repudiation of contracts (0–10 scale)
2. Risk of expropriation (0–10)
3. Corruption (0–6)
4. Law and order tradition (0–6)
5. Bureaucratic quality (0–6)

TABLE A2.1. Groupings according to GDP per Worker in 1997 and the Rule of Law Index (1982–95)

	Group				
	1	2	3	4	5
Income[a]	$56,915–39,511	$37,042–17,061	$15,847–8,241	$7,430–3,489	$2,877–1,163
	Singapore (0.87)	Spain (0.80)	Colombia (0.55)	Indonesia (0.44)	Haiti (0.23)
	United States (0.96)	Sweden (0.98)	Brazil (0.66)	El Salvador (0.34)	Benin[b]
	Belgium (0.96)	New Zealand (0.98)	Tunisia (0.52)	Jamaica (0.51)	Kenya (0.56)
	Ireland (0.88)	Chile (0.64)	Algeria (0.50)	Honduras (0.39)	Zambia (0.41)
	France (0.94)	Greece (0.66)	Ecuador (0.57)	Sri Lanka (0.46)	Nigeria (0.39)
	Norway (0.97)	Portugal (0.79)	Peru (0.42)	Zimbabwe (0.51)	Bangladesh (0.29)
	Austria (0.95)	South Korea,	Guatemala (0.35)	Nicaragua (0.47)	Burkina Faso (0.50)[e]
	Hong Kong (0.81)	Republic (0.69)	Dominican	Cameroon (0.55)	Madagascar (0.48)[e]
	Switzerland (1.00)	Argentina (0.54)	Republic (0.50)	Ivory Coast (0.62)[c]	Niger (0.52)[e]
	Italy (0.80)	Venezuela (0.58)	Thailand (0.67)	Pakistan (0.42)	Mali (0.31)[d]
	Netherlands (0.99)	Mexico (0.58)	Paraguay (0.46)	Senegal (0.48)	Malawi (0.50)
	Japan (0.93)	Uruguay (0.54)	Morocco (0.51)	India (0.58)	Rwanda[b]
	Israel (0.72)	Malaysia (0.71)	Philippines (0.36)	Mauritania[b]	Burundi[b]
	Canada (0.98)	South Africa (0.75)[c]	Egypt (0.50)	Togo (0.43)	
	Denmark (0.98)	Costa Rica (0.65)		Ghana (0.47)	
	United Kingdom (0.94)				
	Australia (0.93)				
	Finland (0.98)				
Number of countries	18	14	13	15	13

Note: Figures in parentheses are the rule of law index (average 1982–95 or closest available period).
[a]Figures are in 1997 current international dollars.
[b]No political risk data available
[c]Average for 1983–95
[d]Average for 1984–95
[e]Average for 1985–95

This data set was assembled by the Institutional Reform in the Informal Sector (IRIS) Center (University of Maryland) from the *International Country Risk Guide,* a monthly publication of Political Risk Services, Inc., of Syracuse, New York. Knack and Keefer 1995, an IRIS working paper, provides descriptions of the variables.

CHAPTER 3

Labor Surplus Economies

All the extensions of the neoclassical growth model discussed in chapter 2 remain within the framework of a one-sector (capitalist) economy, neglecting the coexistence of capitalist and noncapitalist sectors that development economists have generally viewed as a most striking feature of "underdevelopment." I now turn to two-sector growth models in which one of these sectors, the noncapitalist, provides a more or less elastic supply of labor to the capitalist sector. We will consider whether this provides a solution to the failure of the standard prediction, of a falling rate of profit, to come to pass, as noticed by Arthur Lewis (1976).[1] As noted in the previous chapter, this failure is what seems to be behind the empirical shortcomings of the neoclassical model.

The chapter begins with Lewis's classic model with "unlimited supplies of labor." I look at it as a two-sector model with one good and transitional dynamics that turn out to be significantly different from those of the Solow model. I then consider more general assumptions and find that, although the conditions for a perfectly elastic supply of labor are rather restrictive, elasticity of the supply of labor is indeed critical to the nature of the transition (the zero elasticity of the Solow model being another rather restrictive special case). Finally, I extend the model to bring in efficiency wage considerations. A major aim of the chapter is to review and clarify different concepts of surplus labor while bringing them into otherwise neoclassical growth models. Considerable confusion has prevailed in the development literature about the exact meaning of this very influential concept, its relation to the elasticity of the labor supply, and its macroeconomic implications.

The Lewis Model

There are two sectors in the economy, indicated by subscripts S and M. Sector M is a Solow-type capitalist sector. Sector S is noncapitalist in the sense that workers there receive the average product of labor. This sector produces same (composite) good as does the capitalist sector. Thus, it is one in which, to use Haavelmo's expression, workers know "different ways of doing the same thing" (1954, 49). The key difference between the two sectors is that the noncapitalist or subsistence sector uses a negligible amount of capital in production. As stated by Lewis: "The subsistence sector is by difference all that part of the economy which is not using reproducible capital. Output per head is lower in this sector than in the capitalist sector, because it is not fructified by capital" (1954, 147).

The capitalist (or modern) sector uses a technology with constant returns to scale. I assume, for simplicity, a Cobb-Douglas function:

$$M = AK^a(L_M)^{1-a},$$

where M and L_M are output and employment in this sector, K is the capital stock, and A is a productivity variable. In sector S, technology displays constant returns to labor, and output (S) is then given by:

$$S = w_S L_S,$$

where w_S is the given output per worker in the subsistence sector and L_S is the labor force employed in this sector.

Labor markets are competitive in the sense that "the wage which the expanding capitalist sector has to pay is determined by what people can earn outside that sector" (Lewis 1954, 148). More precisely, the wage in the capitalist sector is determined by the wage in sector S plus a wage premium that the capitalist sector has to pay to attract workers from the subsistence sector. This wage premium compensates for the "higher cost of living in the capitalist sector" ("due to the capitalist sector being concentrated in congested towns, so that rents and transport costs are higher") and for migration costs or "the psychological cost of transferring from the easy going way of life of the subsistence sector to the more regimented and urbanised environment of the capitalist sector" (150) There is also a hint in Lewis that the wage premium may be related to efficiency wage considerations (in particular, to the need to reduce turnover costs in the capitalist sector).

The wage premium $(f - 1)$ is constant so that, as long as the two sectors coexist, the capitalist sector pays a real wage, w_M, given by:[2]

$$w_M = fw_s \quad \text{for } L_S > 0. \tag{1}$$

Employment (L_M) in the capitalist sector is determined by the usual profit maximization conditions under the technology constraint. Assuming perfect competition in goods and labor markets, this implies the following demand for labor in the M sector:

$$L_M = [(1 - a)A/w_M]^{1/a}K, \tag{2}$$

where w_M is determined by the wage premium and productivity conditions in the subsistence sector (eq. 1) as long as $L_M < L$.

There is no open unemployment, so workers not employed in the capitalist sector work in the subsistence sector:

$$L = L_M + L_S.$$

Lewis Labor Surplus, Keynesian Unemployment, and the Classical Subsistence Wage

Figure 12 shows the determination of employment in the capitalist sector and, by means of difference from the total labor force, the amount of labor employed in the subsistence sector. When $L_M = L$ and the subsistence sector has disappeared, the real wage will be determined by the intersection of labor demand in sector M and the given overall supply of labor, as in the one-sector model of a mature economy.

What are the necessary conditions for the coexistence of the two sectors? One is fairly obvious, and I have already alluded to it: the average product of labor must be less in the subsistence than in the capitalist sector. Otherwise, the capitalist sector would not be able to generate a surplus, the capital-using technology would not be used, and the whole of the labor force would find employment in the subsistence sector. Lewis takes this condition for granted when he says that "output per head is lower in [the subsistence sector] than in the capitalist sector because it is not fructified by capital" (1954, 147).

The second condition can be derived from figure 12. A positive fraction of the labor force will find it worthwhile to employ itself in the subsistence sector as long as what workers can earn there is more than the marginal product of labor (adjusted for the wage premium) that would result from employing the whole of the labor force in the capitalist sector. That is, a labor surplus will exist as long as the average product of labor of the noncapitalist technology is more than the marginal product of labor (MPL) at full employment in the capitalist sector, equal to the real wage at the intersection of the labor demand curve and the vertical line at L. It is then and only then that at least some workers will be better off working in the subsistence sector rather than searching for jobs in the capitalist sector.

Since the MPL at full employment is an increasing function of the economywide capital-labor ratio, the coexistence of the two sectors will be characteristic of capital-scarce and labor-abundant countries.[3] This is

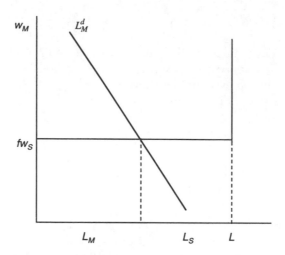

Fig. 12.   Lewis labor surplus

the type of economy that Lewis had in mind and to which he believed the neoclassical model would not apply. In its determination of the real wage, the neoclassical model makes the implicit assumption that the MPL at full employment is higher than the subsistence wage. This Lewis considered appropriate for a "mature economy" — and for "some parts of Africa and of Latin America," where "there is an acute shortage of male labour" (140) — but not for those developing economies in which a capital shortage would give rise to a "labor surplus."

It is worthwhile comparing this notion of labor surplus to two other situations in which the level of employment in the capitalist sector can be said to be demand determined. The first is Keynesian unemployment (see fig. 13). While Lewis's labor surplus is the result of a low level of the economywide capital-labor ratio, unemployment for Keynes derives from a low level of effective demand in the goods market. For Keynes, a deficiency of demand for goods keeps the real wage above the marginal product of labor at full employment and thus gives rise to an excess supply of labor. An increase in effective demand for goods that reduces the real wage — by increasing the price level, given the nominal wage — will then cause an expansion of employment *along* the labor demand curve, thus reducing unemployment.

The similarity with Lewis is that in both cases the real wage is above the MPL at full employment in the capitalist sector. The difference is that in Lewis nothing can be done about it by increasing effective de-

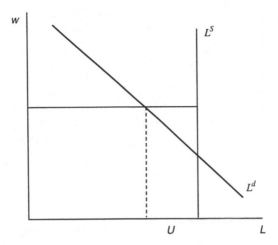

Fig. 13. Keynesian unemployment

mand in the goods market. For employment in the capitalist sector to increase as a result of an expansion in the demand for goods, the real wage would have to fall below the wage in sector S (adjusted for the wage premium). This is prevented by competition in the labor market. The only way to reduce the labor surplus is by expanding not the aggregate demand for goods but the capital stock, an *upward shift* in the labor demand curve rather than a movement *along* it. In modern terminology, the Lewis model refers to a situation of labor market equilibrium with a labor surplus resulting from a "real rigidity." Keynesian unemployment is a situation in which labor market disequilibrium is associated with (even if it is not due to) a "nominal rigidity."

The classical model refers to another distinctive situation. In both Lewis and the classical model, the capitalist sector faces a perfect elastic supply of labor at a "subsistence wage." However, the meaning of *subsistence wage* and the reasons for the elastic supply of labor are very different. The classical is really a one-sector model in the sense that there is no subsistence technology being used by a noncapitalist sector à la Lewis. The labor supply for the economy as a whole is perfectly elastic in a very long run sense. It is through the effects of the real wage on population growth and the operation of the Malthusian principle of population that the labor supply adjusts to the demand for labor at that wage (shown as w in fig. 14), which keeps population at a stationary level.[4] Rather than a subsistence sector, the classical model has an endogenous labor supply and the elastic supply of labor is a locus of a stationary population.

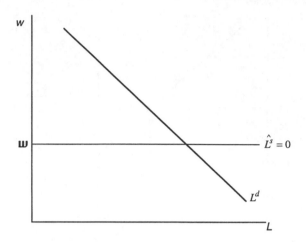

Fig. 14.   The classical subsistence wage

Short-Run Equilibrium and Capital Accumulation

We now derive, as we did in chapter 2 for the Solow model, the schedule of short-run equilibria showing the equilibrium real wage in the capitalist sector (w_M) at different levels of the *economywide* capital endowment per worker (k).

As long as the two sectors coexist, that is, in a labor surplus economy, the equation of the schedule is given by equation 1. The equilibrium wage w_M is independent of k and determined solely by the wage in sector S and the wage premium. The schedule of short-run equilibria in the labor surplus economy is thus a straight line, which is shown in figure 15 as the horizontal segment of the w curve. Changes in the capital-labor ratio determine changes in the employment share of the capitalist sector but leave the real wage unaffected.[5]

When the subsistence sector disappears ($L_S = 0$), the economy becomes a "mature," one-sector economy. The equation of the w curve is now derived from the market-clearing condition that the total labor supply (L) is equal to labor demand in the capitalist sector (L_M). Substituting this condition into equation 2 and solving for w_M, we obtain:

$$w_M = A(1 - a)k^a. \tag{3}$$

For the mature economy, the w curve slopes upward with slope equal to a in ($\log k$, $\log w_M$) space (see fig. 15) and is thus identical to that

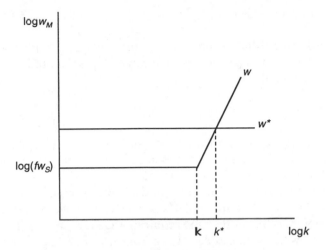

Fig. 15.   The Lewis model

in the Solow model. Let k be the capital-labor ratio at the turning point between a labor surplus and a mature economy. At the turning point, the labor surplus has been absorbed but the wage remains equal to the subsistence wage plus the wage premium. Thus, the value of k can be derived by solving equation 2 for k under $w_M = fw_S$ and $L_M = L$:

$$k = [fw_S/(1 - a)A]^{1/a}.$$

In figure 12, this is the value of the capital-labor ratio for which the MPL at full employment in the capitalist sector is just equal to the average product of labor in the subsistence sector (plus the wage premium).

Consider now the schedule of long-run equilibria. Lewis followed the classical economists in viewing profits as the major source of capital accumulation and workers' aggregate saving as negligible. I adopt this hypothesis, which I later investigate empirically, and assume that workers in both the capitalist and subsistence sectors consume all their earnings. The rate of capital accumulation is then $I/K = s_\pi r - \delta$, where s_π is the savings rate out of profits and r and δ are the profit and the depreciation rates.[6] If we leave aside technical progress, so that the natural rate of growth is equal to the growth rate of the labor force (n), the steady state condition becomes $s_\pi r - \delta = n$.

The profit rate as a function of the wage is derived as in chapter 2. This is:

$$r = aA^{1/a}[(1 - a)/w]^{(1-a)/a}.$$

Substituting from this profit-wage curve into the steady state condition and solving for w_M yields the real wage $(w_M{}^*)$ required to satisfy the steady state condition:

$$w_M{}^* = (1 - a)A^{1/(1-a)}[as_\pi/(n + \delta)]^{a/(1-a)}. \tag{4}$$

This is the equation of the schedule of stationary capital-labor ratios. The schedule, as in the Solow model, is a straight line in (k,w_M) space, shown as the w^* line in figure 15.

Depending on the values of fw_S and w^*, the w and w^* curves may not intersect. This would happen if the subsistence wage adjusted for the wage premium is higher than the required wage $(fw_S > w^*)$. Then the w^* line lies below the w line, and, starting from any initial capital-labor ratio, population growth would outpace capital accumulation. The capitalist sector would be shrinking in relative size, and the economy would tend toward a steady state featuring a subsistence economy with no capitalist sector. In this case, $fw_S > w_M{}^*$, and this implies, using equation 4:

$$w_S > [(1 - a)/f]A^{1/(1-a)}[as_\pi/(n + \delta)]^{a/(1-a)}.$$

Low values of s_π and A along with high values of w_S, f, and n could generate such a path with a shrinking capitalist sector.

If $w^* > fw_S$, the w^* line lies above the horizontal segment of the w curve and the steady state, as shown in figure 15, is at the intersection of the two curves.[7] This is the long-run equilibrium of a Solow model with no technical progress. Starting from an initial capital-labor ratio below this steady state, capital accumulation outpaces labor force growth, as the actual rate of profit is higher than that required by the steady state condition. The capitalist sector then expands in relative size and the capital-labor ratio increases. Eventually, the capital-labor ratio reaches the value k and the subsistence sector disappears. The economy then enters a mature phase, with the capital-labor ratio converging toward its steady state value k^*.

Properties

Lewis focuses on this last case when w^* is larger than fw_S.[8] His view of the process of economic development can thus be interpreted as a transition toward a Solow-type steady state. The transition itself, however, is rather different from that in the Solow model. Even though a Solow-type steady state is the end of the process, the introduction of a labor surplus brings a number of differences into the characteristics of the transition.

First, the growth of the capitalist sector does not proceed at diminishing rates during the transition to the steady state. Rather, it goes on at a constant rate (a function of the distance between the w and w^* lines) until the labor surplus disappears. This constant rate is determined by the savings rate out of profits and the productivity of the capitalist technology (relative to that of the subsistence sector). Then, in the mature phase, capital accumulation continues at a decreasing rate as in the Solow model. The reason for this difference is that during the labor surplus phase the capitalist sector faces an elastic supply of labor. This counteracts the influence of diminishing returns to capital, which accounts for the falling rate of growth during the adjustment process in the Solow model.

The Lewis model, then, implies that the profit rate does not tend to be higher at low-income levels, compared to, say, middle-income levels, as long as the economy remains in the labor surplus phase. Using the production functions of the two sectors, aggregate output ($Y = S + M$) can be written as $Y = L_S + AK^a L_M^{1-a}$, where we set for simplicity $w_S = 1$. Substituting from the labor demand function (eq. 2) under $w_M = f w_S$ and ignoring for simplicity the wage premium (so that $f = 1$), we obtain the following expression for aggregate output:

$$Y = L + A^{1/a}a(1 - a)^{(1-a)/a}K,$$

which shows that even though the technology of the capitalist sector is subject to diminishing returns to capital the Lewis aggregate "production function" during the labor surplus phase displays constant returns to capital.

The constancy of the profit rate during the initial phases of the transition can considerably slow the process of convergence to the steady state. As an example, consider an economy with no population growth where initially the employment share of the capitalist sector is 10 percent. The rate of capital accumulation is such that employment in the capitalist sector grows at an average rate of 3 percent per year. This economy will take 78 years to absorb the whole of the labor surplus into the capitalist sector (this will, of course, take longer if the labor force is expanding). After these 78 years, the economy will not have reached a steady state (at k^*) but only maturity (at k).

During the labor surplus phase, the capital intensity of the whole economy rises, and with it per capita income increases as well. The cause of this growth in per capita income is completely different, however, from that in the mature phase (or in the Solow model). There output per worker rises because the capital intensity in the capitalist sector increases, making each worker in this sector more productive. There is no such increase in the capital intensity of the modern sector during the labor surplus phase. The increase in output per worker is due to the reallocation effects of growth, to the transfer of subsistence sector labor to the capitalist sector, which has higher labor productivity. Indeed, we can write output per worker in the whole economy (y) as a weighted average of output per worker in the two sectors (w_S and y_M, respectively), with the weights being the employment shares of each sector:

$$y = w_S L_S/L + y_M L_M/L = w_S + (y_M - w_S)L_M/L. \tag{5}$$

Alternatively, using the aggregate "production function" derived above and dividing by L (we now let w_S and f be different from 1) yields:

$$y = w_S + ck \quad c = (a + f - 1)[(1 - a)/w_S]^{(1-a)/a}(A/f)^{1/a}. \tag{6}$$

Equation 6 shows average output per worker as an increasing function of the capital-labor ratio in the whole economy: a higher capital-labor ratio increases the employment share of the capitalist sector and, since output per worker is higher there than in the subsistence sector, this reallocation has the effect of increasing output per worker in the whole economy (see eq. 5).

Assuming constant values for w_S and f, equation 6 implies that the growth rate of output per worker (g_y) during the labor surplus phase is:

$$g_y = (1 - w_S/y)g_k,$$

where $g_y = \text{dlog}y/dt$ and $g_k = \text{dlog}k/dt$ is the rate of growth of k. This equation shows g_y as an increasing function of y and g_k. For given values of n and s_π, g_k remains constant during the labor surplus phase, given the constancy of w_M and thus of the rates of profit and capital accumulation. Since y is an increasing function of k (eq. 6), it follows that the growth rate of output per worker increases during the labor surplus phase. Throughout this process, g_y goes from zero (when the employment share of the capitalist sector is so low that its contribution to output is negligible) toward the limit set by the rate of expansion of the capitalist sector. This rate, given that the condition $w^* > fw_S$ is fulfilled, is higher than the natural rate. Then, in the mature phase g_y declines toward the value set by the natural rate. We thus encounter the hump-shaped path of growth rates discussed in chapters 1 and 2.

Who benefits from this growth in per capita incomes during the labor surplus phase? Clearly, with constant earnings per worker in the subsistence sector labor incomes per capita remain constant, except for the presence of a wage premium with little, if any, welfare significance. The gains in output per worker must therefore imply an increasing profit share in total output. This expanding share accounts for the increasing savings rate throughout the labor surplus phase.[9] This is the major stylized fact that Lewis wants to explain:

> The central problem in the theory of economic development is to understand the process by which a community which was previously saving and investing 4 or 5 percent of its national income or less, converts itself into an economy where voluntary saving is running at about 12 to 15 percent of national income or more. This is the central problem because the central fact of economic development is rapid capital accumulation (including knowledge and skills with capital). (1954, 155)

The effects of technical progress on growth and income distribution depend crucially on whether technological change takes place in the capitalist or the subsistence sector. Technical progress in the capitalist sector shifts the w^* line upward and increases profits, leaving real wages constant. At the same time, by raising the profit rate it accelerates the rate of expansion of the capitalist sector and thus speeds up the transition. In contrast, technical progress in the subsistence sector shifts the horizontal segment of the w curve upward and fully benefits workers. Reducing the profit rate hinders the expansion of the capitalist sector.[10]

Are Savings Rates Correlated with Profit Shares?

At the center of Lewis's view of the development process is a rising savings rate. This in turn is attributed to an increasing profit share during the labor surplus phase. Indeed, according to Lewis (1954, 157): ". . . the major source of savings is profits, and if we find that savings are increasing as a proportion of the national income, we may take it for granted that this is because the share of profits in the national income is increasing." Given its popularity, it is surprising that this hypothesis has received little empirical attention. One of the reasons surely must be the difficulty of measuring the share of profits adequately. Another is perhaps that, as Lewis did, it is often taken for granted.[11] We now will look at the relationship between profit shares and savings rates in a cross section of developing countries.

Savings and Profits in Developing Economies

The initial sample has 30 developing countries for which information for
the late 1980s and early 1990s was available from the World Development Indicators (WDI), published by the World Bank. I use the share of
manufacturing profits in GDP as a proxy for the share of modern sector
profits. The appendix describes the data and sources.

Table 12 shows savings rates and the share of manufacturing profits
in GDP for seven country groups ranked according to their savings
rates. Besides a rather close positive correlation between savings and
profit shares, a number of interesting patterns emerge from the table.
First, four East Asian countries (all the East Asian economies in the
sample with the exception of the Philippines) stand out as the only
supersavers. There is a very large gap in savings rates between this group
and the next one, which comprises mainly Latin American countries.
The East Asian economies also have the highest profit shares. These are
the joint outcome of large manufacturing shares, typical of a developed
economy (except for Indonesia), and large profit shares within manufacturing, which are very high even by developing-country standards. Thus,
it is tempting to interpret their very high savings rates as arising from the
coexistence of large and highly productive modern sectors with still
substantial labor reserves. Another salient feature is that most Latin
American countries have savings rates lower than expected given their
profit shares. This feature is what upsets the close relationship when

TABLE 12.   Savings Rates and Profit Shares in Developing Economies

Group	s	π	M/Y	π_M	Countries
1	37.3	19.7	26.0	76.5	Singapore, South Korea, Indonesia, Thailand
2	24.4	17.8	23.6	75.8	Brazil, Venezuela, Peru, Colombia, South Africa
3	21.2	14.6	21.7	66.9	Mauritius, Costa Rica, Ecuador, Turkey, India, Mexico
4	18.5	12.9	19.4	64.1	Cameroon, Kenya, Zimbabwe, Philippines
5	14.0	14.9	20.2	71.6	Uruguay, Argentina, Panama, Honduras, Zambia
6	8.2	9.7	14.7	66.3	Greece, Egypt, Bolivia
7	0.1	8.1	10.8	73.6	Ethiopia, Bangladesh, Jordan

Note: See the appendix to this chapter for sources.
s: Gross domestic savings as a percentage of GDP
π: Share of manufacturing profits in GDP $[=\pi_M(M/Y)]$
M/Y: Share of manufacturing in GDP (%)
π_M: Profit share in manufacturing (100 minus employee earnings as a percentage of value added in manufacturing)

moving from group 4 to group 5, which comprises mostly low savers in Latin America.

It is unlikely that the positive correlation is a result of income levels affecting both savings rates and manufacturing shares. Country groups are rather heterogeneous in terms of income levels, and one finds high- and low-income countries across the spectrum of savings rates. A few examples are low-income Indonesia and India, with much higher savings rates than upper-middle-income Argentina and Greece; Mexico and Turkey have income levels similar to those of South Korea and Thailand but much lower savings rates (a difference of more than 13 percentage points of GDP). It is worth noting also that the information on household savings presented in the appendix—available from UNCTAD (1997) for 10 of the 30 countries in our sample—suggests that, with few exceptions, household saving as a percentage of GDP is remarkably stable at around 9 to 12 percent. This leaves business savings—which originate in profits—as the major source of differences in overall savings rates.

Changes in Savings Rates

We now look at changes in savings rates and profit shares from 1970 to the early 1990s. Our sample is reduced to 25 countries given the absence of information for five countries in our original country sample. Table 13 summarizes the results.

Among the 11 countries with rising savings rates, nine recorded increases in the share of manufacturing profits in GDP, while the other

TABLE 13.   Changes (Δ) in Savings Rates and Profit Shares, 1970–90s (percentage points)

	Δs	$\Delta \pi$	$\Delta M/Y$	$\Delta \pi_M$
Rising savings rates				
East Asia and Mauritius (5)	18.5	7.0	9.4	1.4
Latin America (4)	5.3	0.9	0.9	1.1
India	4.3	3.0	3.0	7.7
Turkey	3.4	6.3	7.0	4.8
Falling or stagnant savings rates				
Latin America (5)	−9.6	0.9	−1.7	9.7
Africa (6)	−7.7	4.5	6.0	1.7
Greece	−11.0	−3.4	−3.0	−8.7
Philippines	−4.7	−1.4	−1.0	−2.3
Bangladesh	−5.0	0.7	1.7	−7.7

Note: Number of countries is in parentheses.

two had stagnant profit shares (a change of one percentage point or less). The four high-saving East Asian countries had staggering increases in savings rates (of more than 12 percentage points and more than 20 points in three countries). The data clearly suggest that the very high savings rates in these countries are a relatively recent phenomenon closely associated with sharply rising profit shares; some 20 years ago their savings rates were about 14 to 21 percent. Mauritius, with an increase in savings of nearly 12 percentage points, also belongs to this group.

There were also four Latin American economies (Brazil, Colombia, Ecuador, and Uruguay) with modest increases in savings rates and profit shares. In all of them, the change in savings is eight percentage points or less (and in one, Uruguay, the change is marginally above 1 percent). India and Turkey are the two other countries with rising savings, of the same order as the Latin American economies, albeit with larger increases in profit shares.

Eleven countries recorded significant declines in savings rates. Among them, eight had falling or stagnant profit shares while three had increases in profit shares (Venezuela, Zimbabwe, and Zambia, the latter with a puzzling change of 17 percentage points). The sharpest declines in savings were largely concentrated in Latin America (Bolivia, Venezuela, Argentina, and Panama), although on average their profit shares stagnated. A similar contrast is present in four African countries, with falling savings and rising profits (albeit only marginally with the exception again of Zambia, which has a puzzling fall in savings of 33 percentage points). The three remaining countries (Greece, the Philippines, and Bangladesh) fit broadly into the pattern of falling savings and falling or stagnant profit shares.

Finally, there were three countries with stagnant savings rates, of which two (South Africa and Cameroon) had stagnant profit shares and one (Mexico) had a rising profit share.

This picture suggests two conclusions. First, we do find, as Lewis argued, that whenever savings rates increased there was an increase in the share of profits: none of the 11 countries with rising savings had a significant decline in profit shares. Second, rising profit shares were not, however, a sufficient condition for an increase in savings rates: overall, countries with falling savings rates had, on average, marginally rising profit shares. This suggests a general downward trend in savings rates among developing countries, a trend from which only those countries with rapidly rising profit shares escaped.

The next question is: under what circumstances did the share of manufacturing profits in GDP increase in those countries with rising savings rates? The answer is easy in the case of the five economies with dramatically rising savings: rapid industrialization. As is shown in table 13, in these economies the change in the profit share within manufacturing is marginal and most of the increase in savings is associated with a large increase in the share of manufacturing in GDP. The answer is less clear in the six other countries since, especially in three Latin American countries (Colombia, Uruguay, and Brazil), the fall in the wage share within manufacturing, rather than the increase in the manufacturing share, played the major role in the rising profit share (or in preventing a more significant decline, as in the case of Brazil).

There are also two different situations in the group of countries with falling or stagnant savings rates. In the African countries, as well as the Philippines and Bangladesh, we tend to find that the fall or stagnation in the share of profits within manufacturing plays a major role. In contrast, deindustrialization—in the sense of a decline in the share of manufacturing in GDP—appears to be the major factor behind the fall or stagnation in profit shares in the Latin American countries (especially Argentina and Panama) and Greece. A possible generalization in the case of Latin America, then, is that the forces causing a fall in savings rates are associated with stagnant or falling manufacturing shares and only countries that significantly reduced the share of wages in manufacturing escaped from the general trend toward lower savings rates.

Surplus Labor and the Elasticity of the Labor Supply

We now relax some of the assumptions adopted in the first section and consider a more general setting. First, we allow for diminishing returns to labor in sector S—which may be due to the presence of a fixed factor such as land in agriculture—and consider the possibility that the marginal product of labor falls to zero at some level of employment (Lo). Thus:

$$S = L_S^{1-b} \quad 0 \leq b < 1 \quad \text{for } L_S < Lo$$

$$S = So \quad \text{for } L_S \geq Lo, \tag{7}$$

where we omit for simplicity the fixed factor. Sen (1966) has analyzed the case in which output is invariant to the number of workers. In its simplest version, households in the subsistence sector take their production and working-time decisions to maximize consumption per family member. As long as work time is less than the total number of hours available for work, maximizing consumption per head implies working until hours of work have a zero marginal product. The removal of a family worker from the household will lead the other members to adjust their working time so that the marginal product of hours of work remains zero. The total output of the household will thus be invariant to the number of family workers.

On the demand side, we now allow for differences in the consumption goods produced by the two sectors (the investment good being produced by the capitalist sector). We retain the assumptions that workers in both sectors do not save and that there is a constant saving propensity out of profits (s_π). Using good M as the numeraire, the value of total consumption is thus:

$$p_S C_S + C_M = w_S L_S + w_M L_M + (1 - s_\pi)P, \tag{8}$$

where w_S is the wage in sector S measured in terms of good M, C denotes consumption, and P is total profit given by:

$$P = aM = [a/(1 - a)]w_M L_M. \tag{9}$$

The elasticity of substitution between M and S goods is constant (corresponding to a constant elasticity of substitution [CES] utility function). Hence:

$$C_M/C_S = B(p_S/p_M)^h, \tag{10}$$

where h is the elasticity of substitution.

Market equilibrium requires two conditions. In the goods market:

$$S = C_S. \tag{11}$$

In the labor market, the equilibrium condition is given, as before, by equation 1; that is, the wage in sector M is in equilibrium equal to what workers can earn in sector S (plus a wage premium). The value of the average product of labor in sector S (w_S) is now determined as:

$$w_S = p_S L_S^{-b} \quad \text{for } L_S < Lo$$
$$\tag{12}$$
$$w_S = p_S So/L_S \quad \text{for } L_S \geq Lo.$$

Determinants of Labor Supply Elasticity

In this more general setting, how elastic is the labor supply to the capitalist sector? The derivation of labor supply elasticity involves the equilibrium conditions and a number of behavioral equations of the model. The

steps are presented in the appendix to this chapter, where the elasticity
($e = \mathrm{d}\log L_M/\mathrm{d}\log w_M$) is shown to be:

$$e = (1 - l_M)/[bl_M + (h - 1)^{-1}] \quad \text{for } L_S < Lo$$

$$\qquad\qquad\qquad\qquad\qquad\qquad\qquad\qquad (13)$$

$$e = (1 - l_M)/[l_M + (h - 1)^{-1}] \quad \text{for } L_S \geq Lo,$$

where l_M is the employment share of the capitalist sector (L_M/L). Equation 13 shows that the elasticity of substitution in consumption between
S and M goods is a critical variable affecting labor supply elasticity. In
particular, for labor supply elasticity to be positive the elasticity of substitution in consumption must be greater than one.[12] Indeed, consider the
case of a unit elasticity ($h = 1$). The consumption shares of the two
goods are then constant. The level of employment in the S sector is then
independent of relative prices (p_S/p_M) and the product wage in sector M,
as is readily verified from equations 8 through 11 using the equilibrium
condition in the labor market. In this case, an increase in labor demand
in sector M will increase the product wage there by exactly the amount
required to keep L_S (and thus L_M) constant. The labor supply to sector M
is then as inelastic as in a one-sector economy. Equation 13 also shows
labor supply elasticity as a decreasing function of the employment share
of the modern sector (and thus increasing with the employment share of
sector S). Indeed, a higher employment share in sector M implies that
the same increase in L_M leads to a larger proportional reduction of
employment in the subsistence sector. The equilibrium product wage
then increases by a larger amount.

We can now address the question of under what conditions the
capitalist sector will face a perfectly elastic supply of labor, or, as Lewis
puts it, when there is "unlimited labor available at a constant real wage."
Besides the existence of a subsistence sector ($l_M < 1$), for e to tend to
infinity the denominator in the expression in equation 13 must be zero.
For this, two conditions are required.

The first condition is infinite elasticity of substitution in consumption. That is, the goods produced by the two sectors must be perfect
substitutes, or, what comes to the same thing, the two sectors must
produce the same good. This is one of the assumptions that was made in
the first section. Suppose that the two sectors produce different goods;
food is grown in the subsistence sector while the capitalist sector produces textiles. Reallocating labor from the subsistence to the capitalist
sector will reduce the output of food and increase the output of textiles,
thus generating an excess demand for food and an excess supply of
textiles at the original relative prices. The terms of trade will move in
favor of the food-producing sector, thus raising the subsistence wage

(and the capitalist sector wage) in terms of textiles. The capitalist sector will thus face an upward-sloping supply curve of labor. The required shift in the terms of trade depends on how substitutable the two goods are. Only when the two goods are perfect substitutes will no change in the subsistence wage be required (provided the second condition is fulfilled). Then, excess demand for the goods produced by the subsistence sector is offset by the extra output generated in the capitalist sector, so that no shift in "relative prices" between the two sectors is needed.

The second condition is that $b = 0$. This is the assumption of constant returns to labor in the subsistence sector that was also adopted in the first section. With diminishing returns to labor in the subsistence sector ($b > 0$), the average product of labor in sector S, and thus the wage in this sector, will increase as labor is withdrawn from this sector. Labor would then be available to the capitalist sector at an increasing real wage, even if the two sectors produce the same good.

How much of Lewis's model survives when the conditions for a perfectly elastic supply of labor are not fulfilled, that is, when we move to a two-good economy? As we have seen, a key reason why the subsistence sector is a reserve of surplus labor for the modern sector (in the sense that it provides a perfectly elastic supply of labor) is that it competes in the goods market with the modern sector by producing the same good. The elasticity of labor supply is infinite because the elasticity of substitution is infinite. More generally, how much a sector has to raise wages to attract additional workers from other sectors depends on how many workers are displaced by the increase in production in that sector, and this depends on how substitutable the goods produced are. Thus, the extent to which the noncapitalist sector provides an elastic supply of labor to the modern one depends on the extent to which it competes with it in the goods market by producing more or less close substitutes.

Consider the case in which the subsistence sector produces goods with a price elastic demand and the elasticity of substitution in consumption is greater than unity. How does Lewis's story change when we adopt this broader notion of labor surplus?[13]

Using equations 2 and 13, the slope of the w curve in ($\log k$, $\log w_M$) space can be written as:

$$\text{dlog}w_M/\text{dlog}k = 1/(e + 1/a), \tag{14}$$

which shows that the higher e is the flatter is the w curve. As already indicated, when $h > 1$ labor supply elasticity is positive. This guarantees that the employment share of the subsistence sector and, thus, the elasticity of the labor supply are decreasing functions of the economywide capital-labor ratio.[14] The slope of the w curve increases with the capital-labor ratio, and, using equations 13 and 14, we have:

$$\text{dlog}w_M/\text{dlog}k \rightarrow a/[a(h-1)+1] \quad \text{for } l_M, k \rightarrow 0, \text{ and } e \rightarrow h - 1$$

$$\text{dlog}w_M/\text{dlog}k \rightarrow a \quad \text{for } l_M \rightarrow 1, k \rightarrow \text{infinity, and } e \rightarrow 0.$$

Thus, the slope of the w curve increases, tending toward the value a of the mature phase in the Lewis model. Although the curve is steeper now at low levels of k than in the Lewis model, it is flatter than before at high levels of k. This is because the elasticity of labor supply always remains positive no matter how large k is. Rather than a sharp turning point from the labor surplus phase to maturity, we now have, as shown in figure 16, an increasing product wage, rising gently at first and more steeply later as the capital-labor ratio increases. The subsistence sector, although shrinking in size as k increases, never disappears (the production technology in sector S implies that productivity tends toward infinity when employment tends toward zero). Therefore, the steady state now features the coexistence of the two sectors.

Labor Supply Elasticity and the Role of Returns to Labor

The role of returns to labor in the subsistence sector deserves further attention. There are several notions of surplus labor in the development literature. We will focus in this section on two of them. One notion, present in Lewis's article (1954), refers to a perfectly elastic labor supply, meaning that labor is available at a constant real wage (equal to the subsistence sector wage plus a constant wage premium). In this case, the labor surplus is the whole labor force in the subsistence sector in the sense that the labor supply to the capitalist sector remains perfectly elastic until this sector has absorbed the whole of the subsistence labor force. The required conditions—constant returns to labor in the subsistence sector and infinite elasticity of subsistence in consumption—are those that yield the properties of Lewis's model: the constancy of the real wage, the effects of technical progress, and the trends in income distribution.

A second notion refers to a situation in which labor is so abundant that, given the technology and other factor supplies available to the subsistence sector, the marginal product of labor in this sector is equal to zero. Under these conditions, a higher level of employment in the capitalist sector will not affect the level of output in the subsistence sector. In this case, the labor surplus is only that fraction of the labor force that,

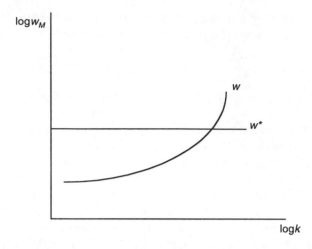

Fig. 16. A two-good, two-sector model with elastic price demands

when withdrawn from the subsistence sector, would make the marginal product of labor positive.[15]

There has been a tendency to assimilate these two notions or, what is perhaps worse, to define surplus labor with reference to both notions simultaneously. According to Little (1982, 87), for example: "In the post war literature, Surplus labor must be taken to mean that, at the prevailing wage, more labor can be taken on in modern sectors of the economy without raising the wage, and without loss of output in the traditional sectors." Yet these are quite different notions that need to be clearly distinguished.[16] As our previous analysis makes clear, a zero marginal product of labor is neither a necessary nor a sufficient condition for a perfectly elastic labor supply.[17] That output in the subsistence sector may remain constant as employment in the capitalist sector increases does not prevent the average product of labor in that sector from rising. In fact, a zero MPL guarantees that the average product of labor will increase since a smaller number of workers will now share the same output in the subsistence sector. Moreover, a comparison of the two expressions in equation 13 makes it clear that labor supply elasticity when the MPL is positive is larger than when it is zero as long as the average product of labor in the subsistence sector determines the supply price of labor to the capitalist sector. In other words, the existence of surplus labor — in the traditional sense that the marginal product of labor in the subsistence sector is zero — makes the labor supply to the modern sector less, not more, elastic. This should not be surprising. A zero MPL implies that the average product of labor in the subsistence sector (APL$_S$) is APL$_S$ = So/L$_S$. The elasticity of the APL$_S$, with respect to an employment decline in sector S, is then:

dlogAPL$_S$/−dlogL$_S$ = 1.

If the MPL is positive, the APL$_S$ is L_S^{-b}, which implies that:

dlogAPL$_S$/−dlogL$_S$ = $b < 1$.

It follows that, in the face of a small reduction in L_S (a small increase in L_M), the proportionate increase in the average product of labor is greater when the marginal product of labor is zero. The subsistence wage, and thus the modern sector wage, rises more, and this means a less elastic labor supply.

A digression is worthwhile here to discuss the major attempt to reconcile the notion of a perfectly elastic supply of labor with a zero MPL in the noncapitalist sector. Fei and Ranis (1964) considered an economy in which landownership is concentrated in the hands of a few landowners and agricultural workers have to work for them as tenants or wage earners. The agricultural production function is such that, given the endowment of land, the marginal product of labor becomes zero at a certain level of employment (L_A^*). Initially, the land and labor endowments are such that the available labor force, L_A, is greater than L_A^* and thus the MPL is indeed zero. In this economy, there is surplus labor, not in the sense of Lewis but in the sense that withdrawing a fraction ($L_A - L_A^*$) of the labor force from agriculture leaves agricultural output unaffected.

In this situation, competition among workers would tend to generate a zero wage equal to the marginal product of labor in agriculture. At the same time, some food output would remain unsold if it is greater than landlords' demand for food (i.e., demand at the saturation level). Fei and Ranis (1964) conclude that under these conditions the agricultural wage will be institutionally determined at a level higher than the MPL in agriculture. Food will be distributed among workers according to the average product of labor in agriculture (less the food consumption of the landlords). The corresponding institutional wage can be seen as the outcome of a noncompetitive market allocation based on social consensus. This is under the initial conditions, when the whole labor force is employed in agriculture. Less convincingly, as will be discussed later, Fei and Ranis then argue that this institutional wage is perpetuated over time by convention and social consensus as long as there is surplus labor in agriculture. They note that "as long as surplus labor continues to exist in the agricultural sector, there is no reason to assume that this social consensus changes significantly" (22).

Given a constant institutional wage in terms of food and an MPL equal to zero in agriculture, the labor supply to the industrial capitalist sector is perfectly elastic during what Fei and Ranis call the labor surplus phase of economic development. In this phase, the reallocation of the labor force from agriculture to industry does not affect food supply given the presence of surplus labor in agriculture. Moreover, the increase in the food demand of industrial workers is just equal to the decline in food consumption within agriculture, on the assumptions of a uniform wage rate and that the income elasticity of food demand of those that appropriate the agricultural surplus, the landlords, is equal to zero.[18] Thus, the expansion of industrial employment, as determined by capital accumulation, generates by itself the required increase in the agricultural surplus as the labor force reallocation reduces food consumption within agriculture. There is no upward pressure on the agricultural terms of trade,[19] and, with a constant wage in terms of food, the model during this phase is indeed very similar to the Lewis model.[20]

As an attempt to reconcile the notion of a perfectly elastic supply of labor to the capitalist industrial sector with a zero marginal product of labor in agriculture, the Fei and Ranis model has a number of shortcomings. The key to this attempt is the introduction of an "institutional wage," which delinks the supply price of labor to the modern sector from the current productivity conditions in agriculture. The meaning of this institutional wage is far from clear, however. The wage is "institutional" in the sense that it is not the outcome of a competitive market allocation. Yet it is not institutional in the sense of being determined by convention: the wage has a definite relationship with demographic and technological factors. If current productivity conditions in agriculture were critical initially, why do they become unimportant later? In other words, why shouldn't the social consensus — on which the institutional wage is built — change significantly as the average product of labor in agriculture changes with the reallocation of the labor force toward the industrial sector? The analytical source of these difficulties seems to be that, in their 1964 book, Fei and Ranis are not fully conscious that they are determining the wage from the equilibrium condition in the food market (as they clearly do in the mathematical appendix to their 1961 article).[21]

In the face of these shortcomings, Jorgenson (1961, 1967) found it easy to argue that in an agricultural sector organized as a more or less egalitarian peasant economy the relationship between the agricultural surplus and the expansion of industry would be inverted. Indeed, suppose that peasants appropriate the agricultural surplus and their income, in terms of food, is equal to the average product of labor in this sector.

Assume also that consumption demands are such that all income is spent on food at income levels below a critical level of food requirement (C_A^*) and that when the income level compatible with C_A^* is surpassed all additional income is spent on industrial goods.[22]

When agricultural productivity is so low that income is below C_A^*, agriculture employs the whole labor force and the economy has no industrial sector. When productivity has risen to the point where income per worker in agriculture is greater than C_A^*, the given food requirements of the population, land endowment, and agricultural productivity determine the equilibrium level of employment in agriculture independently of relative prices, wages, and the capital stock in industry. Combined with the full employment assumption, this feature has the striking implication that the industrial employment share will also be fully determined by these three factors. Jorgenson's is thus a model in which the size of the agricultural surplus determines the level of industrialization. As in the Fei and Ranis model, agriculture must generate an excess of production over its own consumption to feed industrial workers and sustain a given level of industrial employment. Unlike Fei and Ranis's argument, in Jorgenson's model — given the inelastic demand for food — the agricultural surplus can only increase as a result of productivity improvements. These productivity improvements increase the size of the labor force that can be fed outside agriculture and are critical to the expansion of the capitalist sector.[23]

Finally, it is worth noting that some early development theorists were well aware that a zero marginal product of labor in the subsistence sector does not provide a perfectly elastic labor supply to the modern sector. Nurkse (1953), for example, viewed the existence of a zero marginal product of labor as concealing a hidden saving potential that in principle allows for an increase in investment without the need to reduce consumption.[24] He argued then that all sorts of difficulties were likely to be faced in the practical application of that proposition (38). Thinking of labor surplus as rural underemployment, he argued that "Everything depends on the mobilization of the concealed saving potential in the shape of the food surplus that becomes available to the productive peasants when their unproductive dependents go away" (38–39) and that results, we may add, from the increase in the average product of labor in agriculture. Given that "the peasants are not likely to save the surplus voluntarily since they live so close to subsistence level" (43), the mobilization of the saving potential will be incomplete, short of drastic measures by the State[25] or of "a widespread and radical improvement in farming techniques, accompanying the removal of the surplus farm labour, so that total farm output might be substantially increased and not merely held constant" (43).

Efficiency Wages and Kaldorian Underemployment

A more promising approach to freeing the Lewis model from some of its restrictive assumptions than that of Fei and Ranis is to combine the extended Lewis model described earlier to include efficiency wage considerations. Thus, we shall assume that in the capitalist sector the real wage paid by firms affects labor productivity through its influence on nutrition or health. This hypothesis — the efficiency wage hypothesis — goes back to Leibenstein's writing on economic backwardness (1957) and has been discussed in the development literature by Mazumdar
▷ (1959) and Stiglitz (1976) among others.

Technology in the modern sector is now described by:

$$M = K^a(EL_M)^{1-a}, \tag{15}$$

where E is an effort function of the form:

$$E = E(w_M/p) \quad E' > 0; \quad E'' < 0; \quad E(\omega) = 0, \tag{16}$$

where (w_M/p) is the real *consumption wage* in the M sector and ω is the minimum wage required to generate a positive effort from workers. The consumption wage, rather than the product wage (w_M/p_M), is of course the one affecting the services a worker renders whether the channel is nutrition and health or involves other possible influences on a worker's effort. Moreover, we assume that effort increases with w_M/p according to equation 16 as long as the real consumption wage is higher than the average product of labor in the subsistence sector plus the wage premium (fw_S/p). Otherwise, the wage in the M sector is determined by fw_S.

Firms treat prices as given and maximize profits over w_M and L_M subject to equations 15 and 16 and $w_M > fw_S$. The first-order conditions of this maximization program imply the "Solow condition" that the wage elasticity of effort is equal to unity (Solow 1979):

$$E'(w_M/p)(w_M/p)/E(w_M/p) = 1. \tag{17}$$

Solving equation 17 for (w_M/p) yields the equilibrium value of the "efficiency wage" (the real consumption wage that maximizes profits) as a function only of the parameters of the productivity (or effort) function E. Consider, for example, an effort function of the form:

$$E = (w_M/p - \omega)^d \quad d < 1 \quad \text{for } w_M/p > \omega \text{ and 0 otherwise}$$

Using equation 17 and solving explicitly for the efficiency wage yields:

$$w_M/p = \omega/(1 - d). \tag{18}$$

Assume that workers' utility function is of the Cobb-Douglas form: $U = C_S^\alpha C_M^{1-\alpha}$, with a unit elasticity of substitution in consumption. This specification has the advantage of making it possible to derive an exact measure of the real consumption wage. The corresponding price index (p) is:

$$p = p_S^\alpha p_M^{1-\alpha}. \tag{19}$$

Combining equations 18 and 19, we can also solve for the efficiency product wage:

$$w_M/p_M = (p_S/p_M)^\alpha \omega/(1 - d), \tag{20}$$

which shows the efficiency product wage as an increasing function of the efficiency consumption wage, $\omega/(1 - d)$, and the terms of trade between the subsistence and modern sectors (p_S/p_M). It is worth noting that the efficiency product wage increases with the expenditure share of subsistence goods (α).

Earnings in the subsistence sector are determined, as before (eq. 12), by the value of the average product of labor:

$$w_S = p_S L_S^{-b},$$

where L_S is equal to the difference between the total labor force and employment in the modern sector. Clearly, in this model the market-clearing condition, $f w_S = w_M$, will in general not be fulfilled. The reason is that when subsistence earnings, adjusted for the wage premium ($f w_S$), are below modern sector wages as determined by equation 20, competition among workers will not lead to lower wages in the modern sector. It is not profitable for firms to undertake such wage reductions. Wage determination is then compatible with the existence of an excess supply of labor to the modern sector. Even though all workers find employment in one of the two sectors, there is an excess supply of labor in the sense that the earnings differential between the modern and subsistence sectors is larger than the wage premium required to lure workers out of the subsistence sector.[26]

How elastic is the labor supply to the modern sector with this excess supply of labor? It is clear from equation 20 that the answer depends exclusively on how much the terms of trade (p_S/p_M) change as employment in sector M changes. We can find the terms of trade as a function of L_M by combining the goods market equilibrium equations (8 and 11) and the consumption demand functions (eq. 10, when $h = 1$). This yields:

$$p_S/p_M = (1/B)(w_M/p_M)(L_M/L_S^{1-b})(1 - s_\pi a)/(1 - a), \qquad (21)$$

where $1/B$ is now equal to $\alpha/(1 - \alpha)$. Equation 21 shows the terms of trade for the subsistence sector increasing with L_M/L_S. An increase in L_M (which reduces L_S) creates excess demand for S goods, and the relative price of S goods has to increase to clear the goods market.

Using equations 20 and 21 to eliminate (p_S/p_M) and taking logs, total differentiation yields after some manipulation the labor supply elasticity $(\text{dlog}L_M/\text{dlog}w_M)$:

$$e = (1 - \alpha)/\alpha[1 + (1 - b)L_M/L_S].$$

The elasticity of labor supply is a decreasing function of the expenditure share of subsistence sector goods and of the employment share of the modern sector. An increase in these shares turns the terms of trade in favor of the subsistence sector and, even though the real consumption wage is unaffected, the product wage increases.

There are two interesting differences from the labor supply elasticity derived in the previous section. First, positive labor supply elasticity no longer depends on the elasticity of substitution in consumption being more than unity (the elasticity has been derived on the assumption of a unit elasticity of substitution). Second, returns to labor in the subsistence sector now affect labor supply elasticity in a completely different way, one that conforms with conventional wisdom. Indeed, labor supply elasticity now increases with parameter b. This means that elasticity is at its maximum when the marginal product of labor is zero, or $b = 1$, and at its minimum level when $b = 0$ (constant returns to labor). There is here a striking contrast with the model presented in the previous section. The source of the difference is the nature of the labor surplus. The increase in the average product of labor in the subsistence sector — which results from an increase in employment in the modern sector — now has no effect on the modern sector consumption wage (eq. 18 shows the real consumption wage determined only by the parameters of the productivity function). The efficiency product wage rises but only because the terms of trade turn against the modern sector. This terms of trade effect is minimal when the marginal product of labor is zero precisely because there is no output loss in the subsistence sector as a result of the increase in employment in the modern sector. Labor supply elasticity is thus highest when the MPL in sector S is zero.

It is worth noting that if productivity in the subsistence sector is also affected by workers' earnings there — a reasonable assumption in the context of a nutrition-based efficiency wage model — the shift in the terms of trade will have a positive productivity effect on sector S that tends to make the labor supply more elastic. Indeed, this productivity effect moderates the shift in the terms of trade required to clear the goods market as employment in the modern sector increases, thus making the increase in the product wage that the modern sector has to pay smaller.[27] This is an additional reason why, in the presence of efficiency wages, a low MPL in sector S is more likely to be associated with a great elasticity of the labor supply, for such situations are typically associated with labor abundance and widespread poverty in the subsistence sector, and it is then that an increase in subsistence earnings is likely to have a large positive productivity effect.

In the presence of efficiency wages, a labor surplus can develop in the subsistence sector that provides an elastic labor supply to the modern sector. This labor surplus is quite different from the conventional type — since the marginal product of labor in the S sector need not be zero — as well as from the Lewis variety — because now the labor market does not clear. We may refer to it as Kaldorian underemployment since the distinctive feature of Kaldor's definition of labor surplus is its emphasis on a labor market in disequilibrium:

> The best definition I could suggest for the existence of "labor surplus" . . . is one which is analogous to Keynes' definition of "involuntary unemployment": a situation of "labor surplus" exists when a faster rate of increase in the demand for labor in the high productivity sectors induces a faster rate of labor transference even when it is attended by *a reduction, and not an increase, in the earnings differential between the different sectors.* (1968, 386; italics original)[28]

A reduction of the earnings differential (w_M/w_S), as the employment share of the modern sector increases, is precisely what happens when the modern sector faces an excess supply of labor. Combining equation 20 and the expression for the value of the average product of labor in sector S yields:

$$w_S/w_M = (p_S/p_M)^{1-\alpha} L_S^{-b} (1 - d)/\omega.$$

Using equation 21 to eliminate (p_S/p_M) and taking logs, total differentiation yelds:

$$d\log(w_S/w_M) = (1 + L_M/L_S)d\log L_M, \tag{22}$$

which shows that increases in modern sector employment tend to narrow the earnings differential, the impact being greater the larger the employment share of the modern sector is.

As the employment share of the modern sector increases throughout the transition to a steady state, the earnings differential will eventually narrow to the point where it equals the wage premium ($f - 1$). The market-clearing condition ($fw_S = w_M$) is then reestablished. With further increases in the employment share of the modern sector, equation 20 no longer applies and is replaced with the market-clearing condition (eq. 3). The elasticity of labor supply is then determined, as in the previous section, by the elasticity of substitution in consumption. Since this elasticity is one in the present model, the corresponding labor supply elasticity is zero (see eq. 18 when $h = 1$). The earnings differential is now determined by the wage premium and no longer shrinks as the employment share of the modern sector increases. Kaldor refers to this situation as "economic maturity," defined as a state of affairs in which real income per capita has reached broadly the same level in the different sectors of the economy (1967, 8). This notion of maturity is different from that of the Lewis model. Its defining characteristic is the disappearance of an earnings differential among sectors (up to a wage premium with no welfare significance). In the Lewis model, this condition always holds, and the defining characteristic of the mature economy is instead the disappearance of the subsistence sector.

The Kaldorian notion of underemployment is also different from, although not necessarily inconsistent with, the type of unemployment analyzed by modern theories of efficiency wages.[29] In these theories, the wage *relative* to some fallback position plays a prominent role in determining work effort, unlike our specification, which neglects the influence on effort of factors other than the *absolute* level of the real consumption wage. This raises the question of whether the conclusion that the earnings differential falls as employment in the modern sector increases survives when we bring the cost of job loss, or more generally wage relativities, into the determination of the efficiency wage. To address this question, suppose that the minimum wage (ω) in the effort function increases with the real consumption wage in the S sector (w_S/p): the higher this wage, which represents the earnings that workers in sector M will obtain if they lose their jobs, the higher is ω and thus the efficiency wage that firms in sector M have to pay. Let ψ be the elasticity of ω with respect to w_S/p. For simplicity, we may assume that $\omega = (w_S/p)^\psi$. Following a procedure similar to that used to derive equation 22, and noting that ω is no longer exogenous, we have:

$$\mathrm{dlog}(w_S/w_M) = (1 - \psi)(1 + L_M/L_S)\mathrm{dlog}L_M. \tag{23}$$

Equation 23 shows that the wage differential will narrow with an increase in modern sector employment provided that ψ is less than unity. A unity elasticity represents the extreme case in which all that matters is the wage relative to the fallback position (so that, say, a 50 percent reduction in the fallback position [w_S/p] implies a 50 percent reduction in the efficiency wage). This case is clearly inconsistent with Kaldor's definition of labor surplus, since it implies that the wage differential is independent of the employment share of the modern sector. The other extreme case is zero elasticity, in which all that matters is the absolute wage. This is in the tradition of early theories of efficiency wages and is the case examined in this section. Note that for $\psi = 0$ equation 23 indeed simplifies to equation 22. It is interesting that the middle ground between these two extreme cases — when $0 < \psi < 1$ and work effort depends on both the absolute level of the wage and the fallback position — also fits Kaldor's notion of labor surplus: the wage differential narrows when modern sector employment increases, although less than when $\psi = 1$.

APPENDIX

Derivation of Labor Supply Elasticity

Substituting from equation 12 into the labor market equilibrium condition and dividing by p_M yields:

$$w_M/p_M = fL_S^{-b}p_S/p_M \quad \text{for } L_S < Lo$$
$$w_M/p_M = fSoL_S^{-1}p_S/p_M \quad \text{for } L_S \geq Lo.$$
(A.1)

Substituting from equation 10 into A.1:

$$w_M/p_M = f(1/BC_M/C_S)^{1/h}L_S^{-b} \quad \text{for } L_S < Lo$$
$$w_M/p_M = f(1/BC_M/C_S)^{1/h}So/L_S \quad \text{for } L_S \geq Lo.$$
(A.2)

Substituting from equation 9 into 8 and using equations 7, 11, and 12:

$$C_M/C_S = [(1 - s_\pi a)/(1 - a)](w_M/p_M)(L_M/L_S^{1-b}) \quad \text{for } L_S < Lo$$
$$C_M/C_S = [(1 - s_\pi a)/(1 - a)](w_M/p_M)(L_M/So) \quad \text{for } L_S \geq Lo.$$
(A.3)

Substituting from equation A.3 into A.2, we obtain w_M/p_M as a function of L_M and L_S. Taking logs, total differentiation yields, after some manipulation:

$$d\log L_M/d\log(w_M/p_M) = (L_S/L)/[1/(h-1)] + b(1 - L_S/L) \quad \text{for } L_S < Lo$$
$$d\log L_M/d\log(w_M/p_M) = (L_S/L)/[1/(h-1)] + (1 - L_S/L) \quad \text{for } L_S \geq Lo.$$
(A.4)

TABLE A3.1. Savings Rates and Profit Shares in Manufacturing

	Savings Rate			Profit Share		Profits in Manufacturing		Manufacturing Share	
	s 1988–92	s 1970	s_h 1980–84	π 1988–92	π 1970	π_M 1988–92	π_M 1970	M/Y 1988–92	M/Y 1970
Singapore	44.6	18	–	19.5	12.8	68.6	64	28.4	20
Korea	37[a]	15	10.3	21[a]	15.8	71.7[a]	75	29.3[a]	21
Indonesia	34.4	14	–	15.6	7.4	79.6	74	19.6	10
Thailand	33[f]	21	10.4[i]	22.8[f]	11.8	86[f]	74	26.5[f]	16
Brazil	26.8[a]	20	–	22[a]	22.6	78.5[a]	78	28[a]	29
Venezuela	24.8	37	3.8	16.3	11	79	69	20.6	16
Peru	24[g]	17	16.7	20.6[g]	–	86[g]	–	24[g]	20
South Africa	23.2	24	–	12.7	13	50.6	54	25	24
Colombia	23	18	8.6	17.3	15.8	85	75	20.4	21
Mauritius	22.5[a]	11	–	13[a]	9.2	54[a]	66	24[a]	14
Costa Rica	22[f]	14	–	12[f]	–	63[f]	59	19[f]	–
Ecuador	22	14	9.6	13.8	13.1	63.8	73	21.6	18
Turkey	20.4	17	12.1[j]	18.9	12.6	78.8	74	24	17
India	20.3[b]	16	16.6[k]	11.1[b]	8.1	61.7[b]	54	18[b]	15
Mexico	20[a]	19	–	18.8[a]	12.3	80[a]	56	23.5[a]	22
Cameroon	19[e]	18	–	7.6[e]	7.1	54[e]	71	14[e]	10
Kenya	18.8	24	–	6.8	6	57.6	50	11.8	12
Zimbabwe	18.8	21	–	18.8	12	68.2	57	27.6	21
Philippines	17.3[c]	22	10.0[l]	18.4[c]	19.8	76.7[c]	79	24[c]	25
Uruguay	16.3[b]	15	9.2	19.3[b]	17.4	77[b]	74	25[b]	23.5
Argentina	15[h]	25	–	17.8[h]	23	81[h]	72	22[h]	32
Panama	13.5[e]	24	–	4.5[e]	8.8	63.5[e]	68	7[e]	13
Honduras	13	15	–	9.5	–	62.8	–	15.2	14

Zambia	12[a]	45	23.5[a]	6.6	73.5[a]	66	32[a]	10
Greece	9[a]	20	9.5[a]	12.9	59.3[a]	68	16[a]	19
Egypt	8[d]	9	9.3[d]	–	66.5[d]	46	14[d]	–
Bolivia	7.7[c]	24	10.4[c]	8.2	73[c]	63	14.3[c]	13
Ethiopia	5[c]	11	9[c]	6.8	80[c]	76	11.3[c]	9
Bangladesh	2[c]	7	5.1[c]	4.4	66.3[c]	74	7.7[c]	6
Jordan	-6.6	–	10.1	–	74.6	–	13.6	–

Note:

s: Gross domestic savings as a percentage of GDP. Figures refer to the average for 1988–92 (unless otherwise indicated) and 1970. *Source:* Table 9 of World Development Indicators, *World Development Report*, World Bank, various years.

s_h: Households savings as a percentage of GDP. Average for 1980–84 unless otherwise indicated. *Source:* Table 44 of UNCTAD 1997, UNCTAD secretariat estimates, based on national and international sources.

π: Share of manufacturing profits in GDP [= $\pi_M(M/Y)$]

M/Y: Share of manufacturing in GDP (%). Figures refer to the average for 1988–92 (unless otherwise indicated) and 1970. *Source:* Table 3 of World Development Indicators, *World Development Report*, World Bank, various years.

π_M: Profit share in manufacturing = 100 minus employee earnings as a percentage of value added in manufacturing. Figures refer to the average for 1988–92 (unless otherwise indicated) and 1970. *Source:* Table 7 of World Development Indicators, *World Development Report*, World Bank, various years.

[a]1988–91
[b]1990–92
[c]1988–90
[d]1988–90 and 1992
[e]1989–90
[f]1990–91
[g]1988
[h]1992
[i]1981–83
[j]1977–81
[k]1978–82
[l]1983–85

Data Appendix

Table A3.1 presents the available information on gross domestic savings, manufacturing profits, and value added for a sample of 30 developing countries. The data sources utilized are several *World Development Reports* of the World Bank, with the exception of the data from UNCTAD's *Trade and Development Report* (1997) on household savings. Figures A3.1 and A3.2 provide scatter diagrams of savings rates and profit shares at the end of the period and of changes in these variables during the period.

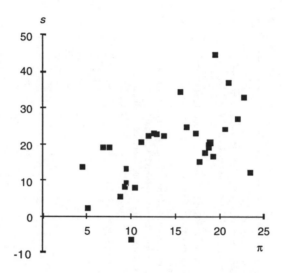

Fig. A3.1.   Savings rates (*s*) and profit shares (π)

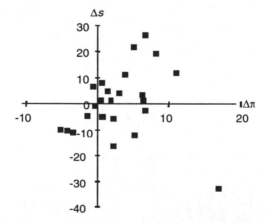

Fig. A3.2.   Changes in savings rates (Δs) and profit shares ($\Delta\pi$)

CHAPTER 4

Increasing Returns, External Economies, and Multiple Equilibria

With the introduction of a labor surplus and an elastic labor supply, Lewis took an important step away from the neoclassical model of a mature economy. This was a major departure, but it was the only one. Implicitly or explicitly, Lewis assumes a constant returns to scale technology and perfect competition in the capitalist sector together with exogenous technical progress. Other contributors to the theory of economic development in the 1940s and 1950s, Rosenstein-Rodan and Nurkse, in particular, took more radical steps and considered the implications of increasing returns to scale in the technology of the capitalist sector.

The source of aggregate increasing returns to scale may be internal or external to the firms operating in the modern sector. In the first case, the firm's technology is itself subject to increasing returns to scale as a result of fixed costs, area/volume relationships and technical discontinuities. The presence of these plant-level economies of scale was seen as characteristic of mass production methods in early development theory writing. Rosenstein-Rodan's work (1943) dramatizes them with the example of a shoe factory that to operate profitably with modern technologies would have to employ no less than 20,000 workers. In Nurkse, the relative convenience of the hammer and stone technologies for Robinson Crusoe depends on the number of nails to be driven.[1] Economies of scale due to indivisibilities and technical discontinuities are also characteristic of the provision of infrastructure (or "social overhead capital"), which "require[s] a minimum high quantum of investment which would serve, say, fifty factories but would cost far too much for one" (Rosenstein-Rodan 1984, 208).

Even if each firm operates individually with a constant returns to scale technology, returns to scale may increase at the sector or economywide level if the firms' activities collectively affect the production conditions of a large number of them. When these external effects are positive, the aggregate production function (at the industry or economy level) may display increasing returns to scale. For Rosenstein-Rodan (1943, 1984), these effects arise from activities such as industrial training. A related example, formalized by Arrow (1962), is learning by

101

doing, which increases the stock of experience as a by-product of production activities. In both cases, the expansion of the economy increases the pool of trained workers and skills on which each firm can rely. This raises the productivity with which modern technologies can be applied to production, so that even if the costs of an individual firm do not fall with its own expansion the firm's costs fall with the expansion of its industry or the economy as a whole. Nurkse suggests another source of external effects when he mentions that the productivity of modern technology depends on the quality of management (or, as he puts it, "the qualities of enterprise and initiative") and that the supply of managers and their quality will tend to increase with the expansion of the capitalist sector (1953, 10).[2]

Whether external to the firm or a result of plant-level economies of large-scale production, many early contributors to development theory viewed increasing returns to scale as characteristic of modern technology. In this chapter, I focus on technological external effects as the source of increasing returns and look at the implications of this assumption when it is combined with the assumption of surplus labor. The next chapter considers increasing returns arising from internal economies.

Increasing Returns to Scale and Efficiency Wages

In the economy to be considered, increasing returns to scale are associated with industrial training à la Rosenstein-Rodan or learning by doing à la Arrow and are external to the firm. This allows us to skip, at this stage, issues of market structure and imperfect competition that will appear in the next chapter when I deal with internal economies of scale.

A Rosenstein-Rodan/Leibenstein Model

Technological external effects are combined with labor surplus à la Leibenstein and Kaldor (see chap. 3). Besides being external to the firm, increasing returns to scale have two features: (1) they arise from the stock of experience, collectively generated and available to firms, and are a function of cumulative output; and (2) they are assumed to be specific to the capitalist sector to emphasize the role of social interaction in the learning process. Making the state of technology a positive function of the economywide capital stock, the production function for the representative firm in the capitalist sector becomes:

$$M = (\tilde{K})^{\mu} K^{a} (EL_M)^{1-a} \quad \mu > 0 \quad E = (w_M/p - \omega)^d,$$

where $(\tilde{K})^{\mu}$ represents the external effect of the average capital stock in the economy $(\tilde{K})$. In equilibrium, the average capital stock will be equal to the capital stock of the representative firm, that is, $\tilde{K} = K$. This specification is virtually identical to a model of learning by doing with the capital stock as a proxy for cumulative output.[3] Alternative specifications would make the state of technology a function of the capital stock per head — in which case technology would not display pure scale effects — as in Kaldor's (1957) "technical progress function" or Romer's (1986) specification of a different type of external effect (discussed in chap. 6).

The other assumptions remain identical to those in the final section of chapter 3. In particular, workers' effort (E) depends on the absolute level of the real consumption wage. With the same effort function, profit maximization by firms yields the efficiency consumption wage given by equation 18 in chapter 3. The Cobb-Douglas demand functions yield the same expression for the consumption price index $(p = p_S{}^{\alpha}p_M{}^{1-\alpha})$ and the same efficiency product wage (given by eq. 20). From the assumed production conditions in sector S, it follows that labor supply elasticity to sector M is given, as before, by

$$e = (1 - \alpha)/\alpha\,[1 + (1 - b)L_M/L_S] \quad \text{for } fw_S < w_M$$

and

$$e = 0 \quad \text{for } fw_S = w_M.$$

From the first-order conditions for profit maximization, employment in the capitalist sector is determined as:

$$L_M = K^{1+\mu/a}(1 - a)^{1/a}E^{*(1-a)/a}(w_M/p_M)^{-1/a} \quad E^* = [\omega d/(1 - d)]^d, \quad (1)$$

where w_M/p_M is the efficiency product wage, given by equation 20 in chapter 3, and E^* is the effort level corresponding to the efficiency wage. In what follows, I choose good M as the numeraire and thus set p_M equal to one.

Multiple Equilibria and a Profitability Trap

It will again be convenient to present the model with the now familiar real wage diagram in $(\log K, \log w_M)$ space. Consider first the w curve, the schedule of short-run equilibria. The slope of this schedule is now given by:[4]

$$\text{dlog} w_M / \text{dlog} K = (1 + \mu/a)/(e + 1/a).\tag{4}$$

Equation 4 is identical to equation 14 in chapter 3 except for the presence of the increasing returns parameter μ. Its presence implies that at any given level of K the slope of the w curve is larger than in the case of constant returns. This steeper w curve means that a given increase in the capital stock (keeping the total labor force constant) raises the market-clearing value of the real wage by more than what would occur under constant returns. This is because, in addition to the greater relative abundance of capital, there are now additional productivity effects of the capital stock due to increasing returns. This tends to increase the MPL at full employment and the market-clearing wage more than otherwise would be the case. Equation 4 shows that the slope of the w curve is inversely related to labor supply elasticity, and thus, as shown in figure 17, it increases with K (since e falls as L_M/L_S increases). More precisely, when K and L_M/L_S tend toward zero, e tends toward $(1 - \alpha)/\alpha$. The slope of the w curve is then $(1 + \mu/a)/[(1 - \alpha)/\alpha + 1/a]$. When $f w_S$ tends toward w_M (and thus e tends toward zero), the slope of the w curve tends toward $(a + \mu)$. Further increases in K leave the slope unaffected. It is worth noting that equation 4 simplifies to $\text{dlog} w_M / \text{dlog} K = a$, the slope of the w curve in the Solow model, when e and μ both equal zero. If e tends toward infinity, we have the Lewis case, in which the w curve is flat for positive values of L_S.

A major change, with respect to previous models, can be seen in the schedule of stationary capital stocks (the w^* curve).[5] Using equation 1 and the production function, the profit-wage curve is now:

$$r = aK^{\mu/a}[(1 - a)E^*/w_M]^{(1-a)/a}.$$

Substituting into the steady state condition, $s_\pi r = \delta$, and solving for the real product wage yields the equation of the w^* curve:

$$w_M^* = (1 - a)E^*(as_\pi/\delta)^{a/1-a}K^{\mu/(1-a)}.$$

The required wage is no longer independent of the capital stock: it is now an increasing function of K, so that the w^* curve in (K, w_M) space is a positively sloped curve (see fig. 17). This is due to the (external) productivity effects of increases in the capital stock. Since the profit rate depends on the real wage and productivity, which in turn depends on the capital stock, the same rate of profit, and thus the same rate of capital accumulation, can now be generated at lower and higher levels of wages and capital stock. There is no longer a unique value of the real wage that can generate

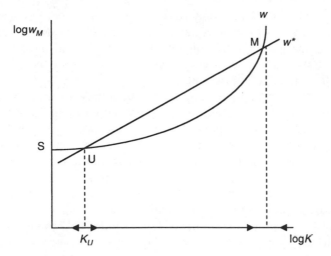

Fig. 17. A Rosenstein-Rodan/Leibenstein model

the steady state rate of accumulation. There is now a locus of (w, K) combinations that generates this equilibrium rate of accumulation.

The novel feature of the model is that it generates multiple equilibria under certain conditions. Given that the capital stock increases when the economy is below the w^* line and contracts when it is above, these equilibria, when they exist, must be as follows: (1) a locally stable, noncapitalist steady state at point S with per capita incomes and wages at subsistence sector levels; (2) a locally stable steady state at point M with high real wages and high capital intensity; and (3) an unstable equilibrium at point U. Depending on initial conditions, the economy moves away from this equilibrium toward either the high- or low-level stable equilibria.

To better understand why the intersection at point U is unstable (and thus why the other two equilibria are stable), consider an initial capital stock below K_U in figure 17. At this low level of capital stock, the market-clearing wage (on the w curve) is higher than the real wage required to generate the steady state rate of accumulation (on the w^* curve). The rate of accumulation is thus less than depreciation, and the capitalist sector shrinks in size over time. The economy's capital intensity declines, thus moving away from K_U and toward the subsistence economy at point S. Similarly, consider an initial value of K above K_U. The market-clearing wage is now lower than the required wage. The rate of capital accumulation is thus higher than its steady state value. The capital intensity of the economy increases over time, increasing the capital stock further away from K_U and toward the steady state at point M. Above M, the wage is again higher than required and the lower profit rate will reduce the rate of capital accumulation until the economy is back to the stable equilibrium at M.

There is a development trap below the low-K intersection at point U. The low-level stable equilibrium at point S is a trap in the sense that it is only a locally stable equilibrium and a sufficiently large departure from it will trigger a self-sustained process of expansion toward the high-level equilibrium. The local stability arises from the fact that below K_U the elastic supply of labor and increasing returns interact negatively to hinder the expansion of the capitalist sector: the elastic labor supply sets a floor to the real wages that the capitalist sector has to pay and, together with the initial conditions of low productivity, this prevents the profitable use of capital-intensive technologies with increasing returns. These interactions can be described as a vicious circle between the inducement to invest and the scale of the capitalist sector. The inducement to invest is weak because the scale of the capitalist sector and, thus, the level of productivity (as determined by K) are small. The size of the sector and productivity remain small because the inducement to invest is weak (profitability is low).

Above the low-level intersection there is, in contrast, a virtuous circle between productivity increases and the inducement to invest. In this case, the interactions between increasing returns to scale and an elastic supply of labor become positive and counteract the influence of diminishing returns to capital. The reason is that the presence of increasing returns to scale strengthens the productivity effects of capital accumulation while at the same time the elastic supply of labor weakens the effects of capital accumulation on the real wage. Growth can then go on with a constant or even increasing rate of return on capital. This virtuous circle may converge to the high-level equilibrium in which labor surpluses have been largely absorbed into the capitalist sector and the economy, with a large capital endowment, is able to generate high real wages. This high equilibrium is the final state of the transition phase toward a mature economy in which the rate of growth would depend exclusively, as in the Solow equilibrium path, on technical progress and labor force growth.

The unstable intersection between the vicious and virtuous circles has to be associated with Rosenstein-Rodan's writing. Indeed, it corresponds to that critical mass of investment that generates the externalities and scale economies required for a big push toward sustained economic development. This critical mass of investment, corresponding to K_U, need not be spontaneously achieved and may require policy action. As

Rosenstein-Rodan stated: "There is a minimum level of resources that must be devoted to . . . a development program if it is to have any chance for success. Launching a country into self-sustaining growth is a little like getting an airplane off the ground. There is a critical ground speed which must be passed before the craft can become airborne" (1984, 210).

The development trap below the low K intersection has to be distinguished from a poverty trap due to insufficient savings. In the savings trap model of chapter 2, the rate of accumulation is low at small levels of K because low incomes, barely enough for subsistence consumption, adversely affect the savings rate. Below the low K intersection in that model, the capital stock contracts because savings, despite the high profitability of investment, fall below depreciation due to the low propensity to save. In the present model, the rate of capital accumulation $(s_\pi r)$ is low at small levels of K because profitability is low. Even though a low savings rate may aggravate the problem, it is the low profit rate, due to the small capital stock, that prevents the rate of capital accumulation from rising above depreciation. It is in this sense that the weakness of the inducement to invest, rather than the scarcity of savings, is the source of the problem and explains why the initial conditions of low productivity and capital scarcity persist. This is an important difference between the two models. Unlike what happens with a savings trap, even a large degree of international capital mobility may now be insufficient to lift a poor economy out of this type of development trap. I shall return to this subject in chapter 9.

The multiple equilibria generated by the model should also be distinguished from an example of multiple equilibria with a nonconvex technology that first appeared in the original Solow article (1956, 71). In the Solow diagram of figure 18, the curve showing gross investment per worker as a function of the capital-labor ratio has the shape of an S, which may then intersect the effective depreciation line at more than one point. In this case, as in related examples in Wan 1971 (chap. 2, sec. 2), Barro and Sala-i-Martin 1995 (sec. 1.3.5), and Azariadis 1996, the technology of the single sector being considered features increasing returns *to capital* over a range of capital-labor ratios (with diminishing returns to capital at higher levels of the capital-labor ratio). The increasing marginal product of capital can generate low- or medium-level unstable intersections and therefore multiple equilibria. This is similar to the present model because in both cases profitability increases over a range of capital stocks. The key difference is that here this is not a property of the production function. The technology of the capitalist sector features diminishing returns to capital over the whole range of capital stocks, and it is the interaction between increasing returns *to scale* and an elastic labor supply that generates multiple equilibria.

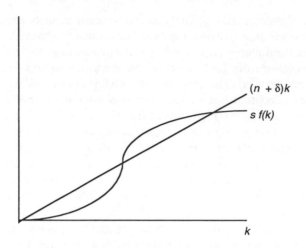

Fig. 18.   A case of multiple equilibria in Solow 1956

The Conditions for Multiple Equilibria

The conditions for the existence of multiple equilibria can be derived from the geometry of figure 17.[6] For the model to generate a low-level intersection, the w curve must be flatter than the w^* locus at low levels of K. This requires $(a + \mu)/(ea + 1) < \mu/(1 - a)$, which implies:

$$\mu(e + 1) > 1 - a. \tag{5}$$

For inequality 5 to be fulfilled, μ must be positive. There must be increasing returns to scale. This condition is evident from figure 17. Otherwise, the w^* curve would be horizontal and, as in the Solow and Lewis models, there would only be a unique equilibrium (in Lewis, either a subsistence or a mature economy equilibrium depending on the position of the two curves). Had we assumed constant returns to scale, there would not be a critical level of the initial capital endowment below which no sustained growth is possible. With constant returns, production can be undertaken at the smallest imaginable scale without any adverse effect on profitability. Then, if profitability is not high enough to generate sustained growth, this will be true no matter how large the initial capital stock is, and, if it is high enough, this will be true regardless of how small the initial capital stock is. In Lewis's model, for example, even the smallest initial capital stock leads to self-sustained growth provided that the propensity to save out of profits is sufficiently high and modern technology is sufficiently productive.

It is worth noting, indeed, that the condition refers to increasing returns rather than positive technological external effects. Technological externalities need to be positive here *only to the extent* that they are the source of aggregate increasing returns. This can be seen more clearly if we do not restrict the sum of the capital and labor coefficients in the firm's production function to unity. With b now being the output-employment elasticity, the condition in inequality 5 becomes:

$$(a + \mu + b - 1)[e(1 - b) + 1] > (a + \mu)b \quad b < 1,$$

which shows that even if $\mu = 0$ (no technological externalities) the condition can be fulfilled if $a + b > 1$ (increasing returns to scale).

For inequality 5 to hold in the absence of increasing returns *to capital* $(a + \mu > 1)$, the labor supply must be elastic $(e > 0)$. There must be surplus labor in the broad sense of an elastic labor supply in order to generate the relatively flat segment of the w curve and thus the low K intersection. Otherwise, there would only be a mature economy intersection (if it exists). This is because without a subsistence sector where workers can work if they do not find employment in the capitalist sector the real product wage would drop far enough to make the capitalist sector profitable.

As inequality 5 makes clear, a *perfectly* elastic supply of labor is not necessary to generate the low K intersection. What the condition implies is that the sum of the parameter of returns to capital $(a + \mu)$ and the product of the increasing returns parameter and labor supply elasticity $(e\mu)$ must be greater than one. This condition is likely to be fulfilled when labor supply elasticity is high at low levels of K even with a small dose of increasing returns. In the present model, e tends toward $(1 - \alpha)/\alpha$ when K and L_M/L_S tend toward zero. The condition in inequality 5 then becomes $\mu > \alpha(1 - a)$.[7]

The condition for the labor supply elasticity implied by inequality 5 is not restricted to the particular type of labor surplus considered in the present model. As shown in Ros and Skott 1997, in a model without efficiency wages, with labor market clearing and CES utility functions, the necessary condition involves a sufficiently high elasticity of substitution between the goods produced by the two sectors. Consider, for example, the w curve of the model presented in the third section of chapter 3. There labor supply elasticity is given in equation 13 as $e = (1 - l_M)/[bl_M + (h - 1)^{-1}]$, for $L_S < Lo$. When K and l_M tend toward zero, e

tends toward $(h - 1)$. The condition for a low K intersection then becomes $\mu > (1 - a)/h$ (see Ros and Skott 1997). Again, in the absence of increasing returns to capital, this condition states that the elasticity of substitution in consumption must be greater than unity and high enough to make the labor supply sufficiently elastic.

While returns must increase to generate the low K intersection at point U, they must not increase dramatically if the model is to generate the high K intersection. As figure 17 makes clear, for this intersection to exist the slope of the w^* line, given by $\mu/(1 - a)$, must be less than the slope of the w curve in the mature phase (given by $a + \mu$). Thus, it is necessary that $\mu/(1 - a) < a + \mu$, which implies $a + \mu < 1$. The increasing returns parameter (μ) must not be so high as to generate aggregate increasing returns to capital. Under such dramatically increasing returns, there would be no mature steady state. After reaching the critical value K_U, the economy would keep growing without bounds. Even in the mature phase, the effects of capital accumulation on productivity would more than outweigh the effects of raising real wages on the profit rate. The profit rate, the rate of capital accumulation, and the capital-labor ratio would go on increasing in a process of endogenous growth similar to that in the Romer's 1986 model, as will be discussed in chapter 6.

Stable Equilibrium with a Small Capitalist Sector

In the previous model, the low-level stable equilibrium is a subsistence economy without a capitalist sector. I now consider a variant of this model that generates a low-level stable equilibrium with a capitalist sector. The key change is abandoning the assumption of constant expenditure shares, which follows from the Cobb-Douglas specification of the utility function, and considering instead changing expenditure shares. I do this in a simple way. Suppose that the expenditure share of the subsistence sector good (α) falls as K increases due to a relatively high income elasticity of demand for the M sector good. At low levels of K, the high value of the expenditure share (α) will moderate the high value of e arising from the low employment share of the modern sector (a low L_M/L_S). If, for example, α tends toward one when K tends toward zero, labor supply elasticity will be zero just as in the mature phase at high levels of capital stock. The slope of the w curve will thus be larger than the slope of the w^* locus (provided returns to capital are not increasing). At intermediate levels of K, the lower value of α tends to increase labor supply elasticity. The combination of a labor surplus and an income-elastic demand for M goods makes the w curve relatively flat. It is then possible that, over a range of K values, the w curve will become flatter

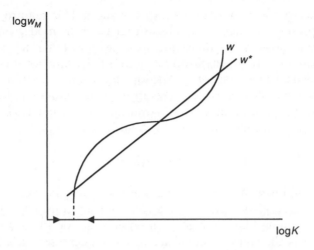

Fig. 19. Low-level equilibrium with a capitalist sector

than the w^* line before becoming steeper again at high values of K. The w curve will thus have the shape of an inverted S, as in figure 19.[8]

The model generates a low-level stable equilibrium at strictly positive values of K. What gives local stability to the low-level intersection is the relatively inelastic labor supply, which exists when K is small. This low labor supply elasticity is due to the small expenditure share of M goods, which implies that the additional income generated by an expansion of the capital stock is mostly spent on S goods. This turns the terms of trade against the M sector, thus raising the product wage in this sector and preventing a self-sustained expansion of the capital stock.

Properties and Extensions

I now turn to discussing some implications of the Rosenstein-Rodan/ Leibenstein model examined earlier. Although the main focus will be on the properties of the transition to the steady state, it is worthwhile to begin by saying something about the determinants of the steady state in the high-level equilibrium.

Determinants of the Mature Steady State

The economy has two sectors, one of which uses a fixed factor and labor under diminishing returns. As discussed in chapter 3, this implies that the two sectors will coexist in the steady state. This feature, together with the presence of increasing returns to scale in the modern sector, has novel implications for the determinants of the steady state.

We can derive the employment share of the modern sector in the mature phase — in the sense of Kaldor (see chap. 3) — from Kaldor's condition of equality between wages in the two sectors (neglecting, for simplicity, the wage premium). Substituting from equation 12 into 22 in chapter 3, we can solve for $l_M* = L_M/L$ under $w_S = w_M$:

$$l_M* = \{1 + [\alpha/(1 - \alpha)](1 - s_\pi a)/(1 - a)\}^{-1}.$$

The employment share of the modern sector remains constant during the mature phase, given our assumption of constant expenditure shares. Assuming that the high-level equilibrium occurs in the mature phase, this is the employment share of the modern sector in the high-level steady state.

Using the steady state condition $w_M = w_M*$, we can solve for the steady state values of the capital-labor ratio ($k*$) and the real consumption wage $(w/p)*$ (where $w = w_M = w_S$):[9]

$$k* = (as_\pi/\delta)^{1/(1-a-\mu)} l_M*^{(1-a)/(1-a-\mu)} L^{\mu/(1-a-\mu)} \tag{6}$$

$$(w/p)* = D^{(1-a)} l_M*^{\mu(1-a)/(1-a-\mu)}(1 - l_M*)^{-ba} L^{\mu(1-a)/(1-a-\mu)-ba} \tag{7}$$

$$D = (1 - a)(as_\pi/\delta)^{(a+\mu)/(1-a-\mu)},$$

where we have set, for simplicity, the value of effort (E) when $w_S = w_M$ equal to unity. Equations 6 and 7 show that, in addition to the determinants of the steady state in the Solow model (savings and depreciation rates), a number of other variables affect the configuration of the steady state. Two features stand out. First, the steady state is not independent of the scale of the economy. The capital-labor ratio is an increasing function of the size of the labor force (L), given the presence of increasing returns ($\mu > 0$). When extended to allow for population growth, the model implies that the steady state value of the capital-labor ratio — and of labor productivity in the modern sector — will be growing at an endogenous rate given by $n\mu/(1 - a - \mu)$, the rate of growth of the labor force (n) times the exponent of L in equation 6.[10] With population growth, the steady state is thus characterized by a situation in which profitability is constant, employment in the modern sector grows at the same rate as the overall labor force, and the rate of capital accumulation is higher than Harrod's natural rate (equal to n in the absence of exogenous technical progress) by an amount that depends on the increasing-returns parameter.[11] The steady state growth rate of the capital stock is endogenous in the sense that it depends on technology parameters (in particular, μ), but not in the sense that it is affected by the savings rate. In this, and unlike in recent endogenous growth models, the present model features one of the key properties of the Solow model—the independence of the steady state growth rate from the savings rate.

The scale of the economy also affects the steady state value of the real wage; however, the sign is now ambiguous. The reason is that, along with the positive productivity effects of a larger scale of the modern sector, operating through increasing returns and the rising capital-labor ratio, there are now negative effects. These arise from the higher terms of trade (p_S/p_M) that result from diminishing returns to labor in sector S. Indeed, in the absence of technical progress in sector S, labor productivity in this sector falls with an increasing labor force and this turns the terms of trade against the modern sector. The real wage then tends to rise or fall depending on whether the net effect of the increasing-returns effect plus the negative terms of trade effect on profitability is positive or negative.[12]

The second distinguishing feature of the steady state is the presence of the employment share of the modern sector (l_M^*) among its determinants. There are two reasons for this. First, the larger the employment share the higher is, for a given scale, the steady state value of the capital-labor ratio and—through the (external) productivity effects of capital accumulation—the higher the steady state real wage tends to be. Second, a smaller sector S implies higher productivity in this sector in the steady state. This effect—reflected in the term $(1 - l_M^*)^{-b\alpha}$ in equation 7—has a positive influence on the real wage and disappears only if $b = 0$ (constant returns to labor in sector S, which implies that productivity is independent of employment). In the present closed-economy model, the long-term equilibrium employment share is largely determined by the consumption shares of the two goods along with savings rates and technology parameters (affecting distribution between profits and wages). In an open economy, as we shall see in chapters 8 and 9, the employment share will primarily be affected by the pattern of specialization in international trade, as determined by resource endowment and policy. For the time being, it is worth pointing out that the presence of the modern sector employment share among the determinants of the steady state is quite consistent with the finding in chapter 1 that differences in incomes per capita across countries are positively associated with the industrial employment share.

The Transition to the Steady State

Some of the more striking implications of the model concern the characteristics of the transition and the possibility of poverty traps. The more general implication is that the adverse effects on productivity and profitability of low capital-labor ratios will inhibit growth at low-income levels and thus weaken the tendency to convergence of neoclassical growth models. Moreover, if multiple equilibria exist, the profit rate and the rate of accumulation in the modern sector are no longer monotonically decreasing functions of the capital-labor ratio. From the profit-wage curve, $r = K^{\mu/a} [(1 - a)E^*/w_M]^{(1-a)/a}$, taking logs and differentiating with respect to $\log K$ and then using the expression for the slope of the w curve (eq. 4) to eliminate $d\log w_M/d\log K$, we obtain:

$$\text{dlog}r/\text{dlog}K = [\mu(1 + e) - (1 - a)]/(1 + ea),$$

where, from the first section:
$$e = (1 - \alpha)/\alpha[1 + (1 - b)L_M/L_S] \qquad \text{for } fw_S < w_M$$
and $$e = 0 \qquad \text{for } fw_S = w_M.$$

Up to the mature phase, elasticity of the labor supply is a decreasing function of the employment share of the modern sector and thus of the capital-labor ratio.[13] If, over a range of low capital-labor ratios, elasticity of the labor supply is sufficiently large so that $\mu > (1 - a)/(1 + e)$, the sign of the derivative $d\log r/d\log K$ is positive and the profit rate is an increasing function of the capital-labor ratio. At higher levels of the capital-labor ratio—and certainly in the mature phase when $e = 0$—labor supply elasticity falls and the profit rate becomes a negative function of the capital-labor ratio (provided that $a + \mu < 1$).

As we did for the Solow model, we can write the transitional component of growth in the modern sector as $s(r - r^*)$, where s here is equal to as_π. Let us define the rate of convergence as the ratio of this transitional component to the log difference between the steady state and the actual values of the real product wage in the modern sector. It follows, then, that when the condition $\mu > (1 - a)/(1 + e)$ is met, and the profit rate follows an inverted U-shaped pattern, the rate of convergence will be low and increasing at low levels of income and relatively high and decreasing as the economy approaches the steady state.[14] The model predicts, under certain conditions, a pattern of conditional divergence followed by convergence, with the highest rates of accumulation occurring in the intermediate rather than the initial stages of the transition, as predicted by the neoclassical model.[15] The key condition is for the profit rate to increase over a range of capital-labor ratios. Since, as the reader may have noticed, this is the same condition for the existence of a low K intersection (inequality 5), and thus for a trap with low profitability, the model also suggests the possibility of divergence between high- and low-income countries. Moreover, if technical progress is largely specific to the modern capitalist sector, the model suggests that the lowest growth rates are to be found in the poorest countries (further away from the high steady state) with negative growth rates for those countries in the poverty trap. It is worth noting that allowing for international capital mobility tends to strengthen these properties of the model, as the low profit rates in the poorest countries imply that capital will flow toward the middle- and high-income economies.

Empirical Evidence

The model has a number of implications that can be checked against the data. I focus here on three of them.

1. Like any other model with increasing returns to scale, this one suggests the presence of significant scale effects in explaining international differences in the levels and growth rates of output per worker.
2. In the presence of multiple equilibria, the model predicts a pattern of conditional divergence at low-income levels, followed by convergence, and suggests absolute divergence at low-income levels if certain conditions are met.
3. The model implies that the pattern of divergence/convergence, with the associated growth acceleration at middle-income levels, arises from the interaction between increasing returns and elastic labor supplies, which makes profitability increase over a range of low and intermediate values of the capital-labor ratio.

Returns to Scale Effects

Consider first the significance of returns to scale effects in explaining cross-country differences in output per worker. We have already met these effects in the cross-country regressions of chapter 1. From table 2 (regression 4), we have:

$$\log(Y/L) = 1.69 + 0.27\log(K/L) + 0.36\log(H/L) + 0.08\log Y$$

$$+ 0.24\log(T/Y) + 0.62\log(L_i/L),$$

where (H/L) is the mean number of years of schooling of the population aged 25 years and above (a proxy for human capital per worker), T/Y is the trade share, and L_i/L is the industrial employment share. Solving for Y in a production function form, we get:

$$Y = AK^{.29}H^{.39}L^{.40},$$

where: $A = (6.3)\ (T/Y)^{.26}\ (L_i/L)^{.67}.$

Two features stand out in this formulation. First, the labor and capital coefficients add up to slightly more than unity (1.08), suggesting the presence of moderate pure scale effects.[16] Thus, an x percent increase in K, L, and H, holding the trade and industrial employment shares constant, results in a $(1.08)\ x$ percent increase in output. This, of course, is simply the counterpart of the coefficient of $\log Y$ in the original regression being positive and implying an aggregate value of the increasing returns parameter of .08 in the production function. Besides these pure scale effects, the coefficients of the trade and industrial employment shares suggest that changes in the reallocation of given resources can produce substantial output gains. A reallocation toward industrial activities or greater international specialization, holding constant the amounts of productive factors, leads to a positive shift in the "efficiency variable" (A). If we can be sure that the trade and industrial employment shares are not capturing such factors as differences across countries in access to technologies, the explanation for these reallocation effects must necessarily involve the presence of economies of scale and specialization and the fact that these play a special role in industrial activities.

Consider now the role of scale effects in explaining differences in growth rates. As is shown in table 14, which uses data from the Penn World Table (see chap. 1), in the regression of output growth on factor accumulation variables, the sum of the coefficients on factor variables exceeds unity by a larger factor than in the regression on income levels. The implied value of the increasing-returns parameter is 0.14 and rises to 0.18 when the 15 high-income countries are excluded. The reallocation of resources toward increasing returns activities is the main candidate for explaining the larger value of the increasing returns to scale effects (i.e., the larger difference between the sum of the coefficients and unity, the expected value under the assumption of constant returns to scale).

In contrast, in the 15 high-income countries the sum of the coefficients is less than one. This suggests that in the postindustrial stage, when the reallocation of resources toward increasing-returns sectors has been largely completed, aggregate scale effects lose the importance that they clearly seem to have in explaining growth differences among the industrializing and preindustrial economies that constitute the rest of the sample. Why should this be so? An explanation has to rely on another interesting contrast between the two groups of countries: the much higher and significant coefficient of labor force growth in the high-income countries, which is the counterpart of the much higher coefficient of (physical) capital accumulation in the developing economies. This strongly points to the importance of reallocation effects under conditions of elastic labor supplies, for it is these conditions that enhance the productivity effects of capital accumulation in the increasing-returns sectors. In this interpretation, the key role of resource reallocation in the growth process is what reduces the coefficient of labor force growth in the initial and intermediate stages.

A recurrent finding in the literature on growth accounting and cross-country productivity performance is that the residual difference between output growth and factor accumulation (total factor productivity growth) tends to be much more significant among developed countries than among developing ones (see Chenery and Syrquin 1975). The positive and significant residual in developed economies is usually taken to reflect a high rate of technological progress, resulting in an "intensive" growth process. The much smaller, and sometimes even negative, rate of factor productivity growth among developing economies would then suggest an "extensive" growth process, which can be fully accounted for by factor

TABLE 14. Cross-Country Regressions

Independent Variable	All Countries (1)	High-Income Countries (2)	Low- and Middle-Income Countries (3)
Constant	−0.0064	0.015	−0.0085
	(−1.16)	(2.27)	(−1.06)
g_K	0.52	−0.04	0.55
	(7.14)	(−0.27)	(6.25)
g_H	0.30	0.35	0.33
	(2.51)	(2.58)	(2.18)
g_L	0.32	0.50	0.30
	(1.72)	(2.22)	(1.25)
N	57	15	42
Adjusted R^2	0.56	0.50	0.52

Source: Penn World Table (Mark 5.6) (see app. chap. 1)

Note: g refers to growth rate (log difference) and K, H, and L to capital, education (H/L times the size of the labor force), and labor force, respectively.

t-statistics in parentheses

Dependent variable: Growth rate of real GDP, 1965–90

accumulation and, when the residual is negative, would indicate an inefficient process of factor accumulation. The notion that even in the fastest-
growing developing economies growth reflects little technical progress is
the basis of the recent reinterpretation of the East Asian growth experience by Young (1995), which suggests that even these apparent "growth
miracles" were largely based on factor accumulation. The regression
results in table 14 illustrate these findings for our country sample and
time period. In the regression of output growth on factor accumulation
variables, the constant term — which may loosely be interpreted as output
growth unaccounted for by factor accumulation — is positive and significant in regression 2, which refers to the high-income countries, and negative and insignificant in the regression for the rest of the sample (regression 3).

Our earlier discussion suggests, however, an explanation of these
results that is based on the role of reallocation effects and is different
from the "extensive growth" interpretation. The size of the constant,
together with the coefficient of labor force growth, suggests that for the
average developing country — with a rate of labor force growth on the
order of 2.5 percent per year — output would stagnate in the absence of
(physical and human) capital accumulation. At the same time, output
per worker would be falling, as the share in employment of the sector
with diminishing returns to labor would be increasing. Rather than an
inefficient process of factor accumulation, the negative constant may
well be reflecting that, in the presence of increasing returns and rapid
growth of the labor force, a certain threshold rate of capital accumulation must be achieved for productivity growth to be positive. In the high-
income countries, the process of resource reallocation toward the increasing returns sectors has been largely completed and the threshold
rate is lower. The size of the constant is then higher.

The Pattern of Divergence/Convergence

As noted in chapter 1, a number of studies have suggested that for low-
income countries the relationship between the initial level of income and
subsequent growth is positive and income levels diverge. Then, beyond
a certain level of per capita income the relationship becomes negative,
implying convergence of income levels, even though incomes continue
to rise at faster rates than in the poorest countries. This pattern of
divergence/convergence is captured by a quadratic equation in which the
income growth rate (g_y) is related to the level and the square of initial
income (y_0 and y_0^2):

$$g_y = a_0 + a_1 y_0 + a_2 y_0^2 \quad a_1 > 0, \ a_2 < 0.$$

The growth rate reaches a maximum at an income level equal to:

$$y^M = -a_1/2a_2,$$

provided that a_2 is negative (the condition for a maximum) and a_1 is positive (so that y is positive). The corresponding maximum growth rate is $g_M = a_0 - a_1^2/4a_2$. The equation also implies a threshold level of convergence, the income level at which the growth rate is equal to that in the highest-income countries (g^*), at:

$$y_C = y^M + [a_1^2 - 4a_2(a_0 - g^*)]^{1/2}/2a_2,$$

which is less than y^M since a_2 is negative.

Table 15 summarizes a number of estimates of such quadratic equations for different periods and data sets and also includes linear regressions of growth rates on initial income for subsamples of high- and low-income countries. The results generally support the pattern of divergence/convergence.[17] The signs of the coefficients are systematically favorable to the hypothesis and suggest that growth rates tend to reach a maximum in the intermediate income range. In Baumol and Wolff 1988, for example, this happens at a per capita income of around $1,900 (in 1975 international dollars), with 17 out of the 72 countries in their sample above this income level. Their equation also implies a convergence threshold—in the sense defined earlier—just 22 percent below the income level corresponding to the maximum growth rate.[18] This suggests a tendency for countries to grow faster than the top-income countries when incomes well beyond the median level are reached.

This last observation needs to be qualified by the fact that, except in Sarkar's (1998) pooled regressions, the linear regressions for lower-income groups show coefficients that, although positive and thus indicating divergence, usually have higher standard errors than the negative coefficients for the upper-income groups. This suggests that the tendency toward divergence at low-income levels is more erratic than the tendency to convergence among the upper-income countries. But, since the positive coefficients are larger in absolute value than the negative coefficients (in all cases), this erratic pattern of divergence should not be taken as evidence of a weaker tendency for incomes to diverge. What the evidence seems to suggest is a clear lack of convergence at low- and middle-income levels together with a convergence threshold that varies widely across countries within an ample income range. In Baumol and Wolff 1988, this income range is between $700 and $1,400.

Finally, Sheehey's (1996) regressions suggest that the evidence for

TABLE 15. Growth and Initial Income Regression Results

Authors and Period	Dependent Variable	C	y_0	y_0^2	R^2	N	Data Set
Baumol and Wolff (1988), 1950–80	$\ln(y_t/y_o)$	0.586 (4.2)	0.00038 (2.1)	$-9.9/10^7$ (2.2)	0.07	72	Summers and Heston 1984
	y_t/y_0	3.3 (7.7)	-0.00038 (−12.5)	—	0.30	17	Upper income group
		2.1 (5.5)	0.0005 (1.3)	—	0.03	55	Lower income group
Sheehey (1996), 1960–88	g_y	—	0.0023 (2.46)	$-7.2/10^7$ (1.93)	0.072	107	Penn World Table (Mark 5)
		—	-0.0006 (−2.14)	—	0.293	13	Upper income
		—	0.0028 (2.7)	—	0.072	82	Low income
Sarkar (1998), 1960–93, pooled regressions for 110 countries and various subperiods	g_y	0.57 (2.67)	0.0026 (4.76)	$-0.10/10^5$ (−4.25)	0.02	867	United Nations 1976 UNCTAD 1994
		5.65 (2.73)	-0.55^a (−1.89)	—	0.02	192	24 upper income
		-4.28 (−3.80)	1.06^a (4.85)	—	0.03	675	86 lower income

Study						N	Source
Easterly and Levine (1997)[b], pooled regressions for 1960s, 1970s, and 1980s	g_y	—	0.09[a] (3.74)	-0.007[a] (-4.58)	0.42	41	World Bank Summers and Heston 1988
Sheehey (1996), 1960–88	g_{yw}	—	0.0001 (1.14)	$-5.4/10^8$ (1.11)	0.012	107	Penn World Table (Mark 5)
			-0.0001 (1.28)	—	0.120	14	Upper income
			0.0002 (1.42)	—	0.026	78	Lower income

Note: g_y is the growth rate of per capita GDP. g_{yw} is the growth rate of GDP per worker. y_t is the end of period level of per capita real GDP. y_0 refers to the initial level of per capita GDP (or GDP per worker in Sheehey 1996 with g_{yw} as the dependent variable). N is the number of observations. In the case of Sarkar 1998, numbers in parentheses are White t-statistics. t-statistics are in parentheses.

[a] The independent variable is $\log y_0$ or $(\log y_0)^2$.

[b] Equation 4 in table 1, which includes a number of other regressors

both divergence at low-income levels and convergence at high levels is weaker in terms of GDP per worker than in terms of GDP per capita. Since the difference in results is due to differential rates of change in dependency ratios across countries, his estimates call attention to the role of high population growth rates (causing rising dependency ratios) in the divergence of per capita incomes among low-income countries. The results also highlight the role of falling dependency ratios in high-income countries in the process of income per capita convergence.[19]

The Rosenstein-Rodan/Leibenstein model discussed in the first section of this chapter implies a pattern of divergence/convergence, and thus the evidence on quadratic equations provides some support for the model. The evidence, however, is only suggestive. The model implies a pattern of divergence followed by convergence that is conditional on very specific determinants of the steady state besides the required existence of multiple equilibria. Controlling for the determinants of the steady state involves a number of difficulties, and for an important one — controlling for the long-run employment share of the modern sector — the relevant factors are very different in an open economy setting from those considered so far, as we shall see in chapters 8 and 9. Moreover, the conditions for multiple equilibria may be met in some countries and not in others. A general specification would have to take into account a host of factors, including cross-country differences in the production conditions of noncapitalist sectors and their degree of openness to international trade (both of which will affect labor supply elasticity), as well as differences in the equilibrium employment share of the modern sector. Moreover, since the savings rate is not constant throughout the transition, investigating the behavior of the rate of convergence would involve a larger number of interactions than we have had to face in previous models. We shall look at other relevant empirical evidence in later chapters. For the time being, I shall limit the discussion to a few, less ambitious questions.

First, how does the presence of increasing returns affect the steady state income gaps across countries? The presence of increasing returns has the effect of enlarging the steady state income gaps compared to those in the neoclassical model. Intuitively, this is because in the neighborhood of the steady state the productivity and profitability effects of increasing returns make the profit rate diminish less strongly than otherwise and allow economies with a higher investment share to reach a higher steady state capital-labor ratio than otherwise (and thus a higher level of income in the steady state). The practical answer depends on how much returns increase. If the effects of increasing returns are moderate, as is suggested by the evidence on scale effects discussed earlier, then the picture may remain largely unaffected. Table 16 presents estimates of the steady state income gaps in a Solow model "augmented" with technological externalities. Using the augmented production function, we can adjust the steady state income gaps in the Solow model for the five country groups of chapter 2 (shown in chap. 2, table 7). The steady state values of output per worker in any given group (i) of countries relative to the steady state value in the high-income economies of group 1 can be estimated from:[20]

$$\log(y_i^*/y_1^*) = [1 + \mu/a(1 - a - \mu)]\log(y_i^*/y_1^*)_S,$$

where $(y_i^*/y_1^*)_S$ is the relative steady state income in the Solow model (see eq. 4' in chap. 2).

The exercise assumes a value of $\mu = 0.2$, and for comparative purposes the table reproduces the steady state income gaps of the Solow model (i.e., the same model with $\mu = 0$). The exercise confirms that the presence of increasing returns has the effect of enlarging the steady state income gaps but that a moderate dose of increasing returns does not make a dramatic difference.

Moreover, the investment share will now tend to rise throughout the transition. This has the opposite effect of narrowing steady state income gaps, as differences in the steady state investment shares are now likely to be much smaller than actual differences. The implication for the Rosenstein-Rodan/Leibenstein model is that actual differences in income levels should largely be viewed, just as in the Solow model, as the result of differences in relative position with respect to the steady state. Under these conditions, the model not only implies a pattern of conditional divergence followed by conditional convergence but also a pattern of absolute divergence/convergence. This broad implication is consistent with the trends reviewed in chapters 2 and 3: convergence

TABLE 16. Actual and Steady State Income Gaps in the Solow Model Adjusted for Increasing Returns

	Averages for Country Groups				
	1	2	3	4	5
Income as a percentage of group 1 (1997)	100	56.7	25.2	10.7	4.3
Steady state income as a percentage of group 1 (Solow model)	100	90.5	92.7	87.6	85.0
Steady state income as a percentage of group 1 (adjusted for $\mu = 0.2$)	100	79.6	84.1	73.9	69.0
Number of countries	18	14	13	15	13

among the OECD economies and a number of middle-income developing economies together with increasing heterogeneity among the developing countries. In particular, the model accommodates two striking
features of postwar development trends. First, the highest growth rates
are found among developing countries and a number of industrial countries that were initially relatively less developed.[21] Second, the lowest
growth rates are typically found among the low-income countries.[22]

A second important question is how much of the inverted-U pattern
of the transitory component of growth survives the inclusion of human
capital variables and other likely determinants of the steady state? To
investigate this issue, I included in the quadratic equation a number of
variables used in Barro 1991: the average investment share, initial enrollments in primary and secondary education, and two political risk and
instability variables (the number of revolutions and coups per year
[REV] and the number of political assassinations per million population
and per year [ASSASS]). The equations were estimated for 1960–89 —
the longest period for which data on all variables were available — and
then separately for 1960–79 and the 1980s, which witnessed a sharp
slowdown in growth in highly indebted middle-income countries.

The regression estimates presented in table 17 are generally favorable to the divergence/convergence hypothesis.[23] They tend to confirm
that, after controlling for differences in investment shares, education,
and political risk variables, the economies of the poorest countries
tended to grow more slowly than middle- and high-income economies
and only after a threshold was there a clear process of income convergence. The coefficients on initial income have the expected signs for the
whole period and the two subperiods, although they are highly significant only for the period 1960–79. Most of the other variables also have
the expected signs and are significant for this last period (especially
investment share and primary education). Two exceptions are one of
the political variables (revolutions and coups, which has a positive but
insignificant coefficient) and secondary education (which has the expected positive sign but is not significant). For the other periods (1960–
89 and 1980–89), REV has the expected negative sign but remains
insignificant and secondary education has a consistently positive and
significant coefficient.

A comparison of the two periods before and after 1980 suggests
that the lack of significance for the whole period (1960–89) of the
coefficients on the initial income terms is due to a sharp increase after
1980 in the standard errors of *both* coefficients — the positive divergence coefficient and the negative convergence coefficient on the
square term. Many factors probably account for this erratic behavior.
There is some indication that slowing growth in highly indebted middle

economies in the 1980s contributed to it. The debt crisis plunged a number of countries into economic stagnation during this period. Being at middle-income levels, they may otherwise have maintained, or even accelerated, their growth processes. The inclusion of a dummy variable, with a value of one for these highly indebted economies and zero otherwise, turns out to be significant and negative for the whole period as well as for the period 1980–89.[24] Its inclusion also tends to reduce the standard errors of the coefficients of the income terms, making the square term significant for the period 1960–89. The overall picture that emerges is one of a lack of convergence at low-income

TABLE 17.   Cross-Country Regressions

Independent Variable	1960–79	1960–89	1960–89	1980–89	1980–89
Constant	−0.195	−0.074	−0.123	−0.021	−0.164
	(−1.57)	(−0.71)	(−1.16)	(−0.11)	(−0.79)
$Logy_0$	.061	0.029	0.014	0.019	0.055
	(1.83)	(1.02)	(1.44)	(0.39)	(1.02)
$(Logy_0)^2$	−0.005	−0.003	−0.003	−0.002	−0.004
	(−2.14)	(−1.49)	(2.46)	(−0.57)	(−1.19)
I/Y	0.0008	0.001	0.001	0.002	0.002
	(2.89)	(3.82)	(3.59)	(3.62)	(3.13)
PRIMo	0.019	0.020	0.022	0.057	−0.059
	(1.86)	(2.29)	(2.46)	(−2.22)	(−2.31)
SECo	0.019	0.026	0.021	0.038	0.036
	(1.42)	(2.31)	(1.91)	(2.15)	(2.02)
REV	0.006	−0.0095	−0.0055	−0.0107	−0.0107
	(0.65)	(−1.14)	(−0.65)	(−0.78)	(−1.53)
ASSASS	−0.054	−0.041	−0.047	−0.018	−0.024
	(−2.04)	(−2.38)	(−2.70)	(−1.18)	(−1.53)
DDEBT	−	−	−0.008	−	−0.014
	−	−	(−1.97)	−	(−1.88)
N	89	89	89	88	88
Adjusted R^2	0.27	0.45	0.47	0.25	0.27

Note:

y_0: GDP per capita in the initial year of the period. *Source:* Penn World Table (Mark 5.6).

I/Y: Ratio of real domestic investment to real GDP (average for the period). *Source:* Penn World Table (Mark 5.6).

   PRIMo: Primary school enrollment rate in the initial year of the period. *Source:* Barro and Lee 1994.

   SECo: Secondary school enrollment rate in the initial year of the period. *Source:* Barro and Lee 1994.

   REV: Number of revolutions and coups per year (average for the period). *Source:* Barro and Lee 1994.

   ASSASS: Number of political assassinations per million population and per year (average for the period). *Source:* Barro and Lee 1994.

   DDEBT: Dummy variable for severely indebted middle-income economies

   t-statistics in parentheses

   Dependent variable: Growth rate of real GDP per capita

levels (a positive but often insignificant coefficient of initial income) followed by convergence at high-income levels (a negative and often significant coefficient of the square income term).

In the quadratic equation, the newly included variables substitute for the constant term (a_0) and therefore affect the convergence threshold — $y_C = y^M + [a_1{}^2 - 4a_2(a_0 - g^*)]^{1/2}/2a_2$ — with a sign that is opposite the one in the growth rate regression (provided that a_2 is negative). The regression results suggest, then, that higher school enrollments and rates of investment tend to reduce the threshold of convergence, while political instability tends to increase it. Moreover, the significance of these variables is the most likely explanation for the contrast between the erratic pattern of divergence among developing countries and the more definite tendency toward convergence among high-income countries. Since the latter are more homogeneous than the former in terms of investment shares and educational variables, the omission of these factors from the linear regressions between growth and initial income has a smaller impact on the standard error of the estimated coefficient of initial income.

The results, needless to say, again call into question the "convergence result" of the empirical literature in support of the neoclassical growth model, according to which "given the human-capital variables, subsequent growth is substantially negatively related to the initial level of per capita GDP" (Barro 1991, 409). The positive coefficient on initial income suggests the presence of strong forces toward divergence, which are offset only at middle and high levels of income.[25]

Growth Acceleration and the Verdoorn Law

A key question still remains: is there any evidence that the pattern of income divergence followed by convergence and the associated growth acceleration in the transition obeys to the mechanisms envisaged by the model? As mentioned in chapter 1, Kaldor viewed the high growth rates characteristic of middle-income countries as an attribute of the process of industrialization. Expressing this view in terms of a regression equation for 12 advanced countries in the period 1953–54 to 1963–64, he found a very high correlation between the rate of growth of GDP (g_Y) and the rate of growth of manufacturing production (g_M). The regression reported in Kaldor 1967 is:

$$g_Y = 1.153 + \underset{(0.040)}{0.614 g_M} \quad R^2 = 0.959$$

(standard error is in parentheses).

In Kaldor's view, the most significant finding was that the coefficient on g_M was (considerably) less than unity, implying that "the faster the overall rate of growth, the greater is the *excess* of the rate of growth of manufacturing production over the rate of growth of the economy as a whole" (1967, 8; italics original). In other words, high overall growth rates are associated with fast rates of industrialization. Kaldor did not view this relationship as being, at least primarily, a demand-side phenomenon: it is not so much that high rates of GDP growth generate high growth in manufacturing, given high-income elasticity of demand for manufactures. Causality runs primarily from manufacturing to GDP growth and more precisely from manufacturing growth to the growth rate of GDP per worker. This is the result of two mechanisms. First, the growth rate of productivity in manufacturing industries itself rises with the rate of growth of output. Second, employment growth in industry tends to increase the rate of productivity growth in other sectors. This is the consequence of diminishing returns to labor in other sectors and the absorption of surplus labor from these sectors as well as of a faster increase in the flow of goods into consumption, which tends to increase productivity in the commerce sector (15).

The first mechanism is Verdoorn's law — named after P. J. Verdoorn, who found a strong empirical relationship (1949) between productivity and output growth in a cross section of industries. A moment's reflection will show that for the mechanism of labor force reallocation envisaged by Kaldor to generate high rates of *overall* productivity growth the Verdoorn relationship must be such that industrial productivity and employment growth are positively correlated. Otherwise, a high rate of manufacturing output growth will not bring about the reallocation of the labor force. This may be the reason why in his interpretation of Verdoorn's law Kaldor placed so much emphasis on the coefficient in the regression of productivity growth on output growth (the Verdoorn coefficient) being positive *and* less than unity. For in this range of values the Verdoorn coefficient implies a positive association between productivity growth and employment growth in industry.[26] Thus, in Kaldor's (1967) original analysis of a cross section of 12 developed countries from 1953–54 to 1963–64, the estimated Verdoorn relationship is:

$$g_p = 1.035 + 0.484g_M \quad R^2 = .826,$$
$$(.070)$$

where g_p and g_M are, respectively, the rates of growth of labor productivity and production in manufacturing. The standard error is shown in parentheses. The value of the Verdoorn coefficient (close to 0.5) meant, as Kaldor (1966) stated it, that each additional percentage point in the growth of output is associated with a 0.5 percent increase in employment and a 0.5 percent increase in the growth of productivity.[27]

As noted by Rowthorn (1979), Verdoorn (1949) derived the relationship between productivity and output growth from a simultaneous equation model in which the parameters of both the production function and the labor supply function affect the relationship. In the appendix to this chapter, I derive the Verdoorn coefficient (v) that links productivity and output growth from such a model, assuming a CES production function in manufacturing. The Verdoorn coefficient is given by:

$$v = (\pi\lambda + \sigma\mu)/[\pi(\lambda + e) + \sigma\mu(1 + e)]$$

$$\lambda = \mu e + \sigma(1 - \mu e),$$

where π is the profit share in manufacturing equal to $a/[a + (1 - a)(K/L_M)^{-\psi}]$, $\sigma[=1/(1 - \psi)]$ is the elasticity of factor substitution, μ is the increasing-returns parameter in the production function, and e is the elasticity of the labor supply to the manufacturing sector.

The coefficient of the productivity and employment growth relationship $[v/(1 - v)]$ is then:

$$v/(1 - v) = (\pi\lambda + \sigma\mu)/[e(\pi + \sigma\mu)].$$

This expression shows that if the elasticity of factor substitution is zero or very small then e and μ must both be greater than zero for productivity and employment growth to be positively correlated. In this case, a positive association between productivity and employment growth must reflect the facts that the labor supply to industry is elastic and returns to scale are increasing. For positive values of the elasticity of substitution, a positive value of μ is no longer a necessary condition for $v/(1 - v)$ to be positive. Yet, if μ were zero, $v/(1 - v)$ would be equal to σ/e, so that a value of $v/(1 - v)$ equal to unity (as implied by Kaldor's results) would require elasticity of factor substitution equal to that of the labor supply. Then, of course, if labor supply elasticity is larger than unity, only in the presence of very high elasticity of factor substitution would a close association between productivity and employment growth be consistent with constant returns to scale.

The evidence for Verdoorn's law provides additional support for the view that growth acceleration at middle-income levels is based on the interaction between increasing returns and elastic labor supplies.[28] It suggests that this is the mechanism generating the close association between overall growth rates and the rate of industrialization and explaining why the productivity effects of industrialization are enhanced at those intermediate stages of the transition when both the demand for manufacturing products and the labor supply to industry are highly elastic.

None of the three sets of empirical evidence discussed previously is only consistent with the increasing returns/surplus labor model discussed in the first section of this chapter. The evidence for scale effects is consistent with any model with (moderately) increasing returns to scale. The pattern of absolute income divergence at low-income levels and growth acceleration at middle-income levels is consistent with a number of other models. The savings trap model of chapter 2 and the Lewis model of chapter 3 both suggest similar patterns, though for different reasons. Reference can also be made to the "technology gap" view of Gomulka (1971) and Abramovitz (1986). For Abramovitz, technological backwardness brings with it a potential for rapid productivity growth. This growth, however, cannot be achieved when certain societal characteristics, which are necessary to absorb the available stock of technology and vary positively with income level, arc lacking. Yet, the three pieces of evidence — scale effects, the pattern of divergence/ convergence, and Verdoorn's law and productivity-employment relationships — together seem to send a clear message. It is both of the model's key departures from the neoclassical model — increasing returns and elastic labor supplies — that seem to make it more consistent than alternative explanations with the data on income and growth differences across countries.

At the same time, the evidence suggests the limitations of the present version of the model. First, the size of scale effects indicates that, although aggregate returns to scale increase moderately, they probably increase more than what can be accounted for by technological external effects. Aggregate increasing-returns parameters of 0.1 to 0.2 imply sector parameters in the increasing-returns activities that may be twice as high, on the order of 0.2 to 0.4, and are likely to reflect the importance of economies of scale internal to the firm. The next chapter will bring these internal returns to scale into the analysis. Second, the evidence points to the importance of human capital — both in the analysis of scale effects and in affecting the patterns of income divergence and convergence. Yet, education and off-the-job acquisition of skills are absent from the formal model of the first section of this chapter. The last section of chapter 6 will attempt to overcome this shortcoming after a discussion of recent theories of endogenous growth.

APPENDIX

On Verdoorn's Law

Verdoorn's law is commonly taken to imply that, in the regression of productivity growth on output growth, the regression coefficient (Verdoorn's coefficient) is positive and less than unity. After Kaldor (1966, 1967) investigated the relationship for a cross section of developed economies, research on the subject included cross-country studies of manufacturing industries and time-series for single countries (for surveys, see Bairam 1987; McCombie 1983; and Thirlwall 1983). The sometimes contrasting results, depending on the particular specification and estimation procedures adopted, have fueled a continuing controversy regarding the appropriate tests and specifications of Verdoorn's law. At the source of much of this controversy are the difficulties of deriving information on returns to scale from the estimated Verdoorn coefficients.

To illustrate these difficulties, consider a common interpretation of the Verdoorn coefficient. Assume the following production function in manufacturing:

$$M = AK^{a+\mu}L^{1-a}.$$

Taking logs and differentiating with respect to time, we can decompose the growth of output (g_M) into:

$$g_M = \beta + (a + \mu)g_K + (1 - a)g_L, \tag{A.1}$$

where $\beta = (\text{dlog}A/dt)\ 1/t$ and g_K and g_L refer to the growth rates of capital and labor inputs, respectively. Then, assuming a constant capital-output ratio, so that $g_M = g_K$, and using $g_p = g_M - g_L$, we can express the rate of growth of output per worker (g_p) as:

$$g_p = [\beta/(1 - a)] + [\mu/(1 - a)]g_M, \tag{A.2}$$

which shows the Verdoorn coefficient, $[\mu/(1 - a)]$, as being determined exclusively by the parameters of the production function (μ and a) and thus a purely technological coefficient. A positive and less than unity Verdoorn coefficient implies that $\mu > 0$ and $a + \mu < 1$, that is, increasing returns to scale and diminishing returns to capital. With $a = 1/3$, a Verdoorn coefficient of the order of 0.5 would imply an increasing-returns parameter of 1/3.

One problem with this interpretation is that equation A.2 holds only in the steady state, when output and the capital stock are growing at the same rate. Off the steady state, some productivity increases will have been due to capital deepening, which, in turn, will be affected by the growth in real wages and labor supply elasticity. This will be the case as long as the elasticity of factor substitution is positive, which is, of course, the case with the log linear production function assumed.

To illustrate this point, consider the Cobb-Douglas technology extended to allow for the technological externalities assumed in the first section of this chapter. Combining equations 1 and 4, that is, the labor demand function and the slope of the *w* curve (which depends on the labor supply function), we can express the growth of employment in sector *M* as a function of the growth of capital stock:

$$g_L = [e(a + \mu)/(ea + 1)]g_K. \tag{A.3}$$

Taking logs in equation 1 and differentiating with respect to time, we obtain an equation similar to A.1 (except that now $\beta = 0$). Substituting from equation A.3 and solving, as before, for the growth of output per worker as a function of output growth, we get:

$$g_p = [1/(1 + e)]g_M.$$

The Verdoorn coefficient is now inversely related to the elasticity of the labor supply, and in fact it turns out to be independent of the nature of returns to scale! Rather than a technological parameter, the Verdoorn coefficient is now exclusively affected by the nature of the labor supply function to sector *M*. An elastic, but less than perfectly elastic, labor supply can then generate a positive and less than unity Verdoorn coefficient.

It does not follow from this that it is impossible to derive any information about returns to scale from the Verdoorn coefficient. We need a more general specification, however, to discover under what conditions we may be able to do so. Consider a CES production function extended to allow for technological externalities:

$$M = A[aK^\psi + (1 - a)L^\psi]^{1/\psi},$$

where $A = (K)^\mu$ represents, as in equation 1, the external effect of the economywide average capital stock and the elasticity of factor substitution is given by $\sigma = 1/(1 - \psi)$. This can be written in intensive form as:

$$p = K^\mu[ak^\psi + (1 - a)]^{1/\psi}, \tag{A.4}$$

where *p* is output per worker (*M/L*) and *k* is the capital-labor ratio (*K/L*). Taking logs in equation A.4 and differentiating, we get:

$$\text{dlog}p = \mu\text{dlog}K + \pi(\text{dlog}K - \text{dlog}L) = (\mu + \pi)\text{dlog}K - \pi\text{dlog}L, \tag{A.5}$$

where π is the profit share equal to $a/[a + (1 - a)(K/L)^{-\psi}]$. To express dlog*p* as a function only of dlog*L* (and then as a function of dlog*M*), we need to derive the employment-capital elasticity to eliminate dlog*K* from equation A.5. Intuitively, this employment-capital elasticity depends on the labor demand function (in particular, the elasticity of substitution, which affects the reaction of labor demand to the change in the product wage) and labor supply elasticity, which affects how much the product wage has to rise for a given increase in employment. Consider, first, the labor demand function. From the first-order conditions for profit maximization, we get:

$$w = K^\mu (1 - a)[ak^\psi + (1 - a)]^{(1-\psi)/\psi}. \tag{A.6}$$

Taking logs in equation A.6 and differentiating and then solving for dlog$L$, we get:

$$\text{dlog}L = (1 + \sigma\mu/\pi)\text{dlog}K - (\sigma/\pi)\text{dlog}w. \tag{A.7}$$

Using equation A.7, together with dlog$L$/dlog$K = e$ (dlog$w$/dlog$K$), we can solve for the employment-capital elasticity:

$$\text{dlog}L/\text{dlog}K = (\pi + \mu\sigma)/(\pi + \sigma/e). \tag{A.8}$$

As is readily verified, this employment-capital elasticity is an increasing function of the elasticity of the labor supply. More surprisingly, the effect of the elasticity of factor substitution depends on whether $e\mu$ is more or less than unity. When $e\mu$ is less than unity, a higher elasticity of factor substitution adversely affects the employment effects of capital accumulation. This is clearly the case when there are constant returns to scale or the labor supply is inelastic. If $e\mu$ is more than unity — due to the presence of increasing returns and high elasticity of the labor supply — the employment effects of capital accumulation turn out to be positively affected by the elasticity of factor substitution.

The reason for this seemingly paradoxical result can be seen from equation A.7, which shows that labor demand is affected in two ways by the elasticity of factor substitution. First, for a given change in the product wage, a higher σ adversely affects the change in labor demand (this effect is $-[\sigma/\pi]$dlog$w$). Second, for a given change in the capital stock, a higher σ positively affects the change in labor demand provided that μ is positive (this effect is $[\sigma\mu/\pi]$ dlog$K$). Indeed, under increasing returns, capital accumulation has the effect of reducing the cost of labor for a given product wage. This reduction of labor costs stimulates labor demand, the more so the higher is the elasticity of factor substitution. When elasticity of the labor supply is high and the productivity effects of capital accumulation (given by μ) are larger than the real wage effects of employment growth (given by $1/e$) — and therefore $\mu e > 1$ — the positive effect of a higher σ on labor demand outweighs the negative effect. Employment-capital elasticity thus rises with σ.

Using equation A.8 to eliminate dlog$K$ from equation A.5:

$$\text{dlog}p = [(\pi\lambda + \sigma\mu)/e(\pi + \sigma\mu)]\text{dlog}L, \tag{A.9}$$

where $\lambda = \mu e + \sigma(1 - \mu e)$.

Using equation A.9, together with dlog$p$ = dlog$M$ − dlog$L$, we find the expression for the Verdoorn coefficient:

$$v = \mathrm{d}\log p/\mathrm{d}\log M = (\pi\lambda + \sigma\mu)/[\pi(\lambda + e) + \sigma\mu(1 + e)]. \qquad (A.10)$$

Equation A.10 shows that a number of variables and parameters in general affect the Verdoorn coefficient. These include the profit share, which depends on the capital-labor ratio; returns to scale (μ); and parameters of both the labor demand function (elasticity of substitution in particular) and the labor supply function (e, which depends on production conditions in the rest of the economy, the composition of employment, and the parameters of the demand functions for goods).

Equation A.10 is a rather complicated expression, but it simplifies in a number of special cases. Consider, for example, the case of an elasticity of substitution equal to one. Setting $\sigma = 1$ in equation A.10 yields $v = 1/(1 + e)$, which is, of course, the same expression that we obtained in the case of a Cobb-Douglas technology extended to allow for technological externalities. No parameters other than labor supply elasticity appear in the expression for v because, with an elasticity of factor substitution equal to one, the wage and profit shares in output remain constant. Output per worker and the product wage then grow at the same rate, and $\mathrm{d}\log p/\mathrm{d}\log L$ is equal to the inverse of labor supply elasticity ($1/e$). As can be readily verified, $v = \phi/(1 + \phi)$, where $\phi = \mathrm{d}\log p/\mathrm{d}\log L$.

Consider now the case of a fixed coefficients technology. Setting $\sigma = 0$ in equation 11 yields (provided that $e > 0$) $v = \mu/(1 + \mu)$. The Verdoorn elasticity is now a pure technology parameter, unaffected by the elasticity of labor supply. Indeed, without factor substitution the change in output per worker is completely delinked from the change in wages. Hence, labor supply elasticity does not appear in the determination of the Verdoorn coefficient. Moreover, without exogenous technical progress output per worker changes only as a result of the presence of increasing returns, and the relationship between labor productivity and output growth reflects exclusively the extent of increasing returns. This, or something very similar, may be what Kaldor had in mind in his interpretation of Verdoorn's law, for in this case there is a strict correspondence between the existence of increasing returns to scale ($\mu > 0$) and a Verdoorn coefficient that is positive *but* less than unity, so that productivity and employment growth indeed rise or fall together. It is worth noting, however, that the increasing-returns parameter would have to be dramatically high ($\mu = 1$) for the Verdoorn coefficient to be on the order of Kaldor's empirical estimates ($v = 1/2$).

CHAPTER 5

Internal Economies, Imperfect Competition, and Pecuniary Externalities

As mentioned in chapter 4, the source of aggregate increasing returns to scale may be external or internal to the firm. Each of these sources of increasing returns is associated with externalities—divergences between social and private costs and benefits. Drawing on a distinction first introduced by Viner (1931) and later developed by Meade (1952), Scitovsky (1954) distinguished between technological and pecuniary externalities. Following Meade (1952), he defined the former as those external economies arising from direct interdependence among producers, a property of the production function.[1] For example, the economies resulting from industrial training or learning by doing, discussed in chapter 4, accrue to a firm directly with the growth of an industry or the whole industrial system. When the firm's production function displays constant returns to scale, it is these effects, external to the firm, that cause aggregate returns to scale to increase and at the same time cause a divergence between social and private costs and benefits. In the case of industrial training, for instance, this divergence arises from the incomplete appropriability of the social returns from this activity (see Rosenstein-Rodan 1943, 1984).

When the source of increasing returns is a property of the individual firm's production function, externalities that are not of a technological nature can also arise. These are pecuniary externalities, in which interdependence among producers takes place through the market mechanism rather than directly, as in the case of technological externalities. As Scitovsky (1954, 300) stated it, all that is necessary for these external effects to take place is that "the profits of one producer are affected by the actions of other producers." Such external effects arise from the expansion of one firm, which, operating under economies of scale, reduces the production costs for other producers (through the reduction of its own costs), or from the expansion of other producers, enlarging the size of the market for the individual firms and thus reducing their production costs. As a result, and even without technological externalities, additional returns would accrue to a firm not only with its own expansion but with the growth of an industry and the whole economy. Fleming

(1955, 283) further distinguished "horizontal" from "vertical" pecuniary externalities, depending on whether interdependence takes place horizontally, through the interrelated markets of final goods industries, or vertically, through industries interacting as suppliers and customers.

In this chapter, I turn to economies in which aggregate increasing returns originate in economies of scale at the firm level and where pecuniary externalities can arise. Combined with elastic factor supplies, economies of scale leading to pecuniary externalities can generate multiple equilibria. In each of the three cases to be examined, the presence of internal economies of scale forces us to abandon the assumption of perfect competition. In the first two cases, pecuniary externalities involve demand spillovers across final goods industries. In Fleming's terminology, these are cases of horizontal external economies. In the third case, external effects involve vertical external economies in the spirit of Hirschman's (1958) "forward and backward linkages."

The Big Push in a Multisectoral Economy

I follow Murphy, Shleifer, and Vishny (1989b) in their formalization of Rosenstein-Rodan's idea of the need for a big push to overcome existing coordination problems when multiple equilibria arise. In this model, economies of scale arise in the production of final consumer goods and the market structure is such that a single firm in each sector has access to the increasing-returns technology.

Consider a multisectoral economy producing n final goods, each of which has an equal and constant share ($1/n$) in final expenditure. There are two techniques in the production of each good: a traditional technique with constant returns to scale (cottage production) and a modern technique with increasing returns to scale (mass production). The modern technique dominates the traditional technique at high levels of output but is less productive at low levels. Letting S and M be the output levels produced with each technique in any given sector, technology is thus described by:

$$S = L_S \tag{1}$$

$$M = k(L_M - F) \quad k > 1, \tag{2}$$

with $M > S$ when $L_M = L_S = L/n$, L being the total labor force. I choose units so that the constant returns to scale technique converts one unit of labor into one unit of output. F is the fixed labor input required to start mass production. With $F > 0$, the modern technique displays increasing returns to scale. Since S and M refer to the same good in each sector, L_S provides a perfectly elastic supply of labor for the production of M.

When it is in existence, atomistic producers operating under perfect competition use the traditional technique. In contrast, a single firm in each sector has access to the modern technique. This firm will charge the same price that traditional producers would, even when it becomes a monopolist. Indeed, the firm would lose all its sales if it charged more and finds it unprofitable to charge less since it faces a demand curve with unit elasticity (given the constant share of each good in the final expenditure). The modern firm has to pay a factory wage premium $(w - 1)$, where the traditional wage is set equal to one and w is the wage paid by the modern firm.

Let Y be aggregate income (measured in traditional wage units). The monopolist profit in any given sector is equal to sales (Y/n) minus total costs, wL_M. Since the price is one (and thus $M = Y/n$), using equation 2 the monopolist profit (π) can be written as:

$$\pi = a(Y/n) - wF \quad a = (1 - w/k), \tag{3}$$

where 1 is the price he or she charges and w/k is his or her unit-variable cost. It is worth noting that the difference between price and variable cost, $a = (1 - w/k)$, must be positive if the factory is to break even, whatever the level of income. This implies that:

$$w < k, \tag{4}$$

that is, that the wage premium must not be so high as to offset the advantages of mass production. Still, even with inequality 4 fulfilled, the monopolist will incur the fixed costs wF only if he or she expects sales (Y/n) to be high enough for the investment in mass production to be profitable.

Monopolist expected sales is a function of the fraction (η) of sectors in the economy that industrialize. Indeed, aggregate income can be expressed as the sum of income in the traditional sectors, $(1 - \eta)L$, and wages and profits in the modern sectors, $\eta(wL + n\pi)$. Spending per sector is then:

$$Y/n = \eta\pi + [1 + \eta(w - 1)]L/n.$$

Substituting into equation 3 and solving for π as a function of η gives:

$$\pi(\eta) = \{a [1 + \eta(w - 1)]L/n - wF\}/(1 - a\eta). \tag{5}$$

What happens to profits as the fraction of sectors that industrialize increases? Differentiating equation 5, we can solve for the slope of the profit function:

$$d\pi/d\eta = a[(L/n)(w - 1) + \pi(\eta)]/(1 - a\eta),$$

which, as can be verified, is positive provided that inequality 4 is fulfilled and the modern technique dominates the traditional technique at high levels of output. Three configurations are then possible: first, $\pi(0) > 0$, in which case the expected profits of a monopolist investing in isolation are positive and no traditional economy equilibrium will exist; second, $\pi(1) < 0$, in which case no industrialization equilibrium will exist since profits are negative even when all firms in all sectors adopt the modern technique; and, third, $\pi(0) < 0$ and $\pi(1) > 0$, which implies that whether the modern technique is profitable or not depends on the fraction of sectors in the economy adopting the modern technique. This is the case shown in figure 20. Then, if the fraction η of sectors that industrialize increases when profits are positive and falls when they are negative, there will be multiple equilibria at $\eta = 0$, and at $\eta = 1$. A traditional economy ($\eta = 0$) with negative expected profits and an industrialization equilibrium ($\eta = 1$) with positive profits will be self-sustaining and consistent with the same parameter values.

As is easily verified:

$$\pi(0) = aL/n - wF \quad \text{and} \quad \pi(1) = k(L/n - F) - wL/n.$$

The conditions required for the existence of multiple equilibria, $\pi(0) < 0$ and $\pi(1) > 0$, thus imply that:

$$F > a(L/n)/w \tag{6}$$

$$F < a(L/n). \tag{7}$$

Figure 21 presents a diagram by Krugman (1992) that will be helpful in analyzing the different configurations. The S and M lines show the value of output (with a price equal to one) as a function of labor input, for each technique. These are simply the graphs of equations 1 and 2, with equation 1 coinciding with the 45-degree line due to the choice of units. As drawn, the condition in equation 2 is met: $M > S$ when the labor force is fully employed in mass production in each sector and labor input is L/n. The ray $0w$ shows total wage costs as a function of labor input when employing the modern technique. Its slope is equal to w since

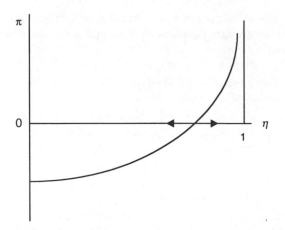

Fig. 20. Profit expectations and multiple equilibria

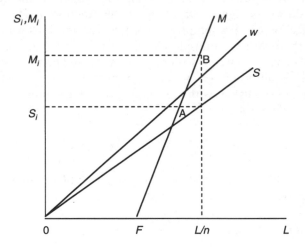

Fig. 21. The big push model of Murphy, Shliefer, and Vishny (1989b)

the traditional wage is set equal to one. The slope of the 0*w* ray is drawn as less than the slope of the M line (*k*), and thus condition 4 is met.

Consider Rosenstein-Rodan's shoe factory. An individual shoe producer adopting the modern technique will be able to sell a level of output equal to S_i by displacing previous sales by traditional producers (with a large number of goods, we can ignore the increase in the demand for shoes arising from the higher wages paid to the workers employed in the shoe factory). Point A in the diagram, on the M line at the level of output S_i, corresponds to the level of employment in a modern sector (the shoe factory) when it sells as much as the traditional producers would when producing at full employment. Point B, on the M line at the level of employment L/n, corresponds to production in the modern sector when it operates at full employment.

Given traditional production elsewhere (i.e., in the production of textiles, food processing, and so on), the adoption of the modern technique in the production of shoes will be profitable if point A is above the $0w$ ray. By merely replacing traditional producers, the shoe factory will find a large enough market to be profitable. Sales are higher than wage costs when the firm invests in isolation, and the same applies to the adoption of mass production methods in other sectors. The use of modern techniques in those sectors will increase the demand for shoes, as a result of the higher wages paid and the profits generated, making it profitable for the shoe factory to increase its output to M_i and employment to L/n (i.e., up to point B). Only an industrialization equilibrium exists with output equal to M_i in each sector. Condition 7 is met; however, condition 6 is not. This is because, given the size of the market (a function of L/n), F and w are so low that the condition is not fulfilled.

Suppose that F is so large that not only point A but also point B, on the M line at the level of output M_i, is below the $0w$ ray. The modern technique is more productive than the traditional in the sense that at high levels of output (with labor input equal to L/n) M is larger than S. Yet, given the wage premium, the potential market is not large enough to take advantage of the simultaneous application of mass production methods let alone the adoption of the modern technique in isolation. Condition 6 is fulfilled, but condition 7 is not. There is only a low-income equilibrium based on traditional techniques.

Between these two extremes there is a range of intermediate values of F for which both conditions are fulfilled and two equilibria exist. This is the case shown in the diagram with point B above the $0w$ ray and point A below it. In isolation, the shoe factory is unprofitable, but a simultaneous adoption of mass production methods would make a level of output at M_i profitable for all modern firms. Given F and w, the potential size of the market is large enough to make a simultaneous application of mass production methods profitable yet insufficient to make any individual modern firm viable. Here multiple equilibria exist, and without a coordinated "big push" the economy may remain stuck in a traditional economy equilibrium.

There are a number of interesting differences between the present model and the one presented in the first section of chapter 4. First, the multisectoral nature of the economy is essential to generating the type of external effects that are behind the coordination problem. If a single good is produced with internal economies of scale, the need for a "big push" cannot arise. Coordination problems will only arise when capital is used in production and there are technological externalities. Thus, in an economy with a single modern firm and no external effects the coordination problem does not exist. There would be a unique equilibrium whose nature depends on whether M is larger or smaller than S when the labor force is fully employed.

Market size also matters in a different way. In chapter 4, cumulative output proxied by overall capital stock matters because it makes modern technology more productive. The external effects are in the nature of technological spillovers. Here, market size matters because it makes modern techniques more profitable. It is in this sense that externalities are pecuniary. Output levels elsewhere have no technological spillovers on the shoe factory (yielding, e.g., a better-trained labor force). They have demand spillovers that make the same technology more profitable.

The presence of a wage premium is now essential for the multiplicity of equilibria, unlike in the model with technological externalities. This is because pecuniary externalities are not sufficient by themselves to generate multiple equilibria. Without a wage premium, there would still be external effects, but these will operate only through profits rather than through the higher wages paid by modern firms. A positive externality would arise only when profits from the individual adoption of the modern technique are positive. Thus, if the adoption of mass production methods is unprofitable in a single sector in isolation, this will also be the case when a simultaneous adoption of modern techniques takes place, and vice versa. This can readily be seen in figure 21. If $w = 1$, the $0w$ ray becomes the S line and there is no configuration in which points A and B can be on two different sides of the $0w$ ray. Thus, there is no conflict between individually and collectively rational behavior. The existence of a high-level equilibrium is sufficient to exclude the possibility of a low-level equilibrium because individual incentives, as mediated by the market, are sufficient to ensure full industrialization.[2]

Economies of Specialization and a Nurksian Trap

We turn now to a model that features monopolistic competition among producers of differentiated consumer goods operating under increasing returns. With free entry in each sector and zero profits in equilibrium, the interactions between economies of scale at the firm level and the gains from specialization result from the expansion of the whole set of consumer goods industries. The specification of technology and market structure follows Dixit and Stiglitz 1977 and Ethier 1982; the interactions involved are close in spirit to Young 1928, Nurkse 1953, and Kaldor 1967. Multiple equilibria can arise from the interaction between economies of specialization and demand elasticities. While the division of labor always makes labor more productive, for this division to be profitable the size of the market for the increasing returns sector must increase pari passu. A low-level equilibrium is then possible, in which the extent to which economies of specialization are exploited is limited by the insufficient elasticity of demands perceived by individual producers and the inelasticity of demands is perpetuated by the deficient exploitation of aggregate economies of scale.

Technology and Demand

Consider an economy with two sectors (S and M) producing consumption goods. Sector S produces under constant returns with labor as the only input: $S = L_S$. As in Ethier 1982, sector M assembles (costlessly) a set of components or differentiated goods (M_i):

$$M = n^a[\Sigma(1/n)M_i^\sigma]^{1/\sigma} \quad a > 1 \quad 0 < \sigma < 1, \tag{8}$$

where n is the actual number of components produced and the restriction on the parameter σ ensures that the M_i components are good substitutes. We can interpret each of these components as a step in the production process. An increase in the number of components (n) implies a finer division of labor. Due to economies of specialization, this greater division makes labor more productive. This is what the specification in equation 8 implies: since $a > 1$, an x percent increase in the number of components, holding (nM_i) constant, generates more units of M than an x percent increase in each component, holding n constant.[3]

Each component is produced under internal economies of scale and identical production conditions:

$$M_i = k(L_i - F), \tag{9}$$

where, as in equation 2, F is a fixed labor input required to start production and L_i is total labor input. Since k and F are common to all goods, units of goods are chosen so that when $L_i = L_j$ the number of units of M_i is equal to the number of units of M_j.

Under the assumption of identical production functions for each differentiated good and given that each of them enters symmetrically in the finished manufacture, all manufactured components will be produced in equal amounts and will require the same labor input (L_i). We can thus express the total amount of labor (L_M) employed in sector M as nL_i. Dividing both sides of equation 8 by L_M and using $L_M = nL_i$, output per worker in sector M is:

$$M/L_M = n^{a-1}[\Sigma(1/n)(M_i/L_i)^\sigma]^{1/\sigma}, \tag{10}$$

where, from equation 9, $M_i/L_i = k(1 - F/L_i)$. Equations 9 and 10 show that there are two sources of increasing returns to scale in sector M. First, as in the model examined in the first section, there are economies of scale related to plant size. Given the number of goods (n), an increase in L_M means a higher input of labor in the production of each M_i good and, from equation 9 this implies a higher output per worker both for each individual good (M_i/L_i) and for the aggregate (M/L_M). Second, a higher level of employment L_M can also lead to an increase in the number of components produced. Then, as shown by equation 10, aggregate output per worker increases even though, at the level of each individual good, output per worker (M_i/L_i) would remain constant. These economies result from an increased division of labor associated with a larger number of components being produced — or, as Kaldor put it, "from increased differentiation, new processes and new subsidiary industries," so that as a result "economies of scale are derived not only from the expansion of any single industry but from a general industrial expansion" (1967, 14). They are external to the firm, although they arise, as we shall see, because in the presence of internal economies of scale (and indivisibilities in the production of goods) the size of the market limits the number of components that can be produced without loss.

Consumption demands for S and M goods are a function of relative prices (p_S/p_M) and the real wage in terms of manufactures (w/p_M):

$$C_M/C_S = zp_S/p_M(w/p_M)^\eta \quad \eta > 0, \tag{11}$$

where p_M $(= p_i/n^{a-1}$ in a symmetric equilibrium) is the price of a bundle of differentiated goods yielding $M = 1$. The specification in equation 11 implies that, given the wage in terms of manufactures, the elasticity of substitution in consumption is equal to one. Changes in the real wage, however, alter expenditure shares: an increase in w/p_M raises $p_M C_M/p_S C_S$ and thus increases the manufactures expenditure share.

Market Structure

Producers in sector S operate under atomistic competition and receive the average product of labor in the sector. This wage also prevails in sector M. Firms there take the wage as given and operate under monopolistic competition in the goods market. For each of the n goods, there is a single firm facing a downward-sloping demand curve:

$$M^d_i = Dp_i^{-\phi} \quad \phi = 1/(1 - \sigma) > 1, \tag{12}$$

where D is a position parameter and ϕ is the price elasticity of demand facing individual producers.[4] The inequality restriction in equation 12 follows from the parameter restriction $0 < \sigma < 1$.

Firms maximize profit subject to equation 12 and the production function in equation 9. The maximization problem implies a pricing decision based on a constant markup over marginal cost, the markup being an inverse function of the price elasticity of demand:

$$p_i = [\phi/(\phi - 1)]w/k. \tag{13}$$

With free entry, the number of firms and of goods produced will expand to the point at which the marginal producer breaks even. With identical production functions, this implies that in a symmetric equilibrium with $p_i = p_k$ all producers break even. This zero-profit condition can be written as $\Sigma p_i M_i = \Sigma w L_i$, or, for a representative producer:

$$p_i M_i = w L_M/n. \tag{14}$$

The zero-profit condition allows us to determine endogenously the number of goods produced. Substituting from equations 9 and 13 into 14 and using $L_M = nL_i$, we can solve for the relationship between n and L_M that will prevail in equilibrium:

$$n = L_M/\phi F, \tag{15}$$

which shows that, for a given level of employment in sector M, both a higher fixed cost (F) and higher elasticity of demand (which reduces the markup) reduce the number of producers that can break even in equilibrium.

Multiple Equilibria

We can now derive the relationship that will prevail between output per worker and aggregate employment in sector M in a producers' equilibrium. First, from equations 8 and 9 we solve for M as a function of L_M (using $L_M = nL_i$):

$$M = n^a k(L_M/n - F).$$

Then, substituting from equation 15 and solving for output per worker (M/L_M):

$$M/L_M = (L_M/\phi F)^{a-1} k(\phi - 1)/\phi, \tag{16}$$

which, given $a > 1$, shows output per worker in sector M as an increasing function of employment (L_M) (see the productivity schedule, M/L_M, in fig. 22). The condition $a > 1$, rather than the existence of economies of scale at the plant level, appears to play the key role because changes in the producers' equilibrium take the form of changes in the number of producers rather than in the size of their plants. The aggregate size of sector M matters by making possible a greater division of labor in the sense of "making room" for additional producers that can break even. Nevertheless, the mechanism involves the presence of economies of scale at the firm level, without which the size of sector M would not limit the number of goods produced (as can be seen from eq. 15, n does not depend on L_M, for $F = 0$).

Consider the relation between the market equilibrium wage and the level of employment in sector M. With zero profits in equilibrium, total income is equal to aggregate wages (wL) and this income is spent on the consumption of S and M goods:

$$wL = p_S C_S + p_M C_M.$$

Equilibrium in the labor market implies:

$$L = L_M + L_S. \tag{17}$$

Using equation 17 and $w = p_S$, and noting that in equilibrium $C_S = L_S$, we have:

$$C_M = (w/p_M)L_M. \tag{18}$$

Finally, combining equations 18 and 11 and using 17 gives:

$$w/p_M = [L_M/z(L - L_M)]^{1/\eta}, \tag{19}$$

which shows the relationship between the wage (in terms of manufactures) and employment in sector M that will prevail in goods and labor market equilibrium. The two are positively related: a higher wage implies a larger fraction of total income spent on manufactures, which requires in equilibrium a higher level of employment in the M sector.

The w schedule in figure 22 shows this equilibrium relationship

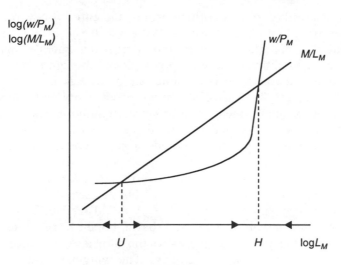

Fig. 22.   A Nurksian trap

between the wage and the level of employment. The curve has a slope equal to $1/[\eta(1 - L_M/L)]$. The curve is thus relatively flat at low levels of L_M, steeper at higher levels, and becomes vertical at $L_M = L$. This shape results from the fact that a reallocation of the labor force from sector S to sector M has two effects on the wage. First, by reducing output in S and increasing it in M, an increase in L_M/L_S generates an excess supply of M and an excess demand for S at the initial relative prices. This puts upward pressure on p_S/p_M and thus also on w/p_M (since in equilibrium $w = p_S$). The second effect arises from a shift in the composition of demand toward M goods. This effect puts downward pressure on p_S/p_M since it reduces the excess supply of M goods and the excess demand for the S good. As L_M increases from initially low levels, the proportionate increase in M output is larger than the proportionate decline in S output, given the high ratio L_S/L_M. Since the proportionate change in demands, $d\log(C_M/C_S)$, is constant with respect to w/p_M, it takes a smaller proportionate change in w/p_M to restore equilibrium at low levels of L_M/L_S. The presence of variable expenditure shares is essential: if $\eta = 0$, the w curve would be vertical at the unique level of employment consistent with market equilibrium.

Full equilibrium requires equality between output per worker and the wage in terms of manufactures and can thus only prevail at the intersection of the two schedules. A wage higher than output per worker implies losses and a contraction of employment. A wage lower than output per worker implies positive profits, the entry of new producers, and the expansion of employment. With $\eta > 0$ and $a > 1$, there is a possibility of multiple interior equilibria, as is illustrated in figure 22.[5] When these equilibria exist, it is apparent from the figure that the high wage equilibrium at point H is stable: an increase in L_M beyond point H would increase the wage above labor productivity and thus cause a contraction of employment. The low-wage equilibrium at point U is unstable: a disturbance that reduces employment lowers the wage by less than it reduces productivity and causes a further contraction of employment.

Below point U there is a poverty trap. The wage is higher than output per worker because the size of the M sector is too small. An increase in aggregate employment (L_M) would tend to close the gap between wages and productivity and, beyond point U, generate positive profits. Yet, the problem appears to the individual producer as one of excessive employment in sector M. The marginal producer cannot break even and leaves the sector. The resulting contraction of employment has external effects on other producers, since the price p_M of the bundle of M_i goods rises and reduces the real wage and, in turn, the consumption of manufactures. Thus, the reduction in the number of producers causes an even larger gap between productivity and wages.

To each of the individual producers the problem appears to be one of high wages or inelastic demands. Below point U, and especially in the low-level stable equilibrium with no M sector, the extent of the price reduction required to displace existing producers seems excessive to the potential entrant since this would make it impossible to recover fixed costs.[6] Demands for each of the M_i goods are inelastic in Allyn Young's sense: that a small increase in their supply does not trigger "an increase in the amounts of other commodities which can be had in exchange for it" (1928, 534).[7] The problem arises because, while each individual producer has a negligible effect on the real wage taken in isolation, together they do not. Together, the wage is in fact too low and the aggregate demand for M is much less inelastic than it appears to the individual producer who takes wages as given, since the relative price p_M/p_S is nothing but the inverse of the real wage. In other words, the size of the market is not given to all producers together. This is why the conflict between what is individually rational to each producer (contract production) and what is collectively rational (expand production) only disappears when the size of the M sector is large enough to generate a wage and a level of consumption that make it possible to generate profits. Additional producers who are attracted now generate similar external effects in reverse. The increase in output and employment causes a fall in the price (p_M) that further increases consumption and output. Here demands appear to be elastic and interact positively with the presence of economies of scale.

The model illustrates Nurkse's insights on the vicious circle of poverty in which the size of the market constrains the level of productivity in any single sector while at the same time it is itself determined by the general level of productivity (1952). Elsewhere, Nurkse emphasized that low levels of productivity outside manufacturing are the source of the problem:

> The relation between agriculture and manufacturing industry offers the clearest and simplest case of balance needed for economic growth. In a country where the peasantry is incapable of producing a surplus of food above its own subsistence needs there is little or no incentive for industry to establish itself. There is not a sufficient market for manufactured goods. (1961, 248)

With little modification, the model illustrates Nurkse's point about the potential role of productivity increases in sector S as a way out of the trap. Suppose that the production and demand conditions are:

$$S = \lambda L_S$$

$$C_M/C_S = z(p_S/p_M)^h(w/p_M)^\eta,$$

where λ is output per worker in the S sector and h is, for a given wage (w/p_M), the elasticity of substitution in consumption between S and M goods. The equation of the w curve is now:

$$w/p_M = [L_M/z\lambda^{1-h}(L - L_M)]^{1/(\eta+h-1)}.$$

With $\eta + h > 1$, the w curve slopes upward as before. With low elasticity of substitution ($h < 1$), the position of the curve depends inversely on productivity in the S sector. Thus, with price inelastic but income-elastic demands for M goods, a higher output per worker in the S sector shifts the w curve downward and reduces the hold of the poverty trap.

Vertical Externalities:
A Rosenstein-Rodan/Hirschman Model

We now consider an economy in which pecuniary externalities arise from the presence of increasing returns in the production of intermediate goods. The specification of technology and market structure in the sector producing intermediate goods follows Skott and Ros 1997 and features a given number of producers of such inputs operating under monopolistic competition. Multiple long-run equilibria can arise as a result of dynamic pecuniary externalities.[8] Because we focus on linkage effects between intermediate and final goods, rather than on demand spillovers across final goods sectors, we simplify and assume that only one final good is produced.[9]

Two sectors compete in the market for the final good. Traditional producers, as before, turn one unit of labor into one unit of output: $S = L_S$. Modern technology is capital intensive. Modern firms, also operating under atomistic competition and constant returns to scale, use capital (K) and intermediate goods (I) to produce output M:

$$M = K^a I^{1-a} \quad 0 < a < 1, \tag{20}$$

where I represents the input of a set of intermediate goods,

$$I = [\Sigma(1/n)I_i^\sigma]^{1/\sigma} \quad 0 < \sigma < 1,$$

where n is the number of intermediate goods, assumed to be given.[10] Production of these intermediate goods is subject to internal increasing returns:

$$I_i = L_i^{1+\mu} \quad \mu > 0, \tag{21}$$

where L_i is labor input. The I_i goods may represent a set of producer services (such as banking and insurance) and manufactured inputs, as in Rodriguez 1996, or a set of infrastructural goods (power, transport, communications, training facilities), as in Skott and Ros 1997.[11] The key difference between traditional and modern sectors is that, while sector M has a Hirschmanian "backward linkage" with sector I, there are no linkages in the case of sector S.

Firms maximize profits, taking input prices as given. Producers in sectors S and M also face given output prices. In sector M, the capital stock is predetermined in the short run and, since producers in this sector are atomistic, a firm's future demand and supply conditions will be independent of its own short-run decisions. Hence, there are no intertemporal complications. As shown in Skott and Ros 1997, the demand function for I goods is given by:

$$I = (1 - a)^{1/a}(p_I/p_M)^{-1/a}K, \tag{22}$$

where p_I ($= np_i$ under symmetry) is the (minimum) cost of a bundle of intermediate goods yielding $I = 1$.

In sector I, producers operate under conditions of monopolistic competition and face downward-sloping demand curves:

$$I^d_i = Dp_i^{-\phi} \quad \phi > 1, \tag{23}$$

where D is a position parameter and ϕ is the price elasticity of demand facing individual producers. This elasticity is a function of σ, a, and n, and for a large n it is given approximately by $1/(1 - \sigma)$.[12] The inequality restriction in equation 23 follows from the parameter restrictions $0 < a < 1$ and $0 < \sigma < 1$.

With a single intermediate good ($n = 1$), the monopoly producer of this good would clearly face an intertemporal optimization problem: the current price p_I would affect the profitability of sector M, which in turn could influence capital accumulation in sector M and thereby future demand for the I good. With multiple I goods, this intertemporal link is weakened and the decisions of an individual producer have only minor effects on the aggregate output of I and profitability in sector M. To simplify, we assume that the number of nontradable inputs is large enough that intertemporal aspects can be ignored. From the conjectured demand function (eq. 23) and the production function (eq. 21), the optimal pricing decision for the I_i producer is a markup over marginal cost:

$$p_i = (1 + \pi)\omega, \tag{24}$$

where: $1 + \pi = [\phi/(\phi - 1)] \qquad \omega = w/(1 + \mu)I_i^{\mu/(1+\mu)}$
w is the wage rate, ω is the marginal cost of labor, and π is the markup over marginal cost.

Equations 23 and 24, by setting $I_i = I^d_i$, can be solved simultaneously for p_i and I_i. Note that, unlike what happens when economies of scale arise only from the presence of fixed costs (as in the first two sections), the marginal cost is not constant but falls with the scale of output.

Short-Run Equilibrium

To derive a short-run equilibrium, equations 23 and 24 are combined with the input demand function in sector M (eq. 22). Assuming symmetry ($p_i = p_j$ and $I_i = I$), these three equations can be solved for I, p_I, and D. We then get:

$$I = [G(1/n)(p_M/w)K^a]^{(1+\mu)/f}, \tag{25}$$

where: $G = (1 - a)(1 + \mu)(\phi - 1)/\phi \qquad f = a - \mu(1 - a) > 0.$

Equation 25 describes a symmetric, short-run equilibrium solution for I. Given a conjectured value of the multiplicative constant D, the first-order conditions for profit maximization determine (p_i, I_i) as a function of D. The actual value of D depends on the pricing decisions of the firm's rivals. As shown in Skott and Ros 1997, stability requires the (empirically plausible) condition $f > 0$.[13] It is worth noting that in this symmetric equilibrium each producer will be willing to sell more goods, at the equilibrium price, if demand is forthcoming.

Consider now the labor market. Let the total work force be L. In equilibrium with $I_i = I_j$, and assuming uniform wages and the absence of unemployment, we have:

$$L = L_S + L_I$$

and

$$L_I = \Sigma L_i = \Sigma I_i^{1/(1+\mu)} = nI^{1/(1+\mu)}, \tag{26}$$

or, substituting from equation 25:

$$L_I = L_I(w/p_M, K). \tag{27}$$

Since $S = L_S$ and (given that there is one final good) $p_S = p_M$,

$$w \geq p_M$$

with equality if $L_S > 0$. That is, the supply of labor to the I sector is perfectly elastic at $w = p_M$ for $L_I < L$.

The labor demand from sector I is determined by equation 27. Combining this equation with the elastic labor supply at $w = p_M$ for $L_I < L$, the short-run equilibrium in the labor market implies that:

$$w = p_M \quad \text{and} \quad L_I = L_I(1, K) \quad \text{if} \quad L_I(1, K) < L. \tag{28}$$

And, if $L_I(1, K) > L$, then labor market equilibrium implies that $L_I = L$ and w/p_M is given by the solution to $L_I(w/p_M, K) = L$. This is:

$$w/p_M = G(1/n)^{1-f}K^a/L^f. \tag{29}$$

With L_I determined, we also have the solutions for $S = L - L_I$ and $M = K^a I^{(1-a)}$. Equations 28 and 29 define the schedule of short-run equilibria. This is shown, in log space, in figure 23. As in the Lewis model, the schedule is a straight line at $w/p_M = 1$, up to the value K, at the turning

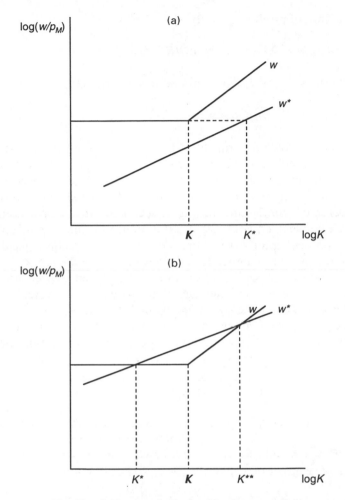

Fig. 23.   A Rosenstein-Rodan/Hirschman model

point between the labor surplus phase and the mature economy, for which $L_I(1, K) = L$, and a line with positive slope equal to a for $K > \text{K}$.

Capital Accumulation and Long-Run Equilibria

Over time, the capital stock changes. We assume a simple formulation in which investment in sector M is financed exclusively out of M-sector profits.[14] The rate of capital accumulation is then equal to $s_\pi r - \delta$, where s_π is the share of profits that is invested.

The rate of profit is given by:

$$r = (p_M M - \Sigma p_i I_i)/p_M K = a(I/K)^{1-a},$$

or, using the value of I as determined in short-run equilibrium (eq. 25):

$$r = aK^{\mu(1-a)/f}[(1/n)G/(w/p_M)]^{(1-f)/f}. \tag{30}$$

Given the wage in terms of M goods, the profit rate increases with the capital stock. Indeed, an increase in the capital stock raises the demand for intermediate goods and reduces marginal costs in the I sector. The fall in the relative price (p_I/p_M) of intermediate goods (for a given value of w/p_M) raises profits in sector M. It is worth noting the similarity between equation 30 and the profit rate function given in the first section of chapter 4. Even though there are no technological externalities, the profit rate depends positively on the capital stock, given the wage in terms of M goods. This is due to the presence of economies of scale in the I sector and the fact that the extent to which they are exploited depends on the size of the capital stock in sector M.

The steady state condition $r = \delta/s_\pi$ defines the equation of the w^* schedule in figure 23. Substituting from equation 30 into this condition and solving for w/p_M yields:

$$(w/p_M)^* = (as_\pi/\delta)^{f(1-f)}(G/n)K^{\mu/1+\mu}, \tag{31}$$

which in $(\log K, \log w/p_M)$ space defines a line with a positive slope equal to $\mu/(1 + \mu)$. The condition $f > 0$ in equation 25 ensures that $a > \mu/(1 + \mu)$, that is, the w schedule, for values of K above K, is steeper than the w^* line. We then have either two intersections or no intersection between the two loci.

Figure 23(a) shows the case in which the two schedules do not intersect. Here $\mathsf{K} < K^*$, where K^* is the solution for equation 31 when $w = p_M$. The subsistence wage is higher than the wage required to generate a positive rate of capital accumulation even when the whole labor force is employed in the modern sector. This case implies that the size of the labor force is so small that industrialization will never be worthwhile given the specification of the production possibilities. There is, then, a unique and stable long-run equilibrium with $K = 0$, $L_S = L$, and $L_I = 0$.

In figure 23(b), $\mathsf{K} > K^*$. The two loci intersect with the slope of the w schedule smaller than the slope of the w^* line at the low K intersection (at K^*) and vice versa for the high K intersection (at K^{**}). It follows that there are two long-run equilibria with strictly positive values of the capital stock as well as an equilibrium with $K = 0$ and $I = 0$. It is readily seen that the equilibrium at K^* is unstable, just like the equilibrium at K_U in the model presented in the first section of chapter 4. Of the two stable equilibria, the low equilibrium without an M sector has an income per worker equal to p_M and zero profits, while the equilibrium at K^{**} necessarily features $w > p_M$ and a positive profit rate. Thus, the real wage and the level of per capita income are unambiguously higher in the industrialized economy.

The similarity of these results to those of the model with technological externalities examined in chapter 4 should not be surprising. In the economy considered, sector S provides an elastic labor supply — or, in fact, a perfectly elastic labor supply since, as in the Lewis model, this sector produces the same final good as the modern sector does. Sectors M and I together use a capital-intensive technology that displays increasing returns to scale. Indeed, combining equations 20 and 26, the "production function" of this "integrated M/I sector" is given by:

$$M = AK^a L_I^{1-a} \quad A = (1/n)^{(1-a)(1+\mu)} L_I^{\mu(1-a)},$$

which shows that, provided that $\mu > 0$, the productivity of this integrated sector depends on its size (the level of employment L_I).

However, unlike the model examined in the first section, there are no technological externalities here. Multiple equilibria are associated with pecuniary externalities, even though these are not a sufficient condition, as figure 23(a) illustrates. The presence of increasing returns to scale in the intermediate goods sector implies that production decisions in sector I, and investment decisions in sector M, have important external effects. An increase in the output of I_i adversely affects the current demand for other intermediate inputs but reduces the price index p_I and raises both the combined input I and the profit rate in sector M. Apart from these static effects, there is a dynamic externality: higher profits in sector M lead to increased accumulation and thus to an increase in the future demand for all I goods. On the investment side, atomistic producers of good M consider all prices given and fail to take into account the external effects of a higher capital stock on increased future demand for I goods and a lower future price p_I.

As a result of these dynamic pecuniary externalities, an initial capital stock below the critical level K^* leads to a cumulative contraction when all firms follow behavior that is individually rational. Because the initial capital stock is small, the demand for I goods is low and I goods are produced at a high cost. As a result, profitability in sector M is so low that the capital stock contracts. This further increases production costs in the I sector and reduces profitability in sector M, moving the economy toward the low-level equilibrium where sectors M and I are absent. This low-level equilibrium is a trap. Rosenstein-Rodan provides an example of the coordination problem involved:

> Low wages should have been a sufficient incentive to create a textile industry in India in the post-Napoleonic era and not in Lancashire, England. Indian wages were 50 or 60 percent lower than the low wages in England. . . . Further analysis revealed, however, that in order to build a factory one would have to build a bridge or finish a road or a railway line or later an electric power station. Each of these elements in the so-called social overhead capital requires a minimum high quantum of investment which could serve, say, fifty factories but would cost far too much for one. (1984, 208)

In other words, the lack of incentives to create a textile industry in India was due to the absence of an I sector, which made textile production unprofitable despite low wages. At the same time, there was no incentive for the production of I goods given the high costs of production in the absence of demand from textile factories. This is why a coordinated effort — a big push aimed at increasing the rate of accumulation above the individually rational level and/or at raising the supply of I goods — becomes necessary to take the capital stock above that critical level (K^* in fig. 23), at which point individual incentives as mediated by the market become sufficient to ensure industrialization.

An important difference from the Rosenstein-Rodan/Leibenstein model examined in chapter 4 is the role of imperfect competition in sector I in the existence of equilibrium and the hold of the development trap. Indeed, the value of the capital stock at the unstable equilibrium (K^*) depends on the position of the w^* schedule, which in turn is affected by the price elasticity of demand for I goods (see eq. 31 and the expression for G in eq. 25). A lower elasticity reduces G and shifts the w^* schedule downward. The hold of the trap increases as K^* becomes larger. Intuitively, a less competitive sector I implies higher markups over marginal costs and thus a higher relative price (p_I/p_M) of intermediate inputs, which reduces the profit rate in sector M. A higher capital stock — which tends to reduce (p_I/p_M) on account of the cost reductions resulting from the higher demand and output of I goods — is then required to generate the profit rate needed for a positive rate of capital accumulation.

Interestingly, the influence of price elasticities in the vicious circle of poverty was emphasized by Nurkse:

> The difficulty is not due fundamentally to discontinuities in the technical forms of capital equipment, though these may accentuate

it. It is due above all to the inevitable inelasticity of demands at low real-income levels. It is in this way that lack of buying power cramps the inducement to invest in any individual industry.

The difficulty is not present, however, in the case of a more or less synchronized application of capital to a wide range of different industries. Here the result is an overall enlargement of the market and hence an escape of the deadlock. (1952, 257)

CHAPTER 6

Endogenous Growth and Classical Development Theory

From the perspective of both early development economics and recent developments in endogenous growth theory, the basic properties of the Solow model are unsatisfactory. What is the major source of these perceived shortcomings? Is it the steady state properties of the model? Is it its answer to the question of what causes steady state growth? Or is it transitional dynamics, with its implications for the question of why some countries grow faster than others? These questions may seem closely related — and they are within the framework of neoclassical growth theory. Yet, they are clearly different questions. The two-sector development theory models reviewed in chapters 4 and 5 clearly have transitional dynamics that are very different from neoclassical growth models — and thus give different answers to the question of why some countries grow faster than others — yet they feature similar steady state properties — for example, that the savings rate has no effect on the steady state growth rate.

Recent endogenous growth theory is more radical in this respect. It objects to the convergence properties of the neoclassical model — capital-scarce countries do not grow faster than capital-abundant countries, differences in rates of return on capital are less than one would expect given the disparities in capital-labor endowments, and capital does not flow internationally toward the poorest countries (see, e.g., Lucas 1988; and Romer 1991). Moreover, it objects to the fact that steady state growth is the result of exogenous forces — labor force growth and technical progress — which are left unexplained by the theory, and to the associated steady state properties. In particular, it objects to the implication that two different economies investing in physical and human capital at different rates will grow at the same rate in the long run provided that they have access to the same technology and their labor forces grow at the same rate. One could say that from the perspective of endogenous growth theory the problems with the transitional dynamics of the neoclassical growth model are a consequence of the steady state properties. The model has the wrong answer to the question of why some countries grow faster than others because it does not have a good answer to the question of what causes steady state growth. And

156

this is perhaps the basic difference between this new strand of growth theory and the earlier two-sector development models.

The objections to the neoclassical growth model expressed in the recent literature have generated the perception that the shortcomings of traditional theory have a common source: a specification of the technology that gives too prominent a role to diminishing returns to capital. If technology could be respecified in such a way as to counteract the influence of diminishing returns, this could in principle overcome the perceived weaknesses of the neoclassical framework. It could generate endogenous growth in the steady state without having to rely on the assumptions of exogenous technical progress and population growth, thus enhancing the explanatory power of the theory. At the same time, such endogenous growth would weaken the strong convergence properties of the traditional model, making the theory more consistent with observed historical experience.

Models of Endogenous Growth

How should technology be respecified to meet these two objectives? Several departures have been attempted in the recent literature. I shall focus mostly on the original articles that triggered the new wave of endogenous growth models.

Increasing Returns to Capital

A first strategy, and one that initially appeared most promising, was to abandon the assumption of constant returns to scale. Increasing returns to scale strengthen the positive effects of capital accumulation on labor productivity, as the effect of a higher capital-labor ratio on output per worker is now enhanced by the positive effect of a larger capital stock and scale of production. This opens up the possibility that the positive productivity effects of capital accumulation offset the negative effects of higher real wages on the profit rate. If, as a result, returns to capital do not diminish, capital accumulation can persist indefinitely even without exogenous technical progress or labor supply growth.

This was the road taken by Paul Romer in his 1986 article. For Romer, knowledge-intensive investments in research and development need not be subject to diminishing social returns. However, their private rate of return can be well below the social rate because the returns on private investments in new technologies are only partially appropriable. As firms develop new technologies, they may make discoveries that many other firms can use at the same time; that is, the information generated is nonrival, unlike ordinary inputs, which are rival — their use by one firm prevents others from using them simultaneously (see Romer 1990b, 1994). Thus, while returns to capital may be diminishing for the individual firm, they may be increasing for the economy as a whole when account is taken of the spillovers from these investments in research and development. These spillovers generate externalities due to inappropriability, as in the case of industrial training à la Rosenstein-Rodan, and, moreover, here they are the source of aggregate increasing returns *to capital.* Capital accumulation, then, feeds itself and generates a self-sustained expansion at an increasing growth rate over time.

We can use our real wage diagram to more formally present the basic result of the Romer model (see fig. 24). Consider a production function with technological externalities in which the multiplicative constant (A) is a positive function of the aggregate capital stock per worker:

$$Y = AK^a L^{1-a} \quad A = (\tilde{K}/L)^\mu, \tag{1}$$

where Y is production at the firm level, K and L the inputs of capital and labor, and $(\tilde{K}/L)$ is the average stock of capital per worker in the economy. If the external effects generated by the average stock of capital per worker are strong enough, so that $a + \mu \geq 1$, the aggregate production function will exhibit nondiminishing returns to capital.

It is easily shown that the equations of the w and w^* curves are now:

$$w = (1 - a)k^{a+\mu} \tag{2}$$

$$w^* = (1 - a)[s/(n + \delta)]^{a/(1-a)}k^{\mu/(1-a)}, \tag{3}$$

where s is the savings rate, n is the rate of growth of the labor force, and k is the overall capital-labor ratio (K/L). Compared to the Solow model, the presence of technological externalities modifies the shape of the two curves in the diagram. In particular, as was discussed in chapter 4, the w^* line is no longer horizontal but positively sloped. With technological externalities, there is no longer a unique real wage but rather a locus of (w, k) combinations that generate the same rate of return on capital: the negative effect of the real wage on the rate of return is here at least partially offset by the (now larger) positive effects of the capital-labor ratio on productivity. Moreover, if external effects are large enough to generate increasing returns to capital in the economy as a whole, it is readily verified from equations 2 and 3 that the w^* line will be steeper than the w line, making the equilibrium at the intersection of the two curves unstable.[1] An economy with a capital-labor endowment greater

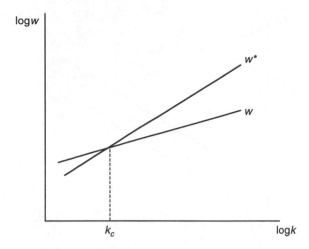

Fig. 24.   A Romer-type model

than k_c in figure 24 will generate a growth path of self-sustained expansion with real wages increasing along the w line and rates of return and capital accumulation (a function of the gap between the two schedules) increasing as well. For this to happen, returns to capital, and not only to scale, must increase. Otherwise, the w^* line will be flatter than the w line and the properties of the model will not be radically different from those of the neoclassical model.[2]

The AK Model

A particular case is the AK model, in which the production function is linear in the aggregate capital stock.[3] In this case, $a + \mu = 1$ in equation 1 and technology displays constant returns to capital. As is readily verified, with $a + \mu = 1$, the w and w^* lines have the same slope (see fig. 25). Provided that the savings rate is higher than $(n + \delta)$, the w^* line is above the w line,[4] and perpetual growth takes place at a constant rate of capital accumulation equal to $(s - \delta)$ (with the production function assumed in eq. 1).[5]

The distinction between transitional and steady state dynamics vanishes. The traditional steady state condition, $I/K = n + \delta$, is never fulfilled since the condition for $w^* > w$, $s > n + \delta$, implies that the rate of capital accumulation will forever remain larger than the rate of labor force growth. Depending on how one wishes to define the steady state, we can say that the economy remains perpetually in transition or, because it

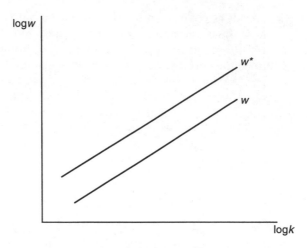

Fig. 25.   The AK model

grows at a constant rate, that there is no transition period, the path along the w line being the steady state growth path.

Unlike what happens in the Solow model, a change in the savings rate now has a permanent effect on the rate of growth of the economy. A higher savings rate shifts the w^* line upward and permanently increases the rate of capital accumulation of the economy. More generally, the parameters affecting the steady state level of income in the Solow model (s, n, and δ) now affect the growth rate of per capita income. With the production function in equation 1, the growth rate of output per worker is now given by $g_y = s - (n + \delta)$.[6] This key difference radically alters the convergence properties compared to those of the Solow model. For example, two AK economies that are identical except for their initial capital-labor ratios will have identical growth rates and therefore will never converge to similar levels of output per worker. Two economies with different savings and population growth rates will tend to have permanently different growth rates of output per worker rather than permanently different income levels, as in the Solow model.

The AK model illustrates very clearly in what sense growth is endogenous. Further comparison with old growth theory will help clarify the distinctive features of the newer approach. In neo-Keynesian and neoclassical growth theory, Harrod's warranted growth rate (sv, the savings rate times the output-capital ratio) adjusts to the exogenously given natural growth rate ($n + \beta$) through changes in either the savings rate (caused by income redistribution; see Kaldor 1956) or the capital-output ratio as a result of changes in factor prices (see Solow 1956). In the AK model, in contrast, the natural rate is no longer independent of the warranted rate: an increase in the investment rate brings about a higher rate of endogenous productivity growth. Provided that returns to capital are constant, this increases the natural rate by exactly the extent necessary to keep it constant at a higher level of growth, which is equal to the new value of the warranted rate. The endogeneity of the natural rate was anticipated by Kaldor when he introduced the technical progress function into the neo-Keynesian model of growth and distribution (Kaldor 1957; Kaldor and Mirrlees 1962).

High Elasticity of Factor Substitution

Sufficiently high elasticity of factor substitution can also counteract the role of diminishing returns to capital and generate sustained growth over time. In this case, the real wage effects on the profit rate are offset, not by the productivity gains resulting from the presence of increasing returns, but rather by high elasticity of substitution, which tends to reduce the demand for labor more than proportionately. This reduces the share of wages in total output. It is then possible that, even under constant returns to scale, high elasticity of factor substitution will make persistent growth possible.[7]

Consider a production function of the form:

$$Y = F(K, L) = A[aK^{\psi} + (1 - a)L^{\psi}]^{1/\psi}, \tag{4}$$

which features constant elasticity of factor substitution given by $\sigma = 1/(1 - \psi)$. If ψ lies in the $(0, 1)$ range, the elasticity of substitution is greater than one. Using equation 4 and setting the marginal product of labor equal to the wage and labor demand equal to the exogenous labor supply yields the equation of the w curve:

$$w = A(1 - a)[ak^{(\sigma-1)/\sigma} + (1 - a)]^{1/(\sigma-1)}, \tag{5}$$

where k is the capital-labor ratio. This can also be written as:

$$w = (1 - a)A^{(\sigma-1)/\sigma}y^{1/\sigma},$$

where y is output per worker, an increasing function of k, as can be seen in equation 4.

Differentiating with respect to k, we can express the slope of the w curve as:

$dw/dk = [(1 - a)/\sigma][ak^{\sigma-1)/\sigma} + (1 - a)]^{-1}aA[a + (1 - a)k^{(1-\sigma)/\sigma}]^{1/(\sigma-1)}$.

It will be useful to look at this expression as the product of two terms.

1. $dw/dy = [(1 - a)/\sigma][ak^{(\sigma-1)/\sigma} + (1 - a)]^{(1-\sigma)/\sigma} = [(1 - a)/\sigma]$ $(A/y)^{(\sigma-1)/\sigma}$, which reflects the extent to which gains in output per worker accrue to wage earners
2. $dy/dk = aA[a + (1 - a)k^{(1-\sigma)/\sigma}]^{1/(\sigma-1)}$, which reflects the extent to which increases in capital per worker raise productivity.

Consider the schedule w^*. The equation of the w^* curve is obtained by substituting the steady state value of the profit rate into the wage-profit relationship. Expressing the profit rate ($= \pi Y/K$, where π is the profit share in output) as a function of k and using equation 5, we can derive the wage-profit relationship:

$$w = [(1 - a)/a]^{\sigma/\sigma-1}[(A^{1-\sigma}/a^\sigma) - r^{1-\sigma}]^{1/(1-\sigma)}, \tag{6}$$

which becomes a linear relationship in the case of a fixed-coefficients technology. With $\sigma = 0$, we obtain $w = A - r$. With unit elasticity of substitution ($\sigma = 1$), the curve is log linear with a slope such that $d\log w/d\log r = -a/(1 - a)$, just as in the Cobb-Douglas case.[8] Assuming, for simplicity, that investment is financed exclusively out of profits, the rate of capital accumulation in the steady state must be such that $s_\pi r = n + \delta$. With a constant savings rate out of profits (s_π), there is a unique value of the required profit rate, $r^* = (n + \delta)/s_\pi$, which is independent of the capital-labor ratio. Substituting this value into equation 6 yields the equation of the w^* curve. This is a horizontal line in (w, k) space, since r^* and thus w^* are independent of k (see fig. 26).[9]

Consider the case of high elasticity of substitution ($\sigma > 1$). As is readily verified, in this case the slope of the w curve falls as k increases. Moreover, the term dw/dy tends toward zero when k goes to infinity, and the slope of the w curve approaches the slope of the w^* line. As illustrated in figure 26, if w^* is higher than w when k tends to infinity, the two curves will not intersect and growth will proceed at a diminishing rate, converging to a constant rate as k tends toward infinity. The rate of accumulation does not converge to Harrod's natural rate, as in the Solow model, because with more than unit elasticity of substitution the profit share increases as k rises and tends toward unity when k tends toward infinity. Then, just as in the AK model, returns to capital become constant since, with $dw/dy = 0$, the negative effect of a higher equilibrium wage on the profit rate no longer counteracts the effect of the larger capital stock on labor productivity.[10] The profit rate remains

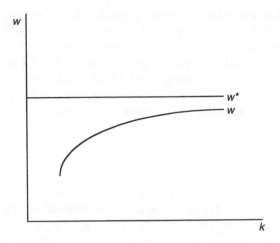

Fig. 26. Endogenous growth with high elasticity of factor substitution

constant and equal to $a^{\sigma/(\sigma-1)}A$.[11] Provided that $s_\pi a^{\sigma/(\sigma-1)}A > n + \delta$, the rate of accumulation approaches a constant value $s_\pi a^{\sigma/(\sigma-1)}A - \delta$, which is greater than the natural rate (n).

This model thus blends features of the AK and Solow models. Two economies that have identical technologies and savings rates but different initial capital-labor ratios will not converge to identical levels of output per worker. They tend to converge to the same rate of growth, and for this reason the initial income gap will not fully disappear. In this aspect, as in the AK model, the strength of convergence is weakened compared to that of the Solow model. At the same time, the transitional dynamics remain similar to those of the neoclassical model since the economy with the lower capital-labor ratio grows at a faster rate.

Human Capital Accumulation

Robert Lucas took another road in a 1988 article. He presents a model in which growth of income per capita is endogenous due to the presence of constant returns to human capital accumulation. The following example illustrates the mechanics of economic growth under these conditions.

Consider an economy with two sectors (Y and H). In sector Y, goods and services are produced with physical and human capital under constant returns to scale:

$$Y = K^a(\gamma H)^{1-a}, \tag{7}$$

where H is the total stock of human capital, γ is the fraction of it devoted to the production of goods, and (γH) is then the input of human capital in this sector.

Sector H produces human capital. The outcome of its activity is to increase the quantity of human capital that can be used in each of the two sectors. Assuming that total human capital (H) grows in proportion to the amount of human capital employed in this sector, $(1 - \gamma)H$, we obtain:

$$dH/dt = \lambda(1 - \gamma)H, \tag{8}$$

where λ is the effectiveness of investment in human capital. If a constant fraction of human capital $(1 - \gamma)$ is devoted to sector H,[12] human capital can grow at a constant exponential rate:

$$\hat{H} = (dH/dt)(1/H) = \lambda(1 - \gamma).$$

The model generates a steady state path in which the rate of accumulation of physical capital is equal to, and determined by, the rate of human capital accumulation. The latter is proportional to society's investment in the sector producing human capital. On this equilibrium path, the rate of return to human capital is constant and income per capita increases continuously — despite the absence of exogenous technological change — as a result of the ever-increasing endowment of human capital per capita. Physical capital accumulation is endogenous, not as a result of the productivity effects of increasing returns, as in the Romer model, but because the continuous accumulation of human capital increases the productivity of physical capital and neutralizes the influence of diminishing returns.

In terms of our real wage diagram, this simple account of the Lucas model results in a representation similar to that of the Solow model (see fig. 27). The w_H curve shows the return to human capital as an increasing function of the ratio of physical to human capital (K/H). The w^*_H curve is horizontal given the technology assumed in equation 7. On the steady state path, the return to human capital and the ratio of physical to human capital remain constant, but because human capital is growing so is physical capital (at the same rate). Using the accumulation equation for K (assuming a given savings rate, s) and the steady state condition ($\hat{K} = \hat{H}$), we can derive the steady state value of the ratio of physical to human capital in sector Y, $[K/(\gamma H)]$. In the steady state, the value of this ratio is:

$$[K/(\gamma H)]^* = \{s/[\lambda(1 - \gamma) + \delta]\}^{1/(1-a)}.$$

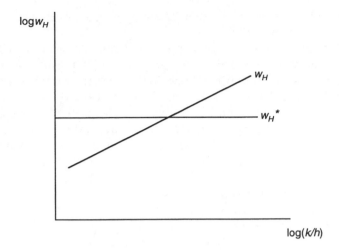

Fig. 27. A Lucas-type model

This expression is identical to the steady state value of capital per effective worker in the Solow model (k^{E*}; see eq. 3 in chap. 2) except that the rate of human capital accumulation, $\lambda \, (1 - \gamma)$, replaces Harrod's natural rate ($n + \beta$). Thus, the two steady state growth rates are identical if the rate of labor-augmenting technical progress (β) is equal to the growth rate of human capital per capita, $\lambda \, (1 - \gamma) - n$. The accumulation of physical capital and output growth are *driven by* the accumulation of human capital, analogous to how in the Solow model capital accumulation in the steady state is driven by technical progress and growth of the labor force.[13]

Other analogies to the Solow model, although more remote, can be noted regarding transitional dynamics. Off the steady state, if the relative endowment of human capital is high (i.e., K/H is low) the economy will converge to the steady state with a growth rate that is initially above the equilibrium rate and vice versa. If initial conditions are such that the ratio of physical to human is relatively high, the economy will converge to the steady state with an initially low growth rate. After a war or an earthquake that has destroyed mostly physical capital, the economy will recover faster than after an epidemic that has destroyed mainly human capital. Another implication, which has drawn considerable attention, is the following: an economy with a relatively low ratio of physical to human capital — for example, a developing country well endowed with human capital — will grow at a relatively high rate compared to the equilibrium path or other developing economies less well endowed with human capital.

A key question is what assumptions in the model generate constant returns to the accumulation of human capital and as a result endogenous growth. In one interpretation (Rebelo 1991), the critical assumption made by Lucas is that the production of human capital only uses reproducible factors. This assumption is obvious in the particular specification used by Lucas (eq. 8): human capital alone enters into the accumulation equation. As shown by Rebelo, the model's properties will remain intact as long as only reproducible factors enter directly or indirectly into the accumulation equation for human capital. As an example, consider the following accumulation equation:

$$dH/dt = s_H Y - \delta_H H,$$

where δ_H is the depreciation rate of human capital and Y is produced under conditions described by equation 7 so that K, along with H, enters into the production of new human capital. Substituting from equation 7 and using the steady state condition $\hat{H} = \hat{K}$, the rate of human capital accumulation in the steady state is still a linear function of H:

$$dH/dt = (s^a s_H^{1-a} - \delta_H)H.$$

The reason is that only reproducible factors, with constant returns to scale, enter into the production of Y (see eq. 7). The model then behaves like the limiting case of the Mankiw, Romer, and Weil extension of the Solow model, in which output elasticities with respect to K and H add up to unity.

In Rebelo's view, the distinctive feature of the model, in terms of the specification of technology, is thus the existence of a "core" reproducible factor that can be produced without the use of nonreproducible factors. This interpretation suggests that the specification in equation 8 is more restrictive than it needs to be. Yet, in another way this is not the case. Equation 8 postulates constant returns to human capital accumulation regardless of whether fixed factors enter into its production — one can imagine, for example, fixed factors entering into the multiplicative constant λ. The justification for the linearity of the human capital accumulation equation has to do, in Lucas's verbal discussion, with the *external effects* of human capital. Lucas discusses two types of external effects of human capital. One is the external effect of human capital in the aggregate production function, which we have neglected in equation 7 because, indeed, it plays no role in generating constant returns to human capital accumulation. Lucas sees the other external effect as crucial to justifying the specification in equation 8, for, as Lucas explains, it is the fact that "human capital accumulation is a *social* activity, involving *groups* of people in a way that has no counterpart in the accumulation of physical capital" that would explain why the initial level of human capital of younger generations is proportional to the level already achieved by older generations (1988, 19; italics original). This external effect is assumed to be internalized through nonmarket mechanisms within small groups, such as firms or families, and in this way creates no gap between social and private returns. But it is nevertheless an external effect that is viewed by Lucas as critical to the linearity assumption in the accumulation equation when applied to infinitely lived families rather than finite-lived individuals.

It is unclear, however, why these external effects should be large enough to generate constant returns to the accumulation of human capital. If sector H largely transmits preexisting knowledge — in schools or within families — returns will eventually diminish in the absence of the production of *new knowledge*. This is why Romer's (1991) interpretation of that sector as a knowledge-producing sector is perhaps the most coherent, assuming that the production of knowledge is not subject to diminishing returns. However, if this is so, the Lucas model does not go much further than replacing the exogenous rate of technical progress in the Solow model with a rate of human capital accumulation that, along with preferences and technology parameters, is critically determined by the exogenous value of λ, the effectiveness of investment in human capital.

Empirical Assessment

It is striking that most recent empirical research has focused on testing the neoclassical growth model, with revisions and extensions, rather than testing the empirical implications of endogenous growth models. This is the case even though, paradoxically, it was the theoretical research on endogenous growth that in part spurred the research that focuses on testing the neoclassical growth model.[14] Part of the explanation, suggested by Mankiw (1995), may be that by emphasizing unmeasurable variables such as knowledge these models have appealed to more theoretically inclined economists, with the result that few attempts have been made to evaluate them. Another explanation arises from the intrinsic difficulty of evaluating models based on large technological externalities in an open economy setting because a crucial question, as we shall see, is whether or not these large external effects (of the physical or human capital stock) are internal to national economies.[15]

As we have seen, recent growth models that rely on technological externalities of physical capital to generate continuous growth tend to assume that the external effects of capital accumulation are so large that they generate nondiminishing returns to capital in the aggregate production function. Taking a very long-term perspective, Romer (1991) finds this assumption attractive because it is consistent with the rising productivity growth rates of technological leaders over the centuries. However, if we try to use this analytical framework to explain cross-country differences in growth rates we immediately face some difficulties. If technological externalities do not cross borders, then — just as diminishing returns to capital in the neoclassical model tend to generate too much convergence — the assumption of increasing returns to capital tends to generate too much divergence, for not only should the gaps in income per capita widen over time but the differences in growth rates themselves should also become larger. Nobody, to my knowledge, has suggested that this is what we observe. The two pieces of evidence — time-series for the productivity leaders and cross sections of countries — can be reconciled if external effects do cross borders, so that the state of technology in, say, Mexico depends on the economywide capital-labor ratio in the United States. However, the transitional dynamics of such a model would not be much different from those of the Solow model. Technical progress, while endogenous in the United States, would still be exogenous in Mexico — a result of shifts in the A variable in the production function and independent of its own investment rate.[16]

The excessive degree of divergence, in models with local externalities, is associated with a difficulty repeatedly pointed out by Solow (1988, 1994). A model with a technology exhibiting increasing returns to capital has a mind-boggling implication: it generates infinite output in finite time. In the example provided by Solow (1994), if we assume an investment rate of 10 percent of GDP and a very small dose of increasing returns to capital, this would happen in 200 years, starting from the current per capita incomes of France or Germany. Even though this observation is not a decisive objection, it seems to set the burden of proof on those who believe in the existence of such dramatically increasing returns.

This particular difficulty is avoided in endogenous growth models that restrict the coefficient on capital in the aggregate production function to unity (the AK model) and thus generate persistent growth at a constant rather than an increasing rate. The properties of these models — persistent growth that depends on the investment rate — may help us to understand the increasing gaps between low- and high-income countries. At the same time, replacing the Solow model with a model lacking transitional dynamics makes it harder to explain the trend toward convergence that has taken place among today's high- and middle-income countries.

As predicted by the Solow model, this process has featured catch-up processes with a significant amount of capital deepening (see the evidence presented in chap. 1; on the period 1950–87, see Maddison 1991). Moreover, the distinctive properties of these models depend critically on returns to capital being exactly constant. This further restricts the assumptions on technology without empirical support. The evidence reviewed in chapter 4 on increasing returns and Verdoorn's law and research on the external effects of capital accumulation suggest the presence of increasing returns to scale *and* diminishing returns to capital, especially in the case of the *aggregate* production function.[17]

Models in which growth is driven by human capital accumulation have been found to be promising for explaining differences in growth rates across developing countries and especially the extraordinary high growth rates recorded in the East Asian miracles (see, in particular, Lucas 1993). Yet, human capital models also seem to imply an excessive degree of divergence across countries. Differences in growth rates tend to persist indefinitely, generating increasing gaps in per capita income levels. If the share of resources invested in human capital increases with per capita income — for example, as a result of the existence of a minimum (subsistence) level of consumption per capita — it will further accentuate the gaps, even though growth rates do not need to diverge (as in models with increasing returns to capital) if the differences in the shares of resources devoted to human capital accumulation decrease over time.

Moreover, as noted by Pack (1994) and Rodrik (1994), the comparative growth performance of East Asia is not easy to reconcile with a human-capital-based explanation of economic growth. Consider the initial conditions in the early 1960s, when growth in East Asia took off at vertiginous rates. The human capital endowment in these countries was rather favorable to growth. Their peoples had levels of education higher than would be expected given their per capita incomes. This is likely to have played a role in their subsequent expansion, but how decisive a role? Rodrik lists four countries (the Dominican Republic, the Philippines, Paraguay, and Sri Lanka) that had the same kind of educational advantage as Korea and Taiwan in 1960 but were unable to grow at rates anywhere near those of the two Asian countries. And what if the initial conditions had not been so favorable? Would there have been East Asian miracles? A simulation by Birdsall, Ross, and Sabot (1995), using a cross-country growth regression, attempts to answer the question: at what rate would the economy of South Korea have grown if its initial level of education had been similar to the developing-country average? Their answer is that South Korea's per capita growth would have been less (close to 5 percent per year instead of close to 6 percent) but still much higher than the developing-country average. We would still have had a Korean economic miracle.

During their process of rapid economic growth, East Asian countries made, in addition, substantial investments in education. Yet the same can be said of many other countries that were unable to grow quickly. The commitment to improving educational standards was almost universal across the developing world. The results of these human capital investments were often very different, but differences in growth rates may have played a major part in these results. This endogeneity problem is illustrated by a comparison between Korea and Mexico (see Birdsall, Ross, and Sabot 1995). In 1970, Korea's public expenditure on basic education per eligible child was only slightly higher than that of Mexico. Two decades later, Mexico's expenditure on education was only 25 percent of the Korean level; secondary enrollment rates were twice as high in Korea, and the gap in tertiary enrollment rates had grown even larger (39 versus 15 percent). Public expenditure policy does not explain this divergence: in fact, by the mid 1970s, after an expansion during the first half of that decade, expenditure in basic education *as percentage of GDP* reached temporarily higher levels in Mexico than in Korea. The explanation of these increasing gaps has to be attributed to the fact that Korea's GDP grew at an annual rate of 9.6 percent, compared to Mexico's 3.5 percent. This difference in growth rates meant that, with the same percentage of GDP invested in education, the resources that Korea was able to invest in this sector expanded at a vastly higher rate. The demographic transition that began earlier in Korea than in Mexico also played a role. This explains why during these two decades the number of school-age children increased by 60 percent in Mexico but fell by 2 percent in Korea.

According to Pack (1994), and unlike today, investments in research and development were of little significance before the mid-1980s in the East Asian developing economies. However, by then these countries had been able to sustain extraordinarily high growth rates for almost three decades. In a recent article (1995), Gustav Ranis tells an interesting and significant story. In the 1960s (from 1960 to 1967), around 15 percent of Taiwan's college graduates went to the United States to undertake postgraduate studies, two-thirds of them in science and engineering. This suggests a very high rate of human capital formation, especially for a country with Taiwan's income in the 1960s. The most revealing part of the story, however, is that only 4.5 percent of those students returned to Taiwan each year. In contrast, by the second half of the 1980s, when Taiwan's industrialization was no longer based on labor-intensive manufactures and was becoming increasingly intensive in science and technology, more than 90 percent of these highly trained graduates were returning to their country. The moral of the story seems to be that reserves of human capital created over the years were a necessary condition for this technology-intensive industrialization to take off but did not by themselves represent a sufficient condition for it.

These observations are difficult to reconcile with the notion that differences across countries in the rate of economic growth are to be explained *primarily* by differences in the levels and rates of human capital formation. More generally, it is hard to reconcile them with a view of the development process in which physical capital accumulation and output growth are essentially driven by human capital formation.

It is worth noting that the difficulties facing growth models that rely on increasing or constant returns to capital are not present in the growth models of early development theory. These models can generate constant or even increasing growth rates over a long transition period without having to rely on restrictive assumptions about technology. The reason is simply that the forces generating constant or increasing growth rates are not exclusively technological. They are rooted in the interaction between a (moderate) dose of increasing returns and a sufficiently elastic supply of labor. As discussed in chapter 4, these interactions do not produce strong, straightforward convergence: given high labor supply elasticity, increasing returns tend to generate divergence, and the fall in labor supply elasticity, as the capital-labor ratio increases, tends to generate convergence. The broad implication is that the highest rates of growth should occur in the intermediate stages of the transition, when increasing returns interact with the continuing high elasticity of the labor supply. This may imply convergence among middle- and high-income countries simultaneous with divergence among middle- and low-income countries. The picture that emerges is consistent with the broad trends reviewed in chapters 1 and 2 and the evidence discussed in chapter 4.

These multiple equilibria models also seem to offer a better alternative than the extensions of the AK model that incorporate the external effects of education or financial development (King and Levine 1993; Berthelemy and Varoudakis 1996) to generate multiple endogenous growth equilibria with associated convergence clubs *in rates of growth*. In Berthelemy and Varoudakis 1996, for example, the real sector uses an AK technology and the financial sector operates under economies of scale and imperfect competition. These economies of scale make the productivity of the financial sector dependent on the size of the real sector, while the total savings intermediated by banks and accumulated in the real sector depend on the margin of intermediation, which is affected by the size of the financial sector. In the presence of AK technology in the real sector, these interactions generate multiple equilibria in growth rates.

This type of interaction and the factors emphasized in this recent literature — financial development and education — are probably important in generating development traps and multiple equilibria. However, the assumption of constant returns to capital in the recent literature is an unnecessary straightjacket. More precisely, one can generate the more plausible multiple equilibria in *levels of income,* rather than rates of growth, by simply replacing the empirically questionable assumption of constant returns to capital with the interactions between increasing returns to scale and elastic labor supplies. We now turn to sketching a model in which these interactions are, in a sense, augmented with further interactions between the goods-producing and educational sectors.

A Development Model with Increasing Returns and Skill Acquisition

In the development models reviewed so far, low productivity and profitability at low-income levels are due exclusively to a low ratio of physical capital to labor in the presence of increasing returns to scale and elastic labor supplies. In the model presented in this section, productivity and profitability are affected not only by the capital-labor ratio but by the level of skill of the work force. In contrast to previous development models, this feature generates development traps in which the initial level of human capital plays a key role.

Consider an economy in which a subsistence sector (S) and a modern capitalist sector (M) coexist while producing the same good. Both sectors use labor with an average level of skills (h), and in addition sector M uses capital. The production functions are:

$$S = hL_S \tag{9}$$

$$M = AK^a(hL_M)^{1-a}. \tag{10}$$

Skilled labor (hL) is analogous to effective labor in the Solow model, so that an increase in h is equivalent to labor-augmenting technical progress, except for the external effects considered below. Technology in sector M features two types of external effect. First, there are learning by doing externalities proportional to the size of the economywide capital stock per worker, as in the Rosenstein-Rodan/Leibenstein model of chapter 4. Second, the average level of skills also features technological externalities, as in Lucas 1988. In the spirit of the Lucas model, these external effects are assumed to be specific to sector M, as they are largely internal to the urban agglomerations of human capital, in which the increasing returns sector is located. The A variable in the production function of the M sector is thus:

$$A = k^\mu h^\beta,$$

where $k = K/L$. Both sectors operate under competitive conditions, and the wage and profit rates must be such that:

$$w = k^\mu h^\beta (1 - a)[K/(hL_M)]^a \tag{11}$$

$$r = k^{\mu/a} h^{\beta/a} a(1 - a)^{(1-a)/a} / w^{(1-a)/a}, \tag{12}$$

where w is the wage per unit of effective labor (analogous to w^E in chap. 2), in terms of the only good produced.

In addition, there is a sector H, where skilled workers (or "teachers") are engaged in the activity of generating and transmitting knowledge that can be utilized in the production of goods and services in sectors S and M. We model the outcome of this sector's activity as enhancing the general level of skills (h), according to an accumulation equation discussed later. The benefits of this activity accrue to the individual firm in the form of purely external economies, so that "teachers" have to be collectively hired by firms. We therefore assume that teachers (L_H) are paid out of a tax (t) on profits:

$$w(hL_H) = trK. \tag{13}$$

The same wage (w) will prevail in equilibrium in sector H and the goods-producing sectors. The total labor force (L) is assumed to be fully employed:

$$L = L_S + L_M + L_H.$$

Short-Run Equilibrium

In the short run, h, K, and L are given, and we can solve the model for the levels of output and employment, the profit rate, and the real wage. The determination of the wage depends on whether sectors S and M coexist. If they do, so that $L_S > 0$, the wage is determined by the production conditions in sector S, as in the Lewis model. From equation 9, using the equality between the wage and the average product of effective labor in sector S, we have $w = 1$, where 1 is the price of the single good produced. The wage per natural unit of labor is equal to h, of course, since from equation 9 h is the average product of labor when labor is measured in natural units. As is readily verified, the behavior of other variables in this case is very similar to that of the Lewis model. In particular, changes in the capital stock affect the employment share of sector M without affecting w, and they affect the profit rate only insofar as there are technological externalities ($\mu > 0$).

When labor in the subsistence sector has been completely absorbed into the M and H sectors ($L_S = 0$), the wage is determined by equation 11 under $L_M = L - L_H$. This implies that $L_H = [ta/(1 - a)](L - L_H)$. Note, therefore, that the ratio L_M/L is fully determined by the tax rate and the parameters of the production function in the M sector. Sector M then operates under a fully inelastic labor supply, as in the Solow model or the mature phase of the Lewis model. Now changes in the capital stock do affect the wage while leaving the employment share of sector M unchanged.[18]

The fraction (L_H/L) of the labor force employed in sector H also depends on the existence of a labor surplus. From equations 13 and 11, we have:

$$L_H/L = [ta/(1 - a)][(1 - a)k^{a+\mu}h^{\beta-a}]^{1/a} \quad \text{for } L_S > 0 \text{ and } w = 1$$
$$(14)$$
$$L_H/L = ta/(1 - a + ta) \quad \text{for } L_S = 0.$$

Equation 14 shows that in the labor surplus economy the resources per worker invested in sector H increase with the overall capital-labor ratio and decrease with the average level of skills provided that $a > \beta$. A higher capital-labor ratio implies, as in the Lewis model, a higher share of profits in total income and thus, with a given tax rate, a higher share of output devoted to sector H. A higher h implies, from equation 13, a higher cost of L_H (in natural units) and thus a reduction in the employment share of sector H, unless the increase in the profit rate due to the external effects of human capital would compensate for the higher cost of L_H.

When the labor supply to sector M becomes inelastic, L_H/L is fully determined by the tax rate and the parameters of the production function of sector M. As indicated earlier, the independence of L_H/L from the capital-labor ratio is due to the unit elasticity of factor substitution assumed in the Cobb-Douglas specification (see note 18).

The determination of the profit rate also differs between the two phases (with and without labor surplus). From equation 12, alternatively setting $w = 1$, or using equations 11 and 14, we have:

$$r = a(1 - a)^{(1-a)/a}k^{\mu/a}h^{\beta/a} \quad \text{for } L_S > 0$$
$$(15)$$
$$r = a[(1 - a)/(1 - a + ta)]^{1-a}k^{a+\mu-1}h^{\beta+1-a} \quad \text{for } L_S = 0.$$

In both phases, the profit rate increases with a higher level of skills, although in the labor surplus phase this is so only in the presence of external effects of human capital ($\beta > 0$). The major difference between the two phases has to do with the effects of k on the profit rate: with $L_S > 0$, the profit rate increases with the overall capital-labor ratio in the presence of externalities resulting from learning by doing ($\mu > 0$). When $L_S = 0$, the profit rate falls as k increases, provided that $a + \mu < 1$, that is, if technology in sector M exhibits diminishing returns to capital.

Capital Accumulation and Skill Acquisition

Over time, the average level of skills and the capital-labor ratio will be changing. The change in h is made to depend on the fraction of the overall labor force employed in sector H and on a depreciation rate (δ_H):

$$dh/dt = \lambda(L_H/L)h^{1-\theta} - \delta_H h \quad 0 < \theta \leq 1,$$

where the restriction on the parameter θ ensures that, given L_H/L, the growth rate of h is a decreasing function of h. Indeed, dividing both sides of the equation by h:

$$\hat{h} = \lambda(L_H/L)/h^\theta - \delta_H. \tag{16}$$

As we shall see in more detail later, this formulation implies that the rate of skill acquisition ($\hat{h}$) is proportional to the gap between the steady state and actual levels of h. It can be justified in a manner similar to explanations of cross-country differences in the rates of technical progress (see chap. 2). Part of the activity of sector H is not the generation of new knowledge but the transmission of existing knowledge. The lower the level of skills, the larger is the stock of existing knowledge that can be transmitted with a given investment of resources in sector H. If this is the case, the lower h is the faster the proportionate rate of growth of h will tend to be. Another, very similar rationale is that the acquisition of basic skills is likely to have a larger *proportionate* effect on the average level of skills than the acquisition of more advanced skills when h is already high.

Substituting from equation 14 into 16, we have:

$$\hat{h} = (\lambda/h^\theta)[ta/(1-a)][(1-a)k^{a+\mu}h^{\beta-a}]^{1/a} - \delta_H \quad \text{for } L_S > 0 \text{ and } w = 1 \tag{17}$$

$$\hat{h} = (\lambda/h^\theta)[ta/(1-a+ta)] - \delta_H \quad \text{for } L_S = 0.$$

The change in the capital-labor ratio is equal to the rate of capital accumulation less the growth of the labor force (n):

$$\hat{k}=s_\pi(1-t)r-(n+\delta), \tag{18}$$

where $s_\pi(1-t)$ is the savings rate out of profits net of taxes and, as in previous development models, there is no saving out of wages. Substituting from equation 15 into 18:

$$\hat{k}=s_\pi(1-t)a(1-a)^{(1-a)/a}k^{\mu/a}h^{\beta/a}-(n+\delta) \quad \text{for } L_S>0$$

$$\hat{k}=s_\pi(1-t)a[(1-a)/(1-a+ta)]^{1-a}k^{a+\mu-1}h^{\beta+1-a}-(n+\delta) \tag{19}$$

for $L_S=0$.

Equations 17 and 19 together imply a strong tendency toward divergence in the labor surplus economy. Consider two economies with different capital-labor ratios (and income levels) that otherwise are identical. From equation 17, h grows at a faster rate in the economy with the higher k: with a higher income and profit share, this economy devotes more resources to sector H (for a given t). From equation 19, k also grows at a faster rate since the profit rate is higher in the high-k economy in the presence of externalities due to learning by doing. It thus follows that the economy with the higher income grows at a faster rate, and a gap in the level of skills will emerge between the two economies. Their growth rates—not only their income levels—will diverge as long as the increase in skills in the high-income economy does not exert sufficiently strong pressure downward on the growth rate of h (eq. 17). It is worth noting that, although this tendency toward divergence does not depend on the presence of externalities due to learning by doing, it certainly accentuates it. With $\mu=0$, the growth of h is still higher in the high-k economy. Provided that β is positive (i.e., that there are external effects of human capital), the increase in h causes a higher rate of accumulation in the high-k economy, which then has more positive feedback on $\hat{h}$.

The tendency toward divergence is reversed when labor in sector S has been absorbed into sectors M and H. Consider again two economies that are identical except for their capital-labor ratios. From equation 17, h grows at the same rate in the two economies and declines over time. With diminishing returns to physical capital, the high-k economy now has a lower profit rate and thus a slower rate of accumulation (see eqs. 15 and 17). With the same growth in h and faster growth in k, over time the low-k economy will be closing its productivity and income gap with the more advanced economy.

At the end of this process of convergence, there is a steady state. Setting $\hat{k}=\hat{h}=0$, the steady state values of h and k are obtained from equations 17 and 19 under $L_S=0$:

$$h^* = (\lambda l_H / \delta_H)^{1/\theta},$$

where $l_H = L_H / L = ta/(ta + 1 - a)$ and

$$k^* = \{[as_\pi(1 - t)/(n + \delta)]h^{*1-a+\beta}l_M^{1-a}\}^{1/1-a-\mu},$$

where $l_M = L_M / L = (1 - a)/(ta + 1 - a)$.

It is worth noting some similarities and differences between this and previous models of human capital formation. The steady state value of k is a function not only of the savings rate (as_π as well as n and δ) but of the employment share of sector H (which affects h^*). This employment share plays a role similar to that of the rate of human capital accumulation (s_H) in the Mankiw, Romer, and Weil extension of the Solow model. This is why k^* can be expressed as the steady state value of the capital-labor ratio in the Solow model, adjusted by a term that is proportional to the steady state level of h. One difference, however, is that a higher employment share of sector H has adverse effects on sector M. A larger sector H implies a smaller employment share of the M sector, which reduces the profit rate at a given level of k (see eq. 15 for $L_S = 0$) and, from equation 18, also has an adverse effect on the rate of accumulation and thus on k^*. A second effect is the adverse effect on savings net of taxes since the posttax profit rate, $r(1 - t)$, falls with an increase in the tax rate. None of these effects must necessarily offset the positive effect — operating through a higher value of h^* — that a higher employment share of the H sector has on k^*. In the presence of moderate external effects (i.e., β is low), the most likely result is that an increase in t, beyond some positive level, increases h^* and reduces k^* and thus has ambiguous effects on per capita income in the steady state.

Another difference from the MRW model is that the steady state value of h does not depend on the share of investment in physical capital. This is partly due, as noted, to the unit elasticity of substitution assumed in the production function of sector M. But more fundamentally (since MRW also assume Cobb-Douglas technology) it is due to the nonsymmetrical treatment of physical and human capital in the present model. In the MRW model, the fraction of the population engaged in the activity of raising the level of skills is indistinguishable from the rest of the labor force. In this respect, the present model is closer to that of Lucas (1988) in which the human capital accumulation depends only on human capital. Unlike the Lucas model, however, we have allowed for diminishing returns in the accumulation of human capital by setting $0 < \theta \leq 1$. This is why the model does not generate endogenous perpetual growth. Note that with $\theta = 0$ the growth rate of h in equation 22 (when

$L_S = 0$) would remain constant over time and the economy would not converge to a steady state.

Long-Run Equilibria

Figure 28 illustrates the solution to the model in $(\log k, \log h)$ space. The schedule $\hat{h} = 0$ shows the (h, k) combinations for which there is no net acquisition of skills. As long as the labor supply is elastic $(L_S > 0)$, the employment share of the H sector rises with the capital-labor ratio and the schedule is upward sloping: a higher k increases $\hat{h}$, and therefore a higher level of h (which reduces h in the absence of dramatic β effects) is required to keep $\hat{h} = 0$. The slope of the schedule is obtained from equation 17:

$$\mathrm{d}\log h/\mathrm{d}\log k = (a + \mu)/[a(1 + \theta) - \beta],$$

which is positive when $\beta < a(1 + \theta)$. When the labor supply becomes inelastic, the employment share of the H sector no longer depends on the capital-labor ratio. There is then a unique value of h, independent of k, which keeps $\hat{h} = 0$. This is the steady state value of h. The schedule is then a horizontal line at $h = h^*$. Above the schedule, h tends to fall, since the level of h exerts an adverse effect on $\hat{h}$. Conversely, the region below the schedule is one of positive acquisition of skills and rising values of h. The arrows in figure 28 indicate the behavior of h off the schedule.

The schedule $\hat{k} = 0$ shows the (h, k) combinations for which there is no net increase in the economywide capital stock per worker. When the labor supply is elastic $(L_S > 0)$, the wage per unit of effective labor remains constant and, in the presence of learning by doing externalities $(\mu > 0)$, the profit rate rises with k. Since an increase in h also has a positive effect on r, and thus on $\hat{k}$, the locus must slope downward (because, to keep $\hat{k} = 0$, a higher k requires a lower h). The slope of the schedule is obtained from equation 19:

$$\mathrm{d}\log h/\mathrm{d}\log k = -\mu/\beta.$$

When the labor supply becomes inelastic, an increase in the capital-labor ratio affects $\hat{k}$ adversely. The locus now slopes upward since an increase in h (which has a positive effect on $\hat{k}$) is required to compensate for the adverse effect of k on $\hat{k}$. From equation 17, the slope of the schedule is:

$$\mathrm{d}\log h/\mathrm{d}\log k = (1 - a - \mu)/(1 - a - \beta).$$

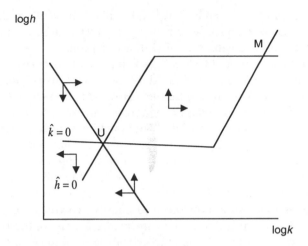

Fig. 28.   A development model with skill acquisition

The model features multiple equilibria. The high-level equilibrium at point M is a Solow-type stable steady state with $h = h*$ and $k = k*$. The low-level equilibrium at point U is a saddle point, with the corresponding saddle path being a downward-sloping locus of (h, k) combinations below which no sustained capital accumulation and acquisition of skills are possible.[19] To the right of the saddle path, there are multiple trajectories converging toward the high-level equilibrium, depending on initial conditions and the relative importance of the different external effects.

Consider, for example, the case in which external effects arise largely from human capital (μ is low and β relatively high; for simplicity, assume that $\mu = 0$ and $\beta > a\theta$). At low levels of k, the growth of k is a function of h but not of k. If the initial values of k and h are such that $\hat{h}$ is positive, then the rate of accumulation will be increasing over time (with k rising at an increasing rate). The growth of h is an increasing function of k/h and h (since $\beta > a\theta$). A country just to the right of the saddle path, with low skills but abundant capital (a high k/h ratio), will follow a growth path with an initially low rate of physical capital accumulation (since h is low) and a fast rate of acquisition of skills (since k/h is high). Its h/k ratio will thus increase over time along a path that features an increasing rate of accumulation and a declining rate of skill acquisition. Then both $\hat{h}$ and $\hat{k}$ decline when, at high levels of k, the labor force in sector S has been fully absorbed. The analysis is symmetrical for a country that starts with a low k/h ratio to the right of the saddle path. Its growth path will feature an initially high rate of physical capital accumulation (because h is high), which increases over time, together with an initially low but increasing rate of skill acquisition.

One may be tempted to label growth as "skill intensive" in the first case, because the h/k ratio rises, and as "capital intensive" in the second case, because the k/h ratio increases. However, these labels would be somewhat misleading. The h/k ratio increases in the first case because the relatively large M sector (associated with the high value of k) provides the resources for the rapid expansion of sector H, so that what makes "skill-intensive" growth possible is in fact the initially high capital intensity of the economy. Similarly, in the second case, it is the initially high level of skills that, by increasing the productivity of sector M, makes the rapid expansion of this sector possible and causes growth to seem "capital intensive." The point is that in the intermediate stage of the transition $\hat{h}$ and $\hat{k}$ tend to converge and when the growth rates of the economy are the highest, the growth path of both economies will feature a rapid process of *both* skill and capital deepening. It is worth recalling the finding in chapter 1 that the fastest growing economies featured both high rates of capital accumulation and rapid rates of educational progress.[20]

Below the saddle path, there is a development trap. Capital accumulation and skill acquisition, or rather the lack of it, interact in a vicious circle, keeping the economy in decline. In contrast to the Rosenstein-Rodan/Leibenstein model of chapter 4, there is no longer a single critical value of k that has to be achieved to make sustained growth possible. Rather, the development trap region is bounded by a multiplicity of k values or, more precisely, of (h, k) combinations. What keeps an economy in the trap may be an excessively low capital stock, despite a rather high level of skills, or an insufficient level of skills, despite a rather high capital stock. Hence, sustained growth may be achieved with a rather low k provided that the level of skills compensates for the small capital stock. The model is thus quite consistent with Azariadis and Drazen (1990), who find that no country in the postwar development experience was able to grow quickly without a critical level of literacy of the labor force (see, however, chap. 1). They interpret this evidence as supporting the notion of "threshold externalities" in the accumulation of human capital. In their model, this threshold is associated with increasing returns to human capital accumulation over a range of human capital levels or to discontinuities in the human capital accumulation function. This yields a critical ratio of human capital to income below which there is an underdevelopment trap. In the present model, the trap is associated with a critical locus of (h, k) combinations, that is, the threshold level of human capital is not independent of the capital-labor ratio. The difference is due to the fact that in the present model there are no increasing returns to human capital accumulation and external effects arise not only from human capital but from physical capital accumulation.

The size of the trap region—which determines what we may call the hold of the trap—depends on the position of the saddle path. A higher rate of labor force growth and a lower savings rate shift the $\hat{k} = 0$ schedule upward and expand the size of the region below the saddle path.[21] A lower value of the parameter λ, which reflects the efficiency with which sector H raises the level of skills, shifts the $\hat{h} = 0$ schedule to the right and thus also increases the size of the trap region. It is worth noting that an increase in the tax rate, which has a positive effect on the rate of skill acquisition but an adverse effect on capital accumulation, shifts the $\hat{k} = 0$ locus upward and the $\hat{h} = 0$ locus to the left. Its effect on the hold of the trap will depend on other parameter values and external effects as well as on initial conditions including the value of t itself.

What are the conditions for multiple equilibria? Clearly, the existence of an elastic labor supply is crucial. Otherwise, figure 28 would consist of a horizontal $\hat{h} = 0$ schedule and an upward-sloping $\hat{k} = 0$ schedule. As in the MRW extension of the Solow model, a unique stable equilibrium would exist, corresponding to the steady state at k^* and h^*. The presence of external effects is also necessary. In their absence, the model at low levels of k is very similar to a Lewis model, with labor augmenting technical progress in sectors S and M. With $\mu = \beta = 0$, the accumulation equation for k, at low levels of k, becomes $\hat{k} = s_\pi(1 - t)a(1 - a)^{(1-a)/a} - (n + \delta)$. The overall capital-labor ratio, just as in the Lewis model, grows at a constant rate that is positive or negative depending on parameter values (but not on the values of h and k). This, of course, simply confirms that an elastic labor supply is insufficient to generate a development trap problem. Increasing returns, or, in the present context, external effects from human capital, are also necessary.

However, both of these effects are not necessary. The existence of a low-level equilibrium depends only on one of this type of effect being present. Consider the case in which β is positive and μ is zero. The major difference from figure 28 is that the $\hat{k} = 0$ schedule would be horizontal at low levels of k instead of being negatively sloped. The vicious circle at low values of k and h involves a low capital-labor ratio that generates an insufficient accumulation of human capital ($\hat{h}$), which in turn would keep h low, with an adverse effect on physical capital accumulation ($\hat{k}$). The difference from the case in which μ is also positive is that the positive feedback effects of k on $\hat{k}$ only include those operating through h but not those operating more "directly" as a result of increasing returns in sector M (in the presence of a perfectly elastic labor supply).

Consider the case in which β is zero and μ is positive. In the accumulation equation for k, at low levels of k, h no longer affects $\hat{k}$. The schedule $\hat{k} = 0$ becomes vertical at that minimum value of k that needs to be achieved to have $\hat{k} > 0$. This value, which is completely analogous to the critical k_U value in the Rosenstein-Rodan/Leibenstein model of chapter 4, depends on parameter values (n, δ, and s_π) and is independent of h. This is because, with $\beta = 0$, an increase in h is exactly analogous to a uniform labor-augmenting technical progress in the S and M sectors. With the increase in h raising labor productivity uniformly in both sectors, and with the wage determined by the productivity of sector S, the higher level of h leaves the profit rate and thus $\hat{k}$ unaffected.[22] The trap is then the whole region to the left of the $\hat{k} = 0$ locus, a vertical line at $k = k_U$. No matter how high the level of skills, capital accumulation cannot get off the ground as long as k is below k_U.

The model presented in this section brings the interactions between skill acquisition and capital accumulation into the analytical framework of early development theory. In doing so, it preserves the transitional dynamics of models based on increasing returns to scale and an elastic labor supply, like those in chapters 4 and 5, and even accentuates the pattern of divergence/convergence characteristic of these models. It also preserves the focus that development theory gave to industrialization and the accumulation of physical capital. It naturally leads us to inquire about the pattern of production and trade specialization that must play an important role in how much returns will increase. At the same time, it points to new research areas and difficult questions, such as the income distribution and demographic factors that may be behind the processes of skill acquisition. Such a research program appears to be a promising avenue for enhancing our understanding of the process of economic development and the differences in growth performance across developing countries. In order to proceed along these lines, we need to turn to the analysis of open economies, which is the setting for the following six chapters.

CHAPTER 7

Trade, Industrialization, and Uneven Development

There are two general ways of looking at the persistence of under-development. One approach is to begin by recognizing that modern techniques have the potential to raise the living standards in less developed countries to the same levels as those found in advanced industrial economies and then ask what prevents the adoption of these techniques in low-income countries. This is the question we have been pursuing up to this point of the book. The answers encountered, except for technology gap explanations, all have the explanation in common that if these techniques are not adopted it must be because they are less profitable than those currently in use. This is the case for the following reasons: (1) the fact that they are intensive in physical (Solow) or human capital (Mankiw, Romer, and Weil), factors that are scarce, and thus expensive, in developing countries; (2) the presence of political risk and the lack of the rule of law, which increase the effective cost of employing these techniques and reduce their expected profitability, especially when access to them requires flows of international investment; and (3) the fact that they are subject to increasing returns to scale or require the use of inputs produced under increasing returns, and are thus unprofitable at low-income levels, which directly or indirectly generate small markets for the increasing-returns activities. It is worth noting that in these views, especially (1) and (3), the ultimate reason for the unprofitability of modern techniques has to do with differences in factor endowments resulting from countries being at different stages in the process of capital accumulation. To state it simply: real wages are lower and capital-intensive techniques less profitable in less developed countries because their economies, having accumulated less capital, are comparatively more labor than capital abundant.

A second approach downplays, in contrast, the role of factor endowments. Indeed, a central proposition of neoclassical trade theory is that, through the international exchange of goods and the equalization of goods prices, competition in domestic factor markets will tend to equalize factor prices among free-trading economies. Real wages will not be lower in labor-abundant countries because free trade — by allowing the labor-abundant economy to specialize in those goods produced with labor-intensive techniques — will cause labor-intensive techniques to be used more extensively than in the previously low-income country. The key questions from this perspective no longer refer to the constraints posed by the stage of capital accumulation but rather to what prevents this tendency to factor price equalization from taking place. Is it the presence of obstacles to free trade and of other sources of resource misallocation, as discussed in the large empirical literature on the relationship between growth and the "outward" or "inward" orientation of trade policy regimes?[1] Or is it that the restrictive conditions required for factor price equalization to operate are rarely met in practice?

We look, in this chapter, for answers to these questions, first considering how openness modifies the convergence properties of the neoclassical growth model. This will provide a useful benchmark, with which we can compare later development models. We turn in the second section to one of the oldest qualifications to the benefits of free trade, the infant industry argument, which I present in the context of a small open economy and in a way that will make its kinship to development trap models clear to the reader. The third section extends the analysis of the argument to the case of different rates of technical progress in a small open economy and the rest of the world. The final section addresses the case of a large economy, using a two-country model in the spirit of Lewis (1969) and Prebisch (United Nations 1950) in which a capital-abundant North and a labor-abundant South have food-producing tradable sectors with very different productivity levels.

Openness and Growth in the Neoclassical Framework

As we know, in the neoclassical model of closed economies, countries converge to different steady states, which depend on savings and population growth rates. Openness in both of its main aspects, international capital mobility and trade, modifies the properties of the neoclassical model in a way that reinforces the tendency of economies to converge to similar income levels. In the steady states of closed economies, profit rates (r^*) will be different across countries. We know from the steady state condition that $r^* = a(n + \beta + \delta)/s$, so that countries with lower savings rates (s) and higher population growth rates (n) would tend to have higher profit rates. This is simply because they will reach lower steady state values of capital per effective worker and, given diminishing returns to capital, the corresponding profit rates will be higher.

Consider the effects of capital mobility. With perfectly integrated capital markets, the differences in profit rates will tend to be wiped away as capital flows from countries with low rates of return to capital to countries where they are high. A uniform profit rate will tend to be established, and the equality $r^* = a(n + \beta + \delta)/s$ will break down for any particular country. Countries with lower savings rates and higher population growth rates will now tend to have the same profit rate that is prevailing elsewhere and therefore, with access to the same technology, will reach exactly the same level of capital per effective worker. Regardless of demographics and savings behavior, a world with perfect capital mobility will feature absolute convergence in terms of output per worker.[2]

Even in the absence of capital mobility, a neoclassical world of trading economies will feature a tendency toward convergence of factor prices across countries. Consider a Heckscher-Ohlin model with two goods produced using two factors in two different countries. The two goods (*M* and *N*) are produced under constant returns to scale using capital and labor, and both countries (1 and 2) have access to the same technologies. Assuming, for simplicity, Cobb-Douglas technologies, the production functions are:

$$M_1 = AK_{M1}{}^a L_{M1}{}^{1-a} \quad N_1 = BK_{N1}{}^b L_{N1}{}^{1-b}$$

$$M_2 = AK_{M2}{}^a L_{M2}{}^{1-a} \quad N_2 = BK_{N2}{}^b L_{N2}{}^{1-b}.$$

Within each country, competition in factor markets establishes uniform wage and rental rates for labor and capital. Profit maximization under perfect competition implies equality between factor prices and marginal products. Moreover, international trade leads to the equalization of goods prices. Together, these tendencies imply that relative wages and capital rentals must conform to certain relationships. Thus, the equality within each country between the product wage in sector *M* and the marginal product of labor, together with the equalization of the price of good *M* through trade, imply that relative wages must be such that:

$$w_1/w_2 = (k_{M1}/k_{M2})^a \quad k_{M1} = K_{M1}/L_{M1} \quad k_{M2} = K_{M2}/L_{M2}, \tag{1}$$

where w_1 and w_2 are the uniform wage rates in countries 1 and 2. Similarly, the relative rentals of capital (r_1, r_2) must be such that:

$$r_1/r_2 = (k_{M2}/k_{M1})^{1-a}. \tag{2}$$

Similar relations apply for good *N* as a result of the equalization of its price through trade:

$$w_1/w_2 = (k_{N1}/k_{N2})^b \quad k_{N1} = K_{N1}/L_{N1} \quad k_{N2} = K_{N2}/L_{N2} \tag{3}$$

$$r_1/r_2 = (k_{N2}/k_{N1})^{1-b}. \tag{4}$$

Equations 1 and 3 imply that:

$$(k_{M1}/k_{M2})^a = (k_{N1}/k_{N2})^b, \tag{5}$$

and, similarly, equations 2 and 4 imply that:

$$(k_{M2}/k_{M1})^{1-a} = (k_{N2}/k_{N1})^{1-b}. \tag{6}$$

Substituting from equation 5 into 6 in order to solve for (k_{M1}/k_{M2}) yields:

$$(k_{M1}/k_{M2})^c = 1 \quad c = (a - b)/b(1 - b), \tag{7}$$

which implies that the capital-labor ratio in the production of good M will be the same in both countries. The same applies to the production of good N, as can be verified using equations 5 and 6 to solve for (k_{N1}/k_{N2}). This is a striking implication: regardless of differences in the overall capital-labor endowments among the two countries, each of the two goods will be produced with the *same* capital intensity in *both* countries. Of course, the labor-abundant country will tend to specialize in the production of the labor-intensive good and will export this good to the capital-rich economy. However, as long as it produces some capital-intensive goods, it will produce them with the same capital intensity that prevails in the capital-abundant country. The value of the marginal product of its labor will be the same as in the capital-rich economy despite its having a comparatively larger labor endowment. Thus, the wage rates in both countries will indeed be identical: equations 1 and 7 imply that $w_1 = w_2$.

Factor price equalization does not imply the convergence of income or output per worker since factor quantities will still differ across countries. However, factor price equalization will imply a stronger tendency toward convergence of incomes than is present in today's world economy: it is hard to imagine a world in which wages are equalized internationally without income gaps being much smaller than what we presently observe. Moreover, the tendency toward factor price convergence takes place independently of whether economies are in the steady state or not (in the Heckscher-Ohlin model, capital is mobile across sectors, but the overall capital stock is given and need not be the steady state stock).

In the analysis that follows in this and subsequent chapters, the tendency toward factor price convergence will not take place. One or more of the several assumptions required for factor price equalization will be violated. I highlight those that are more relevant for our purposes. First, constant returns to scale, as well as both countries having access to the same technology, are essential. With increasing returns, accruing, for example, from external effects of the overall capital endowment, the techniques used by the capital-abundant country will be more productive in both sectors and real wages will accordingly be higher in the capital-abundant country. Second, both goods must be produced in both countries. If the labor-abundant country fully specializes in the production of the labor-intensive good, the link between relative wages and capital intensities in the production of the capital-intensive good will be broken and factor endowments will again play a role in the determination of relative wages. For example, if country 2 is the labor-abundant country and N is the labor-intensive good, specialization of country 2 in the production of N means that equation 1 breaks down. Equation 3 will still hold as a result of the equalization of the price of N, with k_{N2} now being the overall capital-labor ratio in country 2; but there is no reason why the technique used by country 1 in the production of N should be identical to the overall capital-labor ratio in country 2. This technique will generally feature a higher capital-labor ratio, and the wage in the capital-rich country will be higher than that in the labor-abundant economy. Third, both factors must enter into the production of both goods. If, for example, the production of N in country 2 does not use capital, the marginal product of capital in sector M will be delinked from that in country 1. Equation 2 will no longer hold, and the overall factor endowment of country 2 will affect capital rental, and thus the wage, despite the equalization of goods prices.

Multiple Equilibria as a Rationale for the Infant Industry Argument

Consider an economy with two sectors. Sector S produces a labor-intensive good under constant returns to scale (CRS) and without the use of capital. The other sector, M, produces a capital-intensive good under increasing returns to scale (IRS) using capital and labor.[3] We assume here a Cobb-Douglas technology with technological externalities proportional to the size of the capital stock. The two products are good substitutes in consumption. However, only the capital-intensive good can be accumulated as capital. The equilibrium wage rate is uniform across sectors.

The product wage in sector M is an increasing function of the economywide capital-labor ratio (k). In this economy, as in the model of chapter 3 (third section), the w curve is upward sloping with a slope that increases with k. The profit rate in sector M is a decreasing function of the product wage and, given the IRS technology, an increasing function of the capital stock. Thus, the w^* curve of this economy, showing the required value of the product wage in sector M as a function of the capital-labor ratio, is positively sloped. The slope is determined by the strength of the external effects of technology (as in the first section of chap. 4).

Initially, the economy is closed to international trade. Given the assumptions of uniform wage rates and constant returns to labor in the labor-intensive sector, and with an appropriate choice of units, the product wage (w/p_M) is also the relative price ratio (p_S/p_M) between the two goods. We can therefore interpret the w curve as showing the equilibrium-relative prices (p_S/p_M) that would prevail under autarky at different levels of the capital-labor endowment. This is the curve ($p_S/p_M)_A$ in figure 29. In a labor-abundant economy (with a low k), p_S/p_M is low; that is, the labor-intensive good is cheap and the capital-intensive good is relatively expensive, while in a capital-abundant economy p_S/p_M is high because the labor-intensive good becomes relatively more expensive. Under our assumptions, and given in particular that the wage in terms of good S is constant and equal to unity, the wage in terms of good M is a measure (albeit imperfect) of the real consumption wage.

The Gains from Trade

Suppose that this economy opens up to trade and both goods are freely traded in the international market. The economy is small and a price taker for both goods. The relative prices in the international market will thus prevail in the domestic market as well after the economy opens up to trade. These relative prices define the free trade line ($p_S/p_M)_{FT}$ in figure 29. This line is also the w curve of the economy under free trade until the labor force in sector S is completely absorbed into sector M. Then the wage rate is delinked from the price of good S in the international economy and the wage increases with the capital-labor ratio. The w curve of the trading economy is thus horizontal until the economy reaches complete specialization in sector M and then becomes upward sloping. The similarity to the w curve in the Lewis model should not be surprising. The assumption of constant relative prices between the two sectors plays the same role as the one-good assumption in the Lewis model by making the labor supply to sector M perfectly elastic as long as the two sectors coexist.

Consider the case in which the initial capital-labor ratio is below k^{**}, the value of k at the intersection of the free trade line and the w curve under autarky. With such a capital endowment, the economy under autarky produces the labor-intensive good at a lower relative

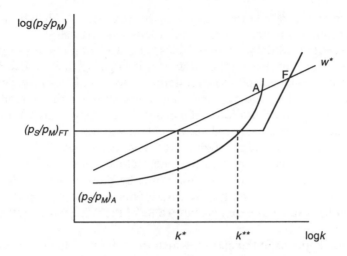

Fig. 29. Short- and long-run gains from trade

price than the rest of the world economy: below k^{**}, $(p_S/p_M)_A$ is less than $(p_S/p_M)_{FT}$. When it opens up to trade, the economy is able to sell its labor-intensive good at the higher relative price prevailing in the international market, that is, in exchange for more units of the capital-intensive good than it can afford to produce domestically (per unit of the labor-intensive good). This is the static (Ricardian) gain from trade: the economy can achieve, through free trade, higher real income by exporting the good in which it has a comparative advantage and importing the good in which it has a comparative disadvantage. Measuring these benefits by their impact on real wages, it suffices to note that real wages increase to the same extent (for the reasons indicated) as does the relative price of the labor-intensive good. These benefits from trade are larger the greater the discrepancy between the relative prices prevailing under autarky and internationally.

The gains from trade are unevenly distributed. Clearly, in the economy considered, all the gains accrue to labor, while capital loses. Given the higher relative price for good S, the product wage in sector M is now higher than under autarky and the profit rate, at the initial level of the capital stock, is lower. As in Stolper and Samuelson (1941), the relatively abundant factor (labor in this case) benefits from the opening to trade, while capital, the scarce factor, loses.[4] Exactly the opposite happens if the economy has a capital endowment above k^{**} and labor is the relatively scarce factor. The economy then has a comparative advantage in the capital-intensive good. When it opens up to trade, it will import the labor-intensive good at a lower price, real wages will fall, and the rate of profit will increase in the capital-intensive industry.

Consider now the long-run effects. The story has a happy ending in the case in which the capital endowment is larger than k^{**}. The higher profit rate stimulates capital accumulation. The capital-labor ratio continues to increase along the free trade line, and eventually the economy will reach complete specialization in the capital-intensive industry. When this takes place, the rate of capital accumulation will still be above its steady state value (since the wage is below w^*). The real wage will then increase along the w curve corresponding to a one-sector economy — the line to the right of the $(p_S/p_M)_A$ curve. In the long run, the short-term losses for labor will be reversed, as the steady state value of the real wage under free trade (at point F) is above the steady state value of the wage under autarky (at point A).

What happens in the case in which the capital endowment is below k^{**}? The answer depends on whether the capital endowment is above or below k^*, the capital-labor ratio at the intersection of the w^* curve and the free trade line. If the capital endowment is larger than k^*, the profit rate falls in the short run and capital accumulation slows. However, the economy still remains below the w^* locus. As a result, the capital-labor ratio will continue to increase, with the economy eventually specializing completely in the capital-intensive good and reaching the high-wage level under free trade.

The long-run implications are quite different if the initial capital endowment is less than k^*, the case of a very labor-abundant economy. The wage under free trade is now above the value of w^* corresponding to this level of capital endowment. As a result, the profit rate in the capital-intensive sector falls below the level that is necessary to generate a rate of capital accumulation equal to the rate of growth of the labor force. Over time, the capital stock of this economy will shrink, relative to the size of the labor force, and the economy will tend to completely specialize in the production of the labor-intensive good. Despite the disappearance of the capital-intensive industry, the economy gains from the free trade pattern of specialization: workers, at least, have a permanently higher standard of living than they had under autarky with the initial capital endowment. This is true, however, only compared to the *initial* pretrade situation. If the economy had continued to develop under autarky, it would eventually have reached the steady state value of the wage under autarky — at the intersection of the $(p_S/p_M)_A$ and the w^* curves. This wage rate, under the assumptions of figure 29, is higher than the one the economy can generate with full specialization in the labor-intensive, CRS industry.

We have here a case in which there are static gains from opening to trade, and yet free trade with specialization in the labor-intensive, CRS industry prevents in the long run the achievement of the higher wage rates that would result from a continued expansion of the capital-intensive, IRS industry. More precisely, we have a case of multiple patterns of specialization under free trade, corresponding to low- and high-wage long-run equilibria with, in between, a critical capital endowment (k^*), which the economy needs to achieve in order to eventually specialize in the capital-intensive, IRS industry.

Infant Industry Protection

Can this labor-abundant economy, with a capital endowment below k^*, do better than either opening up to free trade or remaining under autarky? It can, and this is the essence of the infant industry argument. Suppose the economy has a capital endowment (ko) and opens up to trade while protecting, with a tariff, its capital-intensive industry. As is shown in figure 30, the tariff modifies the international price ratio, shifting the horizontal trade line downward from $(p_S/p_M)_{FT}$ to $p_S/p_M(1 + t)$. This lowers the value of the capital-labor ratio below which the M sector tends to shrink (from k^* to k^*_t in the figure). If the tariff is such that it reduces k^*_t below the economy's capital-labor endowment (ko) and not so high as to reduce the product wage below its autarky level, it will put the economy in that range of k values in which labor gains from

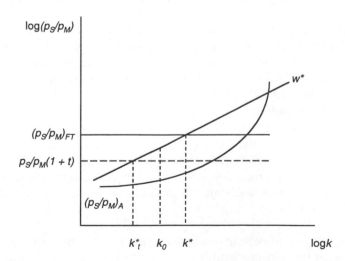

Fig. 30. The infant industry argument

trade while allowing capital accumulation to continue. The economy will then benefit from the static gains from trade — although only partially since the wage rate in the short run will increase less than under free trade — while remaining in a position to exploit the longer term benefits of the continued expansion of its capital-intensive, IRS industry. It is worth noting that this situation provides an argument for temporary protection. When the economy has reached the capital-labor ratio k^*, the capital-intensive industry can survive under free trade and from then on labor would gain in the long run from a reduction in protection.

The case for policy intervention is based on the existence of multiple equilibria, and the conditions for multiple equilibria are similar to those encountered in a closed economy. As noted, the given relative prices in the international economy provide the flat segment of the w curve that is necessary for the k^* intersection to exist. Together with the assumption of constant returns to labor in sector S, these given relative prices make the labor supply to sector M perfectly elastic. The existence of increasing returns in the capital-intensive industry is also a necessary condition (although not a sufficient one, as will be discussed later). If technology displays constant returns in both industries, the w^* locus will be a horizontal line, as is shown in figure 31(a). We will then have two different cases.

1. If the w^* line lies below the free trade line — $(p_S/p_M)_1$ in the figure — free trade is unambiguously superior to both autarky and protection. Then a unique free trade equilibrium with full specialization in the labor-intensive industry yields the highest possible wage rate in the long run.
2. If the w^* line lies above the free trade line, free trade cannot prevent the expansion of the capital-intensive industry. Regardless of how low the capital-labor ratio is, the product wage under free trade remains less than the required wage (w^*). Even if the profit rate falls when the economy opens up to trade — if the capital endowment is below k^{**} in fig. 31 (a) — free trade allows the economy to fully reap the static gains from trade. The wage rate, during the process of expansion of the capital-intensive industry (up to k^{**}), is higher under free trade than under either autarky or protection. There is again a unique free trade equilibrium, in this case with full specialization in the capital-intensive industry.

The argument depends on some form of increasing returns because this is what introduces a wedge between the private and the social costs and benefits of the development of the capital-intensive industry. It is

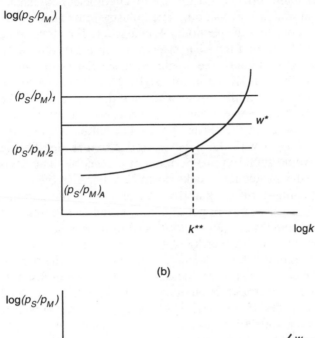

(a)

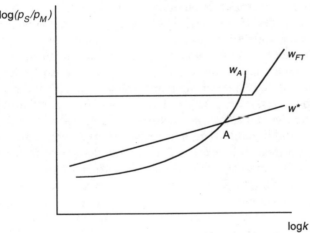

(b)

Fig. 31. Exceptions to the infant industry argument

because the industry generates external effects — in the form of, for example, learning by doing — that free market forces do not guarantee its development. Yet, the existence of technological externalities is not sufficient to warrant protection.[5] The industry must have enough potential, for suppose that the economy's savings rate is so low, or labor force growth is so high, that the highest wage it can achieve under autarky is below the wage under free trade with specialization in the labor-intensive good, as is shown in fig. 31(b). It is then possible, even with full specialization in the M sector, that the survival of the capital-intensive industry would require a wage lower than can be achieved under free trade. In this case, the w^* line, although upward sloping, does not intersect with the w curve under free trade. The survival of sector M would then require permanent protection. The argument for infant industry protection breaks down here because the economy does not have a long-term comparative advantage in the capital-intensive industry. This case is analogous to the one in the Rosenstein-Rodan/Hirschman model when the size of the labor force is so small that industrialization is not viable (see fig. 23[a] in chap. 5).

More generally, for protection to be warranted the industry should be able to meet the Mill-Bastable criterion: the present discounted value of the social costs of protection must be less than the discounted value of the social benefits. If we interpret these costs and benefits as losses and gains to labor, the Mill-Bastable criterion implies that the present discounted value of the costs — due to the lower wages during the period of protection compared to those under free trade — must be less than the present discounted value of the gains, associated with the higher wages the economy generates once it has a comparative advantage in the capital-intensive industry. Two factors play a major role in determining these costs and benefits. The first is the extent to which the economy's capital endowment is below k^*, that is, how far away the current factor endowment is from that required for the protected industry to survive under free trade. This critically affects the size of the costs of protection: in a labor-abundant economy, the costs of protecting a modern aircraft industry may be much larger than the costs of protecting a less capital-intensive textile industry. The second factor is the extent to which the free trade line is below the high-wage equilibrium. This determines how much of a long-term comparative advantage the economy has in the protected industry and thus the value of the benefits from the temporary period of protection.

In our model with two goods, in which the benefits (or costs) from specialization in the IRS industry are permanent while the losses from protection during the transition to the steady state are temporary, the conditions of the Mill-Bastable test will be fulfilled (assuming a zero social discount rate) if the long-term benefits from the expansion of the IRS industry are positive. That is, the test revolves around whether the w^* line intersects the w curve twice under free trade (as in fig. 29) or whether there is no intersection (as in figure 31[b]), that is, whether the conditions for the existence of multiple equilibria are fulfilled or not.

Different Rates of Technical Progress

The small open economy considered so far faces not only *exogenous* but *constant* international prices. The main purpose of this section is to discuss how our previous analysis is modified when the given terms of trade are no longer constant. For simplicity, we now neglect capital accumulation and assume that the economy consists of two labor-intensive sectors.

Two goods are produced with labor under constant returns:

$$Y_1 = h_1 L_1 \quad Y_2 = h_2 L_2,$$

where Y_1 and Y_2 are output levels and h_1 and h_2 are productivity levels, which initially will be taken as given. The total force is fully employed, and a uniform wage rate (w) prevails in the two sectors.

The demand functions for the two goods are derived from a Cobb-Douglas utility function. We can express real income per worker (y) as:

$$y = w/(p_1^{\alpha} p_2^{1-\alpha}), \tag{8}$$

where p_1 and p_2 are the prices of the two goods, and α and $(1 - \alpha)$ are the constant expenditure shares of goods 1 and 2, respectively.

In a closed economy, the two goods are exchanged according to labor input per unit of output. The relative price ratio is thus inversely proportional to the ratio of labor productivities:

$$(p_1/p_2)_A = h_2/h_1, \tag{9}$$

where A refers to the autarkic economy. Suppose that, at the time when this economy opens up to international trade, good 1 is more expensive in the international market than in the local economy under autarky: $(p_1/p_2)_{FT} > (p_1/p_2)_A$, where $(p_1/p_2)_{FT}$ is the relative price ratio prevailing in the international market. The economy has a comparative advantage in sector 1, and under free trade it will fully specialize in the production of good 1 while importing good 2 at the cheaper relative price prevailing abroad. Real incomes will increase as a result. Indeed, using equation 1 and the fact that $w/p_1 = h_1$ in equilibrium (in the open as well as the closed economy), the ratio of real incomes (y_{FT}/y_A) is proportional to the relative price ratios:

$$y_{FT}/y_A = [(p_1/p_2)_{FT}/(p_1/p_2)_A]^{1-\alpha}.$$

Since $(p_1/p_2)_{FT} > (p_1/p_2)_A$, $y_{FT} > y_A$ and the extent to which real income increases is larger: (1) the lower the relative price of the imported good will be (compared to its relative price under autarky); and (2) the larger the fraction of income consumed in the imported commodity will be $(1 - \alpha)$.

The Static Gains from Trade under Increasing Returns

It is worth noting that the static gains from trade are larger in the presence of increasing returns in sector 1 because in that case the expansion of the scale of sector 1 causes productivity gains that are in addition to the more conventional gain from trade arising from the reallocation toward activities with a comparative advantage. Suppose, indeed, that production conditions in sector 1 are described by $Y_1 = L_1^{1+\mu}$ so that labor productivity, $h_1 (= L_1^{\mu})$, increases with employment. Labor productivity is then $L_1^{\mu} = (\alpha L)^{\mu}$ before trade, and equal to L^{μ} after the opening to trade, since sector 1 then employs the whole labor force (L). The ratio of real incomes (y_{FT}/y_A) after and before trade is now:

$$y_{FT}/y_A = (1/\alpha)^{\mu}[(p_1/p_2)_{FT}/(p_1/p_2)_A]^{1-\alpha},$$

which shows that even in the absence of differences in the relative price ratios between the local economy and the international market (i.e., with $p_1/p_{2FT} = p_1/p_{2A}$) free trade brings about gains from specialization that result from the presence of increasing returns. It has long been recognized that these gains from specialization (given by $[1/\alpha]^{\mu}$ when the relative price ratios are the same) may be larger than the more conventional gain from trade. John Stuart Mill, in *Principles of Political Economy* (1848, 99), commented on these gains as follows:

> But there are, besides, indirect effects, which must be counted as benefits of a higher order. One is the tendency of every extension of the market to improve the processes of production. A country which produces for a larger market than its own, can introduce a more extended division of labor, can make greater use of machinery, and is more likely to make inventions and improvements in the processes of production. Whatever causes a greater quantity of any-

thing to be produced in the same place tends to the general increase of the productive powers of the world.

These benefits from trade will be of "a higher order," especially if the relative price structures of the small home economy and the rest of the world were very similar before trade, so that $(p_1/p_2)_A/(p_1/p_2)_{FT}$ was close to unity. In fact, if differences in relative prices were negligible, the *only* benefits from trade would be the gains from specialization associated with the presence of economies of scale.[6]

Dynamic Benefits from Trade

Suppose now that productivity grows over time in both sectors at rates ρ_1 and ρ_2. Using equations 8 and 9, we can express the growth of real incomes on the closed economy path $(\hat{y}_A)$, as a weighted average of ρ_1 and ρ_2:

$$\hat{y}_A = \alpha\rho_1 + (1 - \alpha)\rho_2 = \rho_1 + (1 - \alpha)(\rho_2 - \rho_1). \qquad (10)$$

Assume that productivity in sector 2 grows at a faster rate than productivity in sector 1. To link this to our previous discussion of the infant industry argument, assume that ρ_1 is less than ρ_2 and both productivity growth rates are determined by the presence of increasing returns in sectors 1 and 2, together with labor force growth.[7] We continue to assume that when it opens up to trade the economy has a comparative advantage in sector 1, given the pretrade structure of relative prices. The economy thus specializes in the technologically less progressive sector, giving up its increasing returns industry. Its productivity growth (ρ_1) will be less than it had been previously (and would have continued to be on the closed economy path).

Does this mean that over time the initial static gains from trade will be lost and real incomes in the long run would have been higher under autarky? This is exactly what happened in one of the examples discussed in section 1. There, however, we adopted the assumption that the terms of trade would remain constant, an assumption that is unlikely to hold if productivity growth rates in the two sectors are also different in the rest of the world. If the home economy is too small to influence foreign prices, the terms of trade will move with the ratio of sectoral productivities in the rest of the world (just as in the autarkic economy according to eq. 9). The growth of real incomes under trade will thus be equal to ρ_1 plus any gains (or minus any losses) arising from the evolution of the relative price of the imported commodity:

$$\hat{y}_{FT} = \rho_1 + (1 - \alpha)(\rho^*_2 - \rho^*_1), \tag{11}$$

where ρ^*_1 and ρ^*_2 are the productivity growth rates in sectors 1 and 2 in the rest of the world. A comparison of equations 10 and 11 shows that real income in the trading economy will grow faster than in the closed economy ($\hat{y}_{FT} > \hat{y}_A$) if:

$$\rho^*_2 - \rho^*_1 > \rho_2 - \rho_1. \tag{12}$$

The condition expressed by inequality 12 shows that, even if the economy specializes in the less technologically dynamic sector 1, real incomes grow faster under trade than under autarky provided that the dynamic benefits from the evolution of the international terms of trade ($\rho^*_2 - \rho^*_1$) are larger than the dynamic losses from having specialized in the sector with the lower domestic productivity growth rate ($\rho_2 - \rho_1$). In the example in which sector 1 operates under constant returns and does not have any exogenous productivity growth ($\rho^*_1 = \rho_1 = 0$), real incomes grow faster under trade if $\rho^*_2 > \rho_2$, that is, if the rest of the world has a higher productivity growth rate in sector 2 than does the home economy.

Inequality 12 makes it clear that, for the assessment of the dynamic gains from trade, the relevant comparison not only involves the productivity growth rates in the two sectors within the domestic economy but also the productivity growth differential in the rest of the world. Rearranging inequality 12, the condition reads: $\rho_1 - \rho_2 > \rho^*_1 - \rho^*_2$. The static comparative advantage of the economy (specialization in sector 1) coincides with its long-term advantage if the economy specializes in the sector having the *comparatively largest potential rate of productivity growth*. Pasinetti (1981, 274) stated that

> in order to obtain the highest possible gains from international trade, a country should specialise in producing those commodities for which it can achieve, over the relevant period of time, the highest comparative rates of growth of productivity.

Figure 32 shows on the vertical axis of the growth of productivity under trade (ρ_1, which is equal to the growth of output when the labor force is constant) and, on the horizontal axis, the rate of change of the international terms of trade (measured as $\rho^*_1 - \rho^*_2$, so that the farther we move to the right along the horizontal axis the more adversely the terms of trade move against the home economy). The vertical axis at $\rho^*_1 - \rho^*_2 = 0$ divides the figure into two regions: one of rising terms of trade (to the left of the vertical axis) and one of falling terms of trade (to the right). The line $\hat{y}_{FT} = \hat{y}_A$ is a locus along which the dynamic benefits of trade are nil: the

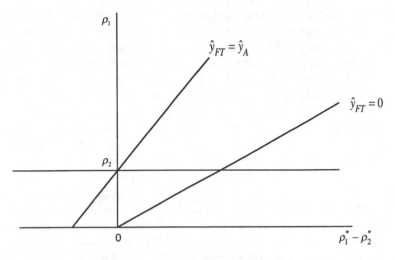

Fig. 32. Terms of trade and dynamic gains from trade

"indirect" benefits (or losses) from the evolution of the international terms of trade exactly compensate for the "direct" losses (or gains) from specializing in sector 1 rather than sector 2. The line slopes upward: the lower the productivity growth of the sector in which the home economy specializes the faster the terms of trade have to increase in favor of the home economy to keep losses and benefits in balance. The line crosses the vertical axis at ρ_2 (the productivity growth rate of sector 2 on the closed economy path). Indeed, if the terms of trade remain constant, trade brings no dynamic benefits or losses when $\rho_1 = \rho_2$. The line $\hat{y}_{FT} = \hat{y}_A$ divides the figure into two regions: above the line the dynamic benefits from trade are positive ($\hat{y}_{FT} > \hat{y}_A$) — since the terms of trade move more favorably than required for $\hat{y}_{FT} = \hat{y}_A$ — and below the line there are dynamic losses. The equation of the line is obtained from equations 10 and 11. As is readily verified, the slope of the line is equal to unity and the intercept equal to ρ_2.

The figure also shows the line $\hat{y}_{FT} = 0$, along which real incomes in the trading economy are constant. Using equation 11, it is easily seen that this line passes through the origin and has a slope equal to $(1 - \alpha)$. The line slopes upward since the more adverse the movement in the terms of trade the faster productivity must grow to keep real incomes constant. It follows that the region above the line is one of rising real incomes, while below, for positive values of ρ_1, there is a region of "immiserizing growth" in the sense that real incomes fall while output volume increases. It is worth noting that the immiserizing growth taking place here is different from the conventional notion (see Bhagwati 1958). This notion refers to the case of an economy exporting a good with inelastic demand and for which it is a large producer in world markets. Growth can be immiserizing in the sense that output growth causes such a large decline in the terms of trade that real incomes fall despite the increase in output. In the region below $\hat{y}_{FT} = 0$, growth is not immiserizing in this sense. It is the *exogenous* and adverse movement of the terms of trade that causes real incomes to fall while the growth of output in itself has no effect on the terms of trade. The fall in real income is the result of a "wrong choice" of specialization, as we shall see, rather than of growth causing the terms of trade to fall.

The figure helps illustrate a number of simple implications of the previous analysis (we confine ourselves to configurations for which both ρ_1 and ρ_2 are positive). First, with constant terms of trade, the dynamic benefits from trade can only be positive if the economy specializes in the sector that domestically has the highest rate of productivity growth. Indeed, with $\rho^*_1 = \rho^*_2$ (along the vertical axis), $\hat{y}_{FT}$ is larger than $\hat{y}_A$ if and only if ρ_1 is higher than ρ_2. If we say that the economy has an absolute dynamic advantage in the sector that has the highest rate of productivity growth domestically, then—in a way analogous to the analysis of the previous section—the absolute and comparative dynamic advantages of the economy coincide when the terms of trade remain constant.

Specialization in the dynamic industry ($\rho_1 > \rho_2$, i.e., specialization according to absolute dynamic advantage) is consistent with dynamic losses from trade: the whole region above the horizontal line at ρ_2 and below the line $\hat{y}_{FT} = \hat{y}_A$ features this combination. For this to happen, the terms of trade must fall. This, of course, is what happens when the rest of the world has a dynamic comparative advantage in the sector in which the home economy has specialized. Similarly, the region below the horizontal line at ρ_2 and above the line $\hat{y}_{FT} = \hat{y}_A$ is one of specialization in the less dynamic sector ($\rho_1 < \rho_2$) but with dynamic benefits from trade. This combination requires that the terms of trade increase in favor of the home economy and increase more the lower the productivity growth rate in the sector in which the home economy has specialized.

The region of immiserizing growth below the line $\hat{y}_{FT} = 0$ is inside the region below the line $\hat{y}_{FT} = \hat{y}_A$. The implication of this is that, under our present assumptions of exogenous terms of trade and positive rates of productivity growth on the closed economy path, immiserizing growth can only arise as a result of dynamic losses from trade and therefore from a "wrong choice" of specialization. This wrong choice may involve specialization according to absolute dynamic advantage or disadvantage, although the latter case requires larger adverse movements in the terms of trade.

Terms of Trade and Uneven Development

"Why does a man growing cocoa earn one tenth of the wage of a man making steel ingots?" asked Arthur Lewis in his Wicksell lectures (1969). The answer that one might be inclined to give would involve looking at the capital endowment per worker as well as the general levels of technology in the cocoa- and steel-producing countries. Thinking of the world economy as comprising two regions trading cocoa and steel, and producing in common a third good, Lewis's answer was highly original and surprising: the productivity conditions in the cocoa- and steel-producing sectors are irrelevant in explaining the wage gap between the two regions. Only the relative productivity levels in the production of the common third good matter.

A couple of decades earlier, Prebisch (United Nations 1950) identified an important problem and asked a similar question. He observed that the Center (or North) of the world economy had grown rich on the basis of rapid technological improvements, but that these improvements had not benefited the periphery (or South) of the world economy to the same extent. Why was it that these productivity gains in the Center had failed to raise the living standards in the South in the form of terms of trade improvements for the periphery? Prebisch also argued that the periphery's terms of trade had in fact been falling, an argument that became known as the Prebisch-Singer thesis on the terms of trade between industrial products and primary commodities. Later empirical studies have found this argument empirically questionable.[8] However, note that Prebisch's question does not lose its relevance as a result because the important question, in my view, is not why the terms of trade had been falling, if they in fact had, but rather why the rapid technical progress in the North had not been reflected in rapid terms of trade improvements in the South. We now turn to an analysis of these issues and the complementarity that, despite their clear differences, exists between the answers given by Lewis and Prebisch.

Lewis's Model of Tropical Trade

Consider a two-country model with three traded goods.[9] The three goods are produced with a "Ricardian technology" using labor alone under constant returns. Both countries produce food (good S). The other two goods (steel and cocoa), which we denote with M and N, are produced in countries 1 and 2, respectively. Output levels and technology are thus described by:

$$S_1 = h_1 L_{S1} \quad M = q_1 L_M$$

$$S_2 = h_2 L_{S2} \quad N = q_2 L_N.$$

A uniform wage rate is assumed to prevail within each country. Measured in terms of food, this wage (w_i/p_S) is equal to the average product of labor (h_i) in the food-producing sector. Thus:

$$w_1/p_S = h_1 \quad w_2/p_S = h_2. \tag{13}$$

In addition, the product wage in sectors M and N must be equal to the average product of labor (q_i) in these sectors:

$$w_1/p_M = q_1 \quad w_2/p_N = q_2. \tag{14}$$

From equations 13 and 14, it is clear that with two countries and three goods — one of which is produced in both countries — relative wages and terms of trade must fulfill two equilibrium conditions. First, given food price equalization, relative wages must be equal to the ratio of the average products of labor in food production. From equation 13, we have:

$$w_1/w_2 = h_1/h_2. \tag{15}$$

We shall refer to equation 15 as the relative wages curve. This is the horizontal line in figure 33. Second, relative wages must be equal to the ratio of the value of average products of labor in sectors M and N. From equation 14, we get:

$$w_1/w_2 = (q_1/q_2)(p_M/p_N). \tag{16}$$

We shall refer to equation 16 as the terms of trade curve. In figure 33, this is a ray from the origin with slope equal to (q_1/q_2). Clearly, in this setting Lewis's question has a simple answer. Since the price of food is the same in both countries, the equality between the wage and the value of the average product of labor in the S sector implies that the ratio of wage rates in equilibrium must be equal to the ratio of productivities in food production (eq. 15). An increase in productivity in sector S_1 raises the wage in terms of food in country 1. In country 2, the price of food

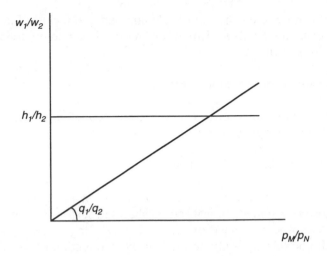

Fig. 33. Relative wages and terms of trade with Ricardian technology

in terms of labor is unchanged, since this only depends on productivity conditions in sector S_2. The wage rate in country 1 relative to that in country 2 must therefore increase. Relative wages are rigidly tied to productivities in the S sectors, and since these are exogenous no other factors, including demand and productivity conditions in sectors M and N, can affect relative wage levels.

This has another consequence. Since changes in the relative productivities of sectors M and N leave relative wages unaffected, it must be the case that compensating changes in the terms of trade (p_M/p_N) take place. As Lewis states it in his explanation of why the wage of a cocoa producer in one country is so much lower than the wage of the steel worker in another:

> Each of these two men has the alternative of growing food. Their relative incomes are therefore determined by their relative productivities in growing food; and the relative prices of steel and cocoa are determined by these relative incomes and by productivities in steel and cocoa. (1969, 17)

This is also the basis for the explanation in <u>Lewis 1954</u> of "<u>why tropical produce is so cheap</u>" and of his policy recommendation that productivity growth be enhanced in the food-producing sectors of the tropical countries rather than in commercial agriculture (sector N).[10] The implication for Prebisch's question is clear: productivity growth in sector M can leave the terms of trade unaffected if technical progress in the North is more balanced between the food and commercial sectors than in the periphery.

An Extension in the Direction of Prebisch

We now assume that goods M and N are produced in capitalist sectors using a Cobb-Douglas technology:

$$M = A_1 K_1^a L_M^{1-a} \quad N = A_2 K_2^a L_N^{1-a},$$

where K and L are capital and labor inputs in each sector and, for simplicity, we assume identical capital shares in sectors M and N. Goods M and N can be consumed or invested. Technology is such that, when invested, good M can only be used in the production of M. The same applies to good N, which can only be used in the production of N. Thus, even though there is international trade in all three goods, there is no trade in capital goods, since there is no use for good M as a capital good in country 2, and likewise for good N in country 1. Under these assumptions, and neglecting savings out of wages, the equality of savings and investment in each country (or the balanced trade condition) implies that:

$$p_M(M - C_M) = s_1 p_M M \quad p_N(N - C_N) = s_2 p_N N, \tag{17}$$

where p and C refer to the prices and consumption levels of each good (consumed locally or abroad) and s refers to the product of the propensities to save out of profits in each country and the profit share in sectors M and N in the competitive equilibrium (equal to a, from the Cobb-Douglas specification of technology).

Since production conditions in the food-producing sectors are assumed to remain the same, the relative wages curve is still the horizontal line at (h_1/h_2). The terms of trade curve is modified because now demand conditions will enter into the determination of the terms of trade. Indeed, from the first-order conditions for profit maximization in sectors M and N, the relative output supply functions of M and N are such that:

$$M/N = A_1^{1/a} K_1 (p_M/w_1)^{(1-a)/a} / A_2^{1/a} K_2 (p_N/w_2)^{(1-a)/a}. \tag{18}$$

Assume a unit elasticity of substitution in consumption between N and M goods:[11]

$$C_M/C_N = B p_N/p_M. \tag{19}$$

Together with equation 17, equation 19 allows us to express the terms of trade between N and M goods as:

$$p_M/p_N = DN/M, \tag{20}$$

where $D = B(1 - s_2)/(1 - s_1)$. Substituting from equation 18 into 20 and solving for the terms of trade gives:

$$p_M/p_N = D^a(w_1/w_2)^{1-a}(A_2/A_1)(K_2/K_1)^a. \tag{21}$$

Equation 21 shows the terms of trade between M and N goods as an increasing function of relative wages. It defines the terms of trade curve shown in figure 34 as the upward-sloping curve (p_M/p_N). Given production and demand conditions in sectors M and N, an increase in relative wages in country 1 increases the relative costs in sector M and thus raises the price of M relative to N goods. The horizontal line at (h_1/h_2) shows, as before, relative wages (w_1/w_2) as determined by relative productivities in food production. The equilibrium terms of trade are determined at the intersection of this line and the terms of trade curve.

Consider in this setting the effects of capital accumulation and technical progress in sector M. In both cases (an increase in either K_1 or A_1), the effect is to shift the terms of trade curve inward and increase the relative price (p_N/p_M) of good N while relative wages remain constant. The effects of technical progress and capital accumulation in sector N are symmetrical. Any of these changes leaves relative wages unaffected. For this reason, and given that a technological improvement in, say, sector M raises wages in country 1 relative to M goods, the same must happen with wages in country 2. Wages in both countries increase in the same proportion (in terms of M goods). The benefits of the expansion of the capitalist sectors in both countries, though not equalizing, are nevertheless evenly spread.[12]

This is the case under the type of technical progress and demand conditions assumed so far, for suppose that technical progress in sector M shifts the demand parameter B in such a way as to reduce the demand for imports from country 2. One such case, the substitution of synthetic for natural products, was a common reference in the literature on the Prebisch-Singer thesis on the terms of trade. The resulting increase in the parameter D in equation 21 tends to shift the terms of trade curve outward and thus to concentrate the gains of technical progress in sector M rather than disseminating them through a lower relative price for M goods. More generally, if goods M and N face different income elasticities of demand (lower for N than for M), there will be a bias in the distribution of the gains from the expansion of sectors M and N in favor

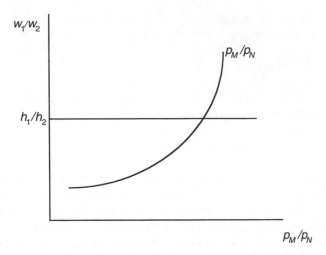

Fig. 34. **Relative wages and terms of trade with capitalistic techniques in the two sectors**

of M producers. This is because the difference in income elasticities of demand will tend to produce an unfavorable evolution of the terms of trade for N goods.

Yet, even in these cases, the adverse movements in the terms of trade do not worsen the wage gap between the two countries. Only relative productivities in the food-producing sectors can enlarge or reduce the gap in labor incomes. This is because the determination of relative wages and terms of trade is not simultaneous: relative wages affect the terms of trade between M and N goods but not the other way around. We now turn to examining circumstances under which changes in the terms of trade due to different demand conditions, capital accumulation, and technical progress outside food production may not leave relative wages unaffected.

Uneven Development: A Prebisch-Lewis Model

We now relax the key assumption that relative productivities in food production are exogenously given. Assume, then, that production conditions in sector S are given by:

$$S_1 = f_1 L_{S1}^{1-b} \quad S_2 = f_2 L_{S2}^{1-b} \quad b \leq 1,$$

where f_1 and f_2 reflect the effects of technology and land endowment on food production. For simplicity, we assume the returns to labor parameter $(1 - b)$ to be the same in both countries. We continue to assume that food production takes place in noncapitalist sectors where labor earns the average product of labor. The equality between the product wage and the average product of labor in sector S in each country implies that:

$$w_1/w_2 = (f_1/f_2)(L_{S2}/L_{S1})^b. \tag{22}$$

The ratio (L_{S2}/L_{S1}) is determined by the demand for labor in sectors M and N and the full employment conditions in each country:

$$(L_{S2}/L_{S1}) = [L_2 - L_N(w_2/p_N, K_2, A_2)]/[(L_1 - L_M(w_1/p_M, K_1, A_1)], \tag{23}$$

where: $L_{N1} < 0,\ L_{N2},\ L_{N3} > 0$ and $L_{M1} < 0,\ L_{M2},\ L_{M3} > 0.$

Equations 22 and 23 define a relative wages curve that is now upward sloping (see fig. 35). The intuition behind this is as follows: an increase in p_M (given p_N) increases labor demand in sector M. Labor market equilibrium in country 1 requires employment in S_1 to fall and thus causes w_1/p_S to increase (due to diminishing returns to labor in sector S). At the same time, employment in S_2 must increase to clear the food market. The increase in p_M thus requires (L_{S2}/L_{S1}) to increase and relative wages (w_1/w_2) to rise.

The terms of trade curve remains determined by equation 21. As is shown in figure 35, the relative wage gap and the terms of trade are now simultaneously determined at the intersection of the two curves. This has some novel implications. Consider the effects of an increase in demand parameter B, which shifts the terms of trade curve outward. As was seen earlier, the relative price of M goods (p_M/p_N) increases. Now, rather than remaining constant, relative wages (w_1/w_2) also increase along the upward-sloping relative wages curve. The mechanisms involved in the change in the terms of trade explain why relative wages have to move in the same direction. The shift in demand toward M goods and away from N goods reduces employment in S_1 and increases it in S_2. As a result, the ratio of labor productivities in food production rises and the gap in relative wages (w_1/w_2) increases.

Consider now the effects of capital accumulation in the Center.[13] Suppose that this is country 1. The expansion of the capital stock in sector M has two effects on relative wages. As before, the increase in the relative supply of M goods tends to reduce the relative price p_M/p_N (at each level of relative wages). This shifts the terms of trade curve inward and tends to narrow the relative wage gap since relative wages fall along the relative wages curve. This is the equalizing effect of the expansion of the Center. In addition, there is a labor force transfer from S_1 to M that

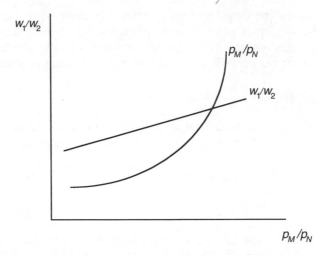

Fig. 35. Relative wages and terms of trade in a Prebisch-Lewis model

now raises the average product of labor in food production. This effect shifts the relative wages curve upward and turns relative wages in favor of country 1 (note that the position of the relative wages curve depends on K_1 in such a way that an increase in K_1 raises $[L_{S2}/L_{S1}]$ and thus shifts $[w_1/w_2]$ upward, given the values of other variables). Can this un-equalizing effect offset the former effect so that the relative wage gap increases when capital accumulation takes place in country 1?

Using the equality between the product wage and the average product of labor in sector S together with the labor demand functions in sectors M and N, we can solve for the (log) change in the terms of trade:

$$\mathrm{dlog}p_M/p_N = -a\mathrm{dlog}K_1 + [(1 + F)/F]\mathrm{dlog}w_1/p_S$$

$$-\{[(1 + bL_N/aL_{S2})]/F]\}\mathrm{dlog}w_2/p_S, \tag{24}$$

where $F = bL_M/aL_{S1}$ and we have held constant, as a first approximation, the price of N goods in terms of food (so that $\mathrm{dlog}p_S/p_N = 0$).

Taking logs in equation 21 and differentiating give us:

$$\mathrm{dlog}p_M/p_N = (1 - a)\mathrm{dlog}w_1/w_2 - [a/(1 - a)]\mathrm{dlog}K_1. \tag{25}$$

Substituting from equation 25 into 24 and solving for $\mathrm{dlog}w_1/w_2$, we obtain:

$$\text{dlog} w_1/w_2 = [aF/(1/a + F)]\text{dlog} K_1 + [b/a(1 + aF)](L_M/L_{S1}$$

$$-L_N/L_{S2})\text{dlog} p_S/w_2.$$

Two effects are involved in the change in relative wages. The first is the "direct effect" of capital accumulation (the first term in the RHS). This effect is unambiguously positive, and its strength depends on F and therefore on the employment share of the M sector in country 1. Since the effects of capital accumulation in country 2 are symmetrical, the implication is that the country with the largest fraction of the labor force in the capitalist sector will tend to "appropriate" the benefits of its own expansion to a larger degree.

The second term in the RHS is affected by the change in the price of food in terms of labor in country 2, $\text{dlog}(p_S/w_2)$. This change is clearly positive: the reduction in agricultural employment in country 1 tends to create excess demand for food, and the clearing of the food market will require a compensating expansion of agricultural employment in country 2. In the face of diminishing returns to labor, the average product of labor in country 2 falls. The sign of this effect depends, then, on whether $(L_M/L_{S1} - L_N/L_{S2})$ is positive or negative. When the expansion takes place in the Center, where most of the labor force is employed in the capitalist sector, the effect will be positive: the reason is that the compensating expansion of employment in S_2 will not increase the wage in terms of N goods and increase the terms of trade for country 2 significantly. The positive effect of capital accumulation on relative wages then tends to be reinforced by a positive (or less negative) effect on the terms of trade for M goods. In contrast, the expansion of sector N on the periphery will generate a compensating expansion of agricultural employment in country 1, which tends to improve the terms of trade for country 1 and tends to offset the improvement in relative wages for country 2.

The analysis shows that with relative productivities in food production endogenously determined the explanation of the large wage differences between developing and developed economies depends, after all, on the capital and labor endowments in these two types of countries. This is all the more true when we take into account the nontraded goods sector. The labor intensity of this sector mirrors the abundance of labor in the economy as a whole. Lewis's reasoning applies here, too: the man growing cocoa has the alternative of working in the nontraded goods sectors, where low wages prevail given the labor intensity of these sectors. To the extent that the nontraded sector provides an elastic supply of labor, the productivity improvements in the export sectors of the periphery will benefit the Center to a larger extent than the productivity gains in the Center benefit the periphery.

Thus, our analysis has some affinity with Prebisch's emphasis on the relative tightness of labor markets in developed and developing countries as a third factor, besides differences in income elasticities of demand and biased technical progress, affecting the evolution of relative incomes and the terms of trade between the two regions. The differences in factor endowments can determine large productivity gaps in food production, and in this sense the analysis is also consistent with the mechanism identified by Lewis as one of the proximate sources of the real wage differences observed.[14]

APPENDIX

The Gains from Trade under Diminishing to Labor in the Traditional Sector

In this section, we consider the analysis of the gains from trade under the more general assumption of diminishing returns to labor in sector S. Suppose, then, that production conditions in sector S are described by:

$$S = L_S^{1-b} \quad 0 < b < 1, \tag{A.1}$$

where S is output and L is employment. As in the text, labor in sector S earns the value of the average product of labor, so that:

$$w = p_S L_S^{-b}, \tag{A.2}$$

where w is the uniform wage rate and p_S the price of good S. Dividing both sides of equation A.2 by p_M, the price of good M, we have:

$$w/p_M = (p_S/p_M)L_S^{-b}. \tag{A.3}$$

We assume Cobb-Douglas demand functions, so that the real wage (w/p) is given by:

$$w/p = w/(p_S^{\alpha} p_M^{1-\alpha}) = (w/p_S)^{\alpha}(w/p_M)^{1-\alpha}, \tag{A.4}$$

where α and $(1 - \alpha)$ are, respectively, the expenditure shares of S and M goods. Substituting now from equations A.2 and A.3 into A.4:

$$w/p = (p_S/p_M)^{1-\alpha}L_S^{-b}. \tag{A.5}$$

Taking logs in equation A.5 and differentiating, we can express the (log) change in the real wage as the sum of two components:

$$\text{dlog}(w/p) = (1 - \alpha)\text{dlog}(p_S/p_M) - b\text{dlog}L_S. \tag{A.6}$$

In the relatively labor-abundant economy with a capital endowment below k^{**} (see the second section), the opening to trade brings about an increase in the relative price (p_S/p_M) and a corresponding gain from trade that is proportional to the expenditure share of the imported good (M in this case). This is the first component of the gain from trade measured in terms of the change in the real wage: $(1 - \alpha)\text{dlog}(p_S/p_M)$. The opening to trade also brings about an increase in employment in sector S, which gives rise to the second component in equation A.6. If returns to labor in sector S were constant ($b = 0$), as was assumed in the second section, the second component in equation A.6 vanishes and the first is the only effect of trade. With diminishing returns to labor ($b > 0$), however, the change in the real wage is reduced by the fact that the expansion of sector S under trade brings about a decline in the productivity of this sector. The intensity of this effect can be derived from the labor demand function in sector M and the full employment condition. With a Cobb-Douglas production function in sector M, this turns out to be:

$$\text{dlog}L_S = [(L_M/L_S)/(a + bL_M/L_S)]\text{dlog}(p_S/p_M), \tag{A.7}$$

where a is the capital share. Substituting from equation A.7 into A.6, the change in the real wage is given by:

$$\text{dlog}(w/p) = [(1 - \alpha) - (bL_M/L_S)/(a + bL_M/L_S)]\text{dlog}(p_S/p_M). \tag{A.8}$$

The change in the real wage, following the opening to trade, turns out to be positive or negative depending on whether the expenditure share of S goods (α) is less or more than $1/[1 + (b/a)L_M/L_S]$. The condition for an increase in the real wage is unambiguously fulfilled in the case of constant returns in sector S ($b = 0$, since α is less than 1). But, with a positive value of b, a small capital share — a labor-intensive M sector so that the increase in the product wage there generates a large decline in employment — may, together with a large expenditure share on S goods, turn the static gains from trade into losses.

CHAPTER 8

Natural Resources, the Dutch Disease, and the Staples Thesis

Does the abundance of natural resources promote or hinder industrialization in an *open economy*? I emphasize *open economy,* as it is only in this context that the most disparate answers have been given to this question. The notion that specialization in resource-intensive goods can be harmful to growth is present in the Prebisch-Singer thesis on the terms of trade for primary commodities and in Bhagwati's model of immiserizing growth. In the literature on the "Dutch disease," a natural resource boom comes close to being a curse. The term *Dutch disease* refers to the adverse effects on manufacturing industries that took place in the Netherlands with the natural gas discoveries of the 1970s and the process of real currency appreciation that followed. Similar "illnesses" affected several oil-exporting countries following the oil price shocks of the 1970s, providing further motivation to a growing literature on the subject.[1]

In contrast, in Hla Myint's (1958) "vent for surplus" approach to trade and development, the opening to trade can provide an outlet for labor and natural resources that were previously underemployed. In this rehabilitation of Adam Smith's views on international trade, the welfare improvements resulting from the expansion of primary exports and the mobilization of previously idle resources are not only beneficial to development but can be much more significant than the Ricardian gains from trade arising from a reallocation of given and previously fully employed resources. Similarly, in the "staples thesis," which originated in the work of Canadian historians, exports of resource-intensive goods (staples) can turn into an engine of growth and transformation. This is an anti–Dutch disease approach in which industrialization is driven by a succession of natural resource discoveries. Against a background of a buoyant world demand for primary commodities and substantial inflows of labor and capital, these exports can lead to a rapid expansion of manufacturing industries and transportation networks, especially if the sectors for primary goods have important domestic linkages. Not surprisingly, Hirschman (1977) found a close affinity between the staples thesis and his own "linkage approach" to development.

Each of these views emphasizes particular mechanisms through which primary exports may help or hurt industrialization. The list is not exhaustive: other political economy considerations and noneconomic mechanisms may also play a role in a full answer to the question.[2] This chapter focuses on economic mechanisms and provides a selective analytical survey of these different approaches. The final section makes an attempt to reconcile them.

On Graham's Paradox

We begin with Graham's paradox. In a celebrated and controversial article, Graham (1923) argued that increasing returns to scale can justify protection. We here focus on another aspect of Graham's discussion. After analyzing a number of examples of two-sector economies featuring increasing costs in the production of one good (wheat) and diminishing costs in the production of the other (watches), Graham noted that:

> The principle just laid down may go far to explain why regions of slender natural resources devoted to manufactures often surpass in prosperity regions of much greater natural resources where extractive industry prevails, tho no great difference exists in native ability of their respective populations. (215)

Graham illustrated his argument with a reference to the prosperous manufacturing East versus the West of the United States at the time when the latter specialized in primary activities. Let us turn to a simple model that reproduces Graham's views, noting that one may find a number of other examples of this paradox in the postwar development experience of the resource-poor manufacturing exporters of Asia in the East and the less prosperous, resource-rich Latin American economies in the West.

A Ricardo-Viner-Graham Model

Consider a small open economy with two sectors, agriculture (A) and manufacturing (M), producing tradable goods. Both sectors use labor (L), and there are two specific factors: land (T) in sector A and capital (K) in sector M. Agriculture operates under constant returns to scale, and there are increasing returns to scale in manufacturing. The production functions are:

$$A = BT^b L_A^{1-b} \quad M = (\tilde{K})^\mu K^a L_M^{1-a},$$

where $(\tilde{K})^{\mu}$ is the external effect of the average capital stock. Both goods are consumed, and in addition good M can be invested. Labor is intersectorally mobile. The model is thus a Ricardo-Viner, or "specific factors," model,[3] except for the assumption of increasing returns in sector M, which is the Graham component. This assumption is introduced, for simplicity, in the form of technological externalities.[4]

Employment in both sectors is determined by profit maximization under competitive conditions.[5]

$$L_A = T[B(1-b)/(w/p_A)]^{1/b} = L_A(w/p_A, T)$$

$$L_M = K^{1+\mu/a}[(1-a)/(w/p_M)]^{1/a} = L_M(w/p_M, K).$$

In full employment equilibrium, we have $L=L_A+L_M$, where L is the total labor force. Free trade prevails. With relative prices (p_A/p_M) determined in the world market and the capital stock being given in the short run, these equations determine output and employment levels in the two sectors and the wage in terms of the good chosen as the numeraire. We choose M as the numeraire. The schedule of short-run equilibria (the w curve)—showing the manufacturing product wage as a function of the capital stock—is derived from the employment functions and the full-employment condition:

$$L = L_A(w, p_A, T) + L_M(w, K) \quad L_{A1}, L_{M1} < 0, L_{A2}, L_{A3} > 0, L_{M2} > 0. \quad (1)$$

As usual, the w curve is upward sloping in $(\log K, \log w)$ space. In equilibrium, a larger capital stock generates higher real wages, all other things being equal (including the endowment of natural resources). The position of the curve depends on the natural resource endowment and relative prices. An increase in the relative price of agricultural goods and an increase in the supply of land both shift the w curve upward: given K, both of these factors increase the demand for labor in agriculture. Labor market equilibrium requires a reallocation of labor away from manufacturing, and the wage in manufacturing must rise in order to make this possible. The result is as expected: a greater abundance of natural resources, given other factor endowments, makes the country more prosperous if we take the real wage, as we shall in what follows, as a general indicator of living standards.

However, other factor endowments will not remain constant, at least not the capital endowment, which changes over time, and in the long run equilibrium will be determined endogenously. Assuming a stationary labor force and no exogenous technical progress, the steady state condition simplifies to the equality between the rate of capital accumulation (I/K) and the depreciation rate of the capital stock (δ): $I/K = \delta$. Investment is determined by:

$$I = s_A R + s_M P \tag{2}$$

$$R = R(w, T, p_A) \quad R_1 < 0, R_2, R_3 > 0$$

$$P = r(w, K)K \quad r_1 < 0, r_2 > 0,$$

where we neglect savings out of wages and let s_A and s_M stand for the propensity to save out of agricultural rents (R) and manufacturing profits (P). Substituting from equation 2 into the steady state condition yields the equation of the w^* curve:

$$\delta = s_A \phi(w, T/K, p_A) + s_M r(w, K), \tag{3}$$

where ϕ stands for rents per unit of capital (R/K), a function such that $\phi_1 < 0$, ϕ_2, $\phi_3 > 0$.

The slope of the w^* schedule depends on the propensities to save out of profits and rents (s_M, s_A) and on how returns increase in manufacturing (parameter μ, which affects the profit-wage curve). Without, or with small, savings out of rents, the curve would slope upward due to the effects of increasing returns in manufacturing. Indeed, as the capital stock increases the profit rate increases, given the wage, and thus the value of the wage that yields constant profit and capital accumulation rates increases. With constant returns, this effect would disappear and the schedule would be either horizontal or downward sloping. An increase in the capital stock lowers rents per unit of capital; even with small but positive savings out of rents, this requires a lower wage to restore a given rate of capital accumulation. We assume in what follows that, given a positive increasing-returns parameter, the difference in savings rates ($s_M - s_A$) is sufficiently large to make the w^* curve slope upward. This is in the spirit of Graham, who, in an argument reminiscent of Marx, viewed the urge to accumulate capital in manufacturing as a consequence of increasing returns:

> Whether by reinvestment of profits or otherwise, this saving through the force of competition is practically compulsory in an industry subject to increasing returns, for the alternative to expansion is bankruptcy. On the other hand in the extractive industries, where an extension of output is likely to be accompanied by a rising unit cost,

this stimulus to expansion and increase in equipment is lacking. (1923, 221)

Graham's Paradox

Consider now two economies that are identical except for their land endowments. The w curve of the land-rich country (w_R in fig. 36) will be above that of the land-poor country (w_P): at each level of capital stock, the greater supply of land generates a higher real wage. The w^* curve of the land-rich country will also be above that of the land-poor country: the larger land supply implies a greater rate of accumulation out of rents, so that, at each level of capital stock, the product wage consistent with a given rate of accumulation will also be higher.

However, the difference in required wages ($w^*_R - w^*_P$) may not be large enough to compensate for the difference in market equilibrium wages ($w_R - w_P$), which tends to reduce the profit rate in the land-rich country (compared to the land-poor country) at each level of capital stock. This is likely to happen with a low propensity to save out of rents.[6] Two results follow. First, in the long-run equilibrium, the land-rich economy has lower real wages than the land-poor country does. The reason is that in the steady state the land-rich economy has a larger natural-resource-intensive sector and a smaller increasing-returns industry. The negative effect on productivity of its smaller manufacturing sector results in lower living standards. Second, off the steady state, at similar levels of capital stock, the land-rich economy has a smaller rate of capital accumulation: the gap between the w^* and w lines is larger for the land-poor country. The land-rich country grows more slowly than the resource-poor country does.

We thus have the paradoxical result that, in comparing two economies identical in all other respects, the rate of capital accumulation — at each level of capital stock — and the long-run steady state level of wages may be higher in the resource-poor economy. The key assumptions required for this result, the presence of increasing returns to scale in the capital-using sector and the role of profits as the major source of capital accumulation, were both explicitly stated in Graham's 1923 article.

The Dutch Disease

Graham's insight has a close affinity to Dutch disease models. The exercise of figure 36 can also be used to illustrate the effects of an export boom of primary products due to either a natural resource discovery or an increase in the relative price of the resource-intensive product.

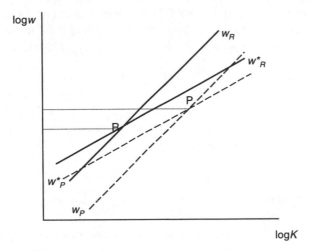

Fig. 36.   Graham's paradox model

Simply think of figure 36 as showing, for the same economy, the long-run equilibrium values of the real wage and the capital stock before and after a natural resource discovery.

The effects stressed in the literature on the Dutch disease are, however, somewhat different and more complex. In the Graham paradox model, the abundance of land has an adverse effect on industrialization because the land-intensive sector and manufacturing compete in the labor market: a larger endowment of land raises labor demand in sector A, thus increasing the product wage in manufacturing and reducing its profitability. This is not, however, the only possible, or even the major, adverse effect that a natural resource boom can have on industrialization. The contribution of the Dutch disease literature is that it brings in other mechanisms, which involve the spending of rents on nontradable goods and the competition in the capital market between manufacturing and the resource-intensive sector. We will now extend the model to allow for the presence of nontradable goods and intersectoral capital mobility. Each of these extensions will be considered separately.[7]

Nontradable Goods

Suppose that, along with sectors A and M, another sector (S) produces nontradable consumer services by means of labor under constant returns:

$$S = L_S. \tag{4}$$

A fraction (q) of the rents (R) generated in sector A is spent on nontradables (we ignore, for simplicity, consumption of services by sector M). Using the expression for R in equation 2, we obtain:

$$p_s S = qR = qR(w, T, p_A) \quad R_1 < 0 \quad R_2, R_3 > 0, \tag{5}$$

where p_s is the price of nontradables in terms of good M. With a uniform wage rate, and given production conditions in sector S, this price is the same as the manufacturing product wage (w). Substituting from equation 4 into 5 and solving for L_s:

$$L_s = (q/w)R(w, T, p_A), \tag{6}$$

which shows the level of employment in the nontradable goods sector as an inverse function of the wage, and an increasing function of the land endowment and the relative price of agricultural goods. Using equation 6 and the full-employment condition $(L = L_A + L_M + L_s)$, the schedule of short-run equilibria is given by:

$$L = L_A(w, p_A, T) + L_M(w, K) + (q/w)R(w, T, p_A). \tag{7}$$

Consider the effects of a more abundant supply of land. This shifts the w curve upward for two reasons. As before, there is a higher demand for labor in sector A. In addition, the increase in land rents generates a higher demand for nontradables. This second effect is the *spending effect* found in Corden 1984. This is the new aspect brought in by nontradable goods, whose presence implies that the w curve would shift upward even if the resource-intensive sector did not use labor directly. The spending out of higher rents leads to a higher relative price of nontradables and thus to real currency appreciation.[8] At the initial level of the capital stock in manufacturing, labor market equilibrium requires a reallocation of labor away from manufacturing and into services. If, in addition to being demanded by sector A, nontradables are used as inputs into manufacturing with a relatively inelastic demand, the adverse effects on manufacturing output and employment will be stronger, of course. The analysis of the longer run consequences of the resource boom is analogous to that in the previous section: the profitability squeeze in manufacturing slows down capital accumulation and can lead to a long-run equilibrium with a smaller manufacturing sector and larger natural resource and service sectors. The presence of nontradable goods (given that the associated shift in the w curve is larger) makes the conditions for a long-run contraction of the capital stock less restrictive.

Intersectoral Capital Mobility

Consider now the effects of a natural resource boom in the presence of intersectoral capital mobility. We leave aside nontradables and modify the production side of our initial model to allow for the use of capital in the resource-intensive sector (and neglect, for simplicity, labor input in this sector). This sector is thus an extractive industry (E) that uses capital and land (mineral land, specific to this sector) with a Cobb-Douglas technology:

$$E = K_E^b T^{1-b}.$$

Manufacturing is identical to the earlier definition, except for the assumption that it operates under constant returns to scale. This assumption will highlight the fact that the mechanisms involved in the reduction of real wages are, unlike in previous models, independent of the presence of increasing returns. We have thus:

$$M = K_M^a L^{1-a}.$$

There are thus two specific factors: land in sector E and labor in sector M, with both sectors now using capital. With no intersectoral capital mobility, profit rates in these two sectors would generally be different since they include quasi rents associated with the given capital stocks. Given the production functions in the two sectors, the short-run profit rates would be such that:

$$r_E K_E = [b/(1 - b)]\theta T \tag{8}$$

$$r_M K_M = [a/(1 - a)]wL. \tag{9}$$

The wage rate (w) and rent per unit of land (θ) are determined by equilibrium in the labor and land markets. Hence, we have:

$$T = T^d = K_E[(1 - b)p_E/\theta]^{1/b} \tag{10}$$

$$L = L^d = K_M[(1 - a)/w]^{1/a}. \tag{11}$$

With capital mobility, quasi rents will tend to disappear and profit rates become equalized. In equilibrium, the amount of capital invested in sector E must yield a profit rate equal to that obtained in sector M. The common profit rate, and the associated composition of the capital stock, must then satisfy:

$$K = K_E + K_M \tag{12}$$

$$K_E = (bp_E/r)^{1-b}T \tag{13}$$

$$r = r_M(w) \quad r'_M < 0, \tag{14}$$

where equation 13, obtained by eliminating θ from equations 8 and 10, expresses the relationship between capital and the profit rate in sector E and equation 14 shows the profit rate in manufacturing as an inverse function of the product wage.

Substituting equation 14 into 13 and using equation 12 yields a schedule of capital market equilibrium:

$$K_M = K - [bp_E/r_M(w)]^{1-b}T. \tag{15}$$

The wage rate and the capital stock invested in manufacturing are inversely related along this schedule (see fig. 37). A higher wage rate implies a lower profit rate in manufacturing (the labor-using sector). Restoring the equality between the two profit rates requires a reallocation of capital toward the resource-intensive sector (which reduces the profit rate there). To determine the wage rate and K_M simultaneously, we need to bring in the locus of labor market equilibrium. This is given by equation 11, which shows the usual positive relationship between the wage and the capital stock.

Consider the effects of a resource boom starting from an initial equilibrium at point A in figure 37. The resource boom is caused by an increase in T or p_E. In either of these cases, profitability in sector E rises at the initial level of the capital stock (K_E). In terms of the figure, the result is an inward shift in the capital market equilibrium locus: for each level of the wage, capital moves from the M to the E sector. The new equilibrium at point B thus features a smaller capital stock in manufacturing and a lower wage. Corden (1984) labels this resource movement *direct deindustrialization* because it is independent of real currency appreciation. Indeed, without nontradable goods there is no spending effect and no change in the price of tradable relative to nontradable goods.

The reduction in real wages from point A to point B is not the result of a decline in manufacturing productivity under increasing returns to scale. The contraction is due to the fact that the higher profit rate in sector E causes labor demand to decrease following the reallocation of capital away from the labor-intensive sector. With the given labor supply, the equilibrium wage falls in order to clear the labor market.

It is easy to see that in the presence of nontradable goods a second resource movement that counteracts the decline in labor demand but

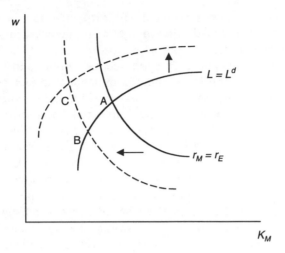

Fig. 37.   The Dutch disease

exacerbates the contraction of manufacturing will take place. The spending effect will increase the relative price of nontradables and wages, causing profitability to decline in manufacturing. Capital then moves from manufacturing to the resource-intensive sector. This is *indirect deindustrialization* (see Corden 1984 and Corden and Neary 1982). Unlike direct deindustrialization, it results from the real currency appreciation caused by the spending effect and depends on its strength. In terms of figure 37, it arises from the upward shift in the schedule of labor market equilibrium that leads to a new equilibrium at point C, which features a higher real wage and a capital stock in manufacturing that is even lower than at point B.

Latin America's Early Import-Substitution Industrialization

An interesting implication of this model is that a fall in exports of primary products may accelerate industrialization. The fall in the profitability of the primary export sector and the resulting contraction in the demand for nontradables will cause resource movements and a real depreciation that can enhance capital accumulation in manufacturing. Since in the model manufacturing is the importables sector, its expansion will appear as a spontaneous process of import substitution. Economists and historians in Latin America have noted these mechanisms in operation during the 1930s. Then the collapse of primary product prices led to sharp real depreciations, which, often coupled with protective tariffs, accelerated the process of import substitution in light manufacturing in a number of Latin American countries.

It was this early phase of spontaneous import substitution that Prebisch observed in the 1930s and recommended accelerating through protectionist measures, in the postwar period. Paradoxically, at first sight Prebisch should have welcomed the lower terms of trade for primary commodities, as this trend was beneficial rather than harmful to industrialization on the periphery. Upon reflection, Prebisch is quite consistent: he saw as harmful the fall in the terms of trade that was *caused* by the expansion of the supply of primary products (as noted in Bhagwati 1985). In the face of inelastic demands for primary goods, this expansion led to a skewed distribution of the gains from trade that favored the industrial centers of the world economy (see chap. 7). In figure 36, the increase in the supply of primary products causes an upward shift of the w curve that inhibits industrialization and, in the face of inelastic demands for these goods, reduces the terms of trade of the country exporting primary products.

This conclusion is quite consistent with the view that a reduction in world demand for primary products could and would change the pattern of specialization of the periphery in favor of manufacturing activities. This is what, in a less traumatic way, a protective tariff on manufactures can achieve: by changing the (domestic) terms of trade against the resource-intensive sector, it induces an expansion of the manufacturing sector. In this case, there is a downward shift of the w curve, as a result of a fall in world demand or the imposition of a protective tariff, which ends up inducing industrialization.

Factor Mobility, Linkages, and the Staples Thesis

The models discussed so far do not fit well the experience of a number of resource-rich countries that have achieved high levels of industrialization. The staples thesis is often cited to make the point that abundance of natural resources and fast growth of exports of primary products need not hinder industrial expansion.[9] A complementary observation is that a severe lack of natural resources may have stunted industrial development in a number of resource-poor countries.

Labor Mobility and the "Regions of Recent Settlement"

As Graham explicitly noted, his discussion assumed the absence of factor mobility. What difference does it make in his model if we allow for the possibility of importing scarce factors? To address this question, we return to the Ricardo-Viner-Graham model and extend it by allowing for international mobility of labor. We assume the rate of migration $(\hat{L})$, the only source of labor force growth, to be an increasing function of the ratio between the domestic market wage (w) and the wage abroad adjusted for costs of migration (w^s):

$$\hat{L} = f(w/w^s) \quad f' > 0 \quad f(1) = 0.$$

We also assume that foreign wages, or migration costs, tend to rise as the number of migrants increases the size of the labor force (L). This makes the supply price of labor (w^s) an increasing function of L:

$$w^s = w^s(L) \quad w^{s\prime} \geq 0, \tag{16}$$

with $w^{s\prime}=0$ as the special case in which, with constant foreign wages and migration costs, the country faces a perfectly elastic labor supply from abroad. The rest of the model remains identical to that presented in the first section. In particular, from equations 1 and 3 we can express the equations of the w and w^* curves as:

$$w = w(K, T, p_A, L) \quad w_1, w_2, w_3 > 0, w_4 < 0$$

$$w^* = w^*(K, s_M/\delta) \quad w^*_1, w^*_2 > 0,$$

where we have set, for simplicity, s_A equal to zero.

Consider the solution to the model in (K, L) space. The schedule of stationary capital stocks shows the (L, K) combinations for which the market wage is equal to the required wage. Setting $w = w^*$, we have:

$$w(K, T, p_A, L) = w^*(K, s_M/\partial). \tag{17}$$

The slope of this $w = w^*$ schedule is positive if there are diminishing returns to capital. Indeed, in (K, w) space, a larger labor force shifts the w curve downward, as the market wage falls for each given level of the capital stock. The new intersection with the w^* curve will feature a higher capital stock if the w^* line is flatter than the w curve. This will be the case unless technological externalities generate increasing returns to capital. Along the $w = w^*$ schedule, the wage increases with K since w^* is a positive function of the capital stock, given the presence of increasing returns (which accounts for the positive effect of K on w^*).[10] Above (below) the locus with a relatively high (low) labor-capital ratio, the market wage is below (above) the required wage and the capital stock is growing (shrinking).

The schedule of stationary labor forces ($\hat{L} = 0$) shows the (L, K) combinations for which the market wage is equal to the supply price of labor. Setting w^s in equation 16 equal to w, and thus $\hat{L} = 0$, we have:

$$w(K, T, p_A, L) = w^s(L). \tag{18}$$

The slope of this schedule is clearly positive: a larger capital stock increases the market wage (at each level of the labor force), and this requires an increase in the labor force, through migration, to bring w and w^s back into equality. The smaller the labor supply response (determined by eq. 16), the flatter is the locus.[11] Above (below) the locus with a relatively high (low) labor-capital ratio, the market wage is below (above) the supply price of labor and the labor force is shrinking (growing).

The two schedules divide the (L, K) space into four regions. At the intersection of the two schedules, the economy is in long-run equilibrium without either migration or capital accumulation taking place. Off this steady state, dynamic adjustments take place in the capital stock and the labor force. These adjustments, as indicated in figure 38, are determined by the region in which the economy finds itself.

We focus, first, on the stable case in which—due to moderate labor supply elasticity—the $w = w^*$ schedule is steeper than the $w^s = w$ schedule. To illustrate the dynamic adjustment to the steady state, consider an economy at point A with an initially low capital stock and no migration taking place. The economy is thus in the high-growth region (since real wages and the capital stock are below their steady state values). The capital stock expands over time. In the absence of labor mobility, and therefore of migration, the adjustment path will be along the horizontal line through point A until the economy reaches point B on the $w = w^*$ schedule. With labor mobility, adjustment will be along a path with an increasing labor force until point C is reached. At C, the capital stock and real wages are both higher than at B (since the $w^* = w$ schedule has a positive slope and w^* increases along this locus). International labor mobility thus allows the economy to reach a steady state with a larger manufacturing sector and higher real wages.

What are the effects of a greater abundance of natural resources? Comparing two economies identical in other respects, the $w^* = w$ schedule of the land-rich economy will be to the left of that of the resource-poor country (see fig. 39). As we have seen, at each level of the labor force the abundance of land reduces the steady state value of the capital stock. The greater abundance of land also shifts the $w^s = w$ schedule upward: at each level of the capital stock, it raises the market wage and,

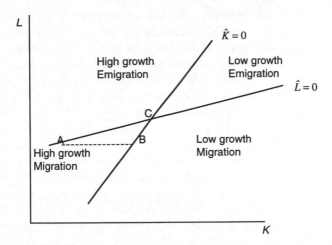

Fig. 38. The dynamics of capital accumulation and migration under international labor mobility

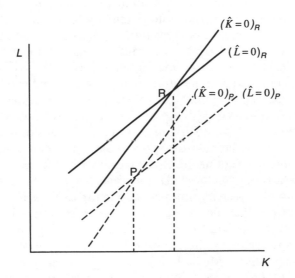

Fig. 39. The effects of natural resources and international labor mobility

with migration, it also increases the size of the labor force. Clearly, the labor supply response is a key determinant of the shift in the $w^s = w$ schedule. With sufficiently high labor mobility, and correspondingly high labor supply elasticity, it is now possible that the abundance of land raises the steady state value of the capital stock and thus of real wages.

This outcome depends on the virtuous interplay between migration and increasing returns in manufacturing. Labor mobility is essential, since otherwise the new long-run equilibrium cannot feature a larger labor force and the economy will remain stuck in a steady state with a small capital stock and relatively low real wages. The presence of increasing returns is crucial, since under constant returns w^* (and thus the steady state value of the wage) is independent of the capital stock.

International capital mobility also makes a difference. Findlay and Lundahl (1994) present a Ricardo-Viner model in which capital is required to advance the land frontier. There the condition that the rate of return on capital required to expand the arable land area must be equal to the profit rate in manufacturing determines endogenously the margin of cultivation. This model presents the interesting possibility that a fall in the international interest rate or an increase in capital mobility (provided that the domestic profit rate is initially higher than abroad) will simultaneously expand the land frontier, increase manufacturing output, and raise the capital intensity of manufacturing. Although the story is not about the effects of a resource boom, it shows the possibility that a general economic expansion with rising real wages and capital deepening in the industrial sector can take place even without labor migration.

The development experience of Canada and Australia, Argentina's industrialization before 1930, and the eventual transformation of the American West into an industrial powerhouse can be cited as examples of how an abundance of natural resources favored the achievement of a large manufacturing sector with high real wages. The expansion of world demand for primary products and improvements in the terms of trade in the pre-1929 period spurred economic growth by attracting large inflows of immigrants and capital and "stirring up dormant resources," drawing them into economic activity for export production (see Nurkse 1961 and Myint 1958). It is interesting that in historians' accounts of these experiences the elasticity of factor supplies, given by the importation of scarce factors, was seen as essential to the development process (see Watkins 1963).

The model also yields some insight into the role of land tenure and policy in the countries of immigration. Economic historians frequently allude to the heavy concentration of land in the hands of a small wealthy elite as a factor retarding Argentina's economic development in comparison with that of Canada and Australia, which followed a much more egalitarian land policy.[12] Compare our model of landlords and tenants with one in which land is evenly distributed among small farmers, who now appropriate the average rather than the marginal product of their labor. In otherwise identical conditions, the market wage will be higher in the country with more egalitarian land distribution. This has the effect of shifting both the $w^s = w$ and $w^* = w$ schedules upward and, with sufficiently high elasticity of the labor supply, of generating a steady state with a larger capital stock and higher real wages in the more egalitarian country.

Development Traps in Resource-Scarce Countries

The combination of labor mobility and increasing returns yields other interesting possibilities. As noted, greater labor supply elasticity makes the $w^s = w$ schedule steeper. The more returns to scale increase, the flatter is the $w^* = w$ schedule. Figure 40(a) illustrates a combination of labor supply elasticity and returns to scale such that the $w^s = w$ schedule is steeper than the $w^* = w$ schedule. The intersection of the two schedules now yields a saddle point equilibrium, as indicated by the dynamic adjustments of K and L. A developing economy with a small initial capital stock and no migration will be in a region of low growth. As the capital stock contracts and the real wages falls, emigration will take place in the presence of high labor supply elasticity. The reduction of the labor force prevents the restoration of profitability that would otherwise have occurred as a result of falling real wages. As in Myrdal (1957), the process is cumulative, since the capital stock continues to contract in the face of a low profit rate. The reader will recognize the situation as one in which the combination of high labor supply elasticity and increasing returns generates a big push problem. The downward-sloping saddle path is the locus of (L, K) combinations that need to be achieved for a process of endogenous growth to take off.

The case in figure 40(a) implies that an economy to the right of the saddle path will keep growing until, presumably, it has absorbed the whole of the world's labor force. Suppose, instead, that well before this takes place the elasticity of the labor supply decreases as the size of the labor force increases. As shown in figure 40(b), the $w^s = w$ schedule then becomes increasingly flatter at high levels of L. This shape yields the possibility of multiple equilibria. The low-K equilibrium is a saddle point, as in figure 40(a), while the high K intersection is a stable equilibrium, as in figure 38.[13]

Consider now the effects of a greater availability of natural

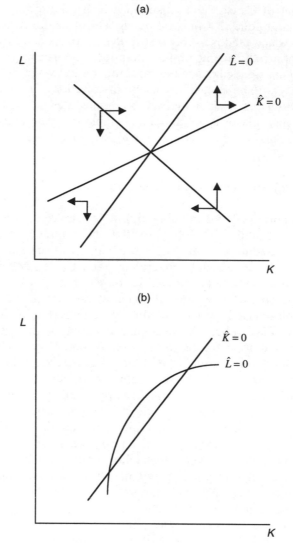

Fig. 40. Development traps in resource-scarce economies

resources. As before, the larger land supply shifts both schedules upward. Given that the elasticity of the labor supply decreases with the size
of the labor force, the shift in the $w^s = w$ schedule is larger at low levels
of L. It is then possible that Graham's paradox applies in the high-K
equilibrium — a relatively large shift of the $\hat{K} = 0$ locus at high levels of

K, implying that the resource-poor economy has a higher real wage and capital stock in the stable steady state. At the same time, the abundance of natural resources tends to reduce the hold of the development trap by shifting the position of the saddle path downward. The large shift of the $\hat{L} = 0$ schedule, at low levels of L, tends to reduce the size of the capital investments and the labor force needed for industrialization to take off. As the reader can verify, similar results apply in the case of a demand expansion for primary products that increases the relative price (p_A) of the resource-intensive good in international markets. This example illustrates how the opening or expansion of trade, whereby previously idle natural resources find productive employment, may be a precondition for industrialization to proceed at a rapid pace.

Linkage Effects

The staples thesis, as well as the literature on the "primary export phase" of Latin America's economic development, also emphasizes the role of linkages generated by different primary export activities. The question that we now address is under what conditions a resource-intensive sector can mobilize domestic economic activity in a manner favorable to industrialization, even without elastic factor supplies from abroad. As we will see, the answer depends on the nature of returns to scale in the sectors that benefit directly from the expansion of exports of primary products.

We can draw on an open economy version of the Rosenstein-Rodan/Hirschman model of chapter 5 to make the basic point. In that model, two sectors (S and M) produce a single final good with different technologies. Alongside them, a sector I, operating under increasing returns and imperfect competition, produces intermediate inputs used in the production of the capital-intensive good (M). Suppose now that the capital-intensive M good and the labor-intensive S good are both traded, while the intermediate inputs, used by sector M and produced under increasing returns, are nontradable. This time, we do not assume that the S and M sectors produce the same good. Nevertheless, the terms of trade between these two goods are determined in the international markets and are thus independent of domestic demand conditions. In addition, there is a resource-intensive sector, producing traded goods, with the same technology as sector A (discussed in the first section). A fraction (γ) of the rents generated in this sector is spent on I goods. Demand for I goods thus has two components: I_M, the demand from sector M, which depends, as before, on the capital stock; and I_A, the demand from sector A, which depends on agricultural rents and therefore on land endowment. Thus, we have:

$$I = I_M + I_A = (1 - a)^{1/a}(p_I/p_M)^{-1/a}K + \gamma R/p_I, \tag{19}$$

where: $R = R(w, T, p_A)$ $R_1 < 0,$ $R_2, R_3 > 0.$

The price of I goods increases with the wage rate and is a decreasing function of the scale of the I sector (see eq. 24 in chap. 5):

$$p_i = w\phi/(\phi - 1)(1 + \mu)I_i^{\mu/(1+\mu)}, \tag{20}$$

where ϕ is the price elasticity of demand facing individual producers and μ is the increasing returns parameter in the production of I goods. The price-wage ratio is a decreasing function of the scale of the I sector (eq. 20), and the demand for I goods increases with the capital stock and rents (eq. 19). Consequently, given the wage and the price of M goods, as determined in international markets, the relative price of I goods (p_I/p_M) is a decreasing function of K and R:

$$p_I/p_M = p_I(K, R, w/p_M)   p_{I1}, p_{I2} < 0;   p_{I3} > 0. \tag{21}$$

Given the production conditions assumed in sector M (a Cobb-Douglas technology with two factors, I and K), the rate of profit can be expressed as a function of only p_I/p_M and the parameters of the production function. Since the profit rate is a decreasing function of the relative price p_I/p_M, we can express it, using equation 21, as:

$$r = r(K, R, w/p_M)   r_1, r_2 > 0   r_3 < 0.$$

As long as it exists, the labor-intensive S sector provides a perfectly elastic supply of labor at a wage (in terms of M goods) equal to the price of the S good ($w = p_s$). This flat segment of the w curve, it may be worth recalling, is not due to the assumption that the M and S sectors produce perfect substitutes (as in the closed economy model of chap. 5). Rather, it is the consequence of the fact that both goods are traded at given international prices and constant returns to labor prevail in sector S.[14] The w curve of the model is thus a horizontal line for $L_S > 0$. When $L_s = 0$, the labor supply is no longer perfectly elastic and the w curve slopes upward. Unlike what happens in the original model, the labor supply is not fully inelastic, given the presence of the A sector. Using the labor demand function in sector A (eq. 3), the elasticity of the labor supply to sector I can be shown to depend on the composition of the labor force and the technology in sector A:

$$\mathrm{dlog}L_I/\mathrm{dlog}w = L_A/bL_I,$$

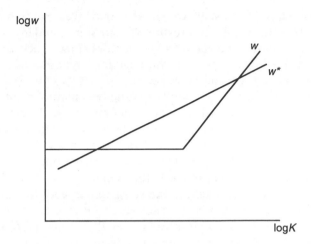

Fig. 41. A "linkage effects" model in an open economy

where w is the wage in terms of good M, the numeraire (and not the product wage in sector I). Since as K increases L_A/L_I falls, the elasticity of the labor supply falls and the w curve becomes steeper. (For simplicity, we draw in fig. 41 the upward-sloping segment of the w curve with a constant slope).

Consider now the w^* schedule. The profit rate increases with the capital stock and is an inverse function of the wage (w/p_M). Thus, the required wage that is consistent with the steady rate of capital accumulation is an increasing function of the capital stock. As in the model of chapter 5, an increase in K raises the demand for I goods and reduces marginal costs in the I sector. The fall in the relative price (p_I/p_M) (for a given value of w/p_M) raises profits in the M sector. The new feature here is that exactly the same thing occurs when there is an increase in the demand for I goods coming from higher spending out of agricultural rents. The profit rate (and thus the required wage) being an increasing function of rents, the position of the w^* curve depends on the abundance of land (and the fraction of rents, γ, spent on I goods).[15]

Multiple equilibria remain a possibility (as shown in the appendix to this chapter). Figure 41 illustrates this case. The low-level, stable equilibrium does not have an M sector. A small I sector coexists with sectors A and S but produces at such high costs that it is unprofitable to invest in sector M. In the high-level, stable equilibrium, there is no S sector: its labor force has been absorbed by a large sector of intermediate inputs producing at low costs for both the M and A sectors. The low-K

intersection shows, as usual, the size of the investments required to make the M sector viable. Interestingly, a greater abundance of natural resources lowers the threshold value of the capital stock required to overcome a development trap, as the resulting expansion of the I sector reduces production costs in the M sector.

More generally, a larger supply of land or a natural resource boom shifts the w^* curve upward. For an economy at low levels of K (but above the low-K intersection), the increase in demand for I goods lowers the relative price of these goods and raises the profit rate and capital accumulation in the M sector. Thus, the spending out of rents has an anti–Dutch disease effect! Indeed, the spending effect in this case is equivalent to real depreciation in the sense that it leads to a lower price of nontradable I goods relative to tradable goods. The boom also has the effect of shifting the w curve inward over that range of K values for which the price of good S no longer determines the wage rate. This inward shift in the w curve reflects the more traditional Dutch disease effect, which in the present model is completely neutralized at low levels of K by the perfectly elastic labor supply.

Figure 42 illustrates a paradoxical outcome. The case in 42(a) depicts a resource-rich economy in which the resource-intensive sector has weak linkages (small γ) with sector I and thus indirectly with sector M. These characteristics cause the value of the capital stock (K^*), at which the w curve slopes upward, to be relatively small (since, with a large share of the labor force employed in the resource-intensive sector, sector S is small from the beginning). At the same time, given the weak linkages of the A sector with the increasing-returns I sector, the required wage (w^*) at that value (K^*) of the capital stock is below the market equilibrium wage. As a result, the two loci do not intersect and there is a unique equilibrium without an M sector.

Figure 42(b) depicts a similar configuration, although for different reasons. Here the economy lacks natural resources and K^* is relatively large. Yet, being resource poor, the required wage (w^*) at that value of the capital stock is also too low to generate an intersection with the w curve. As in figure 42(a), there is a unique equilibrium without an M sector. In both cases, industrialization is not viable due to the small size of the labor force. This is consistent with a land-labor ratio that is very large in the first case and very low in the second. This is why their steady states are bound to be very different, even though neither of these economies will have an M sector. The resource-rich economy will be an exporter of resource-intensive goods and an importer of S and M goods, while the resource-poor economy will be an exporter of the labor-intensive S goods and an importer of the A and M goods.

(a)

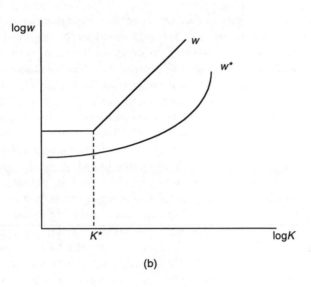

(b)

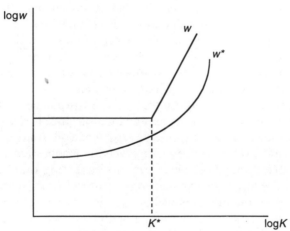

Fig. 42. Low-level equilibria in resource-rich and resource-scarce economies

An Attempt at Reconciliation: Two Hybrid Models

Can these different views of the role of natural resources in development be reconciled? This is the question addressed here. We start by noting that the attempt at reconciliation, in order to have any value, must be consistent with two observations. First, a hundred or more years ago, the abundance of natural resources clearly seemed to be a positive factor in explaining international differences in per capita incomes and even, although to a lesser extent, differences in growth rates. Resource-rich countries (such Australia, Canada, the United States, and Argentina) not only had higher incomes but they were growing faster than most resource-scarce countries, which were not growing at all at the time.[16] Second, as we move closer to today's world, which is increasingly intensive in capital and technology, natural resources not only have ceased to play a significant positive role but one could even argue that their relationship to differences in income and growth is being progressively reversed. When we look at growth rates, we find the highest rates among resource-scarce economies (a relationship that will be further discussed in the next chapter).[17] When we look at the relationship between income and natural resources across *countries* (as we saw in chap. 1, the simple correlation, although hardly significant, is still positive), the statement may not be completely accurate, but it comes closer to the truth when we think of the world economy as comprising different types of areas: the richest areas in the world tend to be *cities,* which are generally the poorest in terms of natural resource endowment.

An analytical framework that is consistent with these observations would have to be such that the abundance of natural resources facilitates development at low-income levels, while at the same time, at later stages of development, higher levels of income are achieved by resource-scarce economies specializing in increasing returns activities. In fact, we have already encountered an example of these properties in our discussion of the interactions between increasing returns and international labor migration. In the model with labor mobility and multiple equilibria of the third section, the low-level trap of the resource-scarce economy involves a vicious circle of emigration and low profitability, while at high equilibrium the same economy may feature a higher income level than that of a resource-rich economy. In what follows, I provide two more examples of models that feature similar properties.

The first is an extension of the linkage effects model of the previous section. In this model, a larger supply of land is favorable to manufacturing because spending out of rents on intermediate goods produced under increasing returns has an anti–Dutch disease effect. This shifts the w^* schedule upward, which tends to increase the value of K in the high-level

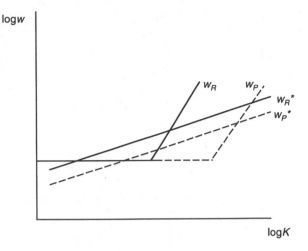

Fig. 43.   Linkage versus Dutch disease effects

equilibrium in addition to reducing the hold of the trap (the value of K at the low-K intersection). Suppose that, in addition to the nontradable I goods, there are other labor-intensive, nontradable goods produced under diminishing returns to labor and that a fraction of rents is spent on these goods (as in the Dutch disease model). A larger supply of land would then strengthen the upward shift in the w curve that occurs at high-income levels when the labor supply to sector I is no longer perfectly elastic. As shown in figure 43, this Dutch disease effect may then cause the high-level equilibrium to feature a lower income level in the land-abundant country, even though the linkage effect (the upward shift in the w^* curve) dominates at low levels of income, where the w schedule is horizontal.

Our second example is a simple extension of the Graham paradox model. Suppose that the savings rate out of rents (s_A) is a nonlinear function of the level of rent income such that:

$$s_A = s_A(R) \quad s_A' > 0 \quad s_A'' < 0.$$

In a manner analogous to the savings function assumed in chapter 2 (fourth section), the w^* schedule will now have a positive and diminishing slope. Multiple equilibria are possible due to the nonlinearity of the savings function, and below the low-K intersection there is a development trap associated with the scarcity of savings (see fig. 44[a]). A greater abundance of natural resources will, as before, shift both the w

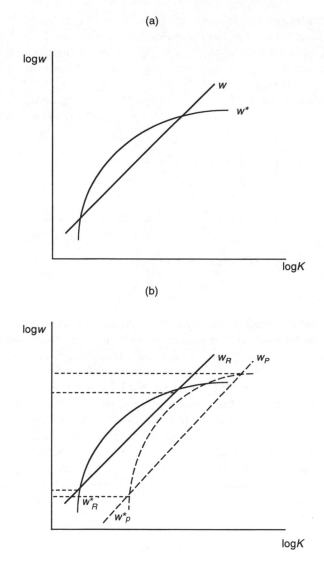

Fig. 44. **Savings traps in resource-scarce economies**

and w^* schedules upward. The upward shift of the w^* schedule will, however, be larger at low levels of the capital stock and output per worker because the positive effect of rent income on savings supply is higher at low-income levels. The abundance of natural resources, as illustrated in figure 44(b), can then reduce the hold of the savings trap at low-income levels (or eliminate it altogether). At the same time, the basic property of the Graham paradox model remains: at high income levels, the upward shift of the w schedule is larger than that of the w^* curve, and the resource-scarce economy reaches a higher income in the high-level steady state.

By relaxing savings constraints on the development of capital-intensive manufacturing, the abundance of natural resources has positive effects on industrialization at low-income levels, where those constraints are most important. In later stages, however, by preventing more complete specialization in the increasing-returns sectors the overall level of productivity and income is adversely affected by the presence of a large resource-intensive sector.

APPENDIX

Derivation of the Slope of the w^* Schedule in the Linkage Effects Model

Consider the determination of the slope of the w^* curve in the linkage effects model. Along the w^* schedule, the profit rate remains constant, and this requires the relative price p_I/p_M to remain constant also. Using equation 20, we can express the proportionate change in p_I as:

$$\mathrm{d}\log p_I = \mathrm{d}\log w - [\mu/(1 + \mu)]\mathrm{d}\log I, \qquad (\mathrm{A}.1)$$

where $\mathrm{d}\log I$ can be expressed as:

$$\mathrm{d}\log I = [1/(1 + I_M/I_A)]\mathrm{d}\log(I_A/I_M) + \mathrm{d}\log I_M.$$

Using the demand functions I_A and I_M in equation 19, together with equation A.1, and setting $\mathrm{d}\log p_I = 0$, we can solve for the slope of the w^* schedule:

$$\mathrm{d}\log w^*/\mathrm{d}\log K = \mu/(1 + \mu)[1 + b(I_A/I_M)].$$

The slope of the w^* curve depends on the increasing-returns parameter in sector I, the output-land elasticity in the agricultural production function and the composition of demand for I goods. Since this composition depends on the level of the capital stock (and, more generally, on the capital-land endowment), the slope is not constant in $(\log K, \log w)$ space. As K increases, I_A/I_M falls (as sector I produces increasingly for the M sector) and the curve becomes steeper. At high levels of K, when I_A/I_M tends toward zero, the slope tends to a constant value, $\mu/$

$(1 + \mu)$, which is the same as in the original model (see chap. 5, eq. 31). When K tends toward zero (and sector I produces exclusively for sector A), the slope goes to zero, which is also the slope of the w curve at low levels of K.

Interestingly, we now have three cases instead of the two seen in the model in chapter 5. In addition to the first case, where the two schedules do not intersect, and the second case, where the schedules intersect twice, it is now possible that a unique high-level intersection exists. This third case occurs here because, unlike in the original model in chapter 5, demand for I goods is not determined exclusively by sector M. Even when there is no sector M ($K = 0$) and I goods are produced at a high cost, there is a demand for them from sector A (this depends, of course, on our assumption that a given fraction of rents is spent on I goods no matter how high their price). Thus, it is always possible, with a sufficiently low wage or a sufficiently productive M sector, to start production of M at low levels of K and avoid the low-level intersection with the w curve.

CHAPTER 9

Trade Specialization and Growth

The analysis in chapter 8 suggests a potentially important role for the pattern of specialization in explaining differences in growth rates. This chapter extends that analysis and looks at the role of policy, in addition to natural resources, in shaping the pattern of specialization. We begin by examining the determinants of trade specialization in a neoclassical model and an extended model with increasing returns to scale. The chapter then shows how different patterns of specialization, consistent with the same factor endowment, can have different dynamic implications in the presence of multiple equilibria. We turn then to the policy implications of our previous discussion and to an empirical analysis. This empirical analysis draws on previous sections and the analysis in chapter 8 to discuss some empirical puzzles that have emerged in the recent research on cross-country growth performance.

Determinants of the Pattern of Specialization

In textbook neoclassical theory, the pattern of specialization is uniquely determined by factor endowments in the sense that, independently of initial conditions, the economy converges to a pattern of specialization that can be fully explained by the economy's factor endowments. At the other extreme of the theoretical spectrum, some new trade theory models treat productivity growth as the result of learning by doing and assume away factor endowments as a determinant of comparative advantage (see, e.g., Krugman 1987). Here the pattern of specialization cannot be determined independently of initial conditions and history. Real shocks like a temporary resource boom or monetary shocks like a temporary currency overvaluation are then all important in its influence on the pattern of trade specialization. Industrial policy also becomes crucial in acquiring new comparative advantages independently of factor endowment. This section discusses the assumptions under which these different possibilities can arise. It is useful to begin with a standard neoclassical model.

The Pattern of Specialization in a Small Open Economy
with Two Tradable Goods

Consider the linkage effects model in chapter 8. We leave aside the
resource-intensive sector (A), and allow for the use of capital in the
production of the labor-intensive good S. As before, M is the capital
good. There are thus two tradable goods $(S$ and $M)$, both of which
require capital. Technology in these sectors is described by:

$$S = K_S^b L_S^{1-b} \quad M = K_M^a I^{1-a},$$

where $a > b$, that is, sector M is more capital intensive than sector S. We
assume here that only sector M uses I goods and later relax this assumption. Labor demand and the profit rate in sector S are given by:

$$L_S = [(1 - b)p_S/w]^{1/b}K_S = L_S(w/p_S, K_S) \tag{1}$$

$$r_S = b(p_S/p_M)[(1 - b)p_S/w]^{(1-b)/b} = r_S(p_S/p_M, w/p_S). \tag{2}$$

We assume now that sector I produces a single good under constant
returns to scale and atomistic competition. Employment in sector I and
the profit rate in sector M are determined as:

$$L_I = [(1-a)p_M /w]^{1/a}K_M = L_I(w /p_M, K_M) \tag{3}$$

$$r_M = a[(1 - a)p_M/w]^{(1-a)/a} = r_M(w/p_M). \tag{4}$$

Given the assumptions about technology and market structure, we
can think of sectors M and I as a vertically integrated sector using capital
(invested in sector M) and labor (employed in sector I). We shall refer,
in this section, to this integrated sector as sector M. Because by assumption M is the capital good, the profit rate in sector S is also a function of
the terms of trade (p_S/p_M). In this section, we choose units such that p_S/p_M
$= 1$. This implies that for the same product wage sector M is always
more capital intensive than sector S.

Equilibrium in the labor market implies a uniform wage between
the two sectors as well as the full employment of the labor force (L): L
$= L_S + L_I$. Consider what happens to the equilibrium wage as capital is
reallocated from sector S to sector M. At any given initial wage, the
reduction of the capital stock in sector S causes a fall in labor demand in
this sector. Using the demand function for L_S, and holding the wage
constant, the reduction in employment in sector S is given by:

$$-dL_S = [(1-b)p_S/w]^{1/b}(-dK_S).$$

The increase in the capital stock in sector M causes an increase in labor demand in sector I. Using the demand function for L_I, the increase in employment in sector I at the initial wage is:

$$dL_I = [(1-a)p_M/w]^{1/a}dK_M,$$

with $-dK_S = dK_M$ since by assumption the reallocation leaves the aggregate capital stock intact. Whether the change creates excess supply or demand for labor depends on the size of $(-dL_S)$ compared to (dL_I). Since sector S is the labor-intensive sector, a reallocation of capital from sector S to sector M tends to create excess supply of labor, and this requires a decrease in the wage in order to clear the labor market.

Figure 45 illustrates how the market equilibrium wage behaves as capital is reallocated to sector M. Formally, this schedule of labor market equilibrium is obtained by substituting from the labor demand functions into the full employment condition: $(L = L_S + L_I)$, setting $K_S = K - K_M$. The schedule slopes downward in (K_M, w) space since an increase in K_M (and a decrease in K_S) creates an excess supply of labor and this requires a decrease in the wage to clear the labor market. Along the schedule the overall stock of capital is held constant. A change in the overall capital stock thus shifts the position of the schedule. For example, an increase in the capital stock, holding the overall labor force constant, shifts the locus upward: a higher overall capital-labor ratio raises the market-clearing value of the wage for each given allocation of the capital stock.

Capital is mobile between sectors S and M. Capital market equilibrium requires the full employment of the aggregate capital stock (K) and equality between the profit rates in the two capital-using sectors (insofar as the two sectors coexist):

$$K = K_S + K_M \quad r_S = r_M.$$

Substituting from the profit rate functions into the condition for profit rate equalization, we can derive a schedule of capital market equilibrium. In (K_M, w) space, this schedule shows, at each given value of the wage, the value of K_M, and the corresponding allocation of the capital stock, that yields the same profit rate in sectors S and M. Under our present assumptions, there is a unique value of the wage, independent of the capital stock in sector M, that satisfies the condition for profit rate equalization. This value depends on technological parameters and the terms of trade but not on factor endowments. A shift in the

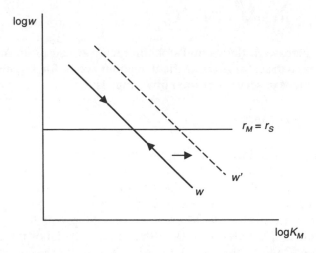

Fig. 45. The pattern of specialization in a neoclassical model

terms of trade in favor of the labor-intensive sector (S) increases the value of the wage required for profit rate equalization.

What happens when the economy is off the locus of capital market equilibrium? Clearly, the profit rates in the two sectors cannot be equal. If the wage is higher than its value on the schedule of capital market equilibrium, the profit rate in the capital-intensive sector is higher than in the labor-intensive sector. Intuitively, the higher wage reduces the profit rate of the labor-intensive sector to a larger extent than in the capital-intensive one. Capital will thus flow toward the capital-intensive sector (M). Below the schedule, the low wage implies that the profitability of the labor-intensive sector is higher and capital thus flows toward sector S. With labor market equilibrium obtaining at all times, and given the negative slope of this schedule, the allocation at the intersection of the two loci is then stable (see fig. 45).

The structure of this economy and the associated pattern of specialization depend on technology and the terms of trade — which affect the schedule of capital market equilibrium — as well as on factor endowments, that is, the overall capital stock and the total labor force — which affect the position of the schedule of labor market equilibrium. Thus, as the capital stock increases the labor market equilibrium schedule shifts up and more capital and labor are allocated to the capital-intensive sector (see fig. 45). The overall capital-labor ratio increases, and as a result the economy allocates more resources to its capital-intensive sector. With no technical progress — so that the capital market equilibrium schedule does not shift—the wage remains constant throughout this process as long as the economy remains incompletely specialized.[1] The reason is that with constant returns to scale in sector S employment in this sector provides an elastic labor supply to sector M. It is only if and when the economy fully specializes in sector M that the wage will tend to increase as a result of the excess demand for labor generated by capital accumulation.

The Pattern of Specialization under Increasing Returns

The model just discussed has a clear-cut answer to the question of what determines the pattern of specialization. Given the technology, terms of trade, and factor endowments, there is a unique allocation of resources that satisfies the conditions of equilibrium in the labor and capital markets. This section extends the model discussed in the previous section to show that under slightly more general assumptions the analysis of the pattern of specialization suffers from a fundamental indeterminancy that opens the door to the role of other determinants, including institutional factors and policies. This extension can be interpreted as an amended neoclassical model that allows for the presence of increasing returns in the production of nontraded inputs. Alternatively, it can be seen as a new trade theory model—such as Krugman's (1987) analysis of the Dutch disease and the "competitive consequences of Mrs. Thatcher"— that abandons the assumption of a Ricardian technology and allows for the presence of nontraded goods.[2]

Nontradable inputs are now produced under internal increasing returns and monopolistic competition. The I sector producing these inputs is identical to that in chapters 5 and 8. As was shown in chapter 5, this implies the following determination of employment in sector I and of the profit rate in sector M:

$$L_I = [(1/n)^{1-f}GK_M^a p_M/w]^{1/f} = L_I(w/p_M, K_M) \qquad (5)$$

$$G = (1-a)(1+\mu)(\phi - 1)/\phi \quad f = a - \mu(1-a)$$

$$r_M = aK^{\mu(1-a)/f}[(1/n)G/(w/p_M)]^{(1-f)/f} = r_M(K_M, w/p_M), \qquad (6)$$

where n is the number of producers in sector I, ϕ is the price elasticity of demand facing individual producers, and μ is the increasing returns parameter in the production of I goods.

Compared to the model presented earlier these assumptions on the market structure and production conditions in sector I have two consequences. First, employment in sector I depends, along with the capital stock in sector M and the wage in sector I measured in terms of M goods, on the number of producers and the extent to which returns increase, both of which affect the efficiency with which the I goods are produced. Second, the profit rate in sector M is now not only an inverse function of the product wage but, given this wage, a positive function of the capital stock invested in this sector. This positive effect of the capital stock is due to the presence of economies of scale in sector I. Indeed, a higher capital stock in sector M raises the demand and output for I goods; the higher scale of output implies an increase in productivity, which, given the wage, reduces the relative price of intermediate goods (in terms of M goods) and thus increases the profit rate in sector M.

As before, equilibrium in the labor market implies a uniform wage and full employment of the labor force. Consider now what happens to the equilibrium wage as capital is reallocated from sector S to sector M. The fall in labor demand in sector S is the same as before. Using the demand function for L_I (see eq. 5), the increase in employment in sector I at the initial wage is now given by:

$$dL_I = [(1/n)^{1-f}Gp_M/w]^{1/f}(a/f)K_M^{(a/f)-1}dK_M.$$

Whether the change creates excess supply or demand for labor (the size of $-dL_S$ compared to dL_I) depends now on the level of K_M, that is, on the initial allocation of the capital stock.[3] When K_M is small, sector I is also small and produces at high costs given the presence of economies of scale in this sector. The relative price of intermediate inputs (p_I/p_M) being very high, the K/I ratio is also very high despite K_M being small in absolute value. With a high K/I ratio, an increase in the capital stock in sector M has small indirect employment effects in sector I. The decrease in labor demand in sector S, then, is larger than the increase in labor demand in sector I. A reallocation of capital from sector S to sector M tends to create an excess supply of labor, and this requires a decrease in the wage to clear the labor market.

In contrast, at high levels of K_M the indirect employment effects of the expansion of sector M can offset the decline in labor demand in sector S. The larger scale of the I sector has made this sector more productive and reduced the relative price of intermediate goods. With a smaller K/I ratio, the expansion of sector M at the expense of sector S can then have the effect of generating excess demand for labor and increasing the market-clearing wage.

We can verify, formally, that a reallocation of capital toward sector M must first reduce the equilibrium wage and later increase it. Substituting from the labor demand functions into the full employment condition, we can derive, as before, a schedule of labor market equilibrium showing the market equilibrium wage under different allocations of the capital stock. Holding K constant, the slope of this locus in $(\log K_M, \log w)$ space is:

$$\mathrm{dlog}w/\mathrm{dlog}K_M = [a/f - (K_M/K_S)(L_S/L_I)]/[1/f + (1/b)(L_S/L_I)],$$

where L_S/L_I, from the labor demand functions, is given by:

$$L_S/L_I = (BK_S/AK_M^{a/f})w^{1/f-1/b}$$

$$B = [(1-b)p_S]^{1/b} \quad A = [(1/n)^{1-f}Gp_M]^{1/f}.$$

As is readily verified, the slope of this locus is negative, tending toward zero, at low levels of K_M and becomes positive, tending toward a, at high levels of K_M (provided that such high values exist given the size of the overall capital stock). The equilibrium value of the wage thus first falls as K_M increases and eventually rises, becoming an increasing function of K_M (see fig. 46).

The condition for profit rate equalization yields, as before, the schedule of capital market equilibrium by substitution from the profit rate functions. The new feature is that the value of the wage that is required for profit rate equalization is no longer independent of the allocation of the capital stock. We now have a locus of (w, K_M) combinations, rather than a unique value of the wage, along which the condition of profit rate equalization is fulfilled. The shape of the schedule depends on whether K_M has to increase or fall, in order to maintain capital market equilibrium, in the face of an increase in the wage rate. Intuitively, the answer to this question depends on which of the two sectors is more labor intensive. The higher wage will tend to reduce the profit rate of the labor-intensive sector to a larger extent. The required reallocation would then depend on the effects of K_M on relative profit rates.[4]

The problem is that it is not clear in this model which of the two sectors is more labor intensive directly *and* indirectly. Even though sector M is more capital intensive than sector S (in the sense that $a > b$), the increasing returns parameter (μ) may be large enough to make the "indirect" labor share of sector M larger than the labor share of sector S. This is due to the presence of economies of scale in sector I, which makes the sum of the capital and labor shares in the "integrated" M/I sector larger than unity.

Formally, the slope of the schedule of capital market equilibrium in $(\log K_M, \log w)$ space is:

$$\mathrm{dlog}w/\mathrm{dlog}K_M = [\mu(1-a)/f]/[(1-a)(1+\mu)/f - (1-b)/b].$$

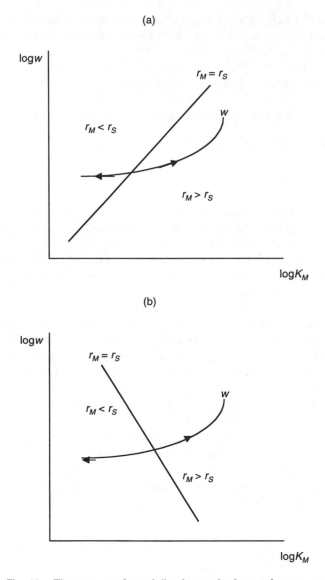

Fig. 46.   The pattern of specialization under increasing returns

We have, indeed, two cases depending on technological parameters in sectors M, S, and I. In figure 46(a), the case of $b > f$ is shown. This implies that $(1-a)(1+\mu) > (1-b)$, which says that the direct and indirect labor share of the M sector is larger than the labor share of sector S.

In this case, a wage increase (given K_M) reduces the profit rate in sector M more than it does in sector S. An increase in K_M (which affects r_M positively) is required to restore the equality of profit rates, which makes the slope of the schedule positive.

In the second case (fig. 46[b]), we have $b < f$. This implies that $(1-a)(1+\mu) < (1-b)$, that is, the direct and indirect labor share of sector M is smaller than the labor share of sector S. An increase in the wage (given K_M) will thus reduce the profit rate in sector S more than it does in sector M. This requires a fall in K_M (which reduces r_M) to restore the equality of profit rates. The slope of the schedule is then negative.

In the configurations shown in figures 46(a) and 46(b), the region to the right of the capital market locus ($r_M = r_S$) is one in which sector M is more profitable than sector S. This is because it is a region where K_M is relatively large, at each level of the wage, and K_M has a positive effect on the relative profitability of sector M. In this region, capital will be flowing toward sector M and thus K_M/K_S will increase. In contrast, to the left of the capital market locus, r_M is lower than r_S and capital is flowing toward sector S. It follows that in both cases the capital allocation at the intersection of the two loci is an unstable equilibrium. As shown in the figures, a capital allocation with a larger value of K_M than at the intersection generates a profit rate in sector M higher than that in sector S. Capital then moves toward sector M and further depresses the relative profitability of sector S. Similar mechanisms, in reverse, operate for capital allocations below the intersection.

We can also verify that when the two schedules intersect this intersection is unique.[5] It follows, then, that if an intersection exists there will be two stable equilibrium allocations in which the whole capital stock is invested in one of the two sectors. In one equilibrium, the economy fully specializes in the production of good S. Since no I sector will exist, not only the capital stock but the whole labor force will be employed in sector S. We shall refer to this capital and labor allocation as the S-equilibrium. In the other equilibrium, the economy specializes in the production and export of good M and, since there will be no S sector, the whole labor force is employed in sector I. We shall call this allocation the M-equilibrium.

In our economy, an S-equilibrium always exists regardless of whether there are multiple equilibria. As we shall see later in more detail, this is due to the assumption that sector S does not use intermediate goods produced under increasing returns. At low levels of K_M, the profit rate in sector M tends toward zero while it remains positive in sector S no matter how large the capital stock is. There are thus some capital allocations, at sufficiently low levels of K_M, for which sector S is more profitable than sector M.

Since an S-equilibrium always exists, it follows that the existence of an M-equilibrium guarantees the existence of an intersection and therefore ensures the presence of multiple stable equilibria. An M-equilibrium, in turn, will exist if profitability in sector M, when the whole of the capital stock is allocated to this sector, is higher than that of sector S (evaluated at the market-clearing wage corresponding to $L_I = L$). Consider, first, the wage in the M-equilibrium (w_M^*). From equation 5, setting $L_I = L$ and $K_M = K$ and solving for the wage, we have:

$$w_M^* = G(1/n)^{1-f}p_M K^a/L^f. \tag{7}$$

Substituting from equation 7 into 6, setting $w_M^* = w_M$ and $K_M = K$, we obtain the profit rate in the M-equilibrium (r_M^*):

$$r_M^* = a(L/n)^{1-f}/K^{1-a}. \tag{8}$$

The profit rate in sector S, evaluated at the M-equilibrium wage, is obtained from substitution of equation 7 into 2:

$$r_M^s = b(p_s/p_M)^{1/b}[(1-b)n^{1-f}L^f/GK^a]^{(1-b)/b}. \tag{9}$$

Note that the profit rate in sector S, evaluated at M-equilibrium wages, r_M^s, is an increasing function of the number of producers of I goods (n). A higher number of producers raises the unit cost of each of the I goods and reduces the demand for labor in sector I. This has a negative effect on w_M^* and therefore tends to increase the profit rate in sector S, which does not use I goods. This negative effect on the wage is offset in the case of the profit rate in sector M, since a higher number of producers implies higher costs for sector M: r_M^* is a decreasing function of the number of producers.

From equations 8 and 9, the condition for $r_M^* > r_M^s$, and thus for the existence of an M equilibrium, is:

$$K^{a-b} > K^{*a-b} = (b/a)^b(p_s/p_M)[(1-b)/G]^{1-b}n^{1-f}L^{f-b}. \tag{10}$$

The existence of multiple equilibria depends on the capital-labor endowment and the terms of trade (p_s/p_M). The aggregate capital stock must be sufficiently large so that, when the whole of it is allocated to sector M, the price of intermediate goods is low enough to make the M sector viable. The threshold value (K^*) of the aggregate capital stock rises with the relative price ratio (p_s/p_M), which increases the profitability of sector S. It also rises with the number of firms (n) in sector I, which adversely affects the profitability of sector M. The effect of the overall labor endowment on the threshold value of K depends on the sign of ($f - b$), that is, on the size of the direct and indirect labor share of sector M compared to that of sector S.

When an M-equilibrium does not exist, and thus there is a unique S-equilibrium, the economy clearly has a comparative advantage in good S and market incentives will lead the economy to specialize in sector S. However, when an M-equilibrium exists, the existence of multiple patterns of specialization consistent with the same factor endowment makes the notion of comparative advantage equivocal. This indeterminacy opens the door to the role of other factors — related to history, exogenous shocks, or institutions and policies — in the determination of the pattern of specialization. Indeed, initial conditions matter now in a way that they did not in the standard neoclassical model since, depending on the initial allocation of resources, the economy will move to one or another of the two patterns of trade specialization and remain locked in it. As we shall see later, temporary shocks can also be decisive, and industrial policy, even when it is transitory, can also make a substantial difference.

Growth and the Pattern of Specialization

When multiple equilibria exist, does it make a difference to the growth rate of an economy whether it adopts one or the other of the two patterns of trade specialization? As we shall see in this section, the pattern of specialization, *for the same* factor endowments, can affect growth through two mechanisms: (1) the effect on the investment share, and (2) the effect of the allocation of investment on the output-capital ratio. Both effects influence the rate of capital accumulation at a given level of the capital stock.

Two Patterns of Specialization Compared

We now assume that the condition for multiple equilibria is fulfilled and compare the wage and profit rates in the two stable equilibria. In an M-equilibrium, the wage and profit rates are given by equations 7 and 8. In an S-equilibrium, we have $K_S = K$ and $L_S = L$. Using equations 1 and 2, the S-equilibrium wage and profit rates are:

$$w_S{}^* = (1-b)p_S(K/L)^b \tag{11}$$

$$r_S{}^* = b(p_S/p_M)(L/K)^{1-b}. \tag{12}$$

Comparing equations 8 and 12 shows that for $r_M{}^*$ to be higher than $r_S{}^*$ requires:

$$K^{a-b} > K_1{}^{a-b} = (b/a)(p_S/p_M)n^{1-f}L^{f-b}. \tag{13}$$

Comparing equations 10 and 13, we can establish that $K^* > K_1$. The assumption of $a > b$ and the second-order condition for a profit maximum among I_i producers ensure this inequality.[6] It follows that when an M-equilibrium exists $(K > K^*)$ the profit rate in this equilibrium is higher than in the S-equilibrium (since then K is also higher than K_1).

Inspection of equations 7 and 11 shows that for $w_M{}^*$ to be greater than $w_s{}^*$ the aggregate capital stock must be such that:

$$K^{a-b} > K_2{}^{a-b} = (1-b)(p_S/p_M)n^{1-f}L^{f-b}/G. \tag{14}$$

From equations 10 and 14, we can establish that $K_2 > K^*$.[7] The existence of an M-equilibrium does not guarantee that the wage in the M-equilibrium will be higher than in the S-equilibrium. This requires that the aggregate capital stock be larger than K_2. In this case, with $K > K_2$, and therefore K larger than K^* and K_1, an M-equilibrium will exist that will feature both profit and wage rates higher than in the S-equilibrium.

Suppose that this last condition $(K > K_2)$ is fulfilled and consider two economies, identical in all respects (including factor endowment, savings rate, and size of the labor force) except for their patterns of specialization. One is specialized in the production and export of S goods, the other in the production of M and I goods. Since it has higher wage and profit rates (with the same capital endowment), the economy that specializes in the production of M and I goods has a higher income per capita than the economy specializing in good S. With identical savings rates (as well as population growth rates), it would appear, according to standard neoclassical growth theory, that the economy with the lower income per capita (that specializing in sector S) should grow at a faster rate: the parameters determining the steady state value of income (savings and labor force growth) are the same as in the M-specialization and, since per capita income is lower, the economy would appear to be further away from the steady state than that with the M-specialization. Yet, it is clear that this last economy is the one that grows at the faster rate: with higher income and the same capital stock and savings rate, its rate of capital accumulation must be higher than in the economy with the S-specialization.

The higher growth rate is the result of the pattern of specialization: it is the associated allocation of the capital stock that raises the rate of capital accumulation for a given investment share (given that for the same capital stock its income level is higher). Moreover, in the presence of international capital mobility this growth advantage is likely to be enhanced since capital will be flowing to the economy with the highest returns to capital and, as we have seen, the existence of multiple equilibria ensures that the profit rate in the M-specialization is higher than that in the S-specialization. With higher profits and capital mobility, the investment share itself is likely to be higher in the M-specialization.

The fact that higher income per worker does not prevent the second economy from growing faster can be seen from a slightly different perspective. The economy specializing in M and I goods is converging to a steady state different from that of the economy producing S goods. In this steady state, the capital-output ratio is the same in both economies since, by assumption, their savings rates and depreciation of the capital stock are the same. Total output, however, is larger in the economy specializing in sector M. The difference is proportional to the difference in output-capital elasticities in sectors M and S.[8] This steady state income gap is the result of their different patterns of specialization, which appears here as an additional determinant of the steady state level of income.

Further Extensions

So far, our discussion has assumed that the technology available to the S sector does not use intermediate I goods. How do the properties and conclusions of the model change when we relax this assumption? Suppose sector S uses I goods although less intensively than sector M does. Demand for I goods will no longer depend exclusively on the capital stock of sector M, just as in the linkage effects model of chapter 8. The capital stock of sector S will now also affect the demand for I goods and the relative price (p_I/p_M) of these inputs. The profit rate in sector M will depend not only on K_M and the product wage but also on K_S and therefore on the aggregate capital stock. There will generally be a sufficiently large capital stock so that when the whole of it is allocated to sector S the profit rate in this sector will be lower than the profit rate in sector M, evaluated at the market-clearing values of the wage and the relative price of intermediate inputs. At this value of the capital stock, the S-equilibrium disappears since sector M is more profitable than sector S, even when $K_S = K$. It is no longer the case that an S-equilibrium always exists regardless of the size of the aggregate capital stock.

We now have three configurations.[9] First, over a range of low values of the aggregate capital stock a unique equilibrium exists. This equilibrium must be that of an economy specializing in S goods in international trade, with a small I sector coexisting with the S sector. Specialization in this case must be in S, and not in M, goods, because S is the sector that uses I goods less intensively and thus is the only one able to survive under the high costs of production prevailing in the small I sector.

Then, over a range of intermediate values of the capital stock, two stable equilibria, with specialization in S and M goods, exist. The size of the capital stock is large enough to generate a productive I sector and make the M sector viable, but only if capital is invested in sector M. If it is allocated to sector S, the market for I goods will be insufficient to make it profitable to invest in sector M. In a related model, Rodriguez-Clare (1996) shows that in the M-equilibrium the profit rate is higher than in the S-equilibrium and the wage rate is at least as high. The M-equilibrium is then unambiguously Pareto superior to the S-equilibrium, not only for $K \geq K_2$, as in the previous model, but over the whole range of K values for which multiple equilibria exist.[10] With a given savings rate, the rate of accumulation on the M-equilibrium growth path is also unambiguously higher than on that of the S-equilibrium.

For high values of the capital stock, we again have a unique equilibrium. The size of the capital stock is sufficient not only to make the M sector viable but to make the S-equilibrium disappear. The low prices of intermediate goods and high wages make it worthwhile for an individual investor to move away from sector S and start production in sector M. By doing so, intermediate goods prices and wages move to reinforce the relative profitability of sector M with eventually all the capital moving away from sector S. This sector becomes unviable at the high wage rates associated with the large capital-labor ratio in the economy.

Another extension of the model would introduce skilled labor and consider differences among sectors in the intensity with which they use skilled labor. This has been done in Rodrik 1994. In Rodrik's model, the sector producing nontradable inputs under economies of scale is intensive in skilled labor. The level of skills then plays a role in the existence of multiple equilibria along with the size of the capital stock. A higher level of skills can partly compensate for the high costs arising from a small market for I goods and thus can reduce the size of the capital stock required for the existence of an M-equilibrium. Similar results follow if sector M, rather than sector I, is intensive in skilled labor: while the high prices of intermediate goods tend to depress the relative profitability of sector M, the abundance of skilled labor tends to raise it, and sector M may be viable depending on the allocation of the capital stock. In any case, multiple equilibria can arise from various combinations of skill levels and capital stocks rather than simply from an intermediate value of the capital stock. In a manner analogous to the development model with multiple long-term equilibria presented in chapter 6, what keeps the economy in low-level equilibrium may be an excessively low capital stock, despite a rather high level of skills, or an insufficient level of skills, despite a rather high capital stock.

Industrial Policy and Transitory Shocks

Many developing countries have adopted industrial policies in an attempt to accelerate the rate of industrialization and economic growth. The results have been mixed if we are to judge from the varieties of growth performance under similar policies. This explains why the effectiveness of these policies is controversial and why widely different views coexist on whether they made a difference and, if so, whether this was positive or negative. This is the case even though observers and policymakers alike have amply documented the role of industrial policy in fostering a fast rate of industrialization in East Asia (see, on the subject, Amsden 1989 and Wade 1990). An important reason for this state of affairs seems to be that consensus is lacking on precisely the key issue of how and under what conditions industrial policy can significantly alter the rate of capital accumulation and growth. The analytical framework presented here will help clarify the questions of how, and under what conditions, changes in trade specialization can affect long-term growth performance.

Industrial Policy, the Capital Stock, and the Level of Skills

In the more general models just discussed, the economy has a clear comparative advantage in the labor-intensive good S and the capital-intensive good M at low and high levels of the aggregate capital stock, respectively. In both cases, a unique equilibrium exists and market incentives lead the economy to specialize in the production of those traded goods in which it has a comparative advantage. This means that when a unique M-equilibrium exists industrial policy is not needed to move the economy toward this pattern of specialization. It also means that when the economy has a unique S-equilibrium industrial policy can hardly improve on the market outcome. Consider, for instance, a policy attempting to reallocate resources toward sector M in an economy that has a unique S-equilibrium. Suppose that policy succeeds in reallocating the whole of the capital stock toward sector M. Because the M-specialization is not an equilibrium, the wage in this economy would fall compared to that in the S-specialization. The profit rate is also likely to fall, especially if the aggregate capital stock is small and the costs of intermediate goods, as a result, are high. With a profit rate in sector M lower than that in sector S—evaluated at market wages and prices of intermediate goods—the policy-induced changes in relative prices required to make sector M viable would imply a further reduction of the wage. The M-specialization, in this case, will not feature a growth rate higher than that in the S-specialization. Ultimately, again, this is due to the fact that an M-equilibrium does not exist.

The scope for policy intervention is very different over that range of intermediate levels of the aggregate capital stock that are large enough to make coordinated development of the M and I industries viable yet insufficient for any individual firm to be profitable in isolation in sector M. Over this range, the economy is in transition between different patterns of trade specialization, a transition in which old comparative advantages are being eroded while new ones are only slowly emerging. In this transition, as long as the low-level equilibrium exists, market incentives are unlikely to move the economy to the high-growth path associated with the superior equilibrium. This is simply because the slow-growth path is a locally stable equilibrium.

The successful policy interventions geared toward accelerating this transition are the basis for Rodrik's interpretation of how "Korea and Taiwan grew rich" (1994). Rodrik argues that, more than their export orientation, the distinguishing feature of these growth experiences was the sharp and sustained increase in their investment rates in the early 1960s. Through an array of government interventions, by subsidizing and coordinating investment decisions, government policy was successful in reallocating resources toward modern capital-intensive industries. With increasing returns in these activities, this reallocation raised the rate of return on capital and pushed the economy into a high-growth path. Outward orientation followed because the higher investment rates increased the demand for imported capital goods. The relatively high level of skills of the labor force in both countries was a condition for the success of industrial policy.

From a broader historical perspective, the very high rates of economic growth achieved by industrializing latecomers in the postwar period can be seen as the result of their having successfully "traversed" the sequence of transitions between different patterns of specialization that were faced in the road to modern industrialization. If our analytical framework has some validity, it is hard to see how, without the policy interventions that accelerated those transitions, a market-driven development model could have produced such extremely high growth rates in East Asia as well as, although growth was slower, the rapid economic development in a few Latin American countries from 1940 to the early 1980s.

The size of the capital stock and the level of skills are not the only factors affecting the existence of multiple patterns of specialization. The condition in equation 8 shows that the existence of multiple equilibria also depends on the terms of trade between S and M goods. To illustrate the role of the terms of trade, consider an economy specialized in labor-intensive goods and suppose that over time the entry of new, low-cost producers in the international market tends to reduce the relative price of S goods. This has the effect of generating an M-equilibrium without necessarily, at the same time, making the economy move toward this high-level equilibrium. The economy is, in a sense, losing its competitiveness in S goods without at the same time acquiring a comparative advantage in M goods. This may describe the situation in a number of semi–industrialized "sandwich economies" facing stiff competition from new, low-wage producers of labor-intensive goods while still being unable to compete with the more efficient producers of capital-intensive goods in the more industrialized economies. If we assume that good S is a primary good, the transition can be interpreted as describing balance of payments problems and eventually the beginning of industrialization in resource-abundant countries facing declining terms of trade for their primary exports.

In any of these interpretations, the economy in transition with declining terms of trade is likely to remain largely specialized in the production of the labor-intensive S goods until it eventually achieves the high levels of the capital stock that make sector M clearly profitable from the point of view of individual investors (unless the price of S goods falls rapidly to such an extent as to eliminate the S-equilibrium). This is so simply because the S-specialization is a locally stable equilibrium: no individual investor in isolation will find the investment opportunities in sector M more attractive than those existing in sector S. In this transition, this economy will suffer a slowdown of its rate of growth as a result of the decline in the relative price of S goods. As shown by equations 2 and 12, the profit rate in this economy is an inverse function of the relative price of M goods. Insofar as the rate of accumulation depends on profitability, the decline in the relative price of S goods will adversely affect accumulation and growth. The slowdown in the accumulation of capital will in turn prolong the transition toward the capital stock necessary to make the production of M goods spontaneously profitable. Under this "slow-growth trap," policy intervention can make a substantial difference in the growth rate in the medium term.

Long-Term Effects of Transitory Shocks

In the neoclassical model with a unique equilibrium, factor endowments, technology, and terms of trade uniquely determine the pattern of specialization. A transitory change in the terms of trade or the availability of natural resources will have transitory consequences. That is, once the terms of trade return to their original level or the newly discovered resources are exhausted the economy will return to the original pattern of specialization.

This is no longer true in a model with multiple locally stable equilibria. Consider, for example, an economy with two equilibria (S and M) that specializes in sector M. A temporary shock changes the terms of trade in favor of sector S. The locus of capital market equilibrium shifts outward. Suppose that the shock makes the M-equilibrium disappear. Market incentives lead the economy to specialize in sector S. Later, when the terms of trade return to their initial level, two equilibria will again exist. However, the economy will remain locked in the S-equilibrium since this pattern of specialization continues to exist and is a stable equilibrium. The reader will recognize here the concerns about the "Dutch disease" if we interpret sector S as a resource-intensive sector and sector M as a manufacturing sector.[11]

The Dutch disease is an example of a transitory real shock. Similar consequences may follow from transitory monetary shocks, which, in the presence of sluggish nominal wage adjustments, lead to a temporary real overvaluation of the domestic currency. This may be caused by a tight monetary policy (as in Krugman 1987) or trade liberalization uncompensated by a devaluation (as in Ros and Skott 1998). Suppose, for example, that a tight monetary policy brings about nominal appreciation of the domestic currency, which, with sluggish wage adjustments, causes a real overvaluation. The price of nontraded goods relative to tradables increases, causing a reduction in the profitability of sector M relative to that of sector S, which uses the nontradable inputs less intensively. A sufficiently large shock of this type can make the M-equilibrium temporarily disappear and push the economy toward the S-equilibrium. When the goods and labor market equilibrium is reestablished, the economy may then remain locked in the S-equilibrium despite the fact that factor endowments, technology, and the terms of trade between S and M goods remained unchanged throughout the process of adjustment.

Trade, Investment, and Growth: An Empirical Analysis

The analysis in the second section suggests two channels through which the pattern of specialization can affect the rate of capital accumulation and growth. First, trade specialization is likely to affect the investment share given that, other things being equal, the rate of return on capital is higher in economies specializing in increasing-returns industries. Second, at the same level of income per worker, specialization in increasing-returns industries is associated with a higher output-capital ratio. Then, for the same investment share, the rate of capital accumulation and growth will be higher when an economy specializes in industries subject to increasing returns. We now turn to an empirical analysis of these implications.

Trade Specialization and Growth

An important practical question is how to measure the pattern of specialization. As a country's income level increases over time, the trade pattern changes. The economy typically moves from being a net importer of manufactures to being a net exporter while manufacturing trade increasingly dominates overall trade. At the same time, the level of income is likely to affect the growth rate in ways independent of the pattern of specialization. For this reason, we would like to have an indicator of trade specialization that isolates the effects of resource endowment and policies and adjusts for the influence of income level on the trade pattern.

Such an indicator is available from Chenery and Syrquin (1986). This is their index of trade orientation (TO), which measures the promanufacturing bias in the composition of commodity exports after adjusting for the country's income and size.[12] That is, it measures, for a given country, the deviation between the observed manufacturing trade bias and that predicted for a typical country of similar income and size. It thus reflects the degree to which the economy specializes in manufactures, as influenced by factors other than size and income (i.e., resource endowment and policies). A 1975 trade orientation index is available for 34 countries, most of which were semi–industrialized in the 1970s. We will also consider a smaller sample of 22 countries for which the TO index as well as Leamer's ratio of intraindustry trade and other trade characteristics are available. These 22 countries were aggregated, according to their trade orientation index, into the following groups: (1) a positive manufacturing export bias (some East Asian and Southern European countries), (2) a moderately positive primary export bias (some Latin American and East Asian countries, Malaysia, the Philippines, and Thailand), and (3) a strongly positive primary export bias (some Latin American countries and the Ivory Coast).

Table 18 summarizes the information available for the small sample, and table 19 presents the cross-country correlations for this group of countries. Table 20 presents cross-country correlations for the large sample.

A positive relationship between the investment share and manufacturing bias in trade is apparent in table 18 for the small sample. For the large sample, as shown in table 20, the correlation coefficient between the two variables is 0.35. The implication of the Graham paradox model of chapter 8 and of the multiple equilibria models presented above is precisely that the pattern of specialization has an effect on the investment share, as investment is enhanced by resource allocation toward increasing-returns industries. This is because of differences in the propensity to invest out profits and natural resource rents, as in the Graham model, or of industrial policy moving the economy to a high-growth path in the presence of multiple equilibria.

A second implication of models with increasing returns refers, as

TABLE 18.   Trade Orientation, Investment, and Growth (22 countries)

	Average Values for Country Groups		
	Manufacturing Bias	Primary Export Bias	
		Moderate	Strong
Trade orientation index	.45	−.10	−.45
Investment share	24.8	19.1	19.5
Growth rate	4.1	2.8	1.5
Trade share	84.8	48.5	39.2
Trade intensity (Leamer's index 1)	.08	.04	−.05
Intraindustry trade ratio	.56	.30	.17
Number of countries	10	6	6

Note: See the appendix to this chapter for country groupings, definitions, and sources.

TABLE 19.   Cross-Country Correlations (22 countries)

	Trade Orientation	Intraindustry	Trade Intensity	Trade Share
Trade orientation	1.00	0.69	0.42	0.35
Intraindustry	—	1.00	0.73	0.71
Trade intensity	—	—	1.00	0.85
Trade share	—	—	—	1.00

Note: See the appendix to this chapter for country groupings, definitions, and sources.

TABLE 20.   Cross-Country Correlations (34 countries)

	Trade Orientation	I/Y_{70-80}	Trade Share	Growth
Trade orientation	1.00	0.35	0.33	0.73
I/Y_{70-80}	—	1.00	0.30	0.54
Trade share	—	—	1.00	0.39
Growth	—	—	—	1.00

Note: See the appendix to this chapter for country groupings, definitions, and sources.

already mentioned, to the effects of the pattern of specialization on the rate of capital accumulation *for a given investment share.* As shown in table 20, the correlation between growth and the manufacturing trade orientation is, interestingly, very high (0.73), which is higher than that between the investment share and the trade orientation index. Also worth noting is the highly significant coefficient of trade orientation in a cross-country regression that includes investment share and the initial level of output per worker:

$$g = 2.02 + 0.09I/Y + 1.47\text{TO} - 0.0002Y/L_{60} \quad R^2 = 0.75,$$
$$\quad (3.73) \quad (4.02) \quad (4.39) \quad (-4.42)$$

where g is the growth rate of output per worker, 1960–90; I/Y is the real investment share, 1970–80; TO is the Chenery-Syrquin trade orientation index, 1975; and Y/L_{60} is the real GDP per worker in 1960. The t-statistics are in parentheses.

The equation indicates that, holding initial income and the investment share constant, countries specializing in manufacturing exports grew at a faster rate than those exporting primary products. If we think of sector S in our model as a resource-intensive sector with few linkages to increasing-returns activities, the equation illustrates the model's basic insight into the growth effects of investment allocation.

The initial level of output per worker also has a highly significant (and negative) coefficient in the regression. This suggests that across this group of 34 semi-industrial countries there was some degree of convergence: other things being equal, countries with a lower initial level of income tended to grow faster. However, as implied by the Graham paradox model (chap. 8) and the models discussed earlier in this chapter, convergence was conditioned by the pattern of specialization: countries exporting manufactures were converging toward high-income levels at a faster rate than were those exporting primary products.

Trade Openness, Investment, and Growth

In their "sensitivity analysis" of cross-country growth regressions, Levine and Renelt (1992) examined the robustness of the empirical linkages between long-run growth rates and a variety of economic, political, and institutional indicators. Their assessment reached pessimistic conclusions. While there are many econometric specifications in which a number of indicators are significantly correlated with per capita growth rates, almost all of these are fragile in the sense that "small alterations in the 'other' explanatory variables overturn past results" (943). Only two relationships pass their test of robustness. One is a positive correlation between growth and the share of investment in GDP. The second is a positive correlation between the ratio of trade to output and the investment share. Table 20 shows for our large sample of 34 countries results consistent with these findings: the positive correlation between growth and investment share (0.54) and that between trade share and investment share (0.30).

The first result is reassuring, as it conforms to standard economic theory. The second is very puzzling and worth exploring further. First, it is important to emphasize that the investment share is not related to trade barriers but to trade share, and therefore the robust relationship does not reflect the effects of trade policy. The relationships between the investment share, or alternatively the growth rate, and a number of indicators of trade barriers or trade policy distortions—Dollar's (1992) "real exchange rate distortion," the average black market exchange rate premium, and Syrquin and Chenery's index of outward orientation—are not robust. Moreover, when controlling for the investment share, there is no robust relationship between trade share and growth (this is so, incidentally, whether the trade indicator is the export share, the import share, or total trade). The fact that the robust correlation is between the trade and investment shares suggests that if trade affects growth it is not through the conventional theoretical channels that involve resource allocation but through less conventional effects that involve enhanced capital accumulation.

What these less conventional effects may be is unclear. Romer (1990a, 1990b) suggested that openness has a positive effect on research and development expenditures and, by increasing the rate of technological change, affects investment share and growth. Other views emphasize the positive effects of openness on technology transfer.[13] Whatever the merits of these views, they can hardly provide a convincing explanation of the Levine-Renelt finding. One reason is that openness in these models does not refer to trade shares, and, therefore, in terms of providing an explanation of the statistical relationship between the trade share and investment, they face an old objection recently restated by De Long and Summers (1991). Trade shares pick up differences in national size and proximity to trading partners. If Belgium and Holland merged, it is hard to see how the combined rate of technical progress would fall (or rise) as a result of this new entity being less "open" than each of the two countries separately.[14]

Even if the objection to viewing trade shares as a measure of openness is not decisive, the puzzle remains: why is it that the robust correlation is only between investment and the trade share and not between investment and other (more appropriate) measures of openness? The analysis in this and the previous chapter suggests a number of channels that can provide a convincing explanation of the positive relationship between trade and investment shares.[15] Our argument will be that the explanation of the trade-investment nexus may run through the pattern of trade specialization as this is determined by policy and factor endowment, including the natural resource endowment.

The main point is that the positive correlation between trade share and investment share is mediated by trade orientation, that is, the explanation of the positive relationship between trade and investment is that both trade and investment shares are positively affected by a pro-manufacturing bias in the trade orientation. We have already discussed and illustrated the effects of trade orientation on the investment share. Consider now the effects of trade orientation on the trade share. A positive relationship between these two variables is apparent in table 18. Tables 19 and 20 show positive correlation coefficients of 0.35 and 0.33.

Why should a manufacturing bias in trade orientation positively affect the trade share? One reason involves the positive effect that specialization in increasing-returns activities can have on trade creation. Increasing returns favor the expansion of intraindustry trade — two-way flows of trade in similar goods subject to economies of specialization. Countries with a stronger bias toward manufacturing in the export bundle typically show higher indices of intraindustry trade. The correlation coefficient between the two indices, as is shown in table 19, is 0.69.

A second mechanism may be the presence of Dutch disease effects in the trade orientation toward primary goods. The implication of the Dutch disease model of chapter 8 is precisely that countries exporting primary goods tend to be less open, other things being equal, since in the long-run equilibrium they have larger sectors producing nontradable goods. In this respect, it is noteworthy that the trade orientation index shows a positive relationship with Leamer's openness index (see tables 18 and 19). The Leamer index is an adjusted trade-intensity ratio that represents the difference between the actual level of trade (as opposed to the pattern of trade) and the level predicted by the Heckscher-Ohlin trade model, including factor endowment and distance to markets. The positive relationship with the manufacturing trade orientation indicates that the more the trade pattern is biased toward exports of primary products the lower the adjusted trade-intensity ratio tends to be. This may well be the result of larger nontradable goods sectors, together with less intraindustry trade, in countries specializing in primary goods.

Cross-country growth studies, with few recent exceptions, have neglected the role of trade orientation and natural resources.[16] Exceptions include Sachs and Warner 1995, 1997; and Sala-i-Martin 1997. It is worth concluding this chapter by pointing out that our results are consistent with their findings on the effects of primary export orientation on growth. In Sachs and Warner 1995, the ratio of resource-intensive exports to GDP has a negative impact on growth, an influence that the authors largely attribute to Dutch disease effects. In Sala-i-Martin 1997, the fraction of primary products in total exports is one of the few economic variables that systematically appear to be correlated with growth (with a negative sign).

APPENDIX

Large and Small Country Samples and Country Groupings

The cross-country correlations presented in table 20 refer to the large sample of 34 countries for which the Chenery and Syrquin index of trade orientation is available. These countries are shown in table A9.1, which also presents information on their trade orientation index and trade share.

The information in tables 18 and 19 refers to a smaller sample of 22 countries for which the TO index and Leamer's ratios of intraindustry trade and adjusted trade intensity are available. Leamer's ratios are shown in table A9.1. In table 18, these 22 countries were aggregated into three groups according to their trade orientation index. These groups are:

1. Countries with positive manufacturing export bias: Egypt, Greece, Hong Kong, Israel, Japan, Morocco, Portugal, Singapore, Spain, and Yugoslavia
2. Countries with a moderate primary export bias: Colombia, Costa Rica, Malaysia, the Philippines, Thailand, and Turkey
3. Countries with a strong primary export bias: Argentina, Brazil, the Dominican Republic, Ecuador, Ivory Coast, and Peru.

TABLE A9.1. Trade Orientation and Other Trade Characteristics

Country	Trade Orientation	Intraindustry Trade	Trade Intensity	Trade Share
Hong Kong	1.19	1.35	0.42	171.0
Taiwan	1.18	—	—	86.8
Korea	0.97	—	—	58.9
Portugal	0.79	0.40	−0.10	58.7
Israel	0.77	0.58	0.12	79.7
Yugoslavia	0.74	0.84	0.04	43.7
Egypt	0.31	0.10	−0.08	52.1
Singapore	0.20	1.08	0.51	302.3
Spain	0.20	0.70	0	30.4
Greece	0.18	0.28	−0.04	39.2
Japan	0.07	0.21	0	23.4
Morocco	0.07	0.09	−0.02	47.0
Costa Rica	−0.01	0.34	0.05	67.0
Malaysia	−0.03	0.45	0.31	87.8
Uruguay	−0.09	—	—	33.4
Colombia	−0.12	0.19	−0.13	29.9
Thailand	−0.12	0.24	0.03	42.8
Philippines	−0.13	0.37	−0.05	45.8
Guatemala	−0.13	—	—	44.3
Turkey	−0.19	0.18	0.05	17.6
Tunisia	−0.23	—	—	65.3
Ivory Coast	−0.29	0.22	0.19	72.2
Peru	−0.34	0.10	−0.21	35.5
Dominican Republic	−0.35	0.10	−0.01	47.8
Mexico	−0.35	—	—	17.3
Chile	−0.40	—	—	39.0
Algeria	−0.41	—	—	62.4
Argentina	0.47	0.28	−0.13	13.6
Syria	−0.48	—	—	49.9
Venezuela	−0.59	—	—	47.3
Ecuador	−0.60	0.02	−0.04	49.3
Iraq	−0.63	—	—	81.1
Brazil	−0.67	0.31	−0.11	17.0
Iran	−1.03	—	—	54.0

Sources:
Trade orientation: Trade orientation index 1975, Chenery and Syrquin 1986
Intraindustry trade: Intraindustry trade ratio, 1982, Leamer 1988
Trade intensity: Adjusted trade intensity ratio, 1982 (Leamer 1), in Leamer 1988
Trade share: (exports + imports)/nominal GDP, average for 1970–80, Penn World Table (Mark 5.6)
I/Y_{70-80}: Real investment share of GDP, average for 1970–80, Penn World Table (Mark 5.6)
Growth: Growth rate of real GDP per worker, 1960–90, Penn World Table (Mark 5.6)

CHAPTER 10

Development, Income Distribution, and Inequality Traps

In previous chapters, I have argued that classical development economics has much to contribute to the explanation of differences in income levels and growth rates across countries (see, in particular, chap. 4). This is so especially when this analytical framework is extended to account for the role of skill acquisition (chap. 6) and the pattern of trade specialization (chaps. 8 and 9). However, there is one aspect of the postwar development experience that remains elusive: the economic setbacks that from time to time are suffered at middle-income levels. These setbacks cannot be attributed to economies falling into classical development traps. According to the development models discussed so far, economies should record an acceleration of growth, rather than a slowdown, at these middle-income levels. This growth acceleration is the result of virtuous interactions between elastic labor supplies and the expansion of increasing-returns activities (see chap. 4), which precisely at an intermediate range of incomes generate a maximum growth rate. The following three chapters take up the issue of economic setbacks. This chapter begins with the role of inequality.

By and large, the societies of developing countries are less egalitarian than those of developed countries. In a merely accounting sense, this higher inequality plays a minor part in explaining why the mass of their populations is poorer than their counterparts in developed economies. If their income distributions were more equal and similar to those found in developed countries, the large differences in income per capita between these two groups of countries would imply that the mass of the populations in many, if not most, developing countries would still live in extreme poverty. Yet, at a deeper level is there not a connection between those two features, the poverty associated with higher inequality and the lower level of economic development? Why is it that we associate underdevelopment with the coexistence of the extremes of wealth and poverty? Could it be, for example, that the greater inequality found in developing countries is *due* to the lower level of development? Or have these countries remained poorer because their societies are less egalitarian?

An old theme in development economics is the Kuznets curve. In

264

the tradition of Kuznets (1955), the answer to the question of whether inequality is due to underdevelopment is affirmative: except for traditional societies that have barely begun the process of modern economic growth, developing countries tend to be less egalitarian because inequality increases in the initial and middle stages of economic development before declining in the more advanced stages. In this view, greater inequality in developing countries simply replicates a feature that characterized today's advanced economies at earlier stages of their development process.

A recent theme in the literature on endogenous growth looks at how income distribution may affect growth.[1] This literature has antecedents among early critics of the Kuznets curve and, in particular, in old arguments about the economic efficiency gains that can arise from greater equality. It gives an affirmative answer to the question of whether inequality is harmful to growth. Other things being equal, economic development is slower in less egalitarian societies. Since today's less developed countries are those that have grown more slowly over the past two centuries, the implication of this view is that one reason these countries are poorer is because they have remained less egalitarian.

This chapter attempts to integrate these two perspectives in a way that, to my knowledge, has not been tried before despite the implications that these two answers must have for each other. In bringing together the interactions between economic development and inequality, we shall see how the relationship between the rate of income growth and the level of income is modified by the adverse effect of inequality on growth. In particular, we shall see "inequality traps" emerging in the process of economic growth at middle- and lower-middle-income levels. These growth slowdowns are the result of Kuznets-curve mechanisms that tend to increase inequality at low- and middle-income levels, together with the adverse effects of inequality on growth emphasized by the recent literature.

This integration requires first assessing how much survives of the old literature and how solid are the contributions of the new approach. After a brief review of some stylized facts on income inequality across the world, we turn to a discussion of the forces affecting the relationship between inequality and income level. The interpretation of the Kuznets curve presented here is based on the evolution of urban-rural economic disparities resulting from the interactions between growth and rural-urban migration under conditions of increasing returns and imperfect labor mobility. We then assess the recent theoretical literature on inequality and growth and related empirical research. The hypotheses on the adverse effects of inequality on growth are evaluated in light of the empirical evidence while "controlling" for the presence of Kuznets curve effects in the cross-country data. Finally, we integrate the two sides of the relationship between economic development and inequality and discuss how growth slowdowns can arise at low- and middle-income levels as a result of inequality traps.

A difference between the two strands of literature is that, while the older one refers to a (controverted) empirical phenomenon (the Kuznets curve) without a good and generally accepted theoretical explanation, the second has a firmer theoretical foundation but is based on limited empirical research. This chapter will also contribute to filling these gaps by emphasizing theoretical aspects in the discussion of the Kuznets curve and presenting new empirical findings in the analysis of the effects of inequality on growth.

Stylized Facts

Less developed countries tend to be less egalitarian than developed countries. Kravis (1960) and Kuznets (1963) originally established empirically the greater inequality found in developing countries. Table 21 presents data for 71 countries in 1990 aggregated into four income levels. It shows that the average Gini coefficients of middle- and low-income countries are systematically higher than those of high-income economies.

The evidence also points, albeit in a less definite way, to the inverted-U pattern between inequality and income across countries: the Kuznets curve. The decline of inequality at higher income levels is clear in table 21 for the country sample as a whole and among European countries. The pattern of rising inequality at low-income levels is weaker but still observable within regions (especially in East and South Asia, sub-Saharan Africa, and North Africa and the Middle East). This weaker pattern of rising inequality at low-income levels explains why cross-sectional studies of the Kuznets curve among *developing countries* have been controverted. In support of it, Adelman and Robinson (1988) concluded their summary of previous findings as follows:

> All these studies agree on one descriptive result: the initial phase of the development process, during which a mostly agrarian economy starts industrialization, is necessarily marked by substantial increases in the inequality of the distribution of income. (958)

Later studies have questioned this evidence (see Anand and Kanbur 1993b and Fields and Jakubson 1994). Fields and Jakubson claim that the finding of an inverted-U pattern depends critically on the choice of

TABLE 21. Income Levels and Inequality in 1990

Gini Averages	High Income ≥ $11,508	Upper-Middle $9,576–$3,250	Lower-Middle $2,922–$1,658	Low Income $1,394–$902	Income ≤ $798	All Countries
Average per income group	34.8 (16)	44.4 (19)	42.3 (13)	43.9 (13)	44.9 (10)	41.8 (71)
Europe	30.8 (8)	32.9 (5)	–	–	–	31.6 (13)
East and South Asia	39.7 (3)	40.2 (4)	36.3 (3)	29.9 (3)	–	36.8 (13)
North Africa and Middle East	–	44.1 (1)	38.2 (5)	–	–	39.2 (6)
Oceania	41.0 (2)	–	–	–	–	41.0 (2)
Sub-Saharan Africa	–	49.5 (2)	–	48.0 (7)	44.9 (10)	46.5 (19)
North and South America	36.6 (3)	53.5 (7)	50.0 (5)	48.2 (3)	–	48.8 (18)

Source: See the appendix to this chapter.

Note: The Gini value is a percentage. The number of countries is in parentheses.

econometric method. While cross-sectional and pooled regressions feature the Kuznets pattern, a "fixed effects model," which allows different countries to be on "parallel" Kuznets curves, shows that inequality falls with the increase in income or even an inverted Kuznets pattern. While their conclusion that the favorable regression results are partly due to middle-income countries with high inequality being in fact on a different (higher) Kuznets curve is reasonable, their claim that the Kuznets pattern disappears in time-series data seems less solid.[2]

The data for our 71 countries in 1990 and for 40 countries in 1965 display a significant quadratic equation typically used to estimate the Kuznets curve. The coefficient on the income term is significant, with the expected positive sign, and the square of the income term has a negative and significant coefficient, implying that inequality first increases and then declines:

1965: GINI $= -280.6 + 87.4\mathrm{Log}y - 5.83(\mathrm{Log}y)^2$
$\qquad$ (-2.52) (2.99) $\quad(-3.08)$

(Adj.) $R^2 = 0.20$ $\quad N = 40$

1990: GINI $= -70.4 + 31.6\mathrm{Log}y - 2.2(\mathrm{Log}y)^2$
$\qquad$ (-1.02) (1.82) $\quad(-2.01)$

(Adj.) $R^2 = 0.15$ $\quad N = 71$.

It is clear, however, that whatever the merits and limitations of Kuznets curve studies, income levels (or the position on the Kuznets curve) can explain at most only a small portion of international differences in inequality. Table 21 points to the importance of these "other factors" by showing the large variation in inequality across regions, with Europe, East Asia, and South Asia being the more egalitarian regions and Latin America — containing the bulk of the middle- and low-income countries in the North and South American group — having the greatest inequality. In our regression results, the adjusted R^2 is of the order of 0.15 to 0.20, indicating that the most important role must be attributed to other factors. In fact, the regression results (in particular, the rather low R^2) suggest that, by far, *deviations from the position on the Kuznets curve* explain most of the cross-country differences in income distribution.

With respect to the time-series evidence, studies for individual countries are scarcer due to unavailability of data for long time periods in all but a few developed countries. Kuznets's original study (1955) relied on data for the United States, the United Kingdom, and Germany, showing a period of stable inequality followed by a decline as incomes increased.

Kuznets hypothesized that inequality may have increased in earlier stages. Williamson (1991) and other economic historians have confirmed that for the United States and the United Kingdom inequality first increased, then stabilized, and later declined over the period of structural transformation that began with the Industrial Revolution. At the same time, Williamson's work shows that the inverted-U pattern, if it existed at all, was much less pronounced in Japan and other East Asian industrializing countries for the more recent time periods for which data are available. Fields and Jakubson (1994) review time-series studies for developing countries and show that the evidence for the Kuznets hypothesis is weaker than in cross-sectional studies. However, in all of these cases the unavailability of data for long time periods makes it difficult to discern any strong patterns or draw firm conclusions.

Recent empirical research on the effects of income distribution on growth, which has proceeded more slowly than the theoretical literature on the subject, has largely consisted in adding inequality measures to the set of other variables that typically appear in standard growth regressions. These so-called reduced form regressions consistently suggest that initial inequality is detrimental to growth, and Clarke (1995) and Perotti (1996) provide strong support for the robustness of these findings. A typical estimate is that a one-standard-deviation decrease in inequality raises the annual growth rate of GDP per capita by 0.5 to 0.8 of a percentage point (Bénabou 1996).[3] It is worth pointing out that the pessimistic conclusions that Levine and Renelt (1992) drew from their "sensitivity analysis" do not apply in this case (see the discussion in chapter 9). Empirical research on the effects of inequality on growth is very recent and was not analyzed by Levine and Renelt.

Table 22 presents my own estimates following this approach. Starting from a typical growth regression (see Barro 1991, 1997), I have added the Gini coefficient to the set of variables considered there and alternatively included and dropped the investment share, which is frequently excluded.[4] The regression coefficient of the Gini variable turns out to be negative and statistically significant in all specifications, with a remarkably stable value of around −0.0005.

As noted by Perotti (1996), a substantial part of the negative association between inequality and growth seems to come from interregional variation in income distribution. The addition of dummy variables for Latin America, Africa, and South-East Asia in Perotti's regressions yields the expected negative signs for the slower growing and more unequal Latin America and African regions and a positive sign for the faster growing and less unequal South-East Asia. The inclusion of these dummy variables makes the coefficient on his measure of equality fall by about 30 percent. In Fishlow (1995), the inclusion of a dummy variable for

Latin America turns the coefficient on the inequality indicator to become statistically insignificant. The results presented in table 23 also tend to confirm that intercontinental variation in income distribution plays a role in the negative association between inequality and growth. Thus, among Latin American and OECD countries, the coefficient of the inequality variable is insignificant (and positive). Still, the negative effects of inequality on growth on the (mostly) low-income countries in Africa and Asia — and the high significance of the coefficient in the case of Africa — suggest that "within-region variation" also has an important role.

Table 24 shows that urban-rural disparities are a most striking feature of inegalitarian developing countries, particularly in Latin America and sub-Saharan Africa.[5] A disproportionate number of the poor in developing countries — 75 to 80 percent in Africa and Asia and 70 percent in Latin America — are located in the rural areas and engage in agricultural activities (see on this subject Todaro 1994, chap. 5). High urban-rural inequality is certainly a major characteristic that distin-

TABLE 22. Inequality and Growth Regression Results, 1960–89

Independent Variable	1	2
Constant	0.094	0.094
	(3.92)	(3.63)
$Logy_0$	−0.012	−0.011
	(−3.14)	(−2.77)
I/Y	0.001	—
	(2.51)	
PRIMo	0.031	0.050
	(2.11)	(3.73)
SECo	−0.002	0.007
	(−0.12)	(0.39)
ASSASS	−0.201	−0.233
	(−1.85)	(−1.95)
GINI	−0.0004	−0.0005
	(−1.71)	(−1.95)
N	37	37
Adjusted R^2	0.47	0.38

Note:

y_0: GDP per capita in 1960. *Source:* Penn World Table (Mark 5.6).

I/Y: Ratio of real domestic investment to real GDP (average for the period). *Source:* Penn World Table (Mark 5.6).

PRIMo: Primary school enrollment rate in 1960. *Source:* Barro and Lee 1994.

SECo: Secondary school enrollment rate in 1960. *Source:* Barro and Lee 1994.

ASSASS: Number of political assassinations per million population per year (average for the period). *Source:* Barro and Lee 1994.

GINI: Gini coefficient circa 1965. *Source:* see the appendix to this chapter.

t-statistics in parentheses

Dependent variable: Growth rate of real GDP per capita

TABLE 23. Inequality and Growth within Regions Regression Results

Independent Variable	All Countries	OECD	Asia	Africa	Latin America
Constant	0.070	0.106	−0.108	0.016	0.045
	(2.65)	(3.77)	(−1.40)	(1.00)	(0.29)
$Logy_0$	−0.0023	−0.0097	0.027	0.011	−0.004
	(−0.82)	(−3.10)	(2.23)	(3.71)	(−0.29)
GINI	−0.0006	0.0002	−0.0011	−0.0015	0.00009
	(−2.40)	(0.81)	(−1.77)	(− 7.36)	(0.08)
N	37	11	13	5	8
Adjusted R^2	0.10	0.45	0.23	0.93	−0.28

Note:
y_0: GDP per capita in 1960. *Source:* Penn World Table (Mark 5.6).
GINI: Gini coefficient circa 1965. *Source:* see the appendix to this chapter.
t-statistics in parentheses
Dependent variable: Growth rate of real GDP per capita, 1960–89

TABLE 24. Income Inequality and Urban-Rural Disparities

	Gini[a]	Urban-Rural Gap[b]	Number of Countries
By income level			
High income	30.1	1.00	7
Upper middle	38.4	1.16	7
Middle income	44.6	1.33	7
Lower middle	43.4	1.94	8
Low income	37.9	2.03 (1.73)[c]	7
By region			
Europe	30.4	1.00	9
North Africa and Middle East	36.2	1.65 (1.28)[d]	5
Asia	38.0	1.40	5
Sub-Saharan Africa	40.3	1.80 (1.57)[c]	10
Latin America	50.9	1.69	7

Note: The sample includes 36 countries for which information was available on basic services and income distribution.
[a]Gini coefficient circa 1990 as a percentage. *Source:* see the appendix to this chapter.
[b]Ratio of the percentage of urban to rural population with access to health care, safe water, and sanitation (each of these indicators was given an equal weight of 1/3). *Source:* UNDP, *Human Development Report*, 1996, World Development Indicators.
[c]Excluding Zambia with an urban-rural gap of 3.85
[d]Excluding Morocco with an urban-rural gap of 3.13

guishes developing from developed economies, which have far more even regional development and more equal income distribution (see table 24). Interestingly, urban-rural disparities replicate to some extent the inverted-U pattern of the relationship between income inequality and income level, although the data also suggest that urban-rural inequality tends to increase more at lower levels of income than does inequality in the overall income distribution.

Economic Inequality and Income Level

We now turn to a discussion of the forces that can cause income distribution to change in the process of economic development. In doing so, we shall distinguish between the forces that may account for an inverted-U relationship between inequality and income level and those that account for deviations from this pattern. Regarding the first set of forces, our focus will be on how the relationship between inequality and economic development is shaped by changes in the structure of factor returns and in urban-rural income disparities. In the second case, we shall look at the role of the distribution of factor endowments and the effects of the pattern of growth.

The Changing Composition of Factor Endowments

Most of the growth models examined in previous chapters would probably agree that one explanatory factor of the relationship between inequality and income level is to be found in the levels of factor endowments and their effects on the functional distribution of income. Developing countries typically have a relative abundance of unskilled labor and a relative scarcity of physical capital and skilled labor. The scarce factors tend to be less equally distributed than unskilled labor. At low levels of education, returns to education are likely to increase and the same may happen with returns to capital as a result of increasing returns to scale in the presence of elastic supplies of unskilled labor. As a result, at very low income levels, the relative scarcity of skilled labor and physical capital may not generate very high returns for these scarce factors. As income increases, the composition of factor endowments changes as economies increase their physical and human capital endowments. The presence of increasing returns to the unequally distributed factors tends to cause inequality to increase over a range of low- and middle-income levels. The abundance of skilled labor and capital will eventually generate diminishing returns to these unequally distributed factors and thus will contribute to a reduction in inequality. Over the corresponding range of income levels, inequality would be inversely correlated with the stocks of physical capital and education per worker.

An inverse relationship across countries between inequality and capital endowments is present in the regression results in table 25. Interestingly, the quadratic specifications in equations 3 and 4, which are consistent with the inverted-U pattern between inequality and income, suggest the presence of factors offsetting the inverse relationship at low-income levels. We have mentioned the role of increasing rates of return on physical and human capital at low-income levels that arises from interactions between increasing returns to scale and elastic factor supplies. In addition, there is an effect of the small share of income of the scarce factors due to their low levels (as suggested by a Lewis-type model).

The Evolution of Urban-Rural Disparities

As suggested earlier, perhaps the most valid generalization about income distribution in developing countries is that income inequality takes the form of a striking contrast between urban wealth and rural poverty (see table 24). We now turn to a model that displays the inverted-U relationship between inequality and income level as a result of the evolution of urban-rural disparities throughout the process of economic development. Our framework combines features of the development models of chapters 4 and 5, and their implications for the functional distribution of income, with insights about the rural-urban distribution of income from the literature on migration and unemployment.

The economy considered is open to international trade and has two

TABLE 25. Inequality and Factor Endowments Cross-Country Results, 1990

Independent Variable	Group 1	Group 2	Group 3	Group 4
Constant	79.3	54.5	−22.0	40.1
	(8.77)	(13.77)	(−0.38)	(5.25)
Log(K/L)	−4.27	—	19.34	—
	(−4.38)		(1.45)	
Log(H/L)	—	−0.81	—	1.43
		(−3.87)		(1.36)
[Log(K/L)]^2	—	—	−1.34	—
			(−1.78)	
[Log(H/L)]^2	—	—	—	−0.07
				(−2.17)
N	46	46	46	46
Adjusted R^2	0.29	0.24	0.32	0.30

Note: K/L and *H/L* refer to the capital-labor force ratio and education, respectively. See the appendix to chapter 1 for sources and definitions.

t-statistics in parentheses

Dependent variable: Gini coefficient

sectors, A and M, which face given world prices, p_A and p_M, in the international market. The agricultural sector (A) is labor intensive and produces under diminishing returns to labor:

$$A = \alpha L_A^{1-b} \quad b < 1. \tag{1}$$

The manufacturing sector (M) is capital intensive and features technological externalities that generate increasing returns to scale:

$$M = (\tilde{K})^\mu K_a L_M^{1-a} \quad a + \mu < 1, \tag{2}$$

where $(\tilde{K})^\mu$ is the external effect of the average capital stock. The inequality restriction in equation 2 rules out increasing returns to capital. For simplicity, we leave aside labor force growth. Agricultural workers earn the average product of labor, and manufacturing workers earn the marginal product of labor. Thus, labor earnings per worker in the two sectors are:

$$w_A = \alpha L_A^{-b} \tag{3}$$

$$w_M = (1-a)K^{a+\mu}L_M^{-a}, \tag{4}$$

where we have chosen units such that $p_A = p_M = 1$.

The migration rate ($m = MR/LF_A$) is an increasing function of the urban-rural wage differential (MR is the number of migrants and LF_A is the rural labor force, including migrants and agricultural workers). A simple version of such a migration function is:

$$L_A/LF_A = (w_M/w_A)^\theta \quad \theta > 0, \tag{5}$$

which implies that $(1 - m)^{-1/\theta} = \omega$, where $\omega = w_M/w_A$.

In the short run, the capital stock is given and there is no labor mobility between the two sectors. The urban labor market clears at a wage determined by the equality between the exogenously given urban labor force and labor demand in industry. The rural wage is determined by the average product of labor at the existing level of agricultural employment, which in turn is equal to the given rural labor force less the migrants.[6] The model gives us solutions for w_A, w_M, and m. From equations 3 and 4, we have:

$$\omega = (1-a)K^{a+\mu}LF_A^{b}(1-m)^{b}/\alpha L_M^{a} \quad \omega = w_M/w_A, \tag{6}$$

which shows a negative relationship between the wage premium and the migration rate. From the migration function in equation 5, we have a positive relationship between the urban wage premium and migration:

$$\omega = 1/(1 - m)^{1/\theta}. \tag{7}$$

Equations 6 and 7 determine simultaneously the short-run equilibrium values of the urban-rural wage differential (ω) and the migration rate (m). Figure 47 illustrates the short-run solution to the model. The $m(\omega)$ curve is the graph of the migration function (eq. 5): it is positively sloped since a higher urban-rural wage differential raises the migration rate. The $\omega(m)$ curve shows the market equilibrium value of the ratio of urban to rural wages at each given level of the migration rate (eq. 6). This curve is negatively sloped: a higher migration rate reduces the level of employment of those engaged in agricultural production and increases the average product of labor in this sector, given the presence of diminishing returns to labor. Thus, the urban wage premium narrows.

The model features unemployment in the short run (the migrants are the unemployed). This may properly be called migration-induced unemployment. It is worth noting, however, that its nature is rather different from that in the well-known Harris-Todaro model: migration is not zero when the economy is in short-run equilibrium. In fact, if there were no migration there would be no unemployment and no wage differential. The wage premium arises from imperfect labor mobility rather than being exogenous as in the Harris-Todaro model.[7]

Consider the effects of changes in the capital stock and the urban-rural composition of the labor force. An increase in the capital stock shifts the $\omega(m)$ function upward (see eq. 6). By raising labor demand in the urban sector, it increases the urban wage premium as well as the migration rate. This unequalizing effect of capital accumulation — in the sense that it increases urban-rural disparities — is analogous to the effect that a higher level of urban employment has on unemployment in a Harris-Todaro model, in which a higher demand for labor in urban areas induces a higher rate of migration and unemployment.[8] As shown by equation 4, the strength of this effect depends positively on the degree to which returns to scale increase in the industrial sector.

An increase in the urban labor supply relative to the rural labor force shifts the $\omega(m)$ curve downward and reduces migration and the urban wage premium (see eq. 6). Urbanization, understood as an increase in the urban labor force and a reduction in the rural labor force, has an equalizing effect on urban-rural disparities. Ultimately, this is due to the presence of diminishing returns to labor in both sectors. It is

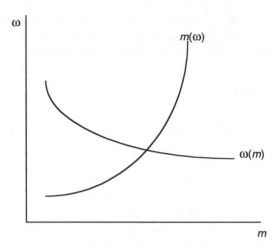

Fig. 47. Short-run determination of migration and the urban wage premium

worth noting that this equalizing effect is not present in the standard Harris-Todaro model, since there the urban-rural wage differential is given.

The reader may also verify that an exogenous increase in the rural labor force and a productivity improvement in agriculture have opposite effects on the urban wage premium. In the first case, the $\omega(m)$ curve shifts upward by reducing the average product of labor in agriculture; in the second case, the $\omega(m)$ curve shifts downward as technological change increases the average product of labor in agriculture. Our analysis in what follows will focus on the effects of capital accumulation and the changing composition of the labor force.

Over time, migration proceeds at a rate that increases with the urban wage premium. We assume that the accumulation of capital is increasing in the industrial profit rate. The resulting changes in the composition of the labor force and the capital stock modify the short-run equilibrium values of urban and rural wages. What is the path of urban-rural disparities as a result of these changes? Clearly, the evolution of urban-rural disparities will depend on the strength of each of the two effects described earlier, the unequalizing effect of capital accumulation and the equalizing effect of urbanization. As we now shall see, the balance of the two effects can be shown to depend on the urban-rural composition of the labor force.

For small values of the urban labor force, the equalizing effects of urbanization associated with the presence of diminishing returns to labor in agriculture are relatively weak. The reason is that with most of the labor force employed in agriculture the reallocation effects of migration have a small effect on rural wages. As a result, the unequalizing effects of capital accumulation operating through the increase in the urban wage premium tend to dominate. This is so whether the initial urban labor force is large or small relative to the capital stock in industry. When the urban labor force is large, the positive productivity effects of industrial employment (associated with increasing returns) translate into positive profitability effects on capital accumulation, which reinforce the growth of the urban-rural wage differential. When the urban labor force is small, those profitability effects are offset by the relatively large impact of capital accumulation on urban wages. In this case, however, the increase in labor demand pulls the urban wage up to such an extent that despite the negative effect on capital accumulation, the urban wage premium increases.[9] Urbanization and capital accumulation, then, go hand in hand with a widening of rural-urban disparities. Because these disparities induce increasing migration rates, we also have in this phase a Todaro-type phenomenon of urbanization tending to outpace the rate of industrialization.

At higher levels of urbanization, the equalizing effects of migration become stronger and capital accumulation proceeds at a slower pace as the profit rate falls. The mechanisms described operate in reverse, and the equalizing effects of migration more than offset the unequalizing effects of capital accumulation. The urban-rural wage differential then tends to fall as urbanization proceeds.

Formally, suppose that the capital stock changes at a rate $(\hat{K})$ that is a positive function of the differential between the domestic rate of profit (r) and an international, risk-adjusted profit rate (r^*):

$$\hat{K} = \phi(r - r^*),\tag{8}$$

where ϕ is a positive parameter. In competitive equilibrium, the profit rate is given by:

$$r = aL_M{}^{1-a}/K^{1-(a+\mu)}.\tag{9}$$

Substituting from equation 9 into 8, we get the dynamic equation for K:

$$\hat{K} = \phi(aL_M{}^{1-a}/K^{1-(a+\ \mu)} - r^*).\tag{10}$$

From equation 10, setting $\hat{K} = 0$, we obtain a locus of (L_M, K) combinations along which the capital stock is stationary:

$$L_M = [r^*K^{1-(a+\mu)}/a]^{1/(1-a)}. \tag{11}$$

Now, using equations 6 and 7 to eliminate ω, we obtain a reduced-form equation for the short-run value of the migration rate. Setting $m = 0$, we obtain a locus of (L_M, K) combinations along which the rural labor force (LF_A), and thus the urban labor force also, is stationary. The equation of this locus is:

$$L_M = [(1 - a)K^{(a+\mu)}LF_A{}^b/\alpha]^{1/a}. \tag{12}$$

Figure 48 shows the long-run solution of the model in $(\log K, \log L_M)$ space.[10] The slope of the $\hat{K} = 0$ locus, obtained by taking logs in equation 11 and differentiating with respect to $\log K$, is a constant less than unity under the assumption of increasing returns $(\mu > 0)$:

$$\mathrm{d}\log L_M/\mathrm{d}\log K = [1 - (a + \mu)]/(1 - a).$$

The slope of the locus $\hat{L}_M = 0$ is derived in a similar way from equation 12:

$$\mathrm{d}\log L_M/\mathrm{d}\log K = (a + \mu)/[a + b(L_M/LF_A)].$$

The slope is thus larger than unity (and larger than the slope of the $\hat{K} = 0$ locus) when L_M is small (for $L_M = 0$, the slope is clearly more than one with $\mu > 0$) and tends toward zero at high values of L_M, when LF_A tends toward zero.

As shown in figure 48, the model features multiple interior equilibria, one of which is a saddle point at the low-K intersection and the other a locally stable equilibrium at the high-K intersection. The downward-sloping saddle path is a critical locus of (L_M, K) combinations below which the economy is in a development trap. In this trap, capital accumulation and urbanization cannot get off the ground. Rural-urban migration is insufficient to offset the negative effects of capital accumulation on profitability. The low profit rate then leads to a contraction of the capital stock, which reduces the urban wage premium and migration. The reader may want to verify that the presence of increasing returns to scale $(\mu = 0)$ is critical for the existence of the trap.

Above the saddle path, and provided that the economy is either below the $\hat{K} = 0$ schedule or above the $\hat{L}_M = 0$ locus, the path toward the high-K equilibrium will feature a negative slope $(\mathrm{d}\log L_M/\mathrm{d}\log K < 0)$ initially. This negative slope is a sufficient condition for the existence of

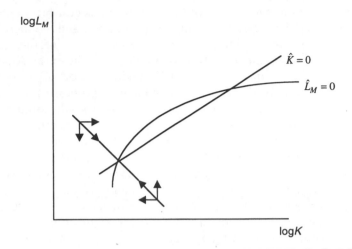

Fig. 48. Long-run dynamics of urbanization and capital accumulation

an initial period in which rural-urban disparities tend to increase. Indeed, solving equations 6 and 7 for the urban wage premium, taking logs and differentiating with respect to $\log K$, we obtain:

$$\text{dlog}\omega/\text{dlog}K = \{[(a + \mu)/(1 + \theta b)] - [a + b(L_M/LF_A)]/(1 + b)\}$$

$(\text{dlog}L_M/\text{dlog}K)$.

With $\text{dlog}L_M/\text{dlog}K < 0$, the process will feature an initial period in which $\text{dlog}\omega/\text{dlog}K$ is positive, and therefore the urban wage premium rises with capital accumulation. When the slope of the actual path becomes positive, the increase in urban-rural disparities slows down and eventually is reversed, as (L_M/LF_A) is sufficiently large to make $\text{dlog}\omega/\text{dlog}K$ negative.

The model generates under certain conditions the inverted-U shape of the Kuznets curve. In this framework, the critical assumptions required to generate this pattern are the following. The first is the presence of imperfect labor mobility. Otherwise, the short-run equilibrium would be characterized by a zero migration rate and the urban wage premium would not change, always being such as to generate the zero migration rate.[11] The second assumption refers to the presence of diminishing returns to labor in agriculture. Indeed, suppose that there were increasing returns in agriculture. The effect of employment growth in the modern sector would unambiguously lead to a widening of urban-rural wage differentials, as the contraction of the agricultural sector brings about a fall in its productivity and both capital accumulation and the increase in the urban labor force tend to have unequalizing effects. Interacting with increasing returns in industry, this worsening of urban-rural disparities would further accelerate the growth of the modern sector and the contraction of agriculture. In this Myrdalian cumulative process of uneven regional development, the growth acceleration phase would continue until the agricultural sector disappears. This process would be accompanied by ever worsening disparities among regions. The third assumption, although not strictly necessary, is the presence of increasing returns to scale in industry. Under these conditions, the impact of the reallocation toward this sector (i.e., of a faster rate of employment growth in the modern sector than in agriculture) during the early stages of the process is to increase the productivity growth differential in favor of industry. Under constant returns to scale in the industrial sector, there would be no tendency for capital accumulation to accelerate in the early stages, and thus the tendency for the urban wage premium to increase would be more moderate.

This account should be distinguished from the more common interpretation of the Kuznets curve, in which the inverted-U pattern arises from the process of reallocation of the labor force from a poor and egalitarian rural sector toward an expanding and inegalitarian urban sector.[12] In that interpretation, the initial stages of the process of labor force reallocation lead to increasing inequality overall, as the share in total income of the poorer and more egalitarian rural sector decreases. This is followed by a leveling off and then a decline in inequality because the share in total income of the middle-income urban classes increases in the later stages of the process. This rather mechanistic process is based on the assumptions that the ratio of the mean incomes between urban and rural areas remains constant and that income distribution remains more unequal in urban than rural areas. The presence of diminishing returns in agriculture and increasing returns to scale in the urban sector play no role there. In contrast, our emphasis on these two assumptions makes the initial increase in inequality result from an increasing ratio of the mean incomes between the urban and rural areas, along with widening disparities within the urban areas. This is followed by a decline in interregional and intraregional disparities. This interpretation is much more Myrdalian in that the unequalizing increasing-returns effects (or "backwash effects" in Myrdal 1957) dominate at low- and middle-income levels and the equalizing diminishing-returns effects (or "spread effects") dominate at higher income levels.[13]

It has often been argued that the upward-sloping section of the Kuznets curve is perfectly escapable or may become a perpetual fate depending on the style of economic development.[14] Our analytical framework has a number of implications concerning the effects of growth on inequality that provide some support for this assertion. The implications that the model has for the effects of the style of growth on inequality can be summarized as follows. First, growth based on physical capital accumulation generates more inequality at low- and middle-income levels, by worsening the urban-rural income distribution, and less inequality at high-income levels by improving urban-rural disparities. As argued earlier, the overall impact of capital accumulation on inequality is likely to vary with the level of urbanization, with the worsening of the rural-urban distribution dominating at low levels of urbanization and the equalizing effects dominating at higher levels. It therefore follows that, *other things being equal,* the impact of growth on the distribution of income varies with the level of development and changes sign from low to high levels of income.

Second, balanced productivity growth between agriculture and industry generates less inequality than does industry-biased productivity growth. A higher rate of land-augmenting technical progress implies a higher rate of growth of rural wages at each level of the urban labor force. Actual urban-rural disparities tend to be smaller. As discussed earlier, the effects on distribution of a higher rate of population growth in rural areas are symmetrically opposite those of agricultural technical progress and will instead worsen the urban-rural income distribution.

Finally, growth based on physical capital accumulation is likely to generate less equality than does skill-based growth. In its simplest version, the accumulation of skills is equivalent in its effects to labor-augmenting technical progress. As such, in a small open economy facing given relative prices it will tend to benefit the labor-intensive sector. If agriculture is more labor intensive than industry, this has a negative effect on the urban-rural wage differential and therefore an equalizing effect. One should add, however, that a number of mechanisms may counteract these equalizing effects, to the extent that educational services are concentrated in urban areas. Under these conditions, the external effects of skill acquisition are larger in the urban than in the rural sector and rural-urban migration is likely to adversely affect the average level of skills in rural areas. This redistribution of skills will prevent the growth in the skilled labor force from being uniform by augmenting the growth of skills of the urban labor force and slowing it down in the rural sector.[15]

The results presented in table 26 support some of these implications. The growth of capital and education per worker both have negative effects on inequality, but only the coefficient of the latter is statistically significant (in regression 2). Moreover, the size of this coefficient is clearly larger in absolute value than the one reflecting the size of the effects of growth in capital per worker on inequality (see, in particular, regression 3). The results in equation 4, although statistically insignificant, show the expected change of the sign of the effects of overall growth on inequality beyond a certain level of income.

Deviations from the Kuznets Curve: The Distribution of Factor Endowments

Although there are good reasons to expect a Kuznets-type relationship between income inequality and income level, the fact is that the position on the Kuznets curve (associated with the level of per capita income) can explain at most only a small part of international differences in inequality. It has been pointed out that in the regression results presented earlier the adjusted R^2 is rather low, suggesting that the forces that account for *deviations from the position on the Kuznets curve* explain most of the cross-country differences in income distribution.

A preliminary discussion of these forces was present in our empiri-

TABLE 26. Changes in Inequality and Growth Regression Results, 1965–90

Independent Variable	1	2	3	4
Constant	9.8	9.46	10.05	11.69
	(1.37)	(1.87)	(1.46)	(1.52)
$g_{(K/L)}$	−0.378	—	−0.09	—
	(−0.54)		(−0.13)	
$g_{(H/L)}$	—	−2.76	−2.71	—
		(−1.81)	(−1.68)	
g_y	—	—	—	2.27
				(0.50)
$(\mathrm{Log}y_0)g_y$	—	—	—	−0.39
				(−0.61)
GINIo	0.75	0.86	0.85	0.73
	(5.57)	(6.87)	(5.98)	(5.09)
N	25	25	25	25
Adjusted R^2	0.61	0.65	0.64	0.60

Source: For y, Penn World Table (Mark 5.6); for *K/L* and *H/L*, see note to table 22.
Note:
$g_{(K/L)}$ = growth rate of capital per worker, 1965–90
$g_{(H/L)}$ = growth rate of human per capital worker, 1965–90
g_y = growth rate of per capita GDP, 1965–90
$\log y_0$ = logarithm of GDP per capita in 1965
GINIo = Gini coefficient circa 1965. *Source:* see the appendix to this chapter.
t-statistics in parentheses
Dependent variable: Gini coefficient circa 1990

cal analysis of the implications of the Kuznets-Myrdal model in the previous section. What other forces can account for deviations from the Kuznets curve? There has been surprisingly little research on this subject. One exception is the early and influential research by Ahluwalia (1974, 1976), who found that, after controlling for the level of income per capita, inequality was negatively associated with the rate of income growth, as well as primary and secondary school enrollments, and positively associated with population growth. As we shall see in the next section, similar associations have recently been found in the new literature on inequality and growth, although here the causation is interpreted in reverse: inequality adversely affects growth and investment in education while inducing higher population growth.

   Another exception is the work of Bourguignon and Morrisson (1990), whose findings highlight the role of the distribution of factor endowments. The following regression results summarize their main findings for two samples of 35 and 20 developing countries:

$$IN = 64 - 0.24S - 0.05V_T + 6.5D_R + 2.9D_A \quad \text{(Adj.) } R^2 = 0.56$$
$$\quad\quad\quad (4.8) \quad (1.5) \quad\quad (3.5) \quad\quad (1.4)$$

$$N = 35$$

$$IN = 63 - 0.16S - 0.11V_T + 6D_R + 2.8D_A + 3.2P \quad \text{(Adj.) } R^2 = 0.49$$
$$\quad\quad\quad (9) \quad (2) \quad\quad (2.1) \quad\quad (2.2) \quad (1) \quad\quad (1.5)$$

$$N = 20,$$

with the *t*-statistics in parentheses.

   The inequality variable (IN) is the income share of the richest 20 percent of the population in the distribution of income. Indicators of the level and distribution of schooling (S)[16] and land distribution (V_T) and the share of agricultural and mineral exports in GDP (D_A and D_R) explain nearly 60 percent of the variance in inequality in the cross section of 35 developing countries. The influence of mineral resources, despite the fact that nowadays these are often publicly owned, is taken to reflect the slowly changing impact on income distribution of the traditionally high concentration of these resources in the hands of a few. In the sample with 20 countries, the authors add an indicator of trade protection (P), which features a positive and significant coefficient in the regressions (not shown here) involving the income share of the bottom 40 and 60 percent. The authors interpret this positive effect as reflecting the fact that protection reduces the returns to the relatively abundant factors — such as unskilled labor in developing countries, which tends to be the most equally distributed — and raises them to the relatively scarce factors — such as capital and skilled labor — which are more highly concentrated (Bourguignon and Morrisson 1990, 1127).

In our analysis, changes in inequality are fully driven by changes in factor returns and regional disparities. It is worth concluding this section by briefly highlighting the role of *endogenous* changes in the ownership structure of factor endowments. Some of these changes generate a tendency toward growing inequality as income increases, such as the "cumulative effects of the concentration of savings," which was perceived by Kuznets (1955) as a major force tending to increase inequality in the distribution of wealth. Others, such as the growth of organized labor movements with the expansion of the modern sectors of the economy and the extension of political rights, generate a tendency toward equality. These changes result in social and economic reforms that modify the posttax income distribution, expand access to education for the mass of the population, and speed up the process of skill acquisition.

The Effects of Inequality on Growth

In chapter 6, I mentioned that four countries (the Philippines, the Dominican Republic, Paraguay, and Sri Lanka), with levels of income and education similar to those of South Korea and Taiwan in the early 1960s, had poor growth performances compared to the two East Asian economies (see Rodrik 1994). In chapter 1, we saw that a number of other developing countries (Argentina, Uruguay, Panama, and South Africa) grew at a slow pace from 1965 to 1997 despite seemingly high levels of education. With the exception of Sri Lanka, what all these countries seem to have in common is a high degree of income inequality, certainly much higher than the relatively low degree of inequality prevailing in Taiwain and South Korea. In recent years, this apparent negative relationship between income inequality and growth across countries, which appears to be strong enough to offset the positive effects on growth of a relatively high level of education, has attracted considerable attention in the endogenous growth literature.

This recent literature focuses on the causation running from inequality to growth. It reaches conclusions opposite those of the classical view, which Williamson (1991) calls the Smithian tradeoff, according to which inequality, by redistributing income toward high savers and thus raising the savings rate, is favorable to growth. It is worth noting that this mechanism is considerably weakened in an open economy, in which the rate of accumulation, even at full employment, is no longer constrained by the domestic savings rate.[17] There is no dearth of analyses supporting the hypothesis of income distribution affecting growth. However, the posited channels through which this takes place vary widely. I begin this section by briefly reviewing these channels. To facilitate the exposition, I will categorize the different approaches under two main headings: (1) those approaches that involve sociopolitical channels, along with economic mechanisms, and affect growth through their influence on physical capital accumulation and productivity; and (2) those approaches that essentially rely on economic mechanisms that affect factor growth (capital, skills, and labor) and thus the rates of capital and skill deepening.

Sociopolitical Mechanisms

Suppose that the rate of physical capital accumulation is a function of the posttax return on capital and a risk-adjusted international profit rate (i.e., the posttax profit rate abroad adjusted for domestic political risk): $I/K = I[r(1 - t) - r^*]$. The following approaches have in common the fact that the link between inequality and growth is forged by sociopolitical factors that affect tax rates or political risk and as a result the rate of investment.

In the fiscal policy approach, income distribution affects growth via its effects on taxation and government expenditure. The key idea is that in democratic political regimes inequality generates pressures for redistribution: inequality lowers the income of the median voter relative to the national average and makes the middle class more likely to ally itself with the poor to press for redistribution. This pressure leads to distortionary taxes, such as a tax on capital, which then discourages the rate of accumulation and growth.[18] Differences within this approach refer to the type of government expenditure they consider: public investment (Alesina and Rodrik 1994), redistributive transfers from rich to poor (Persson and Tabellini 1994), and redistribution from capital to labor (Bertola 1993).

Empirical findings have been disappointing, on balance, for the fiscal approach. This seems to have occurred for two reasons. First, redistributive transfers may have a positive effect on growth by, for example, relaxing constraints on human capital investments by the poor.[19] These positive effects can then offset the negative effects of higher taxation. Second, by reducing social tensions and political instability, fiscal redistribution may have a positive effect on growth, which again counteracts the negative effect of higher taxation (this point is made in Alesina and Perotti 1994).

A second approach focuses on the effects of inequality on sociopolitical instability and conflict (Alesina and Perotti 1994; Alesina et al. 1996). In this view, inequality creates strong incentives for different social groups to engage in rent-seeking activities and leads to social unrest that may make property rights insecure. The resulting uncertainty about the distribution of resources, including an increased expropriation risk, reduces the rate of accumulation and growth. Is this any different from the previous explanation, except that the emphasis is on political risk rather than a tax on capital? Bénabou (1996) points out that in these models the growth rate can be shown to be negatively related to interest groups' rent-seeking *abilities* as well as to income disparities. This means that what really matters for insecurity and sociopolitical instability is not income inequality per se but *inequality in the relative distribution of income and political power.* Greater income inequality accompanied by greater inequality in political power (in the same direction) need not be detrimental to growth. What is detrimental is the asymmetrical situation in which a high degree of income inequality accompanies relative equality in political power. If, as contributors to the fiscal policy approach emphasize (see Alesina and Rodrik 1994), the political economy mechanism of pressure for redistribution is characteristic of democratic political regimes, then these two sets of explanations come very close to one another.

Empirical evidence in support of the importance of inequality in the *relative* distribution of income and political power comes from the fact that growth rates across Latin America are not negatively associated with inequality — unlike what happens with intercontinental differences in inequality and growth.[20] The lack of a negative relationship reflects the fact that some of the least inegalitarian countries — Argentina, Chile, and Uruguay, in the southern cone — were slow-growing economies in the postwar period, while two of the fastest growing (Brazil and Mexico) were among the most inegalitarian countries. However, Brazil and Mexico did not have higher inequality in the relative distribution of income and political power than countries in the southern cone did. Their authoritarian regimes and the weakness of their trade unions implied that their more unequal income distribution was accompanied by greater inequality in political power in the same direction.

A third approach posits that inequality leads to polarization, which in turn undermines the consensus for policy reforms (Haggard and Webb 1993) or the security of property and contractual rights (Keefer and Knack 1997). While the end result is similar to that of previous approaches, the political channel is different here. Drawing on an argument by Esteban and Ray (1994), Keefer and Knack (1997) emphasize the difficulties of collective decision making under conditions of great inequality. The consequence is that inequality reduces the stability and predictability of government decisions by making social consensus more fragile. Potentially, this type of political channel is perhaps the most relevant in explaining cross-country differences in growth *among devel-*

oping countries. The reason is that it is less dependent upon the nature of the political regime than other political explanations. Sociopolitical approaches involving the presence of democratic institutions as crucial to the argument seem less relevant in explaining why relatively egalitarian Korea and Taiwan grew faster than more inegalitarian Latin American economies at a time when most of these countries had authoritarian regimes (with the qualification made earlier on the relationship between growth and inequality across Latin America).[21] Interestingly, what emerges from the empirical research on political instability and growth is a view of Asia as a region with authoritarian but stable regimes, in contrast to the much more unstable political regimes in Latin America (see Alesina et al. 1996).

Economic Mechanisms

Some potential links between income distribution and growth bypass sociopolitical considerations. In the following approaches, inequality affects the rates of factor growth and/or productivity in the use of given factor endowments. The key channels all involve essentially economic mechanisms.

A first approach emphasizes the link between income distribution and investment in education (see Loury 1981; Galor and Zeira 1993; and Birdsall, Sabot, and Ross 1995). Two mechanisms are involved here. The first is the existence of credit constraints that prevent the poor from undertaking the most efficient amount of investment. Less income inequality, then, has a positive effect on human capital investment, as income redistribution relaxes budgetary constraints on the poor. In addition, there is an asset distribution effect. In the presence of diminishing returns to education, which implies that the marginal product of human capital investments by the poor is relatively high, less inequality in the distribution of human capital has a positive asset distribution effect on efficiency. A more egalitarian distribution of education implies, other things being equal, higher productivity of a given stock of human capital.

This imperfect asset markets-cum-diminishing returns argument is similar to the old case for land reform on efficiency grounds. The main difference is that, in the context of models of endogenous growth, the resulting efficiency gains can result in a permanently higher growth rate rather than a once and for all level effect (which nevertheless implies a higher growth rate in the transition to the new steady state). Williamson (1993) presents empirical evidence showing that more egalitarian societies tend to have higher enrollments in secondary education at the same average income level. Perotti's (1996) regression estimates of structural equations also suggest strong support for a positive relationship between income equality and investment in human capital. Birdsall, Ross, and Sabot (1995) present evidence that more equal societies tend to have a more egalitarian allocation of educational expenditures, including public expenditures.

A second transmission mechanism runs from inequality to fertility rates and population growth.[22] As is well known from the literature on the demographic transition, fertility rates tend to fall as per capita income increases. If fertility and income are inversely related, biological constraints must imply that the rate at which fertility increases as income falls must be decreasing. For a given average per capita income more income equality will tend to reduce fertility rates among the poor by more than it increases fertility among the rich (if it increases them at all, given the likelihood of ratchet effects in the behavior of fertility). Fertility and population growth would then be positively influenced by inequality for a given level of per capita income. If population growth reduces the steady state value and transitional growth rate of per capita income (as it does in neoclassical growth and labor surplus models with moderately increasing returns to scale), this provides another channel through which inequality adversely affects growth. Perotti (1996) shows that a larger income share held by the middle class (his measure of income equality) has a strong negative effect on fertility and, through this influence, a positive effect on growth.

Finally, inequality may harm growth by reducing the size of the domestic market for increasing-returns industries. In the recent literature, this mechanism is often associated with Murphy, Shleifer, and Vishny (1989a), who argue that a precondition for industrialization is a limited amount of inequality. In their view, income must be broadly enough distributed to materialize in a higher demand for a broad range of manufactures, which then can complement each other and expand together. This mechanism has often been dismissed in the recent literature as lacking empirical support. This is because the argument is taken to imply the counterfactual prediction that large countries, other things being equal, should grow faster (see Knack and Keefer 1995 and Bénabou 1996). In fact, a big push model with horizontal pecuniary externalities, like the one Murphy, Shleifer, and Vishny have in mind, only suggests that inequality plays a role at low-income levels in strengthening the hold of the low-level trap (or in broadening the set of conditions under which a unique traditional economy equilibrium exists).[23] The fact that the two groups of Asian and African countries in table 23 display the expected relationship of growth being positively affected by income and negatively affected by inequality, in the case of mainly low-income countries, is strikingly consistent with the inequality — market size — growth hypothesis.

Beyond low-income levels, there is no reason to expect an unambiguous and systematic relationship between inequality and growth mediated by the size of the market. Earlier literature in structuralist development economics had in fact developed alternative hypotheses on the effects of income redistribution on growth operating through these channels.[24] More income equality may broaden market demand for the products of leading manufacturing sectors (and through cost reductions stimulate investment in these sectors) — if middle- and low-income groups have high-income elasticity of demand for durable consumption goods produced under increasing returns. Alternatively, it may reduce market demand for manufactures if income elasticities of demand are higher among the rich and the upper-middle class.

Similarly, recent literature on growth and distribution in the Kalecki-Steindl tradition has developed alternative hypotheses concerning the effects of changes in the functional distribution of income on growth (see, on this subject, Dutt 1984, Taylor 1985, Bhaduri and Marglin 1990, and You 1994). In these models, growth may be wage led — in which case the positive effects of redistribution from profits to wages on market demand and resource utilization outweigh the negative effects on profit margins — or profit led — in which case profitability falls with the reduction in profit margins. In the first case, a redistribution from wages to profits, which increases inequality, has "stagnationist" effects on growth, that is, growth is negatively affected as a result of a reduction in demand and capacity utilization. In the second case, redistribution toward profit has "exhilarationist" effects on growth, as investment is stimulated by the higher profit margins.

Shortcomings of the Recent Literature on Inequality and Growth

We now turn to what we regard as some of the main shortcomings of the recent theoretical and empirical research on inequality and growth. A first one is that, with some exceptions (Alesina and Perotti 1994; Perotti 1996), empirical research has relied on "reduced form" regressions that do not distinguish among the specific channels through which inequality affects growth. Perotti (1996) summarizes the scarce available evidence on the specific channels as follows. The transmission mechanism from less inequality to higher growth are essentially three: (1) lower fertility rates, (2) higher rates of investment in education, and (3) greater political and social stability, which favors higher rates of investment. He finds no support for the idea that equality favors growth by generating fewer policy distortions as a result of fewer demands for redistribution.

Another shortcoming, perhaps more important, is that the recent literature fails to distinguish between different sources of inequality and their effects on growth. Our discussion of the determinants of income distribution in the previous section — those associated with the position on the Kuznets curve and those related to deviations from it — intuitively suggests that the different possible sources of inequality may have very different effects on growth. This type of analysis and the associated empirical research are virtually absent in the recent literature, which in a sense has produced one model at a time, each of them focusing on a single hypothesis.

Consider, first, two sources of inequality and the associated effects on growth. The first source depends on the level of factor endowments and affects the structure of factor returns. As argued earlier, this explains, for example, why poor countries (with smaller physical and human capital endowments per capita) tend to be less egalitarian than rich countries. The second source is independent of factor endowments and income levels and is associated with deviations from the "typical ownership structure" of factor endowments, that is, the one corresponding to a simple Kuznets curve (not augmented by factors relating to cross-country differences in the distribution of factor endowments).

Each of these two sources of income inequality may well have different effects on growth (in both size and sign). The effects of inequality on growth associated with the first source — the structure of factor prices for a given distribution of factor endowments — are likely to be *positive* to the extent that high factor returns on physical capital and skilled labor have positive incentive effects on the accumulation of capital and the acquisition of skills. The second component, related to the distribution of factor endowments and policies, is the one that is most likely to have negative effects on growth through either the rates of capital accumulation and skill acquisition or efficiency in the use of factor endowments. This is the type of effect on which the recent literature implicitly focuses.

The failure to distinguish between these two sources in the recent literature is related to neglect of the interactions between income level and inequality (as opposed to income growth and inequality). Yet, the importance of this distinction in the estimation of the effects of inequality on growth in a *cross section of countries* should be obvious, for the sign of the effect will depend on whether international differences in income inequality are due to the first or the second source (as well as on the strength of the two types of effect).

If the Kuznets curve reflects the relationship between the structure of factor returns and the level of per capita income, we can attempt to overcome this limitation by using the results on the Kuznets curve to distinguish between the two effects.[25] In order to achieve this, we can decompose the Gini coefficient into two components: (1) the value of the Gini predicted by the Kuznets curve equation, which, according to our interpretation, is influenced by the structure of factor returns given a "typical" distribution of factor endowments; and (2) the difference between the actual value of the Gini and the value predicted by the Kuznets curve equation, which should mostly reflect the influence on inequality of the deviation of the distribution of factor endowments away from the "typical" distribution on the Kuznets curve. This is the X variable in table 27, and we shall refer to this component as the X-inequality from this point onward.[26]

TABLE 27. Two Effects of Inequality on Growth in "Reduced Form" Regressions

Independent Variable	Group 1	Group 2	Group 3	Group 4
Constant	0.094	0.094	0.055	0.051
	(3.92)	(3.63)	(1.51)	(1.29)
$\text{Log}y_0$	−0.012	−0.011	−0.009	−0.009
	(−3.14)	(−2.77)	(−2.23)	(−1.89)
I/Y	0.001	—	0.001	—
	(2.51)		(2.45)	
PRIMo	0.031	0.050	0.019	0.036
	(2.11)	(3.73)	(1.16)	(2.23)
SECo	−0.002	0.007	0.003	0.012
	(−0.12)	(0.39)	(0.18)	(0.69)
ASSASS	−0.201	−0.233	−0.202	−0.233
	(−1.85)	(−1.95)	(−1.88)	(−2.03)
GINI	−0.0004	−0.0005	—	—
	(−1.71)	(−1.95)		
GINI*	—	—	0.0003	0.0003
			(0.51)	(0.46)
X	—	—	−0.0005	−0.0006
			(−2.13)	(−2.38)
N	37	37	37	37
Adjusted R^2	0.47	0.38	0.49	0.40

Note:
y_0: GDP per capita in 1960. *Source:* Penn World Table (Mark 5.6).
I/Y: Ratio of real domestic investment to real GDP (average for the period). *Source:* Penn World Table (Mark 5.6).
PRIMo: Primary school enrollment rate in 1960. *Source:* Barro and Lee 1994.
SECo: Secondary school enrollment rate in 1960. *Source:* Barro and Lee 1994.
ASSASS: Number of political assassinations per year per million population (average for the period). *Source:* Barro and Lee 1994.
GINI: Gini coefficient circa 1965. *Source:* see the appendix to this chapter.
GINI*: Value of the Gini coefficient (ca. 1965) predicted by the Kuznets curve
X: Value of the Gini coefficient (ca. 1965) due to deviation from the Kuznets curve
t-statistics in parentheses
Dependent variable: Growth rate of real GDP per capita, 1960–89

In the regression equations presented in table 27, we have separately added the two components of the Gini coefficient to standard "reduced form" growth-inequality regressions. The results in the table show the standard negative effect of the Gini on growth (regressions 1 and 2). Regressions 3 and 4 show that the negative effects of inequality on growth are those related to the deviations from the Kuznets curve (X-inequality), while those related to the position on the Kuznets curve (the predicted Gini) are in fact positive (and insignificant).[27]

We should also distinguish between the effects of inequality on two different components of growth: factor accumulation and factor productivity growth. The same source of inequality may have contradictory effects on growth, enhancing some components of growth and inhibiting others. The lack of empirical research on this issue has limited our knowledge of the reasons why inequality may have adverse effects on growth and therefore our understanding of the best policies for improving equality while enhancing growth.

We use a simple framework to distinguish between the effects of inequality on the two components of growth. Consider a "growth-accounting" regression for the 27 countries for which we have data on factor growth and income distribution. The regression estimates are as follows:

$$g_Y = -0.016 + 0.63g_K + 0.28g_H + 0.60g_L \quad \text{(Adj.) } R^2 = 0.67,$$
$$ (-1.87) \quad (5.72) \quad (1.43) \quad (1.81)$$

where g refers to the growth rate from 1965 to 1990; Y to GDP; and K, H, and L to the stock of physical capital, education, and the labor force. Let g_{TFPi} be the residual between the actual value of GDP growth in any given country (g_{Yi}) and the predicted value of GDP growth (g_{Y*i}) from the regression equation above: $g_{TFPi} = g_{Yi} - g_{Y*i}$. This growth rate, g_{TFPi}, is a measure of total factor productivity growth (up to a constant term common to all countries) even though it does not correspond to the conventional definition, since the coefficients in the factor growth variables do not add to unity. The variable g_{TFPi} thus excludes the part of productivity growth that is associated with increasing returns to scale and that, precisely because returns to scale are not constant (the sum of the coefficients is 1.5), should more appropriately be attributed to factor accumulation. Given the definition of g_{TFPi}, we have $g_{Yi} = g_{Y*i} + g_{TFPi}$. Subtracting the growth of the labor force from both sides of this equation, we obtain the growth of GDP per worker as the sum of two terms: $g_{(Y/L)i} = g_{(Y/L)*i} + g_{TFPi}$.

The first term — $g_{(Y/L)*i}$, which is equal to the difference between the predicted growth rate of GDP and the growth of the labor force — is the component of growth due to factor accumulation per worker, while the second is the component that, in our definition, results from total factor productivity growth.

Table 28 presents the results of regressing each of these two components against the initial value of the Gini coefficient (ca. 1965). We also consider, as we did in the regressions reported in table 27, how each of these components of growth correlate with the two components of inequality — the value of the Gini coefficient predicted by the Kuznets curve (GINI*) and the deviation from the Kuznets curve (X).

Two results stand out as particularly interesting. First, the effects of "X-inequality" — inequality associated with deviations from the Kuznets curve — are negative on both components of growth and of a similar order of magnitude. The size of this effect (around 0.0005) is also similar to the one that recurrently appears in the "reduced form" regressions of growth on inequality. The negative effect of X-inequality on total factor productivity growth is surprisingly large. Given that X-inequality is likely to be positively correlated with inequality in the distribution of factor endowments, this effect may be reflecting the adverse asset distribution effects on the efficiency of given stocks of skilled labor and physical capital (as discussed earlier). It may also be the case that the estimated coefficient is picking up the effects on factor productivity performance of other factors closely associated with X-inequality. The

TABLE 28. Effects of Inequality on Factor Growth and Productivity, 1965–90

Independent Variable	Dependent Variable			
	$g_{(Y/L)^*}$	$g_{(Y/L)^*}$	g_{TFP}	g_{TFP}
Constant	0.030	−0.024	0.013	−0.005
	(3.02)	(−1.28)	(1.77)	(−0.30)
GINI	−0.00015	—	−0.0003	—
	(−0.64)		(−1.83)	
GINI*	—	0.0011	—	0.0001
		(2.52)		(0.26)
X	—	−0.0006	—	−0.0005
		(−2.34)		(−2.21)
N	27	27	27	27
Adjusted R^2	−0.02	0.25	0.08	0.10

Note:
$g_{(Y/L)^*}$ = growth rate of GDP per worker due to factor accumulation
g_{TFP} = growth rate of GDP per worker due to total factor productivity growth
GINI: Gini coefficient circa 1965
GINI*: value of the Gini coefficient predicted by the Kuznets curve
X = value of the Gini coefficient due to deviation from the Kuznets curve
t-statistics in parentheses

results in Bourguignon and Morrisson 1990, reviewed earlier, show that inequality is positively correlated with a pattern of primary export specialization and, as discussed in chapters 8 and 9, economies exporting primary goods tend to grow more slowly than manufacturing-exporting countries.[28] This suggests the presence of interactions between the resource base, the pattern of specialization, and income distribution, which are as interesting as they are difficult to disentangle.

A second result is that the effect of inequality on factor accumulation associated with the structure of factor returns, or the position on the Kuznets curve in our interpretation, is positive and highly significant. It is worth noting that it is the presence of this positive effect that makes the negative effect of overall inequality larger and more statistically significant in the case of total factor productivity growth than in the case of factor accumulation per worker. All of this confirms the expectation discussed above and is likely to be explained simply by the fact that high factor returns to physical and human capital enhance factor growth. More surprisingly, however, this positive effect of inequality on growth turns out to be the *strongest* of the different effects estimated in the regression analysis of table 28.

How do we reconcile the result that shows the strongest effect of inequality on growth (associated with inequality in factor returns) to be positive with previous results that show a negative effect of overall inequality on growth? There is, in fact, no contradiction. Less egalitarian societies are not so because they have a more unequal structure of factor returns but because they usually have a more unequal ownership structure of factor endowments (land and human capital, in particular). The negative effects of this X-inequality on growth dominate the positive effects simply because differences in inequality are mainly associated with those factors that have a negative effect on growth. The result is thus quite consistent with the view, supported by the empirical evidence, that differences in inequality across countries are largely associated with deviations from the Kuznets curve.

The contradictory effects that the two sources of inequality have on factor accumulation per worker raise further questions. Is it through population growth (and thus labor force growth), skill acquisition, or physical capital accumulation that these effects operate? Table 29 sheds some light on these questions. It shows the results of regressing population growth, the investment share, and enrollments in secondary education on the Gini coefficient (ca. 1965) and its two components as well as on the *initial* level of GDP per capita. This initial level of income shows highly significant effects, negative in the case of population growth and positive on the two investment shares.

Two results are worth noting. First, the initial level of inequality has a positive and highly significant effect on population growth, clearly show-ing that less egalitarian societies, at similar levels of income, tend to have a higher rate of population growth. This positive effect on population growth in turn implies that inequality, on this account alone, tends to reduce the rates of factor accumulation per worker. Second, the overall effect of the Gini on the investment share is insignificant (and negative), but, quite consistently with the results in table 28, this hides a significant and positive incentive effect of inequality, associated with the predicted Gini, and an adverse effect of the X-inequality. The same expected signs are found in the case of enrollments in secondary education, but here both coefficients are small and far from statistically significant.

How can all these results be summarized? Our conclusions are not in any way radically different from Perotti's (1996) summary of the evidence cited at the beginning of this section. However, we can add a number of qualifications and provisos, which add up to the summary that follows. Less egalitarian societies have higher rates of population growth at any given level of income. This is reflected in lower rates of factor accumulation per capita. In addition, they have lower rates of

TABLE 29. Population Growth, Investment Shares, and Inequality

		Dependent Variable			
Independent Variable	n	I/Y	I/Y	SCHOOL	SCHOOL
Constant	0.057	−11.33	−69.96	−9.01	−15.05
	(7.26)	(−0.76)	(−2.59)	(− 2.03)	(−2.43)
$Logy_0$	−0.007	4.84	8.19	2.23	2.43
	(−7.99)	(3.25)	(1.32)	(4.73)	(4.99)
GINIo	0.0003	−0.33	—	−0.03	—
	(4.18)	(−0.76)		(−0.65)	
GINIo*	—	—	0.61	—	0.09
			(1.93)		(0.92)
X	—	—	−0.23	—	−0.06
			(−2.04)		(−1.32)
N	39	25	25	36	36
Adjusted R^2	0.73	0.42	0.53	0.41	0.43

Note:
y_0: Initial GDP per capita. *Source:* Penn World Table (Mark 5.6).
GINIo: Gini coefficient circa 1965. See the appendix to this chapter.
GINIo*: Value of the Gini coefficient predicted by the Kuznets curve
X: Value of the Gini coefficient due to deviation from the Kuznets curve
n: Population growth rate, 1965–90. *Source:* Penn World Table (Mark 5.6).
I/Y: Ratio of real domestic investment to real GDP (average for the period 1960–79). *Source:* Penn World Table (Mark 5.6).
SCHOOL: Percentage of the working-age population in secondary school (average for the period 1960–85). *Source:* Mankiw, Romer, and Weil 1992.
t-statistics in parentheses

capital accumulation (smaller investment shares at each level of income), which have their source in X-inequality, the kind of inequality rooted in maldistribution of resources that provides no positive incentive effects to the growth process. The mechanism explaining these lower rates of investment in physical capital may be a result of unequal societies being more politically and socially unstable. However, we also found evidence consistent with inequality depressing the market demand for the goods of the increasing-returns sectors and of this having adverse effects on growth at low-income levels. We could not find strong evidence of inequality operating adversely on the *rates* of skill acquisition (once we control for the level of income). The large effects of X-inequality on total factor productivity growth may well be reflecting, however, the negative effects of inequality on growth operating through the *distribution* of human capital.

An implication of our results is that the effects of inequality on growth (both its size and its sign) are level dependent, that is, dependent on the level of inequality. This implication has been neglected in the recent empirical literature, which seems to suggest that more equality is always good for growth no matter how egalitarian a society already is. Yet, unless physical and human capital become as equally distributed as labor, there will be a positive amount of "efficient inequality" arising from the positive (incentive) effects of inequality in factor returns on the rates of factor accumulation. If our previous analysis is correct, these positive effects will emerge in cross-country studies directly if suddenly international differences in income distribution become fully associated with inequalities in the structure of factor returns. However, it would then be incorrect to conclude that equality is harmful to growth, just as it is incorrect to conclude from current cross-country studies that more equality is *always* good for growth.

Finally, it is worth highlighting the importance of the distinction between different sources of inequality for policy design. If the negative effects of inequality on growth largely come from the distribution of factor endowments, then a redistributive policy that fails to change asset distribution and acts exclusively on factor prices will be ineffective (or even counterproductive if the incentive effect of inequality on growth is positive).

Inequality Traps at Middle-Income Levels

The two approaches examined in this chapter do not contradict each other. Consider the following system of two equations:

$$G = a_o + a_1 y - a_2 y^2 + X \tag{13}$$

$$g = b_o + b_1 y - b_2 y^2 - G^\beta \quad \beta > 1, \tag{14}$$

for $g > g^*$ (at high income levels) and $g = g^*$ otherwise. All parameters are positive. The variable G is an index of inequality in income distribution, X refers to X-inequality, y is the natural logarithm of income per capita, and g is the growth rate of income per capita.

The first equation is a Kuznets curve "augmented" with X-inequality, a component of inequality that is assumed to be country specific and independent of the level of per capita income. The second equation is a growth function relating the growth rate of per capita income to the level of per capita income. The inverted-U shape is suggested by the analysis in chapter 4. The function is augmented by the negative effect of inequality considered in the recent literature on inequality and growth and discussed in the previous section. This effect of inequality is assumed to be nonlinear and such that at low levels of inequality a given increase in inequality has a small effect on growth and the effect increases as inequality rises (this is what the inequality restriction on parameter β states). At high-income levels, the quadratic form of the growth function only holds for growth rates above the steady state rate of growth (g^*). When the economy reaches g^*, from above, this steady state rate persists over time.[29]

Equation 14 implies that, for a *given* level of inequality, the growth rate is low at both low- and high-income levels. If looked at from a cross-sectional perspective, it implies a pattern of income divergence at low-income levels followed by convergence at middle- and high-income levels. In this process, as was shown in chapter 4, the growth rate reaches a maximum at an income level equal to:

$$y^M = b_1/2b_2,$$

provided that b_2 is positive (the condition for a maximum) and b_1 is positive (so that y^M is positive). The corresponding maximum growth rate is $g_M = b_o - G^\beta + b_1^2/4b_2$, a negative function of inequality.

The growth function also implies a threshold level of convergence (y_c), the income level at which the growth rate reaches (from below) the growth rate in the steady state (g^*):

$$y_c = y^M - [b_1^2 + 4b_2(b_o - G^\beta - g^*)]^{1/2}/2b_2, \tag{15}$$

which is less than y^M. Equation 15 shows that an increase in inequality raises the convergence threshold or, what comes to the same thing, has the effect of reducing the growth rate at low-income levels.

Consider now equations 13 and 14 taken together. Equation 14 states that growth for a given level of inequality is low at both low- and high-income levels. Since inequality has adverse effects on growth, the fact that inequality is also low at low- and high-income levels (as eq. 13 states) has the effect of smoothing out the inverted-U path of the growth rate. Indeed, taking the total derivative of the growth rate with respect to income yields:

$$g'(y) = g_y - \beta G^{\beta-1} G_y, \tag{16}$$

where: $g_y = b_1 - 2b_2 y$ is the partial derivative of g with respect to y,
and $G_y = a_1 - 2a_2 y$ is the derivative of G with respect to y.

At low-income levels, when G_y is positive, $g'(y)$ is less than g_y, that is, the growth rate increases less with income than if inequality had no effect on the growth rate. At high-income levels, when G_y is negative (and inequality tends to fall as income increases), $g'(y)$ is larger than g_y. The influence of falling inequality then tends to moderate the fall in the growth rate.

A more striking implication of equation 16 is that the maximum growth rate may no longer be reached at middle-income levels. Suppose, indeed, that both the "augmented" Kuznets curve and the growth function are "well behaved" in the sense that over a range of low- and middle-income levels G_y and g_y are both positive. Even then, using equation 16, $g'(y)$ may become negative over this low and middle range of income:

$$g'(y) < 0 \quad \leftrightarrow \quad \beta G^{\beta-1} > g_y/G_y. \tag{17}$$

The inequalities in 17 show that, even though growth tends to accelerate for a *given* level of inequality (g_y is positive), the growth rate may actually fall as income increases over the intermediate range of income levels. "Inequality trap" refers to a situation in which, despite g_y being positive, $g'(y)$ is negative.

Provided that $\beta > 1$, which implies a nonlinear and relatively large effect of inequality on growth at high levels of inequality, the likelihood of inequality traps increases under the following circumstances.[30] First, this will take place if there is a high value of $G^{\beta-1}$ and thus of the level of income inequality generated during the transition toward high-income levels. Other things being equal, in particular the parameters of the g_y and G_y functions, this can only be due to a high level of X-inequality, which is associated with high inequality in the ownership structure of factor endowments. Second, a high value of parameter β would also increase the likelihood of inequality traps. Indeed, the larger is the adverse effect of inequality on growth the more growth is bound to decelerate over the intermediate range of incomes in which income inequality reaches a peak.

A third factor is a high value of G_y, that is, a relatively steep Kuznets curve. As discussed earlier, this is likely to result from a "style" of growth based on physical capital accumulation at the expense of skill acquisition or from industry-biased productivity growth at the expense of agricultural technical progress (with fast population growth playing a role in generating these unbalances). A final factor is whether there is a low value of g_y, which could be determined by a weak response of capital and educational investments to a given increase in the rates of return on capital and education. A strong response of physical and human capital accumulation — as has been present in the East Asian development experience according to Birdsall, Ross, and Sabot (1995) — makes growth relatively elastic to the change in per capita income and thus more likely for the negative effect of inequality on growth to be offset by the positive effect of income on the growth rate (see eq. 4). The interactions between increasing returns and the elasticity of labor supply also play a key role, as in the model presented earlier, with relatively low elasticity of the labor supply tending to generate a low value of g_y.[31]

Faced with a premature growth slowdown, resulting from a combination of these four factors, the conditions of high inequality will tend to be perpetuated by the adverse effect of slow growth on income distribution (see table 26). It is in this sense that the situation can be described as a trap, since the transition to higher income levels is accompanied by a protracted high level of inequality and takes place at a slow pace or may even be interrupted by economic setbacks. Since the highest inequality tends to occur at middle-income levels, such inequality traps are likely to be characteristic of middle-income countries. The counterpart of these traps in egalitarian countries is, in contrast, a virtuous circle of accelerated growth and rapid equalization of incomes.

The empirical literature on political instability and growth provides some evidence on inequality traps. Alesina et al. (1996) find that for the 1960–82 period middle-income and inegalitarian Latin American countries had the highest frequency of major government changes and coups d'état. They also find that these indicators of political instability had a negative effect on growth. Moreover, low growth tends to increase the likelihood of coups according to Londregan and Poole (1990). All of this was reflected in the significantly lower growth rates achieved by Latin America (per capita GDP growth of 2.2 percent per year) in comparison with Asian economies (3.3 percent) and developing countries in Europe (4.1 percent).

Perhaps the best empirical evidence for the implications of our framework comes from the observation that the frequency of both growth acceleration and (although less frequent) economic setbacks is highest at middle-income levels. As discussed in chapter 1, this upward and downward mobility of middle-income countries is the source of the "twin-peaked" distribution in the world economy today, with many poor and rich countries and relatively few in between.[32] What our analysis suggests is that the interactions between growth and inequality, along with the role of the patterns of growth and trade specialization, give rise to this feature. The transition from middle to upper-middle and high incomes is likely to be very rapid in egalitarian countries with a manufacturing bias in their trade orientation, a rapid accumulation of skills, and high agricultural productivity growth. In countries with great social and economic inequality, which have a heavy primary export orientation as well as slower rates of human capital accumulation and technical progress in agriculture, the transition is much slower and protracted. These are, concisely captured, some of the more salient contrasts between the transitions undertaken by the middle-income economies of East Asia and Latin America since 1960.[33]

APPENDIX

Data sources other than those for income inequality are indicated in the text. The source of information on income distribution is the Deininger and Squire (1996) data set, which compiles and compares data based on a diversity of national sources. This data set expands the coverage of previous data sets on Gini coefficients and individual quintile groups' income shares and classifies the information in such a way as to facilitate the selection of high-quality and internationally comparable indexes.

The criteria used in the selection of countries with information on Gini coefficients circa 1965 and 1990 were as follows. In both cases, only national-level data were considered and the high-quality data, as defined by Deininger and Squire, were given priority. Gini coefficients based on tax records were excluded. The high-quality data set for the 1990s had the majority of the estimates calculated on the basis of personal income units. For consistency, these estimates were preferred over those based on household units. The sample of countries circa 1990 was selected among the countries for which information was available between 1987 and 1993, and the sample circa 1965 was selected among those with information available between 1960 and 1970. These criteria give Gini coefficients for 40 countries circa 1965 and 71 countries circa 1990. The composition of the latter 71 countries, by region and income level, is described in table A10.1. The numbers in parentheses are the Gini coefficients in percentage circa 1990.

TABLE A10.1. Gini Coefficients circa 1990

	High Income ≥ $11,508	Upper-Middle Income $3,250–9,576	Lower-Middle Income $2,922–1,658	Upper-Low Income $902–1,394	Low Income ≦ $798
Europe	Finland (26.1) Belgium (26.6) Netherlands (29.6) United Kingdom (32.3) Sweden (32.5) Italy (32.7) Denmark (33.2) Norway (33.3)	Spain (25.9) Yugoslavia (31.9) Ireland (34.6) Greece (35.2) Portugal (36.8)			
East and South Asia	Japan (35.0) Singapore (39.0) Hong Kong (45.0)	Taiwan (30.1) South Korea, Republic (33.6) Malaysia (48.4) Thailand (48.8)	Sri Lanka (30.1) Indonesia (33.1) Philippines (45.7)	Bangladesh (28.9) India (29.7) Pakistan (31.2)	
North Africa and Middle East		Turkey (44.1)	Egypt (32.0) Algeria (38.7) Morocco (39.2) Tunisia (40.2) Jordan (40.7)		

TABLE A10.1. (Continued)

	High Income ≥ $11,508	Upper-Middle Income $3,250–9,576	Lower-Middle Income $2,922–1,658	Upper-Low Income $902–1,394	Low Income ≤ $798
Oceania	New Zealand (40.2) Australia (41.7)				
Sub-Saharan Africa		Mauritius (36.7) South Africa (62.3)		Ghana (36.7) Ivory Coast (36.9) Nigeria (41.2) Senegal (54.1) Kenya (54.4) Lesotho (56.0) Zimbabwe (56.8)	Uganda (33.0) Niger (36.1) Tanzania (38.1) Gambia (39.0) Mauritania (42.5) Madagascar (43.4) Zambia (43.5) Central African Republic (55.0) Guinea-Bissau (56.1) Malawi (62.0)
North and South America	Canada (27.6) United States (37.8) Bahamas (44.5)	Costa Rica (46.1) Puerto Rico (50.9) Colombia (51.3) Venezuela (53.8) Mexico (55.0) Chile (57.9) Brazil (59.6)	Jamaica (41.8) Bolivia (42.0) Dominican Republic (50.5) Panama (56.5) Guatemala (59.1)	Guyana (40.2) Nicaragua (50.3) Honduras (54.0)	

CHAPTER 11

Structural Constraints: Domestic and Foreign Exchange Bottlenecks

Previous chapters have ignored demand constraints on the level of output or, more precisely, constraints arising from a lack of demand in the goods market. In the models examined, the level of output and its growth rate are constrained by factor accumulation and the productivity effects of resource allocation. This seems to be a good approximation of the growth process for most countries from the postwar period to the late 1970s. This was a period when governments were able to follow high-employment policies that effectively removed recurrent effective demand problems except for rather short periods of time. There were some situations, however, both in the early postwar period and especially later, in the 1980s, in which macroeconomic policies were not able to remove these constraints.

This chapter and the following will analyze these situations and their related difficulties. We begin in this chapter with those situations in which the limits to macroeconomic policy arise from a diversity of structural rigidities. Kalecki's writing on developing economies provides the basic analytical framework. In his model, unemployment and excess capacity in a demand-constrained manufacturing sector cannot be removed due to inelasticity of supply in the food-producing sector. We then consider changes in nominal wages and illustrate how a "wage-goods constraint" can give rise to a structural type of inflation. Analogous structural rigidities underlie two-gap models as well as open economy inflation models in the structuralist tradition. We present and discuss these contributions as open economy extensions of Kalecki's two-sector model. Finally, we turn to foreign exchange constraints on domestic supply in a dual economy setting in which domestic firms are directly rationed in the import market, which gives rise to (repressed) excess demand in the domestic goods market.

Domestic Constraints: Kalecki's Dual Economy Model

In its simplest version, Kalecki's model of the macroeconomy of less developed countries consists of a "supply-constrained" agricultural sector

303

with flexible prices, a "demand-constrained" manufacturing sector operating under imperfect competition, and a labor market with fixed nominal wages.[1] The model generates a short-run equilibrium with open unemployment. As we shall see, the nature of unemployment is neither Keynesian — since, under some circumstances, it is not affected by changes in aggregate demand — nor classical, in the sense that it is not associated with downward rigidity of real wages.

The Model

There are two sectors, indicated by A and M. In the first, food output (A) is produced with labor (L_A) and a fixed amount of land (T):

$$A = A(L_A, T) \quad A_1, A_2 \geq 0.$$

This sector operates under atomistic competition. With price-taking behavior, profit maximization yields the following labor demand and output supply functions.[2]

$$L^d_A = L_A(w_A/p_A, T) \quad L_{A1} \leq 0, L_{A2} > 0 \tag{1}$$

$$A^s = A^s(w_A/p_A, T) \quad A^s_1 \leq 0, A^s_2 > 0, \tag{2}$$

where p_A and w_A are the price and nominal wage, respectively, in sector A.

Sector M produces a variety of manufactured goods (M_i), with one producer for each good. Production of these manufactures turns one unit of labor into k units of output up to the full capacity level of output (M_i^*). Production conditions are thus:

$$M_i = kL_i \quad \text{for } M_i < M_i^*$$

$$M = [\Sigma(1/n)M_i^\sigma]^{1/\sigma} \quad 0 < \sigma < 1,$$

where M, as in the intermediate goods sectors of chapters 5 and 9, represents the output of a fixed set of n manufactured goods. The wage in manufacturing (w_M) is equal to the agricultural wage plus a wage premium $(f - 1)$, so that relative wages are given by $w_M/w_A = f$.

In the labor market, firms take wages as given. In the goods market they operate under conditions of monopolistic competition, with each producer facing identical downward-sloping demand curves. Profit maximization here implies that, at a symmetric equilibrium with $p_i = p_j$ and $M_i = M$, pricing decisions follow a markup rule and production is adjusted according to demand:

$$p_M = [\phi/(\phi - 1)]w_M/k \tag{3}$$

$$M = C_M + I, \tag{4}$$

where p_M is the price of a bundle of manufactures yielding $M = 1$, ϕ is the price elasticity of demand facing individual producers, and C_M and I are the consumption and investment demands for manufactures. Note that pricing decisions in sector M determine the product wage, w_M/p_M. Then, given relative wages, the agricultural wage in terms of food varies inversely with the agricultural terms of trade (p_A/p_M).

On the demand side, we treat investment as given and assume, for simplicity, that all profits are saved and all wage income is spent on food or manufactured consumption goods. We also adopt Jorgenson's assumption (1961) of a critical level of food consumption per worker (c_A*) below which all wage income is spent on food and beyond which all additional income is spent on manufactures (see chap. 3). We limit the analysis to a situation in which agricultural wages are less than the critical level of food consumption (c_A*). These assumptions imply that consumption of food (C_A) and manufactures (C_M) are such that:

$$p_A C_A = w_A L_A + p_A c_A * L_M \tag{5}$$

$$p_M C_M = (w_M - p_A c_A *)L_M, \tag{6}$$

where L_M is employment in sector M.

We use a diagram from Basu 1984 (for a similar formulation, see Taylor 1983) to illustrate the short-run equilibrium of the model (see fig. 49). Equilibrium in the food market implies that $A = C_A$. Let AS be the agricultural surplus (food supply minus food consumption by agricultural workers). Using equations 1, 2, and 5, we express the market equilibrium condition as the equality between the agricultural surplus and the demand for food by industrial workers:

$$AS(S, p) = c_A * L_M \tag{7}$$

$$AS(S, p) = A^s(w_A/p_A, T) - (w_A/p_A)L_A(w_A/p_A, T),$$

where $p = p_A/p_M$ and S is a position parameter that depends on land supply, technology parameters, the product wage in manufacturing, and the wage premium.[3] The agricultural surplus is an increasing function of the agricultural terms of trade (p). Higher terms of trade reduce the product wage in agriculture. This raises agricultural employment and the agricultural surplus.

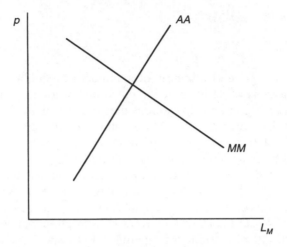

Fig. 49.   Kalecki's dual economy model

Equation 7 defines a schedule of food market equilibrium in (L_M, p) space. This locus (AA in fig. 49, shown as a line for simplicity) slopes upward: a higher level of employment in manufacturing raises food demand by industrial workers, which requires an increase in the terms of trade in order to generate the agricultural surplus necessary to clear the food market. The slope of the locus depends critically on the elasticity of food supply:[4] the lower this elasticity the steeper the locus. The special case of a fully inelastic food supply can be represented by a vertical locus.

Substituting from equation 6 into 4, and choosing units so that $M = L_M$, yields the following equation of a schedule of M sector equilibria:

$$L_M = I/(c_A{*}p + 1 - w_M/p_M) \quad \text{for } M < M^*. \tag{8}$$

Equation 8 shows employment in manufacturing as determined by the level of investment times a multiplier that depends on the terms of trade and the critical level of food consumption. The equation defines a schedule (MM in fig. 49), which shows the effect of the terms of trade on industrial employment. The schedule slopes downward. An increase in food prices causes a fall in workers' real incomes, which, given the inelasticity of food demand, spills over into the manufactured goods market as their consumption of manufactures declines. The lower consumption of manufactures per industrial worker reduces the multiplier and thus the level of production and employment in the M sector.[5]

Unemployment, Effective Demand, and the Elasticity of
the Food Supply

The short-run equilibrium of the model is independent of money wages. This is readily verified from equations 7 and 8. It is also consistent with open unemployment: there is no reason, given the level of investment, why the whole of the labor force would be fully employed. What kind of unemployment have we encountered? Can it be removed by effective demand measures such as, in particular, an increase in investment?

The answer to these questions depends on the slope of the AA schedule, which in the present setting is given by the elasticity of the food supply. Consider, first, the case of a vertical AA schedule, that is, there is a unique level of employment in sector M consistent with equilibrium in the food market. The supply of labor to the industrial sector ($L^s_M = L - L_A$, where L is the total labor force) will also be vertical in this case since agricultural labor demand is inelastic as well. Figure 50 shows this configuration.

What happens if effective demand for M goods increases as a result of a higher level of investment? Since industrial employment is demand determined and there is unemployment and excess capacity in manufacturing, it appears that the higher level of investment should lead to an increase in industrial employment (see eq. 8). Yet, as is illustrated by figure 50, the higher level of investment only raises the agricultural terms of trade without affecting industrial employment. The outward shift of the MM schedule — despite the fact that it implies a higher demand for manufactures at the initial terms of trade — leaves industrial employment and unemployment unchanged.

The reason why the demand for manufactures ends up being the same in both the initial and the final equilibrium is that the increase in effective demand, due to the higher level of investment, is fully offset by the fall in workers consumption of manufactures, resulting from the higher agricultural terms of trade. In fact, the terms of trade increase by exactly the extent necessary to bring effective demand back to its initial level. The result is that effective demand measures cannot cure unemployment and underutilization of industrial capacity. As stated by Kalecki:

> The rise in investment may create a strong pressure on the available supplies of food, while at the same time it is possible to increase the production of industrial consumption goods in line with demand. It may be shown that in some instances the rigidity of food supply may lead to the under utilization of productive facilities in nonfood consumption goods. (1976, 47)

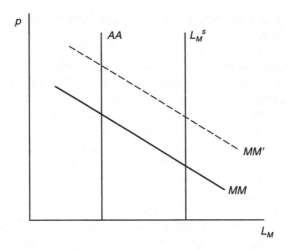

Fig. 50.   The model with an inelastic food supply

Manufacturing employment is demand determined, but effective demand is constrained by the availability of food supplies. Given the inelasticity of food supply, employment in manufacturing is fully determined
by the position of the AA schedule.[6]

Kalecki was well aware that the resulting unemployment is not
Keynesian in its usual sense. It clearly cannot be cured by reducing money
wages and prices, *even if* the price declines raise aggregate demand. If, for
example, a decline in money wages and prices were to shift the *MM*
schedule upward, as a result of real balance effects or Keynesian interest
rate effects on investment, the effect would be to change relative prices
but leave industrial employment unaffected. The ineffectiveness of aggregate demand measures is not due to "real wage rigidity," as in Lewis's
labor surplus, or efficiency wage models. Real wages are, up to this point
in our analysis, fully flexible downward. This type of unemployment is
better described as structural. This is because it involves a maladjustment
between the structure of supply and the structure of demand at full employment, together with structural rigidities on the supply side that im-
pede the adjustment of the structure of supply in the short run. Indeed,
the key assumption behind the results is the inelasticity of the food supply,
which in Kalecki's view is due to the agrarian conditions prevailing in
many developing countries. With an elastic food supply, the AA schedule
will not be vertical. An increase in the terms of trade, following the rise in
investment, will trigger a food supply response. This will allow employ-

ment and capacity utilization to increase in the industrial sector. The fall in real wages does not completely offset the effects of higher investment on effective demand.

The Wage-Goods Constraint, Inflation, and the Structuralist Controversy

Up to this point, we have assumed that reductions in the real wage do not trigger increases in nominal wages. Kalecki also considered real wage rigidity as a source of ineffectiveness of aggregate demand measures. In this case, even though food supply is elastic, the terms of trade at which agriculture will supply the necessary wage goods in order to fully employ the labor force may be so high as to trigger a continuous inflationary process. This idea is the basis of the structuralist models of inflation in the Latin American literature, and it has also played a prominent role in the Indian macroeconomics literature on the "wage-goods constraint" on output and growth.[7]

Suppose, then, that real wages are not fully flexible downward. Due to efficiency wage considerations or to the presence of labor unions, there is a minimum value of the agricultural real wage in terms of food (ω_A) that workers are willing to tolerate without asking for compensating money wage increases (or without the adverse effects on labor productivity that will trigger these wage increases by employers).[8] This minimum wage is affected by labor market conditions. We assume that this wage is an inverse function of unemployment: higher unemployment weakens unions' bargaining power and increases workers' tolerance for low real wages, thus reducing the minimum wage.

$$\omega_A = \omega(U) \quad \omega' < 0 \quad \text{and} \quad U = L - L_A - L_M. \tag{9}$$

This minimum real wage is a threshold: when real wages are above it, money wages remain constant, while below it, money wages increase at a rate that is an increasing function of the gap between the threshold and the actual value of the agricultural real wage ($\omega_A - w_A/p_A$).[9] Since the industrial wage premium is constant, this is also the rate of increase in industrial money wages. Thus:

$$\hat{w} = z(\omega_A - w_A/p_A) \quad \text{for } \omega_A > w_A/p_A$$

$$\hat{w} = 0 \quad \text{for } \omega_A \le w_A/p_A,$$

where z is a positive parameter. Using equation 1 to express L_A as a function of the terms of trade, we can substitute into equation 9 in order to obtain the threshold wage as a positive function of industrial employment and the terms of trade:

$$\omega_A = \omega(L_M, p) \quad \omega_1, \omega_2 > 0. \tag{10}$$

Both a higher level of industrial employment and better agricultural terms of trade (which stimulate agricultural employment) reduce unemployment and thus increase the threshold wage, ω_A. We can now derive a schedule of (p, L_M) combinations along which the actual agricultural real wage is equal to the threshold wage. Using equation 10 and $w_A/p_A = (w_M/p_M)/(fp)$, we obtain:

$$(w_M/p_M)/(fp) = \omega(L_M, p), \tag{11}$$

where w_M/p_M is determined by the pricing decisions in manufacturing. How are p and L_M related along this schedule? Higher agricultural terms of trade lead to a reduction in actual real wages and to a higher threshold wage (as unemployment decreases with the increase in agricultural employment); in order to keep the threshold wage in line with the lower value of agricultural real wages, a reduction in industrial employment is required. Equation 11 thus defines a downward-sloping schedule in (L_M, p) space. The value of the slope depends critically on how sensitive the threshold wage is to labor market conditions, that is, on the ω function. If, for example, unemployment has strong negative effects on workers' bargaining strength, an increase in the terms of trade will only require a small reduction in industrial employment. The schedule will then be rather steep. The smaller are the effects of unemployment on the threshold wage, the flatter is the schedule. Without such effects, the locus becomes horizontal, as in Basu 1984, since there is then a unique value of the threshold wage, and thus of p, for which the actual and threshold wages are equal. It is also worth noting that changes in labor productivity as well as in Kalecki's "degree of monopoly" in manufacturing (determined by the price elasticity of individual demand curves) influence w_M/p_M and thus the position of the schedule.

This schedule of wage and price stability (LL) shows, for each level of industrial employment, the maximum value of the terms of trade that is consistent with stable money wages. Above the locus, the terms of trade are higher than those required for money wage stability. There is thus wage inflation and (given w_M/p_M and p) price inflation. The region below and bounded by the locus is, in contrast, one of money wage and price stability.

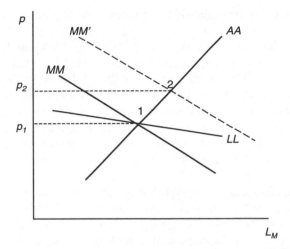

Fig. 51.   Conflict between goods market and labor market equilibria

When we bring the *AA* and *MM* schedules together with the *LL* locus (see fig. 51), the terms of trade, as determined by the equilibrium in the goods market, may turn out to be too high to preserve price stability. For example, an increase in investment that shifts the equilibrium terms of trade from p_1 to p_2 will not only lower real wages and increase industrial employment but will trigger an inflationary spiral because the terms of trade required to keep the goods market in equilibrium are inconsistent with money wage stability in the labor market. As money wages increase, industrial firms react by increasing their prices, while food prices also adjust upward to remove excess demand for food. The rate at which money wages (and prices) increase is a function of the gap between p_2 and the terms of trade on the *LL* schedule at the same level of employment.

Thus, since the agricultural surplus is elastic, effective demand policy can raise employment but only at the cost of higher inflation. If effective demand is constrained to preserve price stability, the maximum level of employment attainable is that at the intersection of the *AA* and *LL* schedules. It is worth noting that this level of employment and the associated rate of structural unemployment do not depend on labor market parameters alone (as does the "natural" rate of unemployment in modern macroeconomic theory). They also depend on the agricultural demand and supply conditions underlying the slope and position of the *AA* schedule. This "inflation barrier" results from the fact that the agricultural sector cannot supply the wage goods necessary to fully employ the labor force at terms of trade that preserve money wage stability in the labor market.

What is the cure for this type of inflation? This was the question debated in the monetarist-structuralist controversies of the 1950s and 1960s (see the Rio Conference volume edited by Baer and Kerstenetzky [1964]). Monetarists argued that, with a stable demand for money, inflation would only continue if the money supply was expanding at a faster rate than output. As for any other kind of inflation, they advocated a tight money policy, which, by shifting the *MM* schedule downward, would eliminate the inflationary pressures associated with a high level of employment.

Structuralists acknowledged that an accommodating monetary policy was necessary for inflation to continue (on this subject, see Olivera 1964). However, they viewed aggregate demand measures that shift the *MM* locus downward as inefficient. Employment would fall and excess capacity would increase. Moreover, the growth of the economy would slow down, insofar as the higher excess capacity in manufacturing would discourage investment in industry and the lower terms of trade would inhibit investment in agriculture. Aggregate demand measures did not address the key problems of low and inelastic food supplies and excess capacity in manufacturing. Thus, the control of inflation through exclusive reliance on these measures was likely to be ineffective in the long run.

In this view, supply-side measures oriented toward increasing food supplies are both more effective and more efficient. By shifting the *AA* schedule to the right, they lead to a reduction in inflation while raising employment and capacity utilization in manufacturing. If these supply-side measures require an increase in investment in agriculture, then it may be preferable to tolerate some inflation in the short run as the price to be paid for dealing effectively with inflation and employment problems in the long run. It is worth noting that in this view there is no long-run tradeoff between inflation and unemployment, although for quite nonmonetarist reasons.

In terms of our diagram, the debate can be interpreted as revolving around two issues. The first involves the elasticities of food supply and demand. A more elastic food demand causes the *MM* schedule to turn clockwise. With sufficiently high price and income elasticities, this schedule would even slope upward (with stability requiring that it be steeper than the *AA* schedule). Then, supply-side measures that shift the *AA* schedule to the right would be less efficient than in the previous case, in the sense of not causing an increase in employment and capacity utilization. Given the elastic food demand, the reduction in the terms of trade

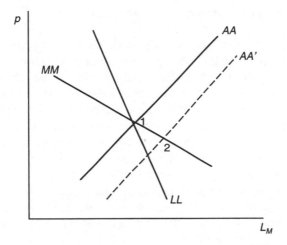

Fig. 52.   A monetarist economy

would then lead to a reduction, rather than an increase, in the consumption of manufactures.

The second issue relates to the slope of the LL schedule. Suppose that the LL locus is steeper than the MM schedule, due to strong effects of unemployment on the threshold wage. As shown in figure 52, the AA schedule shifting to the right will no longer reduce inflation, even though the agricultural terms of trade will still fall with the increase in food supplies. The reason is that the inflationary impact of the increase in industrial employment now offsets the deflationary effects of declining terms of trade. As the monetarist position views unemployment as determined largely by labor market parameters rather than agricultural demand and supply conditions, they can be considered assuming a steep LL schedule. In the extreme case of a vertical LL locus, there is only one level of industrial employment consistent with price stability. The only cure for inflation then is to reduce aggregate demand through a downward shift in the MM schedule.

Some structuralists also emphasized the role of labor market institutions in this type of inflation (see, in particular, Noyola 1956 and Sunkel 1958). Labor market institutions matter insofar as they affect the slope and position of the LL schedule. Later structuralists have built on this insight to advocate income policies that, by shifting the LL schedule upward, can reduce the short-run tradeoff between inflation and unemployment.[10]

Foreign Exchange Constraints and Two-Gap Models

The basic notion underlying two-gap models is that the economy's growth may be constrained by the availability of foreign exchange, as balance of payments disequilibria may not be easily corrected by exchange rate policy. This notion is analogous to Kalecki's view that the expansion of the industrial sector is constrained by the availability of food supplies. This is why two-gap and open economy inflation models in the structuralist tradition can be presented in a framework that is analogous to Kalecki's two-sector model. This is the approach that we will follow here. We will look at two-gap models as a Kaleckian model with two sectors (now domestic and foreign), with the key relative price, instead of the agricultural terms of trade, being the real exchange rate. As we will see, the AA schedule then becomes a locus of external balance and the MM locus becomes a schedule of goods market equilibrium.

Indeed, just as the sources of structural rigidities in Kalecki's model may be the inelasticity of the supply and demand of food (a low response of quantities to relative prices), or an insufficient elasticity combined with a real wage rigidity (a low response of relative prices to changes in nominal prices), two-gap models appear in two analogous versions. In one, which is associated with "elasticity pessimism," the source of the problem (in correcting balance of payments disequilibria) is "limited structural flexibility" (Chenery and Strout 1966, 682)—the low responses of exports and imports to changes in the real exchange rate. If primary goods dominate the export structure and imports are mostly complements, rather than substitutes, of domestic production, import and export price elasticities may be too low for the real exchange rate to significantly affect the trade balance. Given the ineffectiveness of exchange rate policy, the need to preserve external balance will constrain fiscal and monetary policies, which then will be unable to increase the level of employment.

Another version of the two-gap model refers to "real wage resistance" (see Bacha 1984). Here the problem is not one of low responses of quantities to relative prices (low price elasticities) but rather of a structure of relative prices being unresponsive to changes in the nominal exchange rate. If a real devaluation involves distribution effects against wage earners, there may be a minimum level of real wages (and a maximum real exchange rate) beyond which further nominal devaluations are ineffective. If this maximum real exchange rate falls short of the exchange rate required to achieve external balance and full employment, macroeconomic policy will again be unable to meet these two targets simultaneously. The need to maintain external balance forces the economy into a less than full employment equilibrium. As we shall see, this version of the model can generate a type of inflation that is close in spirit to that envisioned by Kalecki.

Elasticity Pessimism

Consider an open economy with two sectors. Sector C uses labor to produce consumer goods for domestic use and exports. Sector I uses labor and imported intermediate goods (with a fixed input-output coefficient) to produce investment goods for domestic use. Technology and market structure are similar to those earlier assumed for manufacturing: production of both goods requires a constant input of labor per unit of output and firms take input prices as given and operate under monopolistic competition in the goods market. Profit maximization again implies that pricing decisions follow a markup rule, while output adjusts to demand:

$$p_C = (1 + \pi_C)w$$

$$p_I = (1 + \pi_I)(w + ep^*\mu),$$

where w is the uniform nominal wage rate, π the markup over unit cost, μ the input-output coefficient for imported intermediate goods, p^* the foreign currency price of these inputs, and e the nominal exchange rate. We choose units such that the labor input-output coefficient is equal to one in both sectors.

We treat investment as given and assume, for simplicity, that all profits are saved and all wage income is spent on consumption goods. Exports (X) are a function of the real exchange rate (p), which we define as ep^*/p_C. These assumptions imply that output C of the consumption goods sector and the trade balance in domestic currency (T) are given by:

$$p_C C = wL + p_C X(p) \quad X' \geq 0 \tag{12}$$

$$T = p_C X(p) - ep^*\mu I, \tag{13}$$

where L is the overall level of employment $(L = L_C + L_I)$. Using $C = L_C$, $I = L_I$, and equation 12, we can express the equilibrium level of employment as a function of $I + X$ times a multiplier:

$$L = [I + X(p)]/(1 - w/p_C), \tag{14}$$

where w/p_C is determined by the pricing decisions in sector C. Using equation 13 and the condition of balanced trade $(T = 0$; we neglect for the time being capital inflows) yields:

$$I = X(p)/(\mu p).\tag{15}$$

Given the level of investment (I), equations 14 and 15 can be solved for p and L, the real exchange rate and level of employment that satisfy the goods market equilibrium and balanced trade. Assume now that the real exchange rate is available as a policy instrument and in addition that the government has fiscal and monetary policy instruments capable of influencing the level of investment. We are interested in the following question: given target values for employment and the trade balance, are there values for I and p such that target values for L and T can be achieved simultaneously? More precisely, if the government wants to achieve full employment ($L = L^s$) and, at the same time, equilibrium in the trade balance ($T = 0$), how should it set its policies to meet these targets? Formally, we are looking for the level of investment and the value of the real exchange rate such that $L = L^s$ and $T = 0$. This amounts to solving the model for I and p given $L = L^s$ and $T = 0$.

Swan's diagram of internal and external balance (1955) illustrates the solution to the problem. Setting $L = L^s$ in equation 14 yields the schedule of internal balance, the locus of (p, I) combinations that keep the economy at full employment. A higher level of investment increases employment. With elastic responses of import and export volumes to changes in the real exchange rate, devaluation is also expansionary. The internal balance schedule will then be downward sloping since a higher exchange rate requires a reduction in investment to keep employment at its target level.

The external balance schedule is given by equation 15, interpreted as a locus of (p, I) combinations that preserve balanced trade. Devaluation has a positive effect on the trade balance, while higher investment has a negative effect, as it increases income and imports. As a result, the external balance schedule has a positive slope. With elastic trade responses, the values of p and I that satisfy the conditions for balanced trade and full employment will then generally exist.

Under our present assumptions, imports are inelastic given the fixed input-output coefficient for intermediate goods imports. If, in addition, exports feature low price elasticities, real devaluation will be effective only within narrow limits. There may be a value of p beyond which the two schedules have the same slope (see fig. 53, where we assume, for simplicity, that the two schedules become vertical beyond p^*). The internal and external balance curves do not cross: the combination of a real exchange rate and an investment level that can simultaneously achieve internal and external balance does not exist. Depreciating the currency beyond p^* is useless. To meet the external balance target, fiscal and monetary policy will thus be constrained to yield the level of investment

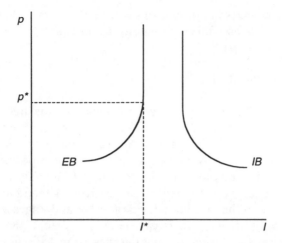

Fig. 53.   Swan's diagram with inelastic trade responses

I^*, the maximum consistent with external balance. Given the need to meet external balance, foreign exchange revenues at $p = p^*$ operate as a constraint on aggregate demand. Macroeconomic policy is then unable to generate the full employment level of output.

Let L^* be the level of employment corresponding to I^*. The value of L^* is given by equation 14. Setting $p = p^*$ and $I = I^*$:

$$L^* = [I^* + X(p^*)]/(1 - w/p_c), \tag{16}$$

where p^* is such that $dX/dp = 0$ for $dp > 0$ and $dX/dp < 0$ for $dp < 0$, and I^* is given by the balance of payments equilibrium condition (eq. 15):

$$I^* = [X(p^*)]/(p^*\mu). \tag{17}$$

A simple extension of the model is to introduce an exogenous level of capital inflows (F). The external balance target (equilibrium in the balance of payments) is now $T + F = 0$ rather than balanced trade. The maximum level of investment consistent with external balance becomes:

$$I^* = [X(p) + F]/(p\mu). \tag{17'}$$

We now look at how these constrained levels of employment and investment respond to changes in exogenous variables and parameters.

Consider first changes in the exogenous level of capital inflows when the economy is at less than full employment. From equation (17'), increases in F raise I^* by $1/(p\mu)$:[11]

$$dI^*/dF = 1/(p\mu) \quad \text{for } L^* < L^s.$$

At some level of capital inflows, the economy reaches full employment. Further increases in F will leave L^* unaffected. What happens to investment under these conditions? A larger volume of capital inflows makes foreign exchange available for an increase in imported inputs and thus in the level of investment. The transfer of labor from sector C to sector I will reduce output C and generate excess demand for goods and labor in sector C at the prevailing level of prices and wages in this sector. If prices and nominal wages increase to the same extent (there is nothing in this situation to prevent nominal wages from keeping up with increases in the cost of living), the increase in prices will lead to a real appreciation of the domestic currency.[12] Indeed, using equation 12, setting $L_C = L^s - I$, and solving for $X(p)$ show that the market for C goods now clears through changes in the real exchange rate (and at levels below p^*):

$$X(p) = (1 - w/p_C)L^s - I. \tag{18}$$

The market-clearing condition in sector C implies an inverse relationship between exports and investment: at full employment, further increases in investment can only be achieved through a real appreciation that causes a reduction in exports. This implies that a portion of foreign exchange made available by the increase in F will be offset by a reduction in exports. As a result, the increase in imported inputs and investment will be less than when the economy is below full employment. Indeed, substituting from equation 18 into 17', we find that:

$$I^* = [1/(1 + p\mu)][F + (1 - w/p_C)L^s], \tag{19}$$

which shows that the multiplier effect of F on I^* is now $1/(1 + p\mu)$ and thus necessarily less than before (see fig. 54).

The result is Chenery's theorem (Chenery and Strout 1966), which states that the effects of capital inflows on investment and growth — or, in Chenery's analysis, the effectiveness of foreign aid — are larger when the economy is constrained by foreign exchange (at less than full employment) than when it is constrained by savings at full employment. The difference is due to the mobilization of domestic savings, which is made possible by additional foreign exchange, when the economy is at less than

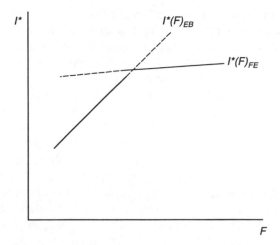

Fig. 54.   Effects of capital inflows on investment

full employment. The constrained level of investment (I^*) can be seen as determined by domestic savings at the foreign-exchange-determined level of employment plus the foreign savings made available by capital inflows. When the economy is at less than full employment, additional foreign savings cause an increase in the level of output consistent with external balance (see eqs. 16 and 17). This output increase leads to higher domestic savings and allows investment to expand to a larger extent than the additional capital inflows do. This mobilization of domestic savings is absent when the economy operates at full employment.

Consider now the effects of an increase in the domestic savings rate. Given our assumptions of savings behavior, we model these effects as resulting from an increase in the "degree of monopoly" that reduces the real wage, w/p_C. At less than full employment, a lower real wage reduces the level of employment while leaving investment unaffected (see eqs. 16 and 17'). The additional savings at the initial level of employment simply reduce consumption demand and employment in sector C without any other consequences.

In contrast, at full employment the lower real wage raises I^*, as is shown in equation 19. The mechanism is as follows. The fall in employment in sector C, which results from the higher savings rate, allows the government to depreciate the currency. Since the economy was initially at full employment, the market for consumption goods was clearing at an exchange rate below p^*. The real depreciation is thus effective in increasing exports. The additional foreign exchange made available by the increase in exports allows the level of investment I^* to increase. In the end, the process involves a reallocation of employment from the production of domestically consumed goods to the production of investment goods and exports (which finance the additional imports of intermediate goods required by sector I).

Policies directed toward increasing domestic savings will thus have a larger impact on investment (and growth) when the economy is at full employment (under a "savings constraint") than at less than full employment (under a "foreign exchange constraint"). It is worth noting that the absence of any effects on I^* at less than full employment is due to our assumption that sector C does not use imported inputs. Otherwise, the fall in output caused by the fall in consumption demand would reduce intermediate goods imports for sector C and make foreign exchange available to sector I for the import of more inputs. In this case, investment can increase, but it will clearly increase by less than it would at full employment. The reason is that, with exports being demand determined and exchange rate policy ineffective, for investment to increase the level of output and employment in sector C must fall — given that it is the reduction in imports to this sector that makes possible the higher imports required to increase investment. The downward adjustment of employment in sector C implies a loss of domestic savings that is absent in the full employment case.

Real Wage Resistance

We turn to the case in which, while exports and imports are elastic, real devaluation is limited by the downward inflexibility of real wages. The economy considered produces a single good that can be consumed, invested, or exported. Imports consist of competing consumer goods. Local producers employ labor with diminishing returns and operate under atomistic competition. As in chapter 3, we assume that the real wage paid by firms affects labor productivity through its influence on nutrition and health. The production function is thus:

$$Y = (EL)^{1-a} \quad 0 < a < 1, \tag{20}$$

and the effort function E has the form:

$$E = (w/p_C - \omega)^d \quad d < 1, \tag{21}$$

where (w/p_C) is the real *consumption wage* and p_C is a consumption price index derived from a Cobb-Douglas utility function of the form $U = C_M{}^\alpha C_D{}^{1-\alpha}$, where C_M and C_D are the quantities of imported and domestically produced consumer goods, respectively. The corresponding consumption price index is then:

$$p_C = (ep^*)^{\alpha} p_D^{1-\alpha},$$

where p_D, p^*, and e are the domestic price, the price of imported consumer goods (in foreign currency), and the nominal exchange rate, respectively.

Firms treat prices as given and maximize profits over w and L, subject to the technology in equation 20 and the effort function (eq. 21). The first-order conditions of this maximization program imply the following employment and wage decisions:

$$(EL)^d = (1 - a)^{1/a} E^{1/a} (w/p_D)^{-1/a}$$

$$w/p_D = p^{\alpha} \omega / (1 - d) \quad p = ep^*/p_D.$$

Labor demand in effective units ($[EL]^d$) is an inverse function of the real wage per effective worker ($[w/p_D]/E$). In equilibrium, all firms pay the same wage, and equilibrium effort is obtained from substitution of the efficiency wage into the effort function.

The efficiency product wage is an increasing function of the real exchange rate and ω, the minimum wage required to generate a positive effort from workers. The profit-maximizing level of employment (L^d) is an inverse function of the efficiency product wage. The two equations combined imply that the profit-maximizing level of employment is an inverse function of the real exchange rate:

$$L^d = L(p) \quad L' < 0. \tag{22}$$

Setting L^d equal to the total labor force, we can solve equation 22 for the unique value of the real exchange rate at which full employment is the profit-maximizing level of employment. The horizontal *IB* line in figure 55 shows the corresponding value of the real exchange rate.

On the demand side, we treat investment as given and assume again that all profits are saved and all wage income is spent on consumption goods. Together with our Cobb-Douglas utility function, this assumption implies the following demand functions for imported and domestic consumer goods:

$$C_M = \alpha w L / (ep^*) \tag{23}$$

$$C_D = (1 - \alpha) w L / p_D. \tag{24}$$

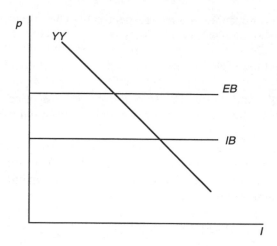

Fig. 55.   Conflict between external and internal balances

Exports are a positive function of the real exchange rate (p) such that:

$$X = X(p) \quad X' > 0. \tag{25}$$

Consider now the goods market equilibrium condition. Using equations 20, 22, 24, and 25, the equality between output supply and aggregate demand $(Y = C_D + I + X)$ implies that:

$$[EL(p)]^{1-a} = (1 - \alpha)L(p)p^{\alpha}[\omega/(1 - d)] + I + X(p). \tag{26}$$

Equation 26 can be interpreted as showing the value of the real exchange rate that clears the goods market at each level of investment. From the RHS of equation 26, a higher level of investment increases aggregate demand and generates excess demand at the initial levels of the real exchange rate and employment. Market clearing requires an increase in aggregate supply and/or a reduction in other components of aggregate demand. This is achieved by the upward pressure on the price of domestic goods and the resulting real appreciation of the domestic currency. From the LHS of equation 26, we can see that the lower real exchange rate, through its effects on the efficiency product wage, increases output supply. In addition, the real appreciation reduces export demand and shifts the composition of consumption demand away from locally produced goods. Eventually, the goods market will clear at a higher level of employment and a lower real exchange rate.

Equation 26 thus defines a downward-sloping schedule of (p, I) combinations that keeps the goods market in equilibrium (the YY schedule in fig. 55). Both a higher exchange rate and increased investment tend to generate excess demand for goods, and therefore the slope of this schedule is negative. Along the schedule, employment increases with the level of investment.

The levels of investment and real exchange rate consistent with goods market equilibrium and required to guarantee full employment are given at the intersection of the IB and YY lines in figure 55. But is this combination feasible? Not necessarily, since the real exchange rate required to guarantee external balance may well imply an efficiency product wage that is too high to induce full employment of the labor force. Consider the external balance condition in this model. Setting the value of imports (ep^*C_M) equal to the value of exports (pX) and using equations 22, 23, and 25, we obtain:

$$L(p)\alpha p^\alpha \omega/(1 - d) = X(p),$$

which can be solved for the value of the real exchange rate that is consistent with external balance, given the wage and employment decisions of firms. This value corresponds to the EB line in figure 55. In the case shown by the figure, this value is higher than the exchange rate required for full employment (corresponding to the IB line). Clearly, the level of employment consistent with external balance and goods market equilibrium—at the intersection of the EB line and the YY schedule—will then be below full employment (since, as noted, along the YY schedule employment increases with the level of investment). If the government then increases the level of investment to induce a higher level of employment, the external balance target will not be met.

The wage and employment decisions of firms, together with the external balance target, will constrain government planners to choose an exchange rate and investment level at the intersection of the EB and YY lines. The result is a less than full employment equilibrium that cannot be corrected through a nominal devaluation or an increase in investment. Any attempt to increase the level of employment in this way would either generate a real wage that is below the efficiency wage, with a corresponding increase in nominal wages, or violate the external constraint. Just as the wage-goods constraint in Kalecki's model results from the fact that the agricultural sector cannot supply the food surplus necessary to fully employ the labor force, structural unemployment here results from a level of competitiveness that is too low to generate the real wage necessary to employ the whole of the labor force.

A higher level of employment can nevertheless be induced by other means. First, higher capital inflows, which for simplicity have been ignored so far, would shift the external balance locus downward and result in an increase in the permissible level of investment and employment. Such a shift induces an increase in employment by reducing the required real exchange rate and thus the equilibrium efficiency *product* wage. Second, an increase in productivity that reduces the efficiency product wage at each level of the real exchange rate would also move the economy closer to full employment. Finally, an import tariff can relax the foreign exchange constraint in the present setting. Under our assumptions, a higher import tariff shifts the *EB* line in figure 55 downward. The reason is that a tariff reduces import demand proportionately more than it increases the efficiency wage. However, this result will not hold if imports are inelastic and their price has a strong effect on the price of consumer goods.

Inflation in the Open Economy

What happens if the level of investment is higher than the level required to maintain external balance given the labor market constraint? To answer this question, we will look at the model in (L,p) space (see fig. 56). Equation 22 defines a downward-sloping employment schedule (LL) in (L,p) space: a higher real exchange rate increases the efficiency product wage and reduces the profit-maximizing level of employment. The goods market equilibrium locus (YY) shows the value of p that makes the volume of output forthcoming at each level of employment equal to aggregate demand. The locus is upward sloping since a higher level of employment, which increases output, requires a higher real exchange rate in order to generate the corresponding increase in aggregate demand. The position of the YY line depends on a given level of investment. The EB line is the locus of real exchange rates and employment combinations that are consistent with equilibrium in the balance of payments. Positive price elasticity of export demand is sufficient for the external balance locus to slope upward.[13] A real devaluation, then, has a positive effect on the trade balance, and an increase in employment, which raises imports, is required to maintain external balance.

As drawn in figure 56, the three loci do not intersect at the same point. The assumed level of investment is not consistent with the external balance and labor market constraints. To examine what will happen in this situation, we need to specify the behavior of prices, the exchange

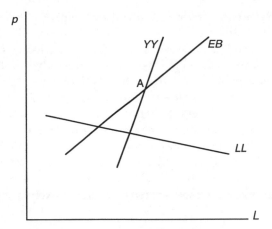

Fig. 56. Conflict between external balance and labor market equilibrium

rate, and nominal wages when the economy is not in equilibrium. As was done earlier, we will assume that domestic prices move instantaneously to clear the goods market and that the nominal exchange rate moves instantaneously to clear the foreign exchange market. Nominal wages, in contrast, adjust sluggishly, with a rate of change that is a function of the gap between real consumption wages and the efficiency consumption wage. These assumptions force the economy to always be at the intersection of the goods market equilibrium and external balance schedules, but they allow for persistent deviations from the *LL* schedule. In a close analogy with the closed economy model examined earlier, this schedule now shows a maximum value of the real exchange rate that is consistent with stable money wages at each level of employment. Above the locus, the real exchange rate is higher than the value required for money wage stability.

In the situation depicted in figure 56, the real exchange rate, as determined by equilibrium in the goods and foreign exchange markets, is too high to preserve price stability. As money wages increase, the nominal exchange rate must depreciate in order to preserve external balance and domestic prices will then increase to maintain equilibrium in the goods market. The rate at which nominal wages (and prices) increase is a function of the gap between point A and the *LL* locus.[14] A reduction in investment that shifts the *YY* locus to the left may be an effective but (as in the earlier analysis) not necessarily the most efficient cure for this type of inflation.

Foreign Exchange Constraints on Domestic Supply

In the two-gap models discussed so far, foreign exchange constraints set a limit to effective demand and, more precisely, to the ability of macroeconomic policies to affect the level of aggregate demand. In some situations — such as those following the terms of trade and debt shocks suffered by some sub-Saharan African countries in the late 1970s and early 1980s — foreign exchange constraints directly affect domestic supply. The low level of domestic supply can then, through mechanisms involving the incentive to export, reproduce the foreign exchange constraint in a self-perpetuating, low-level equilibrium. We now turn to a simple model that addresses this type of foreign exchange constraint.

The Model

The model draws on a number of contributions. One is the literature on "import strangulation" of the manufacturing sector, in which the scarcity of foreign exchange leads to the rationing of essential imports of intermediate and capital goods. It also draws on the analysis of the behavior of rural households under rationing in the goods market, in which the lack of supply of certain "incentive" manufactured goods to rural households can reduce their willingness to engage in the production of cash crops.[15]

The economy considered has two sectors, agriculture and manufacturing. In agriculture, rural households produce an internationally tradable cash crop (A) and a subsistence good (S) for household consumption, with the production functions:

$$A = L_A \tag{27}$$

$$S = L_R - L_A, \tag{28}$$

where A and S are the output of each of the two goods, respectively, and L_R is the rural labor force. The cash crop is fully exported, and rural households decide on their labor allocations by maximizing a utility function:

$$U = \alpha \log C_R + \beta \log S,$$

subject to $p_M C_R = p_A A$ and $C_R \leq \tilde{C}_R$, where p_M is the price of the manufactured good (M), C_R is the rural consumption of M, and $\tilde{C}_R$ is the maximum amount of M that the household can buy when it is rationed in the market. The budget constraint $(p_M C_R = p_A A)$ indicates that all income from cash crop production is spent on manufactures and thus reflects the fact that the rural household does not use the cash crop for any other purpose than to buy manufactures.

From this maximization program, it follows that, when the rural household is unconstrained in the goods market, the amount of labor allocated to the production of the cash crop (L_A) and the household's consumption of good M are given by:

$$L_A = \alpha L_R/(\alpha + \beta) \quad C_R = (p_A/p_M)\alpha L_R/\alpha + \beta).$$

When good M is rationed in the market (and thus the constraint $C_R \leq \tilde{C}_R$ is binding), the amount of labor allocated to cash crop production is given by:

$$L_A = (p_M/p_A)\tilde{C}_R.$$

In this case, a lower price p_A leads the household to allocate more labor to the production of the cash crop so as to be able to make its rationed purchases of good M; and the higher the rationed supply of M to the rural sector the larger the amount of labor that is worthwhile allocating to cash crop production.

The supply of manufactured goods to the rural sector $(\tilde{C}_R)$ is assumed to be a function of the difference between the total production of M and the consumption of M by urban workers (equal to the urban wage bill, $L_M w_M/p_M$):

$$\tilde{C}_R = \Omega[M - (w_M/p_M)L_M] \quad \Omega > 0. \tag{29}$$

In the manufacturing sector, firms produce a nontradable good (M) using labor (L_M) and imported intermediate goods (I). The production function is such that:

$$M = L_M^a I^b \quad 0 < a, b < 1. \tag{30}$$

Firms face U-shaped unit cost curves, and thus at low levels of output $a + b > 1$ and at high levels $a + b < 1$. Firms are rationed in the import market so that at the given price, p_I, they can purchase a maximum amount of imported intermediate goods $(\tilde{I})$. Profit maximization implies the following output supply and labor demand functions:

$$M = (ap_M/w)^{a/(1-a)}\tilde{I}^{b/(1-a)} \tag{31}$$

$$L_M = (ap_M/w)^{1/(1-a)}\tilde{I}^{b/(1-a)}. \tag{32}$$

The rationed supply of imports is such that a balance of payments equilibrium is achieved:

$$p_I \tilde{I} = p_A A + F. \tag{33}$$

Equation 33 states the equality between the value of imports $(p_I \tilde{I})$ and the value of exports (i.e., cash crops, $p_A A$) plus capital inflows net of income paid abroad (F).

Shocks, Setbacks, and Vicious Circles of Economic Decline

Figure 57 illustrates the solution to the model in $(L_A, \tilde{I})$ space. Substituting from equations 31 and 32 into 30 and then using the value of L_A when the rural household is subject to rationing in the manufacturing goods market yields a schedule $L_A(\tilde{I})$. This locus shows how the allocation of rural labor to cash crops varies with the amount of imports available:

$$L_A = (p_M/p_A)B\tilde{I}^{b/(1 - a)} \tag{34}$$

$$B = \Omega(1 - a)(ap_M/w)^{a/(1 - a)},$$

where B is positive since $a < 1$. Given p_A, p_M, and w, L_A increases with $\tilde{I}$. The reason is straightforward: the supply of M goods is constrained by $\tilde{I}$. Thus, a higher level of imports would lead to an increase in M and, given the real wage, to an increase in the supply of M to the rural areas (given that the excess of manufacturing output over wage earners' consumption increases). Since good M is rationed in the market, the increase in the supply of M induces the rural household to allocate more labor to cash crops. The relationship is nonlinear and has the shape of an inverted S-curve. At low levels of $\tilde{I}$ (and thus of M), increasing returns in manufacturing $(a + b > 1)$ imply that the slope of the locus decreases since, with each additional increment in imports, the additional increase in the supply of M to the rural areas (and thus in L_A) becomes larger. At high levels of $\tilde{I}$ (and M), with $a + b < 1$, the slope of the locus increases due to diminishing returns. At high levels of $\tilde{I}$, it is also possible that the market for M goods is no longer subject to rationing (at the given relative price p_M/p_A) so that the level of employment, L_A, no longer responds to changes in $\tilde{I}$. The locus then becomes vertical in $(L_A, \tilde{I})$ space.

Substituting from equation 27 into 33 yields a balance of payments locus (BP) showing the amount of intermediate goods that can be imported at each level of L_A given the exogenous value of net capital inflows (F):

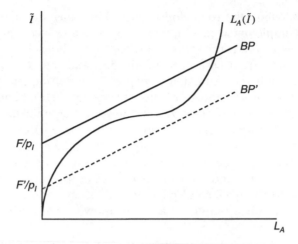

Fig. 57. External shocks under a foreign exchange supply constraint

$$\tilde{I} = (p_A/p_I)L_A + F/p_I. \tag{35}$$

This locus is a straight line with a slope equal to the economy's terms of trade and the intercept given by the purchasing power of net capital inflows in terms of imported goods.

Consider an initial equilibrium with a high level of employment in cash crop production, a small subsistence sector, and a high output level in manufacturing. This high output level in manufacturing is made possible by the large volume of imports that the economy can finance with its exports of cash crops and capital inflows. It is easily verified that the equilibrium is stable. If rural households allocate more labor to cash crops, the economy will be able to import more intermediate goods (the corresponding level of I on the BP line) but less than what is necessary to produce the supply of M goods to the rural areas that makes it worthwhile to allocate the assumed amount of labor to the production of cash crops. Rural households will revise their labor allocation decisions until the economy converges to the equilibrium point.

Subject to a negative external shock—resulting, say, from a decrease in capital inflows from F to F'—the economy may go through a process of economic decline that extends well beyond the proportionate effects that would be expected in comparison with shocks of smaller magnitude—note that the shock considered here is such that the BP line, after the shock, lies below the inflexion point of the $L_A(\tilde{I})$ schedule. In this process of decline, imports of intermediate goods initially decrease following the reduction in F/p_I. This causes a contraction of output and employment in manufacturing, which reduces the supply of manufactures to the rural areas. This leads rural households to reallocate labor away from cash crop production and into the subsistence sector. The result is a reduction in exports that subsequently causes a further contraction of imports, manufacturing output, and employment. The economy eventually stabilizes at a low-level equilibrium, provided that net capital inflows remain positive, with a large subsistence sector and low levels of employment and output in both the manufacturing and cash crop sectors. In the process, the interactions between the production of manufactures and the exports of cash crops have magnified the initial shock to the balance of payments, thus causing the economy to stabilize at a level of output with a much lower level of exports than initially.

How can the economy escape from the low-level equilibrium? In both the initial and final equilibria, the price of manufacturing goods (p_M), and in particular the relative price p_M/p_A, are at disequilibrium levels. It would therefore seem at first sight that the problem of escaping from the low-level equilibrium has an easy solution: letting the price of manufactured goods find its market-clearing level, which would reduce the slope of the $L_A(\tilde{I})$ locus and shift it to the right (even if the real wage, w/p_M, does not change; see eq. 34). With a sufficiently large increase in p_M, the low-level equilibrium would disappear. This would trigger a cumulative process of expansion of the cash crop and manufacturing sectors toward a new, high-level equilibrium.

However, while the fact that p_M remained at a disequilibrium level may have had a role in the process of decline, once the economy has stabilized in the low-level equilibrium the increase in p_M may not be enough to reverse this process. Intuitively, the reason is that the value of I at the inflexion point of the $L_A(\tilde{I})$ locus is independent of p_M, so a higher manufacturing price shifts the value of $(\tilde{I}, L_A)$ at the inflexion point to the right along a horizontal line. While this shift tends to have a positive effect on $\tilde{I}$ and L_A at the low-level equilibrium, it may not eliminate it altogether since the size of the shift is limited by the total labor endowment (L_R) of rural households. The outcome depends critically on the size of the external shock (the size of the reduction in F): if the BP line remains below the inflexion point, then no high-level equilibrium will exist and the economy will remain at the low level.

The situation is somewhat different if the real wage falls. This will not only change the value of L_A at the inflexion point, but it will reduce the value of imports at this point. Two effects are involved here. First, a lower real wage implies that a smaller level of output M (and thus of imports) is needed to generate a given supply of manufactures to the rural areas. Moreover, the lower product wage in manufacturing means that a less import-intensive input mix is required to generate a given level of output (see eq. 31). Yet the wage (w/p_M) need not be at a disequilibrium level at the low-level intersection. Employment in manufacturing has declined, but the subsistence sector has expanded, and this sector sets a floor to the wage in manufacturing. Thus, there are limits to how much the real wage in terms of manufactures can fall by letting the price p_M clear the goods market.[16] A reversal of the process of economic decline may then require a recovery of the level of capital inflows, which would shift the *BP* line upward, or else an improvement in the terms of trade, which would increase the slope of the *BP* line.

CHAPTER 12

Debt Traps and Demand-Constrained Growth

In the 1980s, most countries in Latin America and sub-Saharan Africa suffered economic setbacks that led to a prolonged slump. Factor accumulation models, whether of the neoclassical, endogenous growth, or development theory varieties, do not explain the severe growth slow-down that persisted for over a decade. This is reflected in the common finding that growth rates for Latin American economies and sub-Saharan African countries are lower than those predicted by models with factor accumulation and political variables alone. This is why dummy variables for Latin America, for example, are systematically significant and negative, typically accounting for why growth rates there have been more than one percentage point below what would otherwise be predicted by these models. As stated by Barro (1991, 437): "[T]he results leave unexplained a good deal of the relatively weak growth performance of countries in sub-Saharan Africa and Latin America."[1] The main analytical issue that arises here is why the growth slowdown persisted for such a long period of time and why macroeconomic policies were unable to remove them.

Regardless of their relevance in earlier periods, the two-gap models reviewed in the previous chapter do not provide a fully adequate explanation of the persistence of the slump of the 1980s. While these models may explain the ineffectiveness of macroeconomic policies, they do so under conditions that are at variance with the realities of this period. The notion that relative prices, especially the real exchange rate, have weak and unreliable effects on resource allocation cannot fully account for the problems of a period that witnessed enormous changes in relative prices and substantial quantity adjustments in response to them.[2] Similarly, the assumption of exogenous capital flows cannot be applied to several Latin American countries, where, even though the public sector is subject to rationing in international credit markets, the private sector, which often has most of its financial assets invested abroad, is not in any meaningful sense.

The literature on three-gap models attempts to overcome these limitations and account for the economic stagnation and persistent underutilization of resources that prevailed in Latin American economies during the 1980s.[3] Before turning to this literature, we shall go back to earlier contributions to growth theory. Thus, we will begin by presenting an open economy Harrod-Domar model of capital accumulation and then will extend it by bringing in the insights of the literature on three-gap models. We will then discuss the links between factor accumulation, demand-constrained growth, and long-run convergence by comparing the neoclassical growth path to the demand-constrained growth paths of three-gap models. The chapter then turns to an empirical analysis and an application of the analytical framework developed to explain Latin American growth performance in the 1980s.

An Open Economy Harrod-Domar Model

Technology, Market Structure, and Demand

The economy considered produces a good that can be consumed, invested, or exported. Firms maximize profits: $p_D Z + p_X X - wL$, where Z is domestic sales, X is exports, L is labor input, and p_D and p_X are the price of domestic sales and the price of exports (equal to the international price), respectively. The constraints facing firms involve technology, market structure, and the given capital stock in the short run. Technology is Cobb-Douglas:

$$Y = Z + X = F(L, K) = AK^a L^{1-a},$$

where Y is total output and K is the capital stock. Firms are price takers in export markets and can sell whatever they wish at the international price (p_X). In contrast, in the domestic market they operate under imperfect competition, facing downward-sloping demand curves with a constant price elasticity of demand (ϕ):

$$Z = B(p_i/p_D)^{-\phi},$$

where p_i is the individual price, in equilibrium equal to the average price of domestic sales (p_D, or domestic price for short). From the first-order conditions for profit maximization, the domestic price and employment are determined as:

$$p_D = (1 + \tau)w/F'(L) = (1 + \tau)p_X \quad 1 + \tau = \phi/(\phi - 1) \tag{1}$$

$$w/p_X = F'(L) = (1 - a)AK^a L^{-a}. \tag{2}$$

Equation 1 shows that the domestic price is set as a constant markup (τ) over marginal labor cost $w/F'(L)$. Because firms are price takers in export markets, they sell abroad up to the point where the price of exports is equal to the marginal cost of labor. This implies that the ratio of the domestic to export price is equal to the ratio of the domestic price to the marginal labor cost. Equation 2 shows the determination of employment by the equality between the marginal product of labor and the wage per unit of exports. This implies that the level of employment (and output) is independent of domestic demand. Firms do not increase production in response to higher demand (given w/p_X). Rather, they adjust by reducing exports. The reason is that they face a perfectly elastic demand for exports. Indeed, if they increased production in response to higher domestic demand, their marginal cost would increase above the price of exports. This would induce them to reduce their exports until the marginal cost of production is again equal to the price of exports. This means that a higher domestic demand fully crowds out exports.

Yet, since the price of domestic sales is higher than the marginal cost, the higher volume of domestic sales raises the average markup as well as the profit rate on the given capital stock. From the definitions of the average price on total sales (p) and the profit rate (r), we have:

$$p = (p_D Z + p_X X)/Y$$

$$r = (pY - wL)/p_I K,$$

where p_I is the price of capital goods.

The type of adjustment described implies the following relationship between the profit rate and the share of domestic sales in output (Z/Y):

$$r = [a + \tau Z/Y]\theta v, \tag{3}$$

where v is the output-capital ratio (Y/K), θ equals p_X/p_I, and a is the capital share in output. Equation 3 shows the profit rate as an increasing function of the share of domestic sales in total output and the output-capital ratio, which, given the determination of employment and output, is an increasing function of the ratio of export prices to wages (or the real exchange rate). Note that the profit rate exceeds its competitive equilibrium value ($av p_X/p_I$) by the extent to which the markup (τ) is positive.

Turning to the demand side, assume that there are no savings out of wages and let s_π be the propensity to save out of profits. Consumption (C) is then determined as:

$$p_D C = wL + (1 - s_\pi)(pY - wL).$$

Investment has a domestic (I_d) and an imported (M_k) component:

$$p_I I = p_D I_d + p_M M_k.$$

We assume, for simplicity, that M_k is equal to total imports. The import function is such that there is a fixed amount (μ) of complementary imports per unit of total investment:

$$M_k = \mu I.$$

Equilibrium and the Warranted Growth Rate

The goods market equilibrium condition is:

$$pY = p_D C + p_I I + p_X X - p_M M_k.$$

Substituting from the imports and consumption functions into the goods market equilibrium condition and normalizing by the value of the capital stock ($p_I K$), we can write the equilibrium condition as:

$$s_\pi r = (1 - \theta\mu)g + \theta x \quad 1 - \theta\mu > 0 \quad \text{since} \quad p_M M_k < p_I I, \qquad (4)$$

where g is the rate of capital accumulation (I/K) and x is the export-capital ratio. We choose units such that $p_M/p_I = p_X/p_I (= \theta)$.

We now derive two relationships between the profit rate and the rate of accumulation such that, in a steady state, profit expectations are fulfilled and the rates of accumulation and output growth are constant. The first relationship is obtained from the goods market equilibrium condition. Substituting from equation 3 into 4 and using $Z/Y = (1 - X/Y)$ and $X/Y = xK/Y$ in order to eliminate x, we get:

$$r = [1/(1 + \tau s_\pi)]\{[\tau(1 - \theta\mu)g + [\theta v(a + \tau)]\}. \qquad (5)$$

Equation 5 shows the profit rate that clears the goods market at each level of the rate of accumulation: a higher g raises the value of r through its effect on domestic demand, as was described earlier. This is why higher propensities to import and save (μ and s_π), which reduce domestic demand at each level of g, according to equation 5 have a negative effect on the profit rate. The real exchange rate (p_X/w) has a positive effect on the profit rate by increasing employment and output at each given level of the capital stock and thus the output-capital ratio.

The model is completed with a rate of accumulation function derived from a profit maximization program with adjustment costs:[4]

$$g = \nu(r^e - r^*), \tag{6}$$

where r^e is the expected profit rate and r^* is a risk-adjusted international profit rate.

In a steady state, $r^e = r$. Figure 58 shows the determination of the steady state values of g and r. At the intersection of the two lines, corresponding to equations 5 and 6, the rate of accumulation generates a profit rate that just equals the expected profit rate that induced this rate of accumulation. This equilibrium rate of accumulation is analogous to Harrod's warranted rate, for, in the present open economy context, it is such that the investment forthcoming at the equilibrium profit rate generates an addition to productive capacity such that the increase in domestic demand leaves the composition of total output between exports and domestic sales unchanged.

Above the $r(g)$ line (eq. 5), the rate of accumulation is higher, at each level of the profit rate, than what is required for the domestic market to clear. Firms will thus reduce exports and increase sales in the more profitable domestic market. Thus, as shown in figure 58, the profit rate increases when the economy is above the $r(g)$ line and falls when it is below. To the left of the $g(r^e)$ line (eq. 6), the profit rate is lower than expected and investment decisions will be revised downward, while to the right of the line the rate of accumulation increases.

In the absence of labor supply constraints, the economy will thus converge to the warranted rate if, as in figure 58, the slope of the $r(g)$ line is greater than the slope of the $g(r^e)$ line. The condition for stability is similar to that in Keynesian demand-driven growth models.[5] The propensity to invest out of profits (ν), which affects the slope of the $g(r^e)$ line, must not be too high relative to the leakages from the circular flow of income and expenditure, which affect the slope of the $r(g)$ line. These leakages are here determined by the propensity to save out of profits and the import coefficient (μ). Otherwise, the "accelerator effects" of profits on investment will generate a Harrod's knife-edge instability problem.

There are, however, two important differences to the recent literature on Keynesian growth models. The first is that, unlike what happens in models that assume a technology with fixed coefficients and a variable degree of excess capacity, the steady state in this model features the desired output-capital ratio and there is no reason for firms to revise their investment decisions.[6] This difference is related to the fact that in the present model the level of output plays no role in the adjustment of the goods market (given the real exchange rate). However, this feature

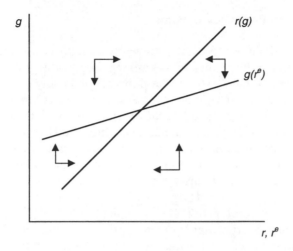

Fig. 58. The warranted growth rate

does not prevent growth from being demand driven: an increase in the response of investment to the profit rate increases the slope of the $g(r^e)$ line and raises the equilibrium values of g and r. Just as in Keynesian models, a decrease in the propensity to save or import tends to increase the steady state values of g and r by shifting the $r(g)$ line outward. These Keynesian features are due to the assumption of imperfect competition in the domestic market. If firms faced perfectly elastic demand curves, the markup over marginal cost would be zero and the rate of profit would be independent of s_π and μ. As the reader can verify, the $r(g)$ line would be vertical at the competitive equilibrium value of the profit rate $(a\theta v)$.

The second difference is that growth is always profit led and cannot be wage led — in Bhaduri and Marglin's (1990) terminology, the growth regime is "exhilarationist" rather than "stagnationist." A reduction in the real wage, due to a devaluation, which increases the real exchange rate (p_X/w), unambiguously increases the equilibrium growth rate by shifting the $r(g)$ line to the right. The reason for this difference arises from the assumptions of a perfectly elastic export demand and a flexible capital-output ratio. Together these assumptions imply that the decline in w/p_X increases employment and output, which has a positive effect on the profit rate and investment. The same happens if the reduction in the real wage is due to an increase in the domestic markup over marginal cost. Since output is independent of the markup (see eq. 2), the result is a purely positive effect on profitability. The higher markup shifts the $r(g)$ line to the right and increases the equilibrium values of g and r.

Demand-Constrained Growth Paths

We now extend our analytical framework to include a government sector and make explicit the financial flows among the private, government, and foreign sectors. Table 30 shows the flows of funds between the sectors, together with each sector's budget constraint (the column equations). The government sector (including the central bank) and the private sector (including domestic commercial banks) are indicated by subscripts G and P. Each of these sectors holds or issues one or more of the following financial assets: money (H), domestic government debt (B), public and private external debt (D), and international reserves (R).

X and M_k refer, as before, to (private sector) volumes of exports and imports, and G refers to real government spending. T, S, and I refer to the government's disposable income, private savings, and investment. These are nominal values deflated by the price of investment goods (p_I). For simplicity, we neglect interest payments on external private debt. The other symbols refer to changes in asset stocks, expressed also in real values and thus to changes in real financial wealth. Since the flows of financial assets refer to changes in the real value of asset stocks, financial surpluses in the last row must also refer to changes in real financial wealth. The inflation tax and the inflationary component of domestic interest payments are therefore subtracted from both the government financial deficit and the private financial surplus.[7]

Goods Market Equilibrium

In the goods market, the value of consumption is now such that:

$$p_D C = wL - \pi H + (1 - s_\pi)(1 - t)(pY - wL) + (1 - s_\pi)r_B B,$$

where t is the tax rate on profits, r_B is the real rate of interest on domestic government debt, and π is the rate of inflation (and thus πH is the inflation tax).[8] Private disposable income now includes the interest income on private holdings of government bonds ($r_B B$) and excludes the inflation tax, which is assumed to be paid by wage earners. There are no

TABLE 30.   Sectoral Financial Flows

Government	Private Sector	Foreign Sector		Total
$-\Delta H$	$+\Delta H$	$+0$	$=$	0
$-\Delta B$	$+\Delta B$	$+0$	$=$	0
$-\Delta D_G + \Delta R$	$-\Delta D_P$	$+\Delta D_G + \Delta D_P - \Delta R$	$=$	0
$T - (1 + \tau)\theta G$	$+S - I$	$+r^* D_G + \theta M_k - \theta X$	$=$	0

other taxes on wages, and wage earners are assumed, as earlier, to have a propensity to consume equal to one.

The goods market equilibrium condition is now:

$$pY = p_D C + p_I I + p_D G + p_X X - p_M M_k,$$

where the import function, as before, is such that there is a fixed amount (μ) of complementary imports per unit of total investment.

Normalizing by the capital stock and substituting from the consumption and import functions into the goods market equilibrium condition, we have:

$$[s_\pi + t(1 - s_\pi)]r = (1 - \theta\mu)g + \theta x + (1 + \tau)\theta q +$$

$$(1 - s_\pi)r_B b - \pi h, \tag{7}$$

where b and h are the ratios of bonds and money to the capital stock and q is the ratio of government expenditures to the capital stock (G/K). As the reader may verify, equation 7 simplifies to equation 4 if $b = h = t = q = 0$. Now, using equation 3 to eliminate x from equation 7, we can derive a new $r(g)$ function and show the profit rate that clears the goods market at each level of the rate of capital accumulation:

$$r = \Delta[(1 - \theta\mu)g + (1 + \tau)\theta q + (1 + a/\tau)\theta v +$$

$$(1 - s_\pi)r_B b - \pi h], \tag{8}$$

where: $\Delta = \tau/[1 + \tau s_\pi + \tau t(1 - s_\pi)]$.

Equation 8 is similar to equation 5 except for the positive effect of government spending (including interest payments on domestic debt) and the negative effects of the inflation tax, which affect the profit rate through their influence on domestic demand.

The presence of taxes on profits modifies the accumulation function. Thus, the rate of capital accumulation is now an increasing function of the posttax expected rate of return:

$$g = v[(1 - t)r^e - r^*]. \tag{9}$$

We also assume that private investment is negatively affected by inflation. One reason is that high inflation makes long-term domestic capital markets disappear, forcing firms to rely more heavily on foreign borrowing at increasing interest rates.[9] Barro (1997) presents empirical evidence from cross-country growth regressions supporting the hypothesis that high inflation has adverse effects on growth. We introduce this influence of inflation on investment by making r^* an increasing function of the inflation rate:

$$r^* = r^*(\pi) \quad r^{*\prime} > 0.$$

The determination of the warranted growth rate is similar to that in the first section except for the effects of government spending, taxes, and inflation. An increase in government spending increases profits by raising domestic demand and shifts the $r(g)$ line outward. The warranted growth rate and the rate of profit increase. Higher taxes on profits reduce growth through two effects: that on the $r(g)$ function, which shifts to the left as a result of the decline in capitalists' consumption, and that on the $g(r)$ function, which shifts downward on account of the negative effects of higher taxes on profitability. Higher inflation has adverse effects on growth and operates in a similar way to higher taxes. It shifts the $g(r)$ function downward by increasing r^*, and it reduces workers' consumption, thus shifting the $r(g)$ line to the left.

Asset Markets Constraints and the Sustainable Fiscal Deficit

So far, the model determines the rates of profit and capital accumulation for a *given* level of government spending. However, the given level of government spending, together with existing tax revenues, may imply an unsustainable path of debt accumulation. This is what, from the perspective of creditors, happened in Latin America in the early 1980s.[10] We are now interested in analyzing what happens after the government has become constrained in credit markets.

Thus, we shall now assume that there is rationing in both the foreign and domestic markets for government debt. Rationing takes the form of a kinked demand function for government debt on the part of domestic and foreign asset holders (see, on this subject, Ros 1991). When $b > \tilde{b}$ or $d_G > \tilde{d}_G$ (where d_G refers to the stock of government external debt as a ratio of the capital stock), the demand for government debt becomes fully inelastic. The maximum amount of debt that the government can issue is thus equal to $g(\tilde{b} + \tilde{d}_G)$. Moreover, when r_B falls below r^* (plus a constant premium, λ), domestic demand for government debt becomes perfectly elastic. This forces the government to set $r_B = (1 + \lambda)r^*$ and to monetize the fiscal deficit whenever it is larger than the increase in the demand for government debt at the interest rates r^* and $r_B = (1 + \lambda)r^*$. But monetization is constrained by seignorage, beyond which international reserves would continuously fall. As a result, the amount that the government can finance by issuing money and without losing reserves is constrained by the increase in the demand for money (gh).

Let us now define the sustainable fiscal deficit as that deficit which is consistent with equilibrium in the overall balance of payments while at the same time keeping the stocks of base money and government debt equal to the constrained levels and growing at the same rate as the capital stock. Thus, consider the sources of finance of the fiscal deficit (the first column in table 30). Set the change in international reserves equal to zero and the growth rate of domestic assets ($\Delta H/H$ and $\Delta B/B$) and external debt ($\Delta D_G/D_G$) equal to the rate of capital accumulation (g).[11] The sustainable fiscal deficit (or the asset market balance condition) is then given as:[12]

$$(1 + \tau)\theta q - (tr + \pi h - r_B b - r^* d_G) = g(h + \tilde{b} + \tilde{d}_G). \qquad (10)$$

The condition expressed by equation 10 constrains the amount of spending that the public sector can undertake. Substituting from equation 10 into 8 in order to eliminate $(1 + \tau)\theta q$ yields:

$$r = \Omega[(1 - \theta\mu + h + \tilde{b} + \tilde{d}_G)g - s_\pi r_B b - r^* d_G +$$

$$(1 + a/\tau)\theta v], \qquad (11)$$

where: $\Omega = \tau/(1 - t)[1 + \tau s_\pi + \pi(1 - s_\pi)]$.

Equation 11 is the $r(g)$ function that satisfies goods market equilibrium as well as the asset market constraints expressed in the sustainable fiscal deficit. The new $r(g)$ line is flatter than before in (r,g) space. In addition to previous effects on profitability, faster growth now increases the constrained level of government spending, which has a positive effect on the profit rate. The reason for this is that a higher growth rate raises the amount of debt and money that the government can issue as well as the amount of tax revenues received. This is why the tax rate now has positive effects on r besides the negative effects operating through capitalists' consumption. It is worth noting that inflation does not affect the position of the $r(g)$ line. With government spending being endogenous, a higher inflation tax raises government spending by the same amount by which it reduces workers' consumption. Moreover, higher interest payments now shift the $r(g)$ line to the left, thus reducing profitability. The reason for this is that higher interest payments reduce the constrained level of government spending. Finally, higher values for h,

$\tilde{b}$, and $\tilde{d}_G$ increase the profit rate by raising seignorage and the level of government spending.

The determination of the growth rate by equations 9 and 11 has a representation in (r, g) space similar to that in figure 58, with, however, a flatter $r(g)$ line. The adjustment dynamics are also similar, although the interpretation of the adjustment off the $r(g)$ line is slightly different. To the right of the $r(g)$ line, the profit rate is higher than that required to clear the goods market at a level of domestic demand consistent with balance of payments equilibrium. The government, now losing reserves, will be forced to reduce its spending. This brings about a decline in domestic demand, which reduces the profit rate.[13]

It is worth noting that while inflation has no effects on the position of the $r(g)$ line, it still adversely affects growth by increasing r^* and shifting the $g(r)$ line down. The resulting growth rate (g_i) can be said to be investment constrained as both private capital inflows and domestic savings, due to unemployment, are below their maximum or potential levels. In contrast to two-gap models, the origin of resource underutilization is not the lack of foreign exchange but rather too low a level of investment. This low level of investment may arise from the asset balance constraints on government spending or from a high inflation rate exerting depressive effects on private investment. In the first case, the closure of the model has a close affinity to the growth path in three-gap models, with a binding fiscal constraint.

There are, however, important differences between the model specification adopted here and the three-gap models. Most of the literature on three-gap (as well as two-gap) models assumes fully exogenous capital inflows and thus credit rationing applies to both the government and private sectors. In our specification, private net capital inflows are endogenous, as they are linked to private savings, asset demands, and private investment through the private sector budget constraint (the second column in table 30). Since the change in net foreign assets plus the net acquisition of domestic financial assets by the private sector must add up to its financial surplus $(s_\pi r - g)$, private capital inflows are determined by:

$$\Delta d_P = g - s_\pi r + g(h + b), \tag{12}$$

where $\Delta d_P = \Delta D_P / K$. For developing countries with substantial capital flight in the recent past, this endogenous determination of private capital inflows appears more appropriate than the assumption of exogenous capital inflows. The present model also differs from standard open economy models in which there is no credit rationing, and both public and private capital inflows are fully endogenous.[14]

The literature on three-gap models emphasizes the role of fiscal constraints in explaining the growth performance of highly indebted countries in the 1980s. In the framework just presented, fiscal constraints are endogenously determined instead by explicitly introducing the medium-term links between sustainable fiscal deficits, capital flight, and private investment. Given the real exchange rate, as well as the parameters of the savings and trade functions, there is nothing that fiscal and monetary policy can do to increase the growth rate. Public investment, in particular, is constrained by the asset balance and external balance conditions. Beyond its endogenous value as determined by the model, increases in public investment would, if undertaken, be inconsistent with those conditions: bond-financed increases in public investment would create an unsustainable increase in domestic interest rates, while money-financed increases would generate unsustainable losses of foreign exchange reserves.[15] This modification allows us to emphasize that fiscal and current account deficits in the medium term are not exogenous but rather are simultaneously determined by private investment, capital inflows, and the rate of economic growth. The "third gap" is an investment constraint, which may or may not originate in a fiscal adjustment problem.

The Foreign Exchange Constraint

In addition to credit constraints on the public sector, it is possible that private capital inflows can reach a maximum value, given the likelihood of credit rationing in foreign financial markets beyond a critical level of private external indebtedness. It is clear that the accumulation function (eq. 9) will no longer determine the growth rate since, at the maximum value of capital inflows, investment demand is constrained and the rate of accumulation must be below the level associated with equation 9. How are investment and growth determined under these conditions?

In this case, investment will be constrained by the level of domestic savings forthcoming at less than full employment and by the, now exogenous, level of private foreign savings. Indeed, with Δd_P equal to the maximum value of private capital inflows ($\Delta \tilde{d}_P$), equation 12 provides the additional equation needed to determine the rate of accumulation.[16] It defines an upward-sloping locus of (g, r) combinations, along which private investment demand is rationed by the availability of foreign exchange:

$$g = [1/(1 + h + b)](s_\pi r + \Delta \tilde{d}_P). \tag{13}$$

A higher profit rate raises g, not because it makes investment more profitable but because it relaxes the credit constraints on investment.

The determination of the growth rate by equations 11 and 13 has a representation similar to that in figure 58. The $r(g)$ line remains unchanged with an endogenous and constrained level of government spending. The adjustment when off this locus is the same as in the case with a fiscal constraint, with the government reducing (increasing) its expenditures whenever the profit rate is higher (lower) than on the locus at a given level of capital accumulation. The $g(r)$ line is now given by equation 13 and shows the foreign-exchange-constrained rate of accumulation at each level of the profit rate. The economy may be assumed to be always on the $g(r)$ line, as a higher rate of growth would imply that the foreign credit constraints on investment are being violated (or else that they are not binding, in which case the economy must be under a fiscal-investment constraint). The economy thus converges to the equilibrium rates of profit and accumulation along the $g(r)$ line. Note also that this schedule no longer involves an expected profit rate, as in the cases examined earlier. This is because the profit rate affects investment through its effects on domestic savings rather than through expected profitability.

The position of the $g(r)$ schedule is affected by the savings rate out of profits and by the exogenous level of capital inflows, both of which shift the schedule upward. An increase in private capital inflows unambiguously raises the growth and profit rates. A higher savings rate out of profits now has contradictory effects: the reduction in capitalists' consumption, which shifts the $r(g)$ line to the left, tends to be offset by the increase in investment resulting from the upward shift in the $g(r)$ function. This model closure has properties similar to those of conventional two-gap models with a binding foreign exchange constraint. One difference, though, is that the downward adjustment of the profit rate, rather than of capacity utilization, is the equilibrating mechanism here.

Longer Run Adjustments: Factor Accumulation and Effective Demand

Growth theory at an early stage was concerned with the adjustment between the growth of aggregate supply and that of aggregate demand, including the problem of how the growth of productive capacity may adjust to the constraints set by the expansion of demand (Harrod 1939). The demand-constrained paths examined in the previous sections are examples of how the growth of productive capacity and aggregate demand are brought into equality through changes in the profit rate and the rate of capital accumulation. This issue was later assumed away in the factor accumulation models of neoclassical theory. It was also ignored by early development theory, as was emphasized in the introduction to this book. It is now time to turn to a discussion of the links between the factor accumulation models in previous chapters and the demand-side models of Keynesian and structuralist macroeconomics in this chapter.

To do so, we need to extend the analysis. The constrained growth paths of the previous section may be seen as a solution of the model for a "medium term" in which we can neglect changes in the employment rate and its potential effects on inflation and the real exchange rate. In order to bring in these effects, consider first the growth of the employment rate over time. Solving equation 2 for L, taking logs and differentiating with respect to time, and then subtracting the rate of growth of the labor force (n) from both sides of the equation, we have:

$$(\widehat{L/N}) = g - n - (1/a)(\hat{w} - \hat{p}_X), \tag{14}$$

where L is employment and N the total labor force. The circumflex (^) over a variable indicates the proportionate growth rate; for example, $\hat{X} = (dX/dt)1/X$.

For the rate of wage inflation, we adopt a Phillips curve specification augmented by the effects of current (or expected) price inflation and the real exchange rate:

$$\hat{w} = \pi + \phi[\omega(L/N), (p_X/w)] \quad \phi_1, \phi_2 > 0. \tag{15}$$

The rate at which money wages increase is affected by the rate of price inflation and is an increasing function of the gap between a target wage (ω) and actual real wages (w/p_D). As in the specification in chapter 11, the target wage increases with the employment rate: $\omega = \omega(L/N)$. Actual real wages are by definition equal to the ratio of export to domestic sales prices (p_X/p_D) divided by the real exchange rate (p_X/w). The first ratio is a constant $(p_X/p_D = 1/[1 + \tau])$, given the price elasticity of demand facing firms in the domestic market. For this reason, equation 15 can also be interpreted as showing the dynamic behavior of the real exchange rate, $(\widehat{p_X/w})$, as an inverse function of the real exchange rate: a higher rate implies faster growth of wages in relation to export prices. The feedback effect on the growth of the real exchange rate is thus negative.

The Factor Accumulation Path

Consider now a case in which the growth rate, as determined by equations 9 and 11, generates growth of employment higher than n, the rate of growth of the labor force. Starting from less than full employment, the employment rate will rise over time and eventually the economy will reach full employment. From then on, the growth of employment will be constrained by the growth of the labor force. If at full employment neither of the two demand constraints is binding, the desired rate of capital accumulation (g^*) will generate an excess demand for labor. The growth of labor demand can be derived from the output supply and labor demand functions, expressed as:

$$\hat{L} = g^* + [1/(1 - a)]\hat{v},$$

where we leave aside technical progress. As a result of an increasing real wage and a declining real exchange rate, a falling output-capital ratio becomes the mechanism through which the labor market clears. In this process, the profit rate and the desired rate of accumulation tend to fall with real appreciation of currency. The economy may then eventually converge to a long-run steady state in which the desired rate of accumulation generates an increase in labor demand that exactly matches the growth of the labor supply.

In this case, the properties of the model closely resemble those of a small open economy Solow-type growth model, with price flexibility and full employment. Both on and off the steady state, the economy is on a full employment path, and off the steady state the rate of output growth is equal to n plus the growth of output per worker resulting from the process of the increasing capital-labor and capital-output ratios. This last property is worth emphasizing. Just as in the Solow model, the process of capital deepening determines a growth rate that is higher than Harrod's natural rate (n in this case).

Degenerate Steady States

Suppose that, starting from less than full employment, the demand-constrained rate of accumulation generates a rate of employment growth that is less than n. Consider first the simpler case of a binding foreign exchange constraint. From equations 11 and 13, we can solve for the equilibrium rate of accumulation (g_F), as a function of exogenous variables and the real exchange rate (p_X/w), which positively affects the output-capital ratio and thus r and g (see eq. 11):

$$g_F = g_F(p_X/w) \quad g_F' > 0. \tag{16}$$

As the employment rate falls, the real exchange rate will eventually increase (eq. 14), and this will have a positive effect on the rate of accumulation. In the (r, g) diagram, the $r(g)$ line shifts to the right and

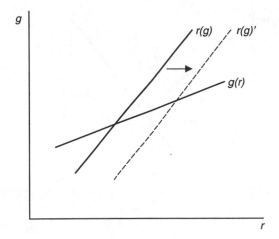

Fig. 59. A degenerate growth path

this raises g along the $g(r)$ line (see fig. 59). Eventually, the rate of accumulation will generate a rate of employment growth equal to n. Still, at the corresponding employment rate the change in wages may be such that the real exchange rate continues to increase. The initial decline in the employment rate will tend to be reversed. However, in contrast to a neoclassical model, there is no reason why the economy, through this process, will reach a full employment position.

To see this point clearly, we have to follow the dynamic behavior of the real exchange rate and employment. Setting $\hat{w} = \pi$ in equation 15, we obtain a locus of $(p_X/w, L/N)$ combinations along which the real exchange rate is stationary:

$$\phi[\omega(L/N), (p_X/w)] = 0 \quad \phi_1, \phi_2 > 0.$$

This is a downward-sloping locus: a higher employment rate tends to raise $\hat{w}$ above π, and this requires a lower real exchange rate, which reduces $\hat{w}$ in order to maintain stability of the real exchange rate. Because the feedback effect of p_X/w on p_X/w is negative (and thus stabilizing), the real exchange rate falls when it is above the locus and increases below it (see fig. 60). The position of the schedule is determined by labor market parameters.

Substituting from equations 15 and 16 into 14 and setting $\hat{L} = n$, we obtain a locus of $(p_X/w, L/N)$ combinations along which the employment rate is stationary:

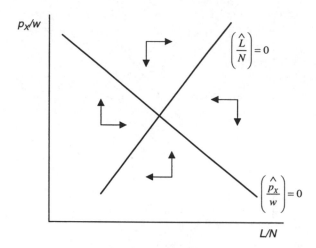

Fig. 60.   Long-term dynamic adjustments in a demand-constrained path

$$g_F(p_X/w) = n + (1/a)\phi[\omega(L/N), (p_X/w)] \quad g_F' > 0, \; \phi_1, \; \phi_2 > 0.$$

The slope of this locus is larger than that of the schedule of stationary real exchange rates, given that g_F' is positive. It is shown as upward sloping in figure 60. Its position is determined by goods market parameters and exogenous variables affecting the $g_F(.)$ function and labor market parameters affecting the $\phi(.)$ function. Because the feedback effect of (L/N) on $(\hat{L/N})$ is stabilizing, the employment rate increases when the economy is to the left of the schedule and falls when it is to the right.

Perhaps the simplest way to see the difference between this model and a neoclassical model is to consider an increase in the rate of growth of the labor force. In a neoclassical model, starting from a long-run steady state, a higher n will reduce the steady state level of output per worker and leave the employment rate unaffected. In the new steady state, the economy will be growing at the new and higher natural rate (n). Under a foreign exchange constraint, the economy will also converge to a higher growth rate (equal to n) through the mechanism described in figure 59 (a higher real exchange rate shifting the position of the $r(g)$ line outward). However, in this process the employment rate will stabilize at a lower level than initially. In figure 60, the higher rate of growth of the labor force implies a leftward shift of the $(\hat{L/N}) = 0$ locus. This leads, indeed, to a higher real exchange rate, which raises the rate of accumulation to the higher level required. But this in turn implies that the long-run value of the employment rate must fall.

The analysis of a fiscal constraint is analogous except for the fact, as the reader can verify, that the position of the $(\widehat{L/N}) = 0$ locus is affected by the inflation rate, since this adversely affects the rate of accumulation at each level of the profit rate (see eq. 9). In both cases, the economy converges to a steady state in the sense that the rate of capital accumulation is equal to Harrod's natural rate and the output-capital ratio, the employment rate, the real exchange rate, and real wages all remain constant over time. Yet, this steady state is degenerate in two ways. First, the path is a less than full employment path. Growth is not supply constrained since the economy is failing to fully utilize its resources, and what prevents it from doing so are precisely the asset market or foreign exchange constraints on effective demand.

Second, and most important, the growth rate converges "prematurely" to the natural rate. Indeed, the economy on its long-run path need not have a capital-labor ratio equal to that of the neoclassical steady state. Then, if the economy differs from a Solow-type steady state not only due to the fact that the unemployment rate is positive but also because the capital-labor ratio is below its steady state value, the growth rate is less than the growth rate that corresponds to the full employment path. As we know from the analysis of the neoclassical model, the difference is proportional to the gap between the actual and steady state levels of income. The implication is that on the demand-constrained growth path (with $g = n$), the economy will not be converging to the Solow steady state, since for this to be the case its growth rate would have to be higher than n rather than equal to it. Convergence is prevented precisely by the constraints on macroeconomic policy and effective demand that keep the economy growing at a rate below the growth rate of factor accumulation models.

The Debt Crisis and Macroeconomic Instability in Latin America

Regional Variables in Cross-Country Growth Regressions

The evidence on the significance of regional dummy variables cited at the beginning of this chapter may be attributable to the fact that demand-constrained growth paths prevented convergence to higher income levels in many parts of Latin America and Africa. If this is so, the lack of convergence should be specific to the period in which asset or foreign exchange constraints have been binding. Moreover, our framework should be able to provide an explanation of the economic setbacks and growth slowdowns suffered by many countries in those regions. We now turn to these questions.

A number of researchers have found significant effects for regional dummy variables in cross-country growth regressions (see, among others, Romer 1989, 1990a; and Barro 1991). The significance of regional variables is likely to reflect the importance of omitted variables. Since these studies include the period of terms of trade shocks and the debt crisis of the 1980s, a reasonable hypothesis is that those shocks threw these countries into a growth path in which demand constraints prevented a full utilization of resources. This section provides some evidence supporting the interpretation that the size and significance of these regional variables is attributable, at least partly, to the inclusion of the 1980s in the period of estimation. The significance of the dummy variable for highly indebted economies in the cross-country regressions of chapter 4 pointed in the same direction.

The exercise presented here consists of estimating cross-country regressions for 1960–69, 1960–75, 1960–79, and 1960–89. The variables chosen for the regressions are strictly based on Barro 1991, noting that the investment share and political variables are averaged over the relevant period. Due to limited data availability, for the two political variables in the period 1960–89 the averages refer to 1960–84. Two variants are estimated depending on whether a dummy variable for the Asian countries is included.[17]

The results are shown in table 31. While the coefficients of the variables for Latin America and Africa are consistently negative and those for Asia are positive (confirming previous findings), none of the dummy variables is statistically significant (at the 5 percent level) for the periods 1960–69 and 1960–75. The dummy variable for Latin America becomes clearly significant when the 1980s are included (i.e., for the period 1960–89), and its significance for the period 1960–79 depends on the inclusion of the dummy variable for Asia. Moreover, the negative coefficient of the dummy variable for Latin America increases considerably in absolute value when the 1980s are included (it nearly doubles in size from the 1960s to the period 1960–89). The dummy variable for Africa becomes significant when the late 1970s and the 1980s are included in the period of estimation (regardless of whether the dummy variable for Asia is included).

Finally, it is worth noting that when the dummy variable for Asian countries is included, this variable only becomes statistically significant when the 1980s are included. This suggests that the performance of Latin America compared to Asia is unambiguously disappointing only after 1980 — disappointing in the sense of being weaker than expected, given differences in other variables such as investment and initial education levels.[18] It also suggests that the interpretation suggested in the introduction may be the only reasonable interpretation. Otherwise, why is it that economies that were converging toward higher income levels before 1980 ceased this development?

Fiscal and Foreign Exchange Constraints in Latin America

The role of the fiscal and foreign exchange constraints discussed earlier may be illustrated by considering the adjustment to the Latin American debt crisis of the 1980s. The debt crisis meant an increase in the foreign interest rate and a reduction in governments' foreign credit. These shocks "opened" a fiscal and a foreign exchange gap as the net inflows of foreign exchange were cut down in both the fiscal and balance of payments accounts. Both of these developments shifted the $r(g)$ line to the left, causing a fall in the rate of accumulation along the $g(r)$ line, and the adjustment to them involved sharp real devaluations and fiscal contraction in all the highly indebted countries. The stabilization and adjustment difficulties that followed differed, however, between two types of economy. In the first, the country's public sector had foreign exchange revenues (e.g., oil revenues in Mexico and Venezuela) and the real devaluations raised the real value of these foreign exchange revenues, contributing to the relaxation of asset balance constraints on public expenditure. In the second, the government had a negative foreign exchange balance as a result of interest payments on foreign public debt (as in Argentina or Brazil). Public savings were adversely affected by real devaluations, and this negative effect exacerbated the fiscal constraints on government spending.

Mexico: Debt Crisis, Inflation, and Investment Collapse

Consider the experience of the first type of economy, which is best illustrated by Mexico. The debt shock there led to an increase in foreign interest payments by the public sector (from 2.6 to 3.9 percent of potential output) and a reduction in foreign lending to the government (from 1.7 to −0.7 percent). To this, the decline in oil prices in 1986 further added to the reduction of the government's foreign exchange revenues by cutting oil export revenues from 5.4 to 3.2 percent (after having reached a peak of 9.6 percent in 1983).

According to the model presented in the second section, the real devaluation that followed contributed unambiguously to relaxation of the foreign exchange constraint in this case. Without it, closing the foreign

TABLE 31. Cross-Country Growth Regressions: The Significance of Regional Variables

Independent Variable	1960–69	1960–75	1960–79	1960–89	1960–69	1960–75	1960–79	1960–89
Constant	0.062	0.068	0.073	0.086	0.058	0.055	0.058	0.070
	(2.35)	(3.35)	(3.69)	(5.68)	(2.05)	(2.54)	(2.76)	(4.48)
$\text{Log}y_{60}$	−0.009	−0.010	−0.009	−0.011	−0.008	−0.008	−0.007	−0.009
	(−2.08)	(−3.26)	(−2.94)	(−4.95)	(−1.83)	(−2.51)	(−2.08)	(−3.74)
I/Y	0.0009	0.0011	0.0007	0.0007	0.001	0.0012	0.0008	0.0007
	(2.49)	(3.78)	(2.24)	(2.35)	(2.48)	(4.02)	(2.50)	(2.50)
$PRIM_{60}$	0.030	0.034	0.027	0.028	0.029	0.028	0.020	0.021
	(2.38)	(3.38)	(2.71)	(3.52)	(2.05)	(2.55)	(1.86)	(2.55)
SEC_{60}	−0.001	−0.011	−0.009	−0.001	−0.001	−0.011	−0.009	0.0005
	(−0.07)	(−0.82)	(−0.70)	(−0.01)	(−0.07)	(−0.79)	(−0.65)	(0.05)
REV	−0.003	0.006	0.003	−0.014	−0.003	0.005	0.001	−0.017
	(−0.26)	(0.66)	(0.31)	(−1.88)	(−0.26)	(0.62)	(0.16)	(−2.30)
ASSASS	−0.011	−0.038	−0.025	−0.020	−0.014	−0.034	−0.019	−0.016
	(−0.26)	(−1.65)	(−0.96)	(−1.26)	(−0.22)	(−1.47)	(−0.75)	(−1.03)
PPI_{60}	0.00003	0.00003	.000002	−.000009	0.00003	0.00004	0.00002	.000005
	(0.42)	(0.56)	(0.05)	(−0.25)	(0.49)	(0.89)	(0.41)	(0.13)
DLA	−0.007	−0.008	−0.012*	−0.015*	−0.007	−0.005	−0.009	−0.012*
	(−1.30)	(−1.74)	(−2.65)	(−4.26)	(−1.07)	(−1.05)	(−1.89)	(−3.36)

	(1)	(2)	(3)	(4)	(5)	(6)	(7)	(8)
DAF	−0.011	−0.008	−0.015*	−0.017*	−0.010	−0.006	−0.012*	−0.014*
	(−1.65)	(−1.57)	(−3.02)	(−4.63)	(−1.47)	(−1.07)	(−2.39)	(−3.80)
DAS					0.003	0.010	0.012	0.013*
					(0.34)	(1.54)	(1.89)	(2.82)
N	89	89	89	89	89	89	89	89
Adjusted R^2	0.25	0.37	0.32	0.58	0.24	0.38	0.34	0.62

Note:

y_{60}: GDP per capita in 1960 (1985 international prices, Laspeyres index). Source: Penn World Table (Mark 5.6).

I/Y: Ratio of real domestic investment to real GDP (average for the period). Source: Penn World Table (Mark 5.6).

$PRIM_{60}$: Primary school enrollment rate in 1960. Source: Barro and Lee 1994.

SEC_{60}: Secondary school enrollment rate in 1960. Source: Barro and Lee 1994.

REV: Number of revolutions and coups per year (average for the period). Source: Barro and Lee 1994.

ASSASS: Number of political assassinations per million population per year (average for the period). Source: Barro and Lee 1994.

PPI_{60}: Deviation of the 1960 PPP for investment from the sample mean. Source: Penn World Table (Mark 5.6).

DLA: Dummy variable for Latin American countries

DAF: Dummy variable for African countries

DAS: Dummy variable for Asian countries

t-statistics in parentheses

Dependent variable: Growth rate of real GDP per capita

*Statistically significant at the $p = 0.05$ level (for the regional dummy variables) exchange gap would have required even larger investment and output losses. Indeed, to the positive effects of devaluation, operating through the export-capital ratio and the output-capital ratio, we can add the positive effects of a higher exchange rate on the real value of the government's foreign exchange balance. This effect acts like a change in (d_G) in equation 11, and, indeed, it is equivalent to an increase in the (rationed) amount of additional foreign debt that the government can issue. As a result of these effects, the $r(g)$ line shifts to the right. This tends to relax the foreign exchange constraint on the rate of accumulation. The locus of combinations showing the foreign-exchange-constrained rate of accumulation at each level of the real exchange rate is thus upward sloping (see fig. 61[a]).[19]

The real devaluation, due to its effects on the $r(g)$ line, also tends to relax the fiscal constraint. However, the higher inflation associated with the devaluation has an adverse effect on private investment, thus causing a downward shift of the $g(r)$ line. At low levels of inflation, this effect may be small and the positive fiscal effects of devaluation may dominate. At high levels of inflation, the negative effects of inflation on investment may well dominate and set a limit to how much the government can offset this decline using additional real revenues. Note again that the positive effects on the inflation tax will not do the trick (quite independently of the likely reduction in the tax base): its effects on government spending are offset (under our assumptions fully offset) by the decrease in workers' consumption. Figure 61(a) illustrates the limits of real devaluation in offsetting the initial shocks over the medium term. The locus of $(g_I, p_X/w)$ combinations — showing the medium-term value of the investment-constrained rate of accumulation at each level of the real exchange rate — takes the form of an inverted-U curve. This shape sets a limit in the medium term to how much the government, through real devaluations, can recover the rates of growth that prevailed before the shocks.

The sharp decline of private investment in Mexico, from 17.4 to 11.6 percent (as a fraction of potential output), is consistent with the role of the investment constraint. It followed sharp cuts in public investment and rapid acceleration of inflation in an economy with no financial indexation and a high degree of international capital mobility (see Ros 1987). As a result, output growth, which in 1980 for a third consecutive year had been above 8 percent, was barely more than 1 percent in 1988 (having been on average zero for the period 1982–88).

Large current account surpluses and continuing capital flight accompanied the collapse of investment and the growth slowdown. Thus, neither the low level of potential domestic savings nor the lack of foreign exchange can explain the sharp contraction of investment. The crucial

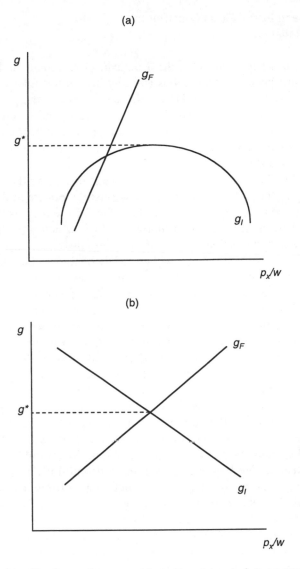

Fig. 61. Foreign exchange and investment constraints on growth

role of the investment constraint is also confirmed by events after 1988. The 1989 debt relief agreement, the reduction of inflation following a successful heterodox program, and the decline in foreign interest rates were the major factors behind the recovery of private investment rates and capital repatriation after 1989.

Argentina and Brazil: Fiscal Constraints
and Hyperinflation

Despite its large foreign debt, the Mexican government had a foreign exchange surplus during the 1980s (largely accounted for by the public sector's oil export revenues). Under these conditions, the positive fiscal effects of real devaluations facilitated fiscal adjustment. Other highly indebted countries, such as Argentina and Brazil, with deficits in the government's foreign exchange balance, found themselves in a much more difficult position.

Consider the effectiveness of devaluation in closing the foreign exchange gap in these deficit countries. The positive effects of devaluation on the trade balance will now tend to be offset by the increase in the real value of government's foreign exchange outlays, which shift the $r(g)$ line to the left. As shown in figure 61(b), if the schedule of $(g_F, p_X/w)$ combinations remains upward sloping, it will certainly be flatter than in the previous case. As a consequence, it takes larger devaluations to relax the foreign exchange constraint, and these have the effect of exacerbating the fiscal gap. The locus of $(g_I, p_X/w)$ combinations is now clearly downward sloping. This is the result of the effects of inflation on private investment being added to the negative effects of devaluation on the fiscal accounts and government spending. Thus, as illustrated in figure 61(b), the relationship between medium-term growth and the real exchange rate takes the form of an inverted V in these deficit countries.

Above the inverted V defined by the two loci of $(g, p_X/w)$ combinations — where g here is the minimum of g_I and g_F — the overall balance of payments is in deficit and below it is in surplus. Suppose that the economy is in the region below the foreign exchange constraint but above the fiscal constraint. The balance of payments disequilibrium has its origin in a fiscal gap, that is, in a gap between actual government spending and its sustainable level (since the economy is above the fiscal constraint). In the absence of a fiscal adjustment that increases public savings, the resulting disequilibrium in the balance of payments will put upward pressure on the exchange rate. Exchange rate depreciation will aggravate the fiscal gap by reducing public savings (the fiscal constraint is downward sloping). This, in turn, will exacerbate the balance of payments disequilibrium and can eventually lead to hyperinflation.

These difficulties become insurmountable through domestic policy if the fiscal adjustment required to bring the economy back to the fiscal constraint is not socially viable. Suppose that, given foreign interest rates and the external debt-GDP ratio, the fiscal adjustment required to prevent a continuous increase in the external debt-GDP ratio is not socially viable. The foreign exchange and fiscal constraints intersect at a growth rate that is not feasible. In the absence of either a reduction in the value of external debt or a decrease in foreign interest rates, the economy may remain for a prolonged period of time on the brink of either a debt moratorium or hyperinflation. Together with Bolivia and Peru, which also fall in the category of nations with a deficit in the government's foreign exchange balance, Argentina and Brazil were precisely those countries in Latin America that suffered hyperinflation episodes in the 1980s.

CHAPTER 13

In Defense of Development Theory

Development economics as it appeared in the 1940s and 1950s in the writings of Rosenstein-Rodan, Nurkse, Prebisch, Hirschman, Leibenstein, and others stressed the barriers to industrialization and capital formation in underdeveloped countries. Successful development required overcoming various inhibiting factors, including the presence of externalities and some form of increasing returns to scale. In focusing on these problems, the classical literature of development economics generated a view of the development process in which increasing returns to scale and elastic labor supplies played key roles. This approach had a lot to say about why poor countries are poor and what they need to do in order to escape underdevelopment. It is puzzling why, in attempting to address the same issues, modern growth economics has largely ignored development theory and proceeded by making tabula rasa of these earlier contributions. This concluding chapter addresses this puzzle and makes the case for a unified research program that merges old and new insights and contributions.

The Empirical Case: Closing Arguments

As was argued in chapter 2, the neoclassical model, with its extensions (technology gaps, human capital, international capital mobility, and political risk), fails to provide a satisfactory explanation of international differences in *both* income levels and growth rates. The theory appears to face the following dilemma. When it views income gaps as differences in the relative position with respect to the steady state, the model — as in the simple Solow version — grossly overstates the growth rates of poor countries. This is so especially under the assumption of international capital mobility, which reinforces the strong convergence properties of the model. When it interprets income differences as a result of steady state gaps — as in the Solow model augmented with human capital (Mankiw, Romer, and Weil 1992) or in technology gap interpretations — the model fits somewhat better the observed differences in growth rates. But then it overstates the differences across countries in the relative returns to skilled labor or relies on unreasonable differences in access to technology.

Other evidence also points to the empirical flaws of the neoclassical model. The key feature of the model — the negative relationship between initial output per worker and subsequent growth — is simply not statistically robust. As shown by Levine and Renelt (1992), the relationship has been absent in the period since the mid-1970s or when OECD countries are excluded from the sample. The estimates of quadratic growth functions in chapter 4 point in the same direction: there is no convergence, either absolute or conditional, at low-income levels. Moreover, the fit of the neoclassical model relies too heavily on continental dummy variables or else on macroeconomic variables that reflect the particular history of different regions of the world, such as high inflation in Latin America. As was argued in chapter 12, these results are at variance with the basic premises of factor accumulation models.

Much work on cross-country growth regressions appears to have proceeded on the assumption that rejection of the convergence properties of the neoclassical growth model provides support for the new growth theories and vice versa. Yet this, of course, need not be the case. Without further revisions and extensions, new growth theory does not pose a serious empirical challenge to the augmented neoclassical models. The empirical assessment of the theory — with its implications of excessive divergence and reliance on human-capital-driven growth — proves to be rather disappointing, as was discussed in chapter 6. The theory appears to face a dilemma, which, although of a very different nature, seems no less serious than that of the neoclassical theory. This is the knife-edge problem that was pointed out by Solow (1994). If returns to capital are increasing, the technology assumed generates infinite output in finite time. If returns to scale increase but returns to capital are diminishing, the qualitative implications are no different from those of the Solow model. Within this recent literature this leaves the AK model as the only viable and rather fragile alternative to the neoclassical model, as it relies on there being exactly constant returns to capital.

The vision of the development process that one finds in the classical literature of development theory has implications for cross-country growth performance that go far in overcoming the shortcomings of neoclassical models while being free of the objections that can be raised against endogenous growth models. In modern technical terms, the key features of this vision involve a nonrepresentative agent methodology, rich transitional dynamics, and the existence of multiple equilibria.

The economies considered by the classical literature of development theory had little to do with the Robinson Crusoe parable.[1] The economies are populated by firms, working-class households, landlords, peasants, and urban self-employed, each of which perform different functions and face different constraints. The departure in this respect is clear, for example, in the view of profits as the source of and motive for the accumulation of capital by firms. Firms' investment decisions are far removed from the intertemporal preferences of consumers, which govern the process of capital accumulation in optimal growth models (see chap. 2). They take these decisions under competitive pressures that are exacerbated in the presence of increasing returns. Lewis adopted the classical view of profits as the main source of savings and investment. As discussed in chapter 3, the evidence largely supports this view. A key feature of the fast-growing developing economies has been the rising share of profits in total income brought about by the expansion of modern industries and leading to a gradual and substantial increase in savings rates.

The transitional dynamics in the models of classical development economics are different from those found in neoclassical models, in which growth proceeds at diminishing rates. They are also different from the growth process, at constant or even increasing rates, envisaged by endogenous growth models. The distinctive feature of the transition to a mature economy in development models is a pattern of divergence followed by convergence at middle- and high-income levels. After a certain threshold of income has been achieved, the presence of increasing returns to scale magnifies the initial productivity advantages that more advanced countries have and determines a tendency toward absolute divergence in the early stages of development. The interplay between increasing returns and elastic labor supplies leads to high growth rates in the intermediate stages of the transition. Then, in the later stages, when labor surpluses have been largely absorbed into the modern sectors of the economy, the existence of diminishing returns to capital eventually generates a tendency toward conditional convergence.

These implications find substantial empirical support in both cross-sectional estimates and long-time series. The pattern of growth in a cross section of countries features a hump shape with growth acceleration at middle-income levels. This pattern, as suggested by our findings in chapter 4, stands the inclusion in growth regressions of other variables (investment rate, education, and political variables). Empirical evidence on scale effects and productivity-employment relationships (Verdoorn's law) lends additional support to an explanation of the hump shape based on a model with increasing returns to scale and elastic labor supplies.

Turning to time-series, the process of growth in the world economy over the last century has been characterized by absolute divergence in per capita incomes. However, over the last 50 years the dispersion of per capita incomes has considerably narrowed within the club of today's rich economies, which largely overlaps the early industrializers. In the last three decades, some late industrializers — the successful East Asian economies and for a while a few countries in Latin America — joined the convergence club and moved rapidly toward middle- and high-income levels. A few among them, most notably Hong Kong and Singapore, had reached by the mid-1990s per capita income levels similar to those of the average of OECD economies. The rest of the developing countries, mostly in sub-Saharan Africa and South Asia, have barely begun the process of modern economic growth and continue to lag behind the middle- and high-income economies. These patterns lend support to the transitional dynamics envisaged by development models.

The neoclassical model ignores the existence of development traps and multiple equilibria. Taken literally, this model suggests that at some early stage, when countries had similar levels of per capita income, positive shocks to savings rates, human capital investments, and population growth in some countries triggered a process of divergence. Some countries moved to a new and higher level of steady state income while others remained in the previous equilibrium and lagged behind. The problem with this interpretation is that it explains very little once we recognize that investment rates and population growth are to a large extent affected by levels of income.[2]

A more fruitful approach, even though it may not seem so at first sight, is to start with the seemingly banal proposition that countries are poor because they are poor (Nurkse 1952) and then ask what mechanisms keep them in poverty. The answer given to this question by early development theory involved two processes. First, factor growth rates (of primarily capital and labor) at low-income levels are such that they perpetuate the low level of income. Malthusian and savings traps must have existed in the past. They may even be relevant for some countries in the present. More importantly, however, and more relevant in our world of open economies, is that poor countries tend to have low rates of return for both labor and capital.

This fact generates multiple equilibria associated with profitability traps. These equilibria are different from those considered in the endogenous growth literature. There, the AK technology assumed leads to multiple equilibria in growth rates so that countries converge to different growth rates and therefore their per capita incomes diverge indefinitely. The approach taken by classical development economics appears to be on more solid empirical ground, as was argued in chapter 6. Of course, it is not necessarily the case that the profitability trap is associated exclusively with a low level of physical capital — as in the model with technological externalities of chapter 4 — or with the lack of infrastructure and the narrowness of the domestic market — as in the models with pecuniary externalities of chapter 5. Extending the models to bring other, no less important development traps is essential to the understanding of underdevelopment. Yet, the interactions between increasing returns to scale and elastic labor supplies, as I shall argue, remain important for the existence of a low-level equilibrium.

Multiple Equilibria and the Profitability Trap: Some Misinterpretations of Early Development Theory

Given its conformity with a number of stylized facts, why did early development theory drift away from the mainstream of the economics discipline? One reason was certainly ideological. The normative implications that were derived from the initial framework became progressively unfashionable from the 1960s onward, first in the profession and later among policymakers (see Stiglitz 1992). But there were also analytical reasons. In the beginning, development theory spurred a revolt against the established core of economic theory. As I have repeatedly insisted, the key departures involved increasing returns and surplus labor. The rebellion the pioneers initiated against traditional neoclassical theory was continued by second and third generations of development economists, but the accent was increasingly placed on technological rigidities, inelastic demands, nonoptimizing agents, and effective demand problems. Whatever the merits of these later developments (and there were certainly important contributions), they had the unfortunate consequence of moving development economics in a different direction from that taken initially, and in doing so they moved the field further away from the neoclassical mainstream. In these developments, misinterpretations of the early theoretical contributions played a major role. What were these misinterpretations?

Elasticity Pessimism?

The counterrevolution in development theory that began in the 1960s argued that, except for the (rather unlikely) event of very low price and income elasticities of export demand, free trade was unambiguously good for developing countries and would obviate the need for a big push. Consider Bhagwati's interpretation of Rosenstein-Rodan's classic (1943) paper:

> The underdeveloped economy was trapped in a low level equilibrium with no effective inducement to invest: e.g., the entrepreneur invest-

ing in shoes was not sure about selling the shoes unless others invested simultaneously in textiles etc. This dilemma would, of course, disappear if the country faced constant terms of trade at which these entrepreneurs could atomistically sell what they wished. Therefore, a necessary condition for Rosenstein-Rodan's analysis and prescription is, of course, elasticity pessimism. (1985, 299)

Thus, in the real world of open economies big push arguments and poverty traps were at best intellectual curiosities in which the bright pioneers of development theory happened to be interested when they began to think about development problems. According to this viewpoint, their mistaken "export-elasticity pessimism" led the pioneers to focus on closed economies and to fail to notice that openness presents a solution to the problems of industrialization. Arguably, it was this line of argument, more than the difficulties of formalizing models with increasing returns and imperfect competition (as claimed by Krugman [1992]), that led to the resurgence of the perfect competition and constant returns to scale paradigm. Because in an open economy, if increasing returns do not play the crucial role that they may do in a closed economy, then, contrary to the beliefs of early development theorists, little is lost by adopting the simpler assumption of constant returns. Stiglitz (1992) in his comment on Krugman's article makes a similar point, which, incidentally, shows the vitality of the "export pessimism" interpretation of the big push argument. He noted that

had Rosenstein-Rodan (1943) succeeded in formalizing his ideas, I doubt that those ideas would have been more palatable. In his model the income effects associated with increasing returns leave the economy stuck in a low-level equilibrium. As Krugman points out, the problem arises from a lack of demand, but once we open the economy to international trade, this argument loses its force. (41)

Before looking at the role that "elasticity pessimism" may have played in the early literature, it is worth noting that both Bhagwati and Stiglitz have in mind a version of the argument in which horizontal pecuniary externalities are the source of the problem. If the source of external economies is technological, the big push argument remains intact whether the open economy faces constant terms of trade or not. The infant industry argument for protection is based precisely on these types of learning by doing externalities. The formalization of this argument in chapter 7 yields a "big push model" in that the combination of increasing returns and an elastic labor supply generates multiple equilibria and a development trap.[3] As we shall see, this type of development trap is, in fact, more likely to appear in an open than in a closed economy. The "linkage effects" model of chapter 8 illustrates how a big push problem can arise in a small open economy in the absence of technological externalities. It illustrates, in fact, that the case of technological externalities is no different from that of pecuniary externalities arising from increasing returns in the production on nontradable goods.

We shall return to these issues later. It is now worth noting that the interpretation based on elasticity pessimism can hardly be reconciled with the original argument in the literature. One of the most influential papers, for instance, was Rosenstein-Rodan's 1943 article. After discussing the self-sufficient "Russian model" and its "several great disadvantages," he (203–4) argues that:

> The alternative way of industrialization would fit Eastern and South-Eastern Europe into the world economy, which would preserve the advantages of an international division of labour, and would therefore in the end produce more wealth for everybody. . . . Clearly this way of industrialization is preferable to the autarkic one.

He goes on to discuss the difficulties involved in the implementation of this process of industrialization. Primary among these difficulties, he argues, are externalities of various kinds and the presence of increasing returns to scale in many activities. At no point is it suggested that low export elasticities will be critical.[4]

All this is not to deny that trade pessimism prevailed at the time. Low elasticities were seen as an obstacle to higher levels of economic development in less developed countries, but elasticity pessimism applied largely to exports of primary products. In the present context, the important point is that this kind of export elasticity pessimism does not seem to have played a significant role in the big push argument.

A Demand Deficiency?

The interpretation based on elasticity pessimism is not confined to the neoclassical resurgence in development economics. Similar conclusions came from more sympathetic accounts of development trap arguments that emphasized a "lack of demand" as the source of the problem. In one version, low-level traps are linked to Keynesian effective demand problems. This interpretation, and a counterreaction to it, appears to have been widespread in the early postwar period.[5] Other, less Keynesian accounts also led to an excessive emphasis on demand deficiencies. Basu (1984) provides a formalization of the Nurksian vicious circle in which monopolistic firms in the modern sector of the economy face kinked demand curves for their products and an elastic supply of labor. The economy may get stuck in a demand-constrained equilibrium in which the low real incomes associated with a low level of resource utilization hold back the expansion of modern firms. Not surprisingly, the vicious circle breaks down when the economy opens to international trade and modern sector firms face given terms of trade in international markets.[6]

Curiously, Krugman (1995) provides another example. After an illuminating discussion of the sources of multiple equilibria in terms of increasing returns *and* the elasticity of factor supplies, when summarizing the argument, he refers to the circular relationship between low productivity and small market size.[7] The division of labor is limited by the extent of the market, and the extent of the market is constrained by the division of labor. In this view, increasing returns can become an obstacle to development at low levels of productivity since the small size of the domestic market reduces the profitability of increasing returns technologies, with an adverse impact on the inducement to invest.

If these interpretations were fully correct, the pioneers would have had little to add to Adam Smith. Indeed, Smith explicitly noted that:

> By means of [foreign trade], the narrowness of the home market does not hinder the division of labor in any particular branch of art or manufacture from being carried to the highest perfection. By opening a more extensive market for whatever part of the produce of their labor may exceed the home consumption, it encourages them to improve its productive powers. ([1776] 1904, 1:413)

By opening the economy, the second component of the circular relationship breaks down — because it is no longer true that the domestic level of productivity constrains the size of the market — and the need for a big push disappears. Unfortunately, Nurkse's writing, although not Rosenstein-Rodan's, provides some ground for this "excessively Smithian" interpretation of the argument.

What is missing in this demand-based interpretation of the big push argument? As was discussed in chapter 4, the conditions for multiple equilibria in a closed economy involve a sufficiently elastic labor supply and the presence of increasing returns to scale. Unless returns to capital increase, increasing returns to scale alone are not sufficient to generate a development trap. An elastic labor supply is essential in providing local stability to the low-level equilibrium. If the labor supply is inelastic, the product wage will tend to fall until increasing-returns technologies become profitable, even at low levels of the capital endowment. It is the combination of an elastic supply of labor, which sets a floor to the wage that the modern sector has to pay, with a small capital stock and increasing returns that produces a vicious circle. Similarly, the same interactions between increasing returns and an elastic labor supply produce a virtuous circle if a sufficiently large capital endowment has been achieved.

Fleming (1955) clearly saw that the "balanced growth doctrine," as he phrased it, does not depend only on increasing returns, and he complained that the literature had insufficiently stated the assumption of elastic factor supplies:

> In order really to salvage the doctrine of external economies under examination, however, it is necessary to drop the assumption that the supply of factors of production is fixed in favour of the assumption that the supply varies positively with real factor prices. . . . [O]f our authors, only Rosenstein-Rodan explicitly assumes an elastic supply of labour in his illustration of the doctrine, though Nurkse, in arguing in terms of the inducement to invest, is in effect assuming some elasticity in the supply of capital. (248)

By emphasizing the elasticity of factor supplies, Fleming early perceived what was to become a major source of the misinterpretation of development trap arguments. The next section will argue that elasticity of factor supplies, which is a necessary condition for multiple equilibria, is in fact enhanced in an open economy setting.

Openness and Development Traps

Does the need for a big push survive in an economy that is open to international trade and capital movements or would openness to trade and capital movements be sufficient to overcome all poverty traps? Without exaggeration, these questions have haunted development economics since its inception. The reason is that they impinge upon the broader question of whether the analytical framework of early development theory, with its emphasis on labor surpluses, increasing returns, and imperfect competition, is at all useful and valid in the real world of open economies.

We have already discussed at several points in this book the fact that capital mobility can do little good when the source of the problem is the presence of increasing returns holding back the inducement to invest. The reason is, of course, that the development trap in this case — unlike the savings trap, which has its origins in the scarcity of domestic savings (due to a low level of income relative to subsistence consumption) — arises from a low rate of return to capital. Nurkse seems to have been fully aware of this point. He observed that capital does not flow to the poorest countries and argued that this is quite consistent with his argument: it is because these countries are in a poverty trap, arising from the lack of inducement to invest, that capital does not flow to them. He concluded that capital mobility is not a sufficient condition to overcome the development problem (1952, 574, 583).

What about trade openness? Can free trade overcome the development traps that can stunt industrialization in a closed economy? Although by now this question has been largely answered, this section provides an opportunity to recapitulate. The argument developed in this section, concisely stated, is as follows. Openness increases the elasticity of factor supplies, which in turn facilitates the existence of multiple equilibria and development traps, especially in the presence of technological externalities or vertical pecuniary externalities involving nontradable goods. At the same time, it also makes demand curves more elastic, thus reducing the demand spillovers arising from horizontal pecuniary externalities and, in turn, coordination problems among producers of traded goods.

Openness and Factor Supply Elasticity

Consider the effects of trade openness on the elasticity of the labor supply. In a closed dual economy model, an elastic labor supply will require sufficiently high elasticity of substitution between the goods produced by the modern and traditional sectors. In an open economy, this condition on the elasticity of substitution is no longer required if both goods are traded, *especially* if the economy is small and takes prices as given in the international market. With fixed terms of trade between the two goods, the expansion of the modern sector does not, as it would in a closed economy, shift the terms of trade in favor of the traditional sector. If, for example, this is a labor-intensive sector producing under constant returns, as in the infant industry model of chapter 7, the modern sector will face an elastic supply of labor at a constant product wage (determined by the given terms of trade). The opening of the economy makes the terms of trade behave as if the two goods were perfect substitutes so that the modern sector faces a perfectly elastic supply of labor as long as the two sectors coexist.[8] This is why, with the exception of the upward-sloping w^* curve, the model of the infant industry argument in chapter 7 is so reminiscent of the Lewis model. In both, the w curve is a straight line as long as the two sectors coexist: in Lewis because the two sectors produce the same good, in the infant industry model because the two sectors produce traded goods with fixed terms of trade.

The model in chapter 7 assumes constant returns to labor in the traditional sector (S). Suppose instead that there are diminishing returns to labor. With equalization of labor earnings in the two sectors (S and M), we have:

$$w_M/p_M = (p_S/p_M)L_S^{-b},$$

where the employment-output elasticity in sector S is $(1 - b)$. Taking logs and differentiating, the labor supply elasticity to sector M is:

$$\mathrm{dlog}L_M/\mathrm{dlog}(w_M/p_M) = [1 - \mathrm{dlog}(p_S/p_M)/\mathrm{dlog}(w_M/p_M)]/b(L_M/L_S).$$

In a closed economy $\mathrm{dlog}(p_S/p_M)$ will generally be positive (unless the elasticity of substitution between the S and M goods is infinite). In a small open economy, this term is zero, making elasticity of the labor supply higher than in the closed economy case.[9]

Efficiency Gains and the Hold of the Trap

By making the w curve flatter at low levels of the capital stock, trade openness may generate a trap or increase the hold of the trap where it already exists. However, this argument needs to be qualified if trade brings gains (such as allocative efficiency gains) that affect the w^* curve. What difference would it make to our conclusions if allocative gains were present? Suppose that the modern capital-intensive sector produces two goods, one exportable and one importable. Alongside this sector, sector S produces a nontradable good using labor subject to diminishing returns. With two traded goods, trade will allow the economy to obtain importable goods at lower costs. These efficiency gains are equivalent to a one-time technological improvement and can be modeled as an upward shift in the multiplicative constant in the production function of sector M. An increase in this multiplicative constant, as a result of the opening to trade, shifts the w and w^* loci upward. Assuming a Cobb-Douglas production function with technological externalities, the shifts in the w and w^* curves (holding K constant) are given by:

$$\mathrm{dlog}(w_M/p_M) = [(1 - a)/(1 + ea)]\mathrm{dlog}A \qquad (1)$$

$$\mathrm{dlog}(w_M/p_M) = \mathrm{dlog}A, \qquad (2)$$

where A is the multiplicative constant and e is labor supply elasticity. Comparing these two expressions, it is readily seen that the shift in the w^* locus (given by eq. 2) exceeds that of the w locus (given by eq. 1). The difference depends on labor supply elasticity. The intuition behind this is simple: the profit rate is an increasing function of the state of technology, given the capital stock. A technological improvement must therefore increase the required wage by more than the market equilibrium wage. The more elastic the labor supply, the less the market equilibrium wage increases and the larger the increase in the profit rate. In fact, if the labor supply is perfectly elastic the w curve will not shift at all.

Given that the upward shift in the w^* curve exceeds that of the w curve, the low-K intersection in the open economy will feature a smaller capital stock than in the closed economy. Hence, the efficiency gains from trade reduce the hold of the development trap. The same argument can be made for other sources of gains resulting from changes in market structure or the transmission of international external effects. However, it is interesting to note that these gains do not eliminate the low-K intersection: the slopes of the loci, in ($\log K$, $\log w_M/p_M$) space, are independent of A. If the condition for multiple equilibria was fulfilled in the pretrade situation, it will also be met after the opening to trade.[10]

Pecuniary Externalities and Demand Spillovers

Consider now the effects of trade openness on pecuniary externalities. This is, of course, the aspect that Bhagwati's and many other interpretations of the big push argument emphasize. In the formalization of the big push argument by Murphy, Shleifer, and Vishny (1989) discussed in chapter 5, demand conditions facing the monopolist in any given sector can be described by a kinked demand curve (see Basu 1997). As is shown in figure 62, before the kink, demand is perfectly elastic at a price equal to the cost of production of traditional producers. After the kink, the demand curve becomes downward sloping with unit price elasticity, given that each good has an equal share in final expenditure. As a result, marginal revenue falls to zero at the kink and beyond.

The position of the kink for, say, a shoe producer, depends on whether monopolists in other sectors invest in modern techniques. When the shoe factory considers investing in isolation, the position of the kink is determined by traditional production since this is the volume of output that the shoe factory can expect to sell by displacing existing producers. Let this volume of output be represented by point A in figure 62. In the presence of positive pecuniary externalities, the adoption of modern techniques in other sectors (textiles, for instance) has the effect of shifting the position of the kink outward (from point A to point B). It is this outward shift in the position of the demand curve, resulting from the actions of other producers, that creates the possibility of multiple equilibria. Given the position of the unit cost curve (AC), it is then possible that the adoption of the modern technique would be unprofitable in isolation. On the other hand, the shoe factory would be able to

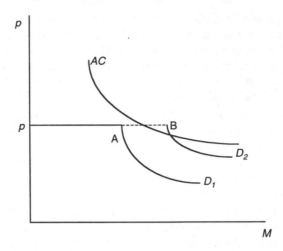

Fig. 62. The effect of pecuniary externalities on demand and unit costs

recover fixed costs if modern firms were simultaneously investing in other sectors.

Suppose that this economy opens to foreign trade and faces given relative prices in the international market. As Bhagwati notes in the quote above, the shoe producer will now be able to sell all he or she wishes at given prices and the demand for his or her product no longer depends on the textile producer adopting the modern technique. The adoption of modern techniques in textile production still affects the domestic demand for shoes, but the domestic demand for shoes no longer constrains the profitability of modern techniques in domestic shoe production. The kink in the demand curve disappears, and the demand for shoes becomes perfectly elastic at the international price.

More generally, by making demand curves more elastic trade reduces the external effects of the modern textile producer on the shoe factory. In our example of given relative prices in international markets, demands become perfectly elastic and the external effects disappear altogether. This is the basis for Bhagwati's criticism, which is clearly valid in the context of "horizontal pecuniary externalities" involving (in the closed economy) demand spillovers *across* final producers of (potentially) traded goods. In the open economy facing given terms of trade, the shoe factory may or may not be profitable, but its profitability does not depend on other sectors adopting increasing-returns technologies. It does not follow, however, that export pessimism is a condition for the existence of *pecuniary externalities* in an open economy or even for the existence of *horizontal* pecuniary externalities in this setting.

Let us note first the fact that horizontal externalities retain practical importance in the absence of export pessimism, unless by this we were to mean anything less than infinite elasticities of demand. The investment decision of the textile producer will still affect demand and profits in the shoe industry, unless, indeed, the shoe factory can sell whatever it wishes at the international price. The fact is, however, that in reality trade is not free and costless: based on the findings of Chenery and Syrquin (1975, 1986) on medium-sized and large countries, Murphy, Shleifer, and Vishny (1989b) emphasize the significance of domestic markets as a source of demand for domestic industry.

Consider now the following setting. Price elasticities of demand for tradable goods are infinite, but each of the modern firms in the multisectoral economy of Murphy, Shleifer, and Vishny uses a technique that requires nontradable inputs produced under increasing returns (as with the I goods in the vertical externalities model of chap. 5).[11] When the shoe factory invests in isolation, intermediate inputs (e.g., services or infrastructure) are produced at a high cost. These high costs may keep the unit cost of the shoe producer above the international price, even at high levels of output. The AC_1 curve in figure 63 shows the unit cost of the shoe producer in this case. When firms in other sectors adopt modern techniques, the market for intermediate goods is expanded. As a result, intermediate inputs are produced at lower costs, which has the effect of reducing the unit cost for the shoe factory. The unit cost curve of the shoe producer shifts from AC_1 to AC_2. It is then possible that the adoption of the modern technique would be unprofitable in isolation, while the shoe factory would be able to recover fixed costs if modern firms were simultaneously investing in other sectors. The possibility of multiple equilibria remains because the cost curve shifts as a result of the actions of other producers.

Vertical pecuniary externalities can thus lead to multiple equilibria in an open economy, even if the shoe producer faces a perfectly elastic demand at the international price (p^*). Other examples that illustrate this conclusion are the linkage effects model of chapters 8 and 9. These examples also suggest that the transmission of vertical externalities is, in fact, more likely in an open than a closed economy. The reason, as argued earlier, is that an open economy makes the labor supply more elastic and these vertical external effects require that the sector producing intermediate inputs must face an elastic labor supply.

It is somewhat ironic that early critics of the "balanced growth" implications of the presence of horizontal pecuniary externalities based their skepticism on the view that vertical externalities were of much

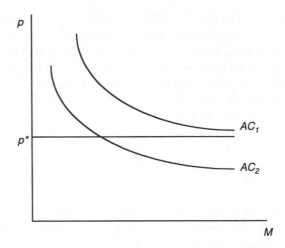

Fig. 63.   Vertical pecuniary externalities in an open economy

more practical relevance than horizontal externalities. As Fleming (1955, 250) argued:

> There can be little doubt but that the conditions for a "vertical" transmission of external economies — whether forward from supplying industry to using industry, or backward from using industry to supplying industry — are much more favourable than for a "horizontal" transmission between industries at the same stage.

He attributes the emphasis given to horizontal externalities by Rosenstein-Rodan and Nurkse to the neglect in the earlier literature (by Marshall and his commentators) of this type of externality at the expense of vertical external economies. He suggests that this neglect may have been due precisely to the greater practical importance of vertical pecuniary than horizontal externalities.[12]

The relative importance of horizontal and vertical externalities impinges on the question of the relative merits of balanced versus unbalanced growth strategies. The multiple equilibria model of chapter 9 helps to illustrate this point. The policy implication of the model is certainly not to develop the S and M sectors simultaneously but rather to *concentrate* resources in the M and I sectors, which comes close to advocating unbalanced growth. The reason is not the same as the one advanced in Hirschman's advocacy of unbalanced growth, which was based on the scarcity of administrative and entrepreneurial capabilities in developing countries.[13] The reason in this case (in which Hirschman's considerations do not play a role) is that multiple equilibria arise from the presence of vertical externalities. If there had been horizontal external effects between sectors M and S, the policy implications would have been different and closer to a balanced growth strategy. The example, then, suggests that policy implications of a big push model can take the form of either balanced or unbalanced growth depending on the type of external effects involved. However, it is interesting to note that the example points to the ambiguity of the terms *balanced* and *unbalanced growth:* a policy oriented toward shifting resources from sector S to sectors M and I (unbalanced growth) is also one aiming at the balanced development of sectors M and I.

Toward a Unified and Extended Research Program

Having defended development economics on empirical and theoretical grounds, it must be recognized that the original framework of development theory largely overlooked the role in underdevelopment of factors other than physical capital, infrastructure, and the narrowness of domestic markets, let alone the effective demand failures that became crucial in the 1980s, as was discussed in chapter 12. The empirical literature on convergence and the theoretical work on endogenous growth have brought attention to the role of human capital, research and development expenditures, and income inequality as well as political risk and instability. These variables affect the steady state level of income in augmented neoclassical models and the growth rate in endogenous growth models. All of these are important considerations, and we have investigated throughout this book how they can enrich and modify the framework adopted by classical development economics.

"Augmenting" a development model with skill acquisition, as was done in chapter 6, fits nicely with the growth experience of developing countries in Europe and East Asia, which featured rapid processes of *both* skill and capital deepening (see chap. 1). This model suggests, indeed, that the high rates of capital accumulation and educational progress reinforced each other: a higher skill level increases the rate of capital accumulation and a higher capital-labor ratio increases the rate of acquisition of skills. This is probably an important reason why certain economies in East Asia and Europe, and *not* other countries with similar initial conditions in education but lower investment rates, were the success stories of the last 30 years. The model in chapter 6 also features a development trap that fits well with the observation in chapter 1 that, with very few exceptions, no country was able to grow rapidly without a critical initial level of schooling.

Introducing the role of income inequality affects the steady state level of income and modifies the transitional dynamics of a development model. The road to high-income levels becomes far less smooth than what is suggested by a superficial reading of the evidence on growth acceleration at middle-income levels. The reason, I believe, is that, while there is certainly a tendency for growth to accelerate in the inter-mediate stages of the transition, inequality also tends to increase over that range of incomes, with negative effects on growth. A rapid and successful transition requires, then, the degree of initial inequality to be limited. Otherwise, inequality traps may emerge that generate economic setbacks and political instability. The integration of old and new insights on the relationship between inequality and development, as was dis-cussed in chapter 10, sheds light on the contrasting development experi-ence of middle-income economies in Latin America and Asia.

The original framework of development theory can also be ex-tended in ways that have received less attention. Chapters 8 and 9 discuss the key role of trade specialization and the channels through which it affects the rate of economic growth. These chapters also ad-dress the varying role of natural resources at low- and high-income levels and how the domestic linkages of the resource-intensive sectors of the economy influence this role. The analysis also clarified the scope and limitations of industrial policy in changing the pattern of trade specialization and in stepping up the rate of capital accumulation. In the presence of multiple equilibria, transitory shocks brought about by accidents of history were shown to have potentially long-lasting conse-quences on economic growth.

Not only can the original approach of development economics be extended in these new directions, but bringing these other factors into this particular framework sheds new light on their role in the develop-ment process. Indeed, these factors not only affect the steady state level of income, as they do in a neoclassical model, but, more importantly from the perspective of underdeveloped countries, they affect the hold of the development trap at low-income levels and the threshold level of income that needs to be achieved before a process of convergence can begin. Thus, we saw in chapter 6 that a low level of schooling may reinforce the hold of a development trap that is also due to low levels of physical capital. Chapter 8 illustrated how the scarcity of natural re-sources at low-income levels and the absence of domestic linkages in resource-rich countries can both stunt industrialization. We also dis-cussed how inequality (chap. 10) and the pattern of specialization (chap.

9) affect the threshold of convergence at which poor countries start catching up with rich ones.

Surely, not everything in development macroeconomics can be explained by extending the original framework of development theory. The contributions of later development economists, in particular, remain relevant to the short- and medium-term problems of developing countries, as was discussed in chapters 11 and 12. Yet, I believe that by extending the approach of classical development theory and blending it with the contributions of modern growth economics we can make further progress in answering two fundamental questions: why are some countries richer than others and why do some economies grow so much faster than others?

Notes

Introduction

1. This was "Avant la lettre," one might add, since most of these writings preceded the neoclassical model of growth at least as it was formalized by Solow in the mid-1950s.

2. I believe it fair to say that only Rosenstein-Rodan fully perceived the general equilibrium implications of these two assumptions taken together.

3. An example is the recent book by Barro and Sala-i-Martin (1995). The only reference there to early development theory is to Lewis's classic work (1954), which, strangely, is regarded as a big push model. There are, no doubt, exceptions, and the contributions of that early period have been the object of renewed interest in recent years (see Murphy, Shleifer, and Vishny 1989b; Krugman 1992, 1995; Rodrik 1994; Ciccone and Matsuyama 1996; Rodriguez-Clare 1996; and Skott and Ros 1997).

4. Chapter 2 addresses the empirical shortcomings of the Solow model. Mankiw (1995) summarizes them well by saying that the predictions of Solow model: (1) understate differences in incomes per capita across countries, (2) overstate the rate of convergence to the steady state, and (3) overstate differences in the rates of return on capital among capital-rich and capital-poor countries.

5. The recent book by Aghion and Howitt (1998) covers this field extensively.

6. I use the term *counterrevolution* in development theory, or in other places *neoclassical resurgence,* to indicate the partial abandonment in the 1960s of the labor surplus–increasing returns paradigm in development economics. Both of these terms are somewhat misleading, however, as there was no neoclassical development economics before the 1940s.

7. The view that the scope of classical development economics is limited to a closed economy has different sources. One of them, perhaps the most popular, is confusion between a savings trap (low income leading to low savings and investment) and a profitability trap (a low profit rate limiting investment opportunities). While the first poverty trap is easily overcome through international capital mobility, the second is not and in fact may be exacerbated by capital mobility. For a discussion of the topic, see chapters 2, 4, and 13.

8. There is in this respect an interesting analogy with Keynes's original writing and how Keynesian economics evolved over time, as captured by Leijonhufvud (1968).

9. It is worth noting the difference with Adam Smith's notion that the

division of labor is limited by the extent of the market. For Young, productivity increases with the extent of the market because the high fixed costs of increasing returns technologies can only be recovered in large markets rather than because workers can specialize in more specific tasks. It is in this sense that Young says that Smith "missed the main point" (1928, 530): the productivity gains from economies of specialization are of a second order compared to the productivity increases arising from more "roundabout" methods of production becoming profitable.

10. It is also present, and certainly fully explicit in a rather pure state, in Kaldor's later writing on economic development. For Kaldor (1967, 27–28), growth is "the result of a complex process of interaction between demand increases which have been induced by increases in supply, and increases in supply caused by increases in demand. . . . The speed of the chain reaction will be greater, the truer it is that consumers choose to buy more of those goods with a large supply response and the larger the response on the demand side caused by increases in production."

11. As discussed in chapter 6, growth is then endogenous under very restrictive assumptions such as dramatically increasing returns to scale (generating nondiminishing returns to capital as in Romer's 1986 model or the AK model), the presence of self-reproducing factors (as in Lucas's 1988 model of growth driven by human capital accumulation), or very large elasticities of substitution in production (as in Jones and Manuelli 1990).

Chapter 1

1. See, in particular, Maddison 1982, 1991, 1993.

2. These 62 countries are those for which data on the capital stock per worker are available in the Penn World Table (or Summers and Heston data set). See the appendix to this chapter.

3. Other measures such as school enrollment ratios reflect current flows of education, and adult literacy rates do not capture skills obtained beyond elementary education. For a discussion, see Barro and Lee 1993.

4. Even then, differences in natural resource endowment may have led to differences in population more than in per capita income. According to Kaldor (1967, 3): "If we go back a few hundred years for example, to 1700 or 1750, we do not find, as far as we can tell, such large differences in real income per capita between different countries or regions. The populations of most countries lived at about a subsistence level—they all had the appearance of underdeveloped countries, by present-day standards. Differences in natural endowment in climate or the fertility of the soil were fairly well balanced by differences in the density of the population; and the great majority of the population of *all* countries derived their living from primary production, that is, from agriculture."

5. In the case of the industrial employment share, the high correlation derives from the inclusion of the middle- and low-income groups (3 through 6). As shown in table 1, industrial employment shares are very similar among

groups 1 through 3 and in fact are higher in group 3 than in the high-income groups (1 and 2).

6. Data on capital per worker and mean years of schooling are not available beyond the early 1990s. This constrained the analysis of growth rates in most of this section to the period 1965–92. Later in this chapter and in chapter 2, the analysis goes beyond 1992 whenever the relevant data are available.

7. Equation 1′ is obtained by solving regression 1 for the growth rate of capital per worker, $g(k)$ and then substituting into $g(k/y) = g(k) - g(y)$. The positive and less than unit coefficient of $g(k)$ in regression 1 ensures that capital deepening is faster the higher the growth of output per worker.

8. On the development experience of Botswana, see Griffin 1989. A stable macroeconomic framework and a high savings and investment rate made possible by large natural resources rents (mining) appear to be the key to the fast rate of economic growth in Botswana.

9. See De Long 1997 and Maddison 1995. There were, however, significant changes in the rankings within this group. For example, the highest level of per capita income in 1870 was Australia's, which outpaced the United Kingdom's, in second place, by a large margin. In 1993, the United States had the highest level of per capita income, while Australia and the United Kingdom were no longer among the five richest countries.

10. For a fuller discussion, see Pritchett 1995 and De Long 1997.

11. See Kristensen 1974; Chenery and Syrquin 1975; Syrquin 1986; Baumol 1986; Abramovitz 1986; Baumol and Wolff 1988; and Lucas 1988.

12. It is worth noting that the statistical significance of this variable does not disappear when, as in regression 1, we include factor accumulation variables in the growth equation.

13. On Kaldor's laws, see Cripps and Tarling 1973 and Kaldor 1966, 1967. Chapter 4 reviews the mechanisms involved and the evidence for the Verdoorn law, which relates to the growth of productivity and output in manufacturing.

14. In any case, according to Temple (1999, 116), the correlation between growth in output per worker over the period 1960–75 and that between 1975 and 1990 is just 0.17 for the whole sample in the Summers and Heston data set.

15. This applies to Swaziland and Botswana (1989) and Nepal (1986).

Chapter 2

1. Demand is not a factor because, strictly speaking, this is a one-good, nonmonetary economy; under a more generous interpretation, monetary policy can be assumed to solve any effective demand problems that may arise.

2. The theory is also about the conditions for the existence and uniqueness of the steady state. These conditions were specified by Inada (1963; see also on this subject Wan 1971). The models in chapters 4 through 6 illustrate situations in which some of these conditions (for either existence or uniqueness) are not fulfilled.

3. Setting $E = 1$ for simplicity, the equilibrium wage can be written as w

$= b(L^{a+b-1})k^a$, where b is the output elasticity of labor in the production function. The wage does not depend on L if b is equal to $(1 - a)$, which implies constant returns to scale $(a + b = 1)$.

4. We can also look at the schedules of short- and long-run equilibria in $(\log k^E, \log y^E)$ space. The corresponding equations are 1 and 4. As the reader can verify, a comparison with equations 5 and 8 shows that the y^E and y^{E*} lines would look exactly like the w^E and w^{E*} lines in figure 9 except that their position is shifted upward by the term $\log[1/(1 - a)]$, which is positive (since $a < 1$).

5. Strictly, this is so if $s/(n + \beta + \delta) > 1$. Since $s/(n + \beta + \delta)$ is the steady state value of the capital-output ratio, the lack of fulfillment of this condition would imply implausibly low values of the capital-output ratio in the steady state and even more so below the steady state.

6. The form of equation 11 to be used is (see Mankiw, Romer, and Weil 1992):

$$g_y = (\log y^E t - \log y^E{}_0)/t = \beta + (1 - e^{-\Omega t})(\log y^{*E} - \log y^E{}_0)/t,$$

where zero refers to the initial year and t to the final year.

7. This assumption does not seem controversial given that the consistency of the Solow model with the postwar growth trends in OECD economies is generally accepted.

8. At least, this must be the case if we are to remain in the context of a one-sector model, with a fixed savings rate and a constant returns to scale technology.

9. From equations 5 and 7, the profit rate can be expressed as $r = a(E/k)^{1-a}$. Substituting this expression into equation 6, and then using $\hat{y}^E = a\hat{k}^E$ and $g_y = \beta + \hat{y}^E$, yields equation 12.

10. It may be worth recalling that we are still assuming constant returns to scale. Under this assumption, there are no obstacles, strictly speaking, to the adoption of the superior technologies no matter how small the amount of capital available to an individual investor.

11. As is readily verified, the slopes of the schedules $\hat{k}^E = 0$ and $\hat{h}^E = 0$ are respectively $(1 - a)/b$ and $a/(1 - b)$. Stability requires that the schedule $\hat{k}^E = 0$ be steeper than the schedule $\hat{h}^E = 0$. This in turn implies that $a + b < 1$. With constant returns to all capital $(a + b = 1)$, for example, the slopes of the schedules would both be equal to unity and the economy would undergo a self-sustaining process of expansion or decline depending on whether the schedule $\hat{h}^E = 0$ lies above or below the schedule $\hat{k}^E = 0$.

12. This is the variable HUMAN (in Barro and Lee 1993) that was used in chapter 1. This measure is more comprehensive than the one used by MRW since it includes schooling at all levels (primary, secondary, and higher), both complete and incomplete. The values shown in the table are averages for the period, as reported in Islam 1995.

13. Phelps cites the finding by Benhabib and Spiegel (1994) that the stock of human capital contributes negatively to a country's output per worker but positively to the rate of growth in its productivity.

14. The same point is made independently by Temple (1999, 135).

15. Compare this with the 2 percent convergence rate claimed by MRW

(1992) and other empirical studies (Barro 1991, 1997), which implies that each country moves halfway toward its steady state in thirty-five years.

16. From equation 20, the derivative of s with respect to y is:

$ds/dy = y^{-2}[(1 - \phi)\psi - \delta\kappa]$, which is positive if $(1 - \phi) > \delta\kappa/\phi$.

17. Two conditions affect the sign of the slope of the w^* schedule. First, D in equation 21 is positive if $(1 - \phi) > a\delta\kappa/\phi$. Since a is less than one, the condition for the savings rate to be an increasing function of income guarantees this inequality. The other condition involves the denominator in equation 21. For it to be positive requires $(1 - \phi)(y - \psi) + \delta k > 0$. This condition states, as is readily verified from equation 20, that income per worker must not be so low that savings per worker are negative.

18. In figure 11, the slope of the w schedule of short-run equilibria remains equal to a, the capital share. The slope conditions for multiple equilibria are guaranteed by the specification in equation 20, together with the fulfillment of the condition that the savings rate increases with income per worker. Indeed, as k tends to infinity the slope of w^* tends to zero and the w^* locus is flatter than the w schedule. When k tends to κ, the w^* locus is steeper than the w curve. The slope of w^* then tends to D/κ, which, as is readily verified, is greater than a provided that $(1 - \phi)\psi/\delta\kappa > 1$, which is the condition for the savings rate to increase with income per worker. The w^* locus is thus steeper than the w schedule at low values of k and flatter at high values of k.

19. Referring to the role of political risk in the failure of capital movements to equalize factor prices, Lucas asks: "Indeed, why did these capital movements not take place during the colonial age, under political and military arrangements that eliminated (or long postponed) the 'political risk' that is so frequently cited as a factor working against capital mobility?" (1988, 16–17).

20. Factors specific to the period 1982–95—such as the fact that many Latin American economies with relatively low RLIs were during the 1980s in the worst of the debt crisis—may, however, also have much to do with this result.

Chapter 3

1. According to Lewis: "All schools of economics have tried their hand at this [what will happen to distribution], but their favourite forecast—the falling rate of profit—has not yet come to pass" (Gersovitz 1983, 452).

2. Because it is constant, the wage premium may, if one likes, be assumed to be equal to zero (so that $f = 1$) without making any significant difference in the analysis that follows.

3. From equation 2, setting $L_M = L$, the marginal product of labor at full employment (MPL$_F$) is given by: $\text{MPL}_F = (1 - a)Ak^a$, where k is the economywide capital-labor ratio (K/L). MPL$_F$ is thus an increasing function of k.

4. A simple formulation of the idea is to make the change in the labor force an increasing function of the gap between the actual real wage and the subsistence wage: $\hat{L} = f(w - \mathsf{w})$ with $f' > 0$ and $f(0) = 0$.

5. Dividing both sides of equation 2 by L, we have:

$$L_M/L = [(1 - a)A/w_M]^{1/a}k,$$

when $L_M/L < 1$, $w_M = f w_S$ and changes in k affect L_M/L, leaving w_M constant. In contrast, when $L_M/L = 1$, w_M is determined by $w_M = (1 - a)Ak^a$ and increases in k then raise w_M.

6. As in chapter 2, the rate of capital accumulation is $I/K = (s/a)r - \delta$. The savings rate (s) is $s = s_\pi a + s_w(1 - a)$, where a and $(1 - a)$ are the profit and wage shares and s_π and s_w are the savings rates out of profits and wages, respectively. With $s_w = 0$, s equals $s_\pi a$. Substituting into the expression for the rate of accumulation yields $I/K = s_\pi r - \delta$.

7. A third possibility is that $f w_S$ happens to equal w^*. Then the initial value of k will persist over time and the two sectors will coexist indefinitely.

8. There is in Lewis's article (1954) some discussion of the factors that may bring about the fulfillment of this condition. He views technological innovations (an increase in A, which shifts the w^* locus upward) rather than an increase in thriftiness (which increases s_π) to be the mechanism that historically triggered the expansion of the capitalist sector. However, his analysis focuses on what happens after the initial expansion has taken place.

9. The savings rate (s) is equal to the savings rate out of profits times the share of profits in total output ($\pi = P/Y$, where P is total profit and $Y = M + S$). Using $a = P/M$ and $w_M = (1 - a)y_M$ together with equation 5, we can express the savings rate as $s = s_\pi a/[1 + L_S/L_M(1 - a)/f]$, where the term multiplying s_π is the profit share, an increasing function of the employment share of the capitalist sector. The savings rate thus tends toward zero (when L_M tends toward zero) and increases, throughout the labor surplus phase, toward the value $(s_\pi a)$, which prevails when the subsistence sector has disappeared.

10. Lewis has an interesting discussion of the political consequences of this: "The fact that the wage level in the capitalist sector depends upon earnings in the subsistence sector is sometimes of immense political importance, since its effect is that capitalists have a direct interest in holding down the productivity of the subsistence workers. Thus, the owners of plantations have no interest in seeing knowledge of new techniques or new seeds conveyed to the peasants" (1954, 149).

11. Exceptions include Chenery and Syrquin 1975 and, more recently, Akyüz and Gore 1996 and UNCTAD 1997.

12. Equation 13 can be written as $e = (h - 1)/[1 + (1 - b + bh)L_M/L_S]$. Since $b \leq 1$ and $h \geq 0$, the denominator of this expression is always positive. For the numerator, and thus for e, to be positive, h must be greater than one.

13. If the elasticity of substitution in consumption is unity or less, little remains of the Lewis model unless additional assumptions are introduced (more on this later). In what follows, we shall focus on the case $b < 1$ and neglect population growth. The analysis would proceed analogously in the case of a growing labor force if equation 5 were reformulated to avoid pure scale effects, so that $S = L(L_S/L)^{-b}$. We will return to the role of returns to labor in sector S later.

14. From equations 13 and 14, we have $d\log l_M/d\log k = e/(e + 1/a)$. A positive e guarantees that l_M is an increasing function of k.

15. A related, but not identical, notion is that surplus labor is the fraction of the labor force, which, when withdrawn, would make the marginal product of labor equal to that in the capitalist sector. In this case, surplus labor exists until the two sectors' MPL are equal, and therefore no output gain can be obtained by reallocating the labor force between sectors. This seems to be the sense in which Fei and Ranis (1964) use the concept.

16. Lewis himself seems ambiguous regarding the notion of labor surplus being used. This ambiguity, however, largely disappears once we recognize that there are in fact two different models in his article (1954). They have sometimes been characterized as the model without trade between the two sectors and the model with trade between the two sectors (see Lewis 1972 and Leeson 1979). My analysis suggests that a better characterization would be a one-good, two-sector model and a two-good, two-sector model.

17. As we shall see, this may imply something similar if one adds some additional but rather arbitrary assumptions about the determination of the subsistence wage.

18. If any of these assumptions, not all explicit in Fei and Ranis 1964, is violated, the increase in the agricultural surplus will fall short of the expansion in food demand outside agriculture and the terms of trade will move against industry.

19. One exception is worth noting: technical progress in agriculture now tends to reduce the real wage in terms of manufactures as the increase in food supply lowers the terms of trade. It thus stimulates employment in industry and raises the profit rate and capital accumulation.

20. The first phase is followed by one in which the MPL in agriculture becomes positive but remains below the wage in terms of food. Fei and Ranis (1964) assume that the wage remains constant as landlords have no incentive to bid it up (letting workers leave agriculture is profitable since the output lost from a worker leaving agriculture is less than the wage in terms of food that the landlord has to pay him or her). The third (or commercialization) phase begins when the MPL in agriculture eventually catches up with the wage in terms of food. The economy now behaves as under a neoclassical model with two capitalist sectors.

21. Remaining consistent with this procedure does not, however, solve all the problems since as soon as an industrial sector emerges this determination of the agricultural wage leaves the terms of trade between agriculture and industry undetermined.

22. In addition, Jorgenson assumes that the agricultural production function displays substitution possibilities between land and labor so that the MPL remains positive no matter how large the agricultural labor force is. This assumption is not critical, however, as we shall see later in Nurkse's argument.

23. It is beyond the scope of this section to discuss the shortcomings of Jorgenson's model. It may nevertheless be worth pointing out that its conclusions are critically dependent on the assumption of a closed economy.

24. Nurkse distinguished this situation from one of Keynesian unemployment, in which both investment and consumption can expand simultaneously, and from the classical situation in which, in order to increase investment, consumption must necessarily be reduced.

25. Nurkse gives the examples of Japan's "stiff land tax" in the nineteenth century and Soviet Union's system of collective farms as responses to the problem of mobilizing the savings potential.

26. The fact that $fw_S < w_M$ implies that $(w_M - w_S)/w_S > f - 1$, that is, the earnings differential is higher than the wage premium and there are no mechanisms to bring them into equality.

27. Formally, if the production conditions in sector S are given by: $S = (FL_S)^{1-b}$, where F is a productivity function of the form $F = (w_S/p)^\phi$, output per worker in sector S is given by $S/L_S = (w_S/p)^{\phi(1-b)}L_S^{-b}$, which increases with L_M for two reasons: (1) the fall in L_S raises productivity due to the presence of diminishing returns to labor in S; and (2) as the terms of trade shift in favor of sector S, F increases.

28. Although it is analogous to Keynesian unemployment in the sense that there is an excess supply of labor, this type of underemployment, just like Lewis labor surplus, is completely resilient to changes in the aggregate demand for goods.

29. See, in particular, Akerlof and Yellen 1985, 1986; and Bowles 1985.

Chapter 4

1. See Nurkse 1953, chap. 1; and Young 1928.

2. Nurkse's suggested external effects are an example of social interactions, associated with the expansion of the capitalist sector, leading to changes in attitudes and motivation. These, together with the effects of social interactions on technological diffusion and innovation, are sometimes described as dynamic technological externalities (see Stewart and Ghani 1992).

3. Arrow's (1962) original model of learning by doing makes productivity a function of cumulative gross investment.

4. Equation 4 is derived as follows. The slope of the w curve can be written as:

$$\mathrm{dlog}w_M/\mathrm{dlog}K = (\mathrm{dlog}w_M/\mathrm{dlog}L_M)(\mathrm{dlog}L_M/\mathrm{dlog}K)$$

$$= (1/e)(\mathrm{dlog}L_M/\mathrm{dlog}K). \tag{2}$$

Taking logs in equation 1 and differentiating with respect to $\log K$ yields:

$$\mathrm{dlog}L_M/\mathrm{dlog}K = (a + \mu)/a - (1/a)(\mathrm{dlog}w_M/\mathrm{dlog}K), \tag{3}$$

using $\mathrm{dlog}E^*/\mathrm{dlog}K = 0$, since the efficiency consumption wage is independent of K. Substituting from equation 3 into 2 and rearranging yields equation 4.

5. I continue to neglect, for simplicity, labor force growth.

6. This discussion will be restricted to the slope conditions for the existence of multiple equilibria. If the two schedules do not intersect, no equilibrium

with a positive capital stock will exist. In chapter 5, I will discuss this case and the reasons why it may arise.

7. The economic interpretation of this inequality is as follows. The expenditure share of the subsistence sector (α) and the labor intensity of modern sector technology $(1 - a)$ both have a positive influence on the product wage of the modern sector. In the first case, because the larger α is the more the terms of trade turn in favor of sector S, this tends to raise the product wage. In the second case, because the higher the labor intensity the more labor demand in the modern sector tends to increase, this puts upward pressure on the real wage. The condition in inequality 5, then, says that the productivity effects due to increasing returns must be large enough to offset the effects of capital accumulation on the product wage. It is then that a low K intersection—above which there is a virtuous circle of capital accumulation and profitability—will exist.

8. The following formulation generates a shape similar to that in figure 19: $(1 - \alpha)/\alpha = zw_M{}^{\eta}$. Assuming for simplicity that $b = 0$ (constant returns to labor in the S sector), the elasticity of the labor supply becomes:

$$e = [\eta + \Delta(L_M/L_S)^{\partial}]/(1 + L_M/L_S),$$

where: $\partial = \eta/[(1 - \alpha)/\alpha - \eta]$ $\Delta = [w/(1 - d)]^{\partial}/\alpha[(1 - s_{\pi}a)/(1 - a)]^{\partial}$.

When $\alpha = 1$, ∂ is negative and e falls as L_M increases. The slope of the w curve increases with L_M. When $(1 - \alpha)/\alpha > \eta$, ∂ is positive and e increases over a range with L_M. The slope of the w curve falls as L_M increases. Eventually, as α tends toward zero, ∂ tends toward zero and e falls again as L_M increases. The slope of the w curve then increases with L_M. Two low-level equilibria with positive capital stocks (one stable and one unstable) can result from this shape of the w curve.

9. Setting $w_M = w_M{}^*$ in the labor demand function (eq. 1), we can solve for K^* and k^*. Solving for the real wage involves the equality $(w_M/p)^* = (w_M/p_M)^*(p_M/p_S)^{\alpha}$ together with equation 21 in chapter 3.

10. This feature is akin to Arrow's (1962) model of learning by doing, in which the rate of per capita output growth in the steady state increases with the rate of growth of population. This implication has often been considered empirically questionable (see, e.g., Romer 1986), and this would certainly be the case if it were taken to mean that high productivity growth rates should be observed in countries with a fast-growing labor force. It is worth noting, however, that this objection seems to neglect the fact that the implication applies only to the steady state. Moreover, in the present model with two sectors the implication applies to the growth of labor productivity in the modern sector but not to aggregate output per capita, as will be discussed later.

11. From equation 6, the steady state value of the capital stock is given by:

$$K^* = (as_{\pi}/\delta)^{1/(1-a-\mu)}l_M{}^{*(1-a)/(1-a-\mu)}L^{(1-a)/(1-a-\mu)},$$

which shows that with labor force growth the steady state rate of expansion of the capital stock is:

$$n[(1 - a)/(1 - a - \mu)].$$

This is thus higher than n by an amount that depends on the size of the parameter of increasing returns.

12. It is worth noting that the real wage becomes independent of scale for $\mu = 0$ and $b = 0$ (under constant returns to scale in sector M and constant returns to labor in sector S).

13. I am neglecting, for simplicity, growth of the labor force.

14. Formally, the rate of convergence (Ω) can be written as:

$$\Omega = as_\pi r^*(r/r^* - 1)/(\log w^* - \log w).$$

Substituting from the profit-wage curve yields:

$$\Omega = as_\pi r^*[(K/K^*)^{\mu/a}(w^*/w)^{(1-a)/a} - 1]/(\log w^* - \log w),$$

where w is the product wage in the modern sector and (w^*/w) is a decreasing function of the employment share of the modern sector (and thus of K).

15. In terms of figure 17, the rate of accumulation is the highest when the gap between the w^* and w curves is the largest.

16. The scale effect, albeit small, is statistically significant, as can be seen in chapter 1, table 2.

17. Evidence in Baumol, Blackman, and Wolff 1989, Dollar 1992, and Easterly 1994, as well as that presented in chapter 1, tends to conform to the same pattern.

18. The calculation of the convergence threshold assumed a growth rate (g^*) of 1.5 percent per year.

19. As the author notes, the results may be influenced by the quality of labor force data, which vary considerably from country to country. Moreover, it is unclear whether the regressions were estimated without a constant and what the implications of this may be.

20. For simplicity, I reformulate the influence of technological externalities to avoid pure scale effects. The production function is then $Y = (\tilde{K}/L)^\mu K^a (EL)^{1-a}$. The equations of the y^E and y^{E*} curves are given by:

$$y^E = k^{Ea+\mu} \quad \text{and} \quad y^{E*} = [s/(n + \beta + \delta)]^{a/1-a} k^{E\mu/a}.$$

From these equations, we can solve for the steady state value of output per effective worker:

$$y^{E*} = [s/(n + \beta + \delta)]^{(a+\mu)/(1-a-\mu)} = [(s/(n + \beta + \delta)^{a/1-a}]^{[1+\mu/a(1-a-\mu)]}.$$

This expression is very similar to the steady state value of y^E in the Solow model (see eq. 4 in chap. 2). The difference has to do with the increasing returns parameter, whose presence enhances the positive effects of savings rates and the negative effects of labor force growth on the steady state level of income. Indeed, the effect of the increasing-returns parameter on the steady state level of income is identical to that of enlarging the capital share in the Solow model.

21. On this subject, see also Barro and Lee 1993. In the period 1965–85, the economies in the highest quintile of growth in the World Bank data reported by Barro and Lee were all developing economies with the exception of Malta, Japan, Portugal, Norway, Greece, Italy, and Finland.

22. Again according to the World Bank data reported in Barro and Lee

(1993), most of the economies in the lowest quantile of growth for 1965–86 (16 out of 22 economies) were those of low-income countries in sub-Saharan Africa and Asia. See also Sen 1993: out of the 16 countries with the lowest growth rates reported by Sen, 12 were low-income countries in sub-Saharan Africa.

23. Easterly and Levine (1997) provide support for the inverted-U pattern in regressions that include other regressors besides the log of initial income and the square term (see table 15).

24. These are the countries in our sample defined by the World Bank's *World Development Report* (1990) as severely indebted middle-income economies: Argentina, Bolivia, Brazil, Chile, Costa Rica, Ecuador, Honduras, Mexico, Nicaragua, Peru, Uruguay, Venezuela, Senegal, the Philippines, and Morocco.

25. Other findings are consistent with this pattern. Levine and Renelt's (1992) analysis of the robustness of cross-country growth regressions shows that the conditional convergence result (a negative coefficient on the initial level of per capita income) is not robust over the period 1974–89 or when OECD countries are excluded (958). This is consistent with our results since the exclusion of the set of OECD countries—which largely overlaps the set of high-income countries—leaves the country sample with (mostly) middle- and low-income economies. According to our analysis, we would not expect conditional convergence in such a country sample. Levine and Renelt's analysis and main conclusions are reviewed in chapter 9.

26. Let g_p, g_L, and g_M, respectively, be the growth rates of productivity, employment, and output. Substituting from $g_M = g_p + g_L$ into $g_p = c + vg_M$, we have $g_p = c/(1 - v) + [v/(1 - v)]g_L$. In order to have a positive relationship between productivity and employment growth, coefficient v must be less than unity.

27. In contrast, the nonindustrial sectors tend to feature negative relationships between productivity (g_p) and employment growth (g_L). For example, Cripps and Tarling's (1973) pooled regressions for developed economies in the period 1950–70 yield the following results for agriculture and mining:

Agriculture: $g_p = 2.153 - 0.919g_L$ $R^2 = .172$ $N = 42$
                              (.319)

Mining: $g_p = 2.961 - 0.799g_L$ $R^2 = .417$ $N = 42.$
                         (.160)

Standard errors are in parentheses.

28. This would include, I would argue, the weaker evidence for Verdoorn's law for cross sections of developed countries in later periods. See on this subject Cripps and Tarling 1973, which found a failure of Verdoorn's law in the period 1965–70, probably as a result of a tightening of labor markets in developed countries during this period.

Chapter 5

1. The beekeeper-orchard example, provided by Meade (1952), illustrates this direct interaction between producers. The laundry-factory example

and many other environmental effects illustrate cases of negative technological externalities (see, on this subject, Stewart and Ghani 1992).

2. Formally, as can readily be checked, when $w = 1$ there are no values of F and L for which conditions 6 and 7 can be fulfilled simultaneously.

3. This may be seen more clearly by reformulating equation 8 as $M = n^{a-1}[\Sigma(1/n)(nM_i)^\sigma]^{1/\sigma}$.

4. From equation 8, the individual demand curve facing each producer can be shown to have the following form:

$$M^d_i = \xi Y p_i^{-1/1-\sigma}/\Sigma p_k^{-\sigma/(1-\sigma)},$$

where ξ is the share of manufactures in consumption and thus $\xi/(1 - \xi) = z(w/p_M)^\eta$. The elasticity of demand facing individual producers is then implicitly given by:

$$(\mathrm{dlog}M^d_i/\mathrm{dlog}p_i)[1 + \eta(1 - \xi)/n] = -1/(1 - \sigma) + \sigma/(1 - \sigma)n - \eta(1 - \xi)/n.$$

The first term on the RHS represents the effect on demand of an individual price change while holding the average price, as well as the manufactures expenditure share, constant. The second term adjusts the first for the effect on the single producer's demand that results from the change in the average price. This effect is of opposite sign since it involves a change in the average price in the same direction as the individual price. The third term relates to the change in the expenditure share as a consequence of the change in p_i: since this share increases with the fall in the average price, the fall in p_i contributes to this increase to an extent that depends inversely on the initial expenditure share and the number of goods. We assume n to be sufficiently large so that each individual producer neglects the effects on the elasticity of the second and third terms. This implies, however, that demand appears to them to be less elastic, especially at low levels of the manufactures' expenditure share, than it actually is.

5. The key condition for the existence of multiple equilibria is that at low levels of L_M the w curve is flatter than the productivity curve. Since the slope of the w curve when $L_M \to 0$ is $1/\eta$, the condition is $a > 1 + 1/\eta$. Note, however, that at low levels of L_M (and n) it is no longer possible to ignore the effect of the number of producers on the price elasticity of demand facing individual firms (see note 4). I address the implications of this issue later.

6. From the expression for the price elasticity of demand in note 4, it is readily shown that, when $n = 1$, $\phi = 1$ and, from equation 16, $M/L_M = 0$. Taking into account the effects of n on ϕ would affect the shape of the productivity schedule but leave the mechanisms involved in the poverty trap at low levels of L_M largely intact. A monopolist ($n = 1$) cannot overcome the trap due to the nature of the external effects: even though this single producer is the whole M sector, he or she will not internalize the beneficial effects of expansion. These effects accrue to others, that is, to the additional producers who find it worthwhile to enter the sector and who, by doing so, keep the scale of the original monopolist largely intact.

7. See also Kaldor 1967, 27.

8. Related models are the "infrastructure model" in Murphy, Shleifer,

and Vishny 1989b and the models in Rodrik 1994 and Rodriguez-Clare 1996, which have multiple short-run equilibria in open economies (see chap. 9).

9. Qualitative results are unchanged if the *S* good is a good substitute for the *M* good or if there is surplus labor à la Leibenstein-Kaldor in sector *S*.

10. Qualitatively similar results can be derived from a Dixit-Stiglitz-Ethier type of specification like that used in the previous section.

11. The properties of the model are also similar to those in Berthelemy and Varoudakis 1996, except for the assumption in their model of an AK technology (see chap. 6). In Berthelemy and Varoudakis the equivalent of our *I* sector is a banking system that intermediates savings. Because it operates under economies of scale, the size of this sector is critical to the productivity of the whole economy.

12. As shown in Skott and Ros 1997, the price elasticity is given by $-\partial \log I_i/\partial \log p_i = 1/(1 - \sigma) - (a + \sigma - 1)/n(1 - \sigma)a$.

13. The condition is realistic, as it implies that economies of scale are not dramatically large.

14. Profits in the *I* sector are thus consumed. This simplifying assumption is unnecessary in an open economy with capital mobility, as we shall see in chapter 9.

Chapter 6

1. With $a + \mu > 1$, the slope of the w^* line—given by $\mu/(1 - a)$—is greater than the slope of the w line given by $a + \mu$.

2. The point that the neoclassical model can accommodate increasing returns to scale, provided that these do not generate increasing returns to capital, has been made by Solow (1988, 1994).

3. On the AK model, see Barro 1990 and Rebelo 1991.

4. For $\log w^*$ to be larger than $\log w$, the term $a/(1 - a)\log[s/(n + \delta)]$ must be positive. This in turn requires $s > n + \delta$.

5. The profit rate can be expressed as:

$$r = ak^{\mu/a}[(1 - a)/w]^{1-a/a}.$$

Substituting from equation 2 and setting $a + \mu = 1$, we obtain $r = a$. The rate of accumulation, $I/K = (sr/a) - \delta$, is thus equal in this case to $(s - \delta)$. More generally, with a production function $Y = AK$, the rate of accumulation is $sA - \delta$.

6. In intensive form, and assuming that $a + \mu = 1$, the production function is $Y/L = K/L$. The growth rate of output per worker is thus equal to the rate of capital accumulation $(s - \delta)$ minus the growth rate of the labor force (n).

7. On this subject, see Solow 1956, 70–71, as well as the contribution of Jones and Manuelli (1990).

8. More generally, the slope of the wage-profit curve can be expressed as $dw/dr = -[a/(1 - a)]^\sigma (w/r)^\sigma$.

9. The shape of the w^* curve depends on the assumption about the sav-

ings rate. Otherwise, the steady state condition would imply that $(s/\pi)r = n + \delta$, where s is the overall savings rate. Since the profit share (π) varies with the capital-labor ratio, whenever the elasticity of factor substitution differs from unity, the required value of r will also vary with k and w^* will thus not be independent of the capital-labor ratio. Although this formulation would appear to be more general, the assumption that the overall savings rate (s) remains constant in the face of changes in factor shares is in fact rather implausible.

10. As can be seen by manipulating equation 4, as k goes to infinity, F approaches a function that is linear in K: $Y = Aa^{1/\psi}K$. The marginal product of capital falls as k increases but, unlike the Solow model, it does not converge to zero. The key difference is that high elasticity of substitution makes neither capital nor labor essential for production in the sense that $F(K, L) = 0$ when $L = 0$ or $K = 0$.

11. The profit rate can be written as $r = \pi Y/K = \pi A[a + (1 - a)k^{(1-\sigma)/\sigma}]^{\sigma/(\sigma-1)}$ when k goes to infinity, π tends to 1, and r approaches $a^{\sigma/(\sigma-1)}A$.

12. This fraction is derived endogenously by Lucas, under the condition of equality between the rates of return on human and physical capital, and in his model it is constant only in the steady state.

13. Another interesting analogy, pointed out by Srinivasan (1994), is to the two-sector model of Mahalanobis (1955) and Feldman (1928, as described in Domar 1957). There, the sector producing physical capital goods uses only reproducible factors (physical capital goods). The model then generates endogenous growth without having to rely on increasing returns to scale. The equilibrium growth rate is determined by the share of investment devoted to capital accumulation in the sector producing capital goods.

14. I say "in part" because empirical research by Baumol (1986), followed by criticisms by Abramovitz (1986) and De Long (1988), was at the origin of the recent work on convergence and also motivated the initial theoretical research on endogenous growth.

15. In what follows, I restrict the discussion to models based on increasing returns and human capital accumulation. As noted, the transitional dynamics of models relying on a high elasticity of factor substitution are similar to those of the Solow model.

16. This observation does not apply (potentially) to the neo-Schumpeterian brand of endogenous growth theory in which the extent to which a developing country internalizes the external effects of technological innovations by productivity leaders may depend on investment rates. However, the focus on explaining technological advances makes these Schumpeterian models mostly relevant, so far, to highly advanced industrial countries (see Grossman and Helpman 1991, 1994; and Aghion and Howitt 1998).

17. For evidence on East Asia that strongly suggests diminishing returns to capital, see Young 1992, 1995.

18. It is of some interest to note that this is due to the Cobb Douglas technology assumed in equation 10. From equation 13, the ratio L_H/L_M is equal to the tax rate times the ratio of the profit share to the wage share in sector M (as indicated earlier). With less than unit elasticity of factor substitution, an increase

in the capital stock will, by raising wages, reduce the profit share. The equilibrium ratio L_H/L_M will thus fall and the employment share of sector M will increase.

19. The reader may verify that with a $\hat{k} = 0$ schedule that is steeper than the $\hat{h} = 0$ schedule the model in the mature phase looks like an MRW model. In the labor surplus phase, the $\hat{h} = 0$ schedule is steeper than the $\hat{k} = 0$ schedule and the model looks like an MRW model with increasing returns to all capital.

20. It is worth noting that the effect of learning by doing externalities (a positive value of μ) is largely to accentuate the virtuous circle between capital accumulation and skill acquisition. One of the broad implications of the model is then that the more returns increase in sector M (the higher μ is) and the stronger the external effects of human capital (the larger β is) the higher the growth rates observed during the transition phase will be and the faster the rates of skill deepening and of convergence toward high-income levels.

21. If we take a view of λ and δ_H such that a higher rate of population growth reduces λ and increases δ_H, a higher n also shifts the $\hat{h} = 0$ locus to the right and further accentuates the outward shift of the saddle path. For evidence supporting the view that educational achievement is adversely affected by high population growth, see Hanushek 1992 (cited in Temple 1999).

22. It is only when the S sector has disappeared, at high levels of k, that an increase in h has a positive effect on $\hat{k}$ even if $\beta = 0$.

Chapter 7

1. See, on the subject, Little, Scitovsky, and Scott 1970, Helleiner 1992, Edwards 1993, and Agosin and Ffrench-Davis 1993.

2. We are leaving aside differences in political risk (see chap. 2). Even then, income per worker will still differ because high-savings countries will be receiving dividend and interest flows from low-saving countries and incomes per capita can also differ due to variations in activity rates.

3. See Skott and Larudee 1998 for a similar dual-economy model and its application to the analysis of the liberalization of trade and capital flows in Mexico.

4. It is possible, as is shown in the appendix to this chapter, that with diminishing returns to labor in sector S and labor earnings there being the average, rather than the marginal, product of labor, both labor and capital may lose from trade. The reason is that the contraction of employment in sector M (following the opening to trade) can lead to such a fall in productivity in sector S (through, in practice, the expansion of underemployment) that, even though the product wage in sector M increases, the real consumption wage falls. The assumption of constant labor productivity in sector S (constant returns to labor) rules out this interesting and important case, which is not our main focus here.

5. This is the case independent of the fact that a second-best argument for protection must exist. Otherwise, the optimal policy intervention is a production subsidy to the capital-intensive industry. See, on this subject, Bardhan 1970.

6. If the expanding sector operated under diminishing returns to labor, these static gains would turn into losses (see the appendix to this chapter).

7. For a broader discussion, under alternative specifications of productivity growth functions, see Ros 1986. Lucas (1988) presents a model along similar lines with different rates of learning in the two sectors.

8. See, on this subject, Haberler 1961, Meier 1963, and Spraos 1980.

9. For previous formalizations and extensions of Lewis 1969, see Findlay 1981 and Bardhan 1982.

10. This is also the crux of Lewis's argument about the long-term evolution of the terms of trade between manufactures (the M good) and tropical products (the N good) as a result of faster productivity growth in the food-producing sectors of industrialized countries.

11. This assumption does not imply that changes in the relative price of food leave the consumption levels of goods N and M unaffected. Rather, its implication is that an increase, say, in the relative price of food increases (or reduces) the consumption shares of M and N goods in exactly the same proportion.

12. It is worth noting that the independence of relative wages from anything other than productivity conditions in the S sectors also applies to the long-run equilibrium (unless one of the two countries imports all the food it consumes from abroad). The long-run equilibrium terms of trade curve is obtained from the steady state values of the product wages in sectors M and N:

$$(w_1/p_M)^* = (1 - a)A_1^{1/1-a}(s_1/\delta)^{a/1-a}$$

$$(w_2/p_N)^* = (1 - a)A_2^{1/1-a}(s_2/\delta)^{a/1-a}.$$

It is easily verified that these equations generate an upward-sloping line, with unit slope, in $(w_1/w_2, p_M/p_N)$ space. As before, a technological improvement or a higher savings rate in country 1 does not increase the wage in country 1 relative to that of country 2. It increases wages in both countries to the same extent.

13. The analysis of neutral technical progress is analogous.

14. Equation 24 is derived by neglecting a secondary effect of capital accumulation and assuming the constancy of p_S/p_N. The price of food in terms of N goods (p_S/p_N) can be expressed as the product of p_S/w_2 and w_2/p_N. We know that the p_S/w_2 ratio increases. For the food market to clear, the product wage in the N sector (w_2/p_N) must increase in order to release the labor force required to expand food production in country 2. Thus, p_S/p_N must increase. This effect tends to reduce the supply of N goods and thus to moderate the potentially favorable terms of trade effects of K_1 on M goods.

Chapter 8

1. For a survey, see Corden 1984. The term has also been applied to what was perhaps the first Dutch disease: the transformation of Spain into an importer of manufactures from, ironically, the Netherlands following the large inflows of gold and silver from its colonies in the New World.

2. See Lane and Tornell 1996 and Tornell and Lane 1999 for recent models in which a natural resource boom encourages rent-seeking behavior and leads to a slowdown in economic growth. Empirical evidence and case studies lending support to these channels are in Gelb 1988, Auty 1990, and Tornell and Lane 1999. Sachs and Warner (1995) investigate this and other noneconomic and economic mechanisms, in a cross section of countries for the period 1971–89, but they find weak evidence of links between natural resource abundance (measured by the ratio of primary exports to GDP) and growth operating through bureaucratic inefficiency and corruption. We shall refer to their main conclusions later in this chapter and in chapter 9.

3. On the "specific factors" model, see Samuelson 1971, Jones 1971, and Dixit and Norman 1980.

4. Alternative specifications involving internal economies of scale in the production of nontraded inputs are considered later in this chapter and in chapter 9.

5. In agriculture, landlords hire workers, or, alternatively, tenants hire land from landlords, and competition in factor markets reduces their income to the level of manufacturing wages.

6. Without savings out of rents the w^* line is the same for both countries. Then, the fact that w_R is above w_P implies, unambiguously, that in long-run equilibrium the land-poor country has higher real wages than the land-rich economy.

7. A key aspect of the Dutch disease is that, in the presence of multiple equilibria, a *temporary* resource boom can move the economy away from high-level equilibrium. It can then remain locked into the low-level equilibrium even after the resource boom is over. Analysis of this phenomenon will be undertaken in chapter 9.

8. The real exchange rate is defined as the price ratio between tradable and nontradable goods.

9. On the staples thesis and Canada's economic development, see Innis 1930, 1940; and Watkins 1963. The approach was later applied to other "regions of recent settlement," including the United States (North 1966), Australia (McLean 1989), and Argentina in the pre-1929 period (Diaz-Alejandro 1984; Cortés Conde 1985). See Findlay and Lundahl 1994 for a survey of these contributions.

10. Under constant returns, the slope of the $w = w^*$ locus is positive, but the wage does not increase with the capital stock along the locus, since w^* is independent of the capital stock. In this case, w^* is only a function of s_M and δ.

11. With no labor mobility and an inelastic labor supply function, the locus becomes a horizontal line in (L, K) space at the exogenously given value of the labor force.

12. For a comparison of land tenure systems in Canada and Argentina in the early nineteenth century, see Solberg 1985.

13. Chapter 10 presents an explicit analysis of this case in the context of a two-sector open economy model.

14. See the infant industry model of chapter 7.

15. The presence of a resource-intensive sector affects not only the posi-

tion but also the slope of the w^* curve. The derivation of this slope is shown in the appendix to this chapter.

16. According to Maddison (1982), these four nations were among the 12 countries with highest per capita incomes in 1870, with Australia at the top of the list (with an income nearly 60 percent higher than that of the United Kingdom, the second country on the list). These countries were growing at relatively high rates, with the exception of Australia, which, as Carlos Diaz-Alejandro (1985) once observed, "was born rich." From 1870 to 1979, Australia grew at an average rate of 1.06 percent per year (Maddison 1982; compare this to the U.S. growth rate of 1.9 percent).

17. For the period 1971–89, Sachs and Warner (1995) find a negative relationship across countries between growth and the ratio of natural resource exports to GDP in the initial year (1971), a relationship that remains after controlling for other determinants of growth.

Chapter 9

1. More precisely, capital accumulation increases the wage at the initial allocation, but the increase in the wage itself implies that the initial allocation no longer satisfies the condition of profit rate equalization. The reallocation of capital toward the capital-intensive sector then brings the wage back to its initial value.

2. Related models may be found in Rodrik 1994, Rodriguez-Clare 1996, and Ciccone and Matsuyama 1996.

3. Note that the change in labor demand in sector I is an increasing function of K_M ($\mu > 0$ ensures that $a > f$).

4. If there is no effect, that is, if K_M does not appear in the profit-wage function, there will be no reallocation capable of restoring the equality of profit rates. The schedule will then be a horizontal line at the unique value of the wage that is consistent with the equality of profit rates. As can be readily verified, this is the case if $\mu = 0$, that is, when the technology of the integrated M/I sector exhibits constant returns to scale. This is the case examined in the previous section.

5. In figure 46(a), this is because the locus of the capital market remains steeper than the locus of the labor market at high levels of K_M. Necessary and sufficient conditions are $a > b$ and $f > 0$. In figure 46(b), the intersection is unique because the locus of the capital market is steeper, at low levels of K_M, than the locus of the labor market (when the latter is relatively flat).

6. For $K^* > K_1$, the following condition must be fulfilled:

$$(1 - b)/b > [(1 - a)/a](1 + \mu)(1 - 1/\phi).$$

The assumption $a > b$ implies that $(1 - b)/b > (1 - a)/a$. For the second-order condition for profit maximum among I_i producers to be fulfilled, it is necessary that $(1 + \mu)(1 - 1/\phi) < 1$ (see chap. 5). Taken together, these inequalities ensure the fulfillment of the condition above.

7. This requires, as in the previous case, that:

$$(1 - b)/b > [(1 - a)/a](1 + \mu)(1 - 1/\phi).$$

The fulfillment of this inequality is guaranteed by the same conditions as before ($a > b$ and the second-order condition for profit maximum among I_i producers).

8. In the presence of differences in the size of the labor force, the difference in the steady state level of income would also be proportional to the size of the labor force (due to the existence of increasing returns to scale in sector I).

9. Three configurations also exist in the linkage effects model and for the same reasons (see the appendix to chap. 8).

10. One source of this difference is the adoption by Rodriguez-Clare of a Dixit-Stiglitz-Ethier specification in sector I, with a preference for variety and an ever-expanding number of I goods (and with a zero profit condition in equilibrium; see chap. 5 for this type of specification).

11. For an analogous example with a Ricardian technology and a continuum of goods, see Krugman 1987.

12. In Chenery and Syrquin 1986, the trade orientation index measures the primary export bias. I use this index multiplied by minus one. This yields the manufacturing export bias.

13. At the same time, it is possible to argue that the effects of openness are dependent on the pattern of specialization that it induces (as in the model in the first section). In some North-South models, such as Young's (1991), openness can even lead to a lower rate of technological change for the South. Moreover, foreign direct investment is a major vehicle of technology transfer and there is no clear positive relationship between openness to trade and openness to foreign investment.

14. It is worth emphasizing that De Long and Summers's observation is not an objection to models in which openness—in the sense of the absence of trade barriers—has a positive effect on investment. It is an objection to using trade shares as a measure of openness. The implication, however, is that we should not interpret the correlation between investment and trade shares as evidence supporting models in which openness enhances investment.

15. I have already mentioned Rodrik's (1994) argument that a higher investment share may lead to a higher trade share as a result of increased imports of capital goods in industrializing economies. Our main focus, however, will take a different direction, partly because in Rodrik's argument causality runs from investment to trade and not the other way around.

16. This line of research is very recent, and Levine and Renelt did not include variables reflecting trade specialization in their sensitivity analysis (1992).

Chapter 10

1. For a review and synthesis of the main arguments and empirical evidence in this recent literature, see Bénabou 1996 and Perotti 1996.

2. A look at their data shows that most of their low-income countries have constant or increasing inequality over time (seven countries) or that their data are limited to one observation (six countries).

3. Interestingly, the negative association between growth and inequality in a cross section of countries was present in earlier studies on the Kuznets curve. In order to explain what factors other than per capita income affect inequality, Ahluwalia (1974, 1976) found that a higher income growth rate, along with higher enrollment rates in primary and secondary education, were associated with less inequality, given the level of income per capita.

4. The variable REV (revolutions and coups) is omitted here, for it was not statistically significant.

5. For recent case studies suggesting an important role for urban-rural disparities, and more generally for regional disparities, in explaining income distribution in Mexico and Brazil, see Bouillon, Legovini, and Lustig 1999 and Ferreira, Lanjouw, and Neri 1998.

6. Because migration takes time, higher migration reduces the level of employment in agriculture in the current period without increasing the labor supply in the urban industrial sector.

7. Unlike in previous chapters, the short-run equilibrium does not feature the equalization of labor earnings across sectors ($w_M = w_A$). This is because migration is costly and labor mobility is imperfect. The model also differs from the Harris-Todaro model, wherein the urban-rural wage differential is exogenous and the short-run equilibrium features the equalization of the expected urban wage and the rural wage. In this model, the expected urban wage, in turn, is an inverse function of the urban unemployment rate, as the probability of being employed falls as unemployment rises.

8. This is not due, however, to the increase in urban employment initially raising the probability of being employed but rather because, with imperfect labor mobility, a higher urban demand for labor raises the urban wage, which leads to a higher migration rate.

9. It is only over an intermediate range of levels of the urban labor force (relative to the capital stock) that the urban wage premium does not increase. In this range, the labor force is sufficiently small to offset the positive profitability effects on capital accumulation but too large for the upward pressure on urban wages to generate an increase in the wage premium.

10. The reader will recognize here the model of chapter 8 (third section). The particular migration function assumed yields the case with multiple equilibria (see fig. 40[b] in chap. 8).

11. In this setting, the wage premium may actually fall throughout the process of urbanization to the extent that increasing migration costs raise the supply price of labor to industry.

12. See Robinson 1976, Anand and Kanbur 1993, and Kuznets 1955.

13. This analysis does not, however, give a full account of the mechanisms envisaged by Myrdal.

14. On the role of the pattern of growth and its influence on income distribution and poverty, see among others, Griffin 1989. For a survey of recent research on the subject, see Lipton and Ravaillon 1995, sec. 5.

15. This unequalizing influence has the same effect as increasing returns in agriculture because agricultural productivity tends to decline with a decrease in the agricultural labor force. As noted in my reference to Myrdal, this redistribution of skills tends to prolong the phase of increasing inequality as well as raising the level of inequality at which the "turning point" occurs.

16. The schooling variable (S) is the rate of secondary school enrollment. It is taken to be a measure of both the level and distribution of human capital because for a sample of countries where the enrollment rate is almost always below 50 percent a measure of the distribution of schooling, $S(1 - S)$ is a monotically increasing function of S.

17. It may still be the case that a higher rate of return on capital causes both greater inequality and more growth, but the causation here does not run from inequality to growth as in the classical view. The classical view should not be confused with Kaldorian and other post-Keynesian growth models. Contrary to what is often asserted in the recent literature (see, e.g., Perotti 1996, 175; and Birdsall, Ross, and Sabot 1995, 477), the functional distribution of income does not determine investment and growth in these models and greater inequality does not cause more growth. Instead, causation runs the other way: growth and investment are the determinants of income distribution. In Kaldor 1956, for example, income distribution is the dependent variable: higher growth leads to redistribution toward profits precisely in order to generate endogenously the savings needed to finance the higher rate of accumulation. (Again, in an open economy this mechanism is partly offset by the adjustment of foreign savings).

18. Inequality is thus harmful to growth, as it leads to a more progressive redistribution of income. The nice dialectics of this reasoning is somewhat perplexing and raises at least two related questions, which were originally left unanswered in this approach: why should redistributive measures take the form of taxes that discourage investment and why cannot redistributive government spending, if applied, say, to the enhancement of human capital accumulation by the poor, be favorable to growth?

19. Perotti (1993) finds positive, albeit insignificant, coefficients on transfers in growth regressions.

20. See table 23. If anything, the relationship across Latin America is positive.

21. It is worth noting that Clarke's (1995) comprehensive analysis of "reduced form" regressions concludes that the negative correlation between inequality and growth holds for both democracies and nondemocracies. As already mentioned, empirical research on the effects of inequality operating through fiscal policy has been disappointing.

22. For recent models on endogenous fertility and its relationship to human capital and income distribution, see Becker, Murphy, and Tamura 1990; and Galor and Zang 1993.

23. On this subject, see chapter 5.

24. See Furtado 1969, Tavares and Serra 1971, Taylor and Bacha 1976, and Lustig 1980.

25. One shortcoming of this procedure is that the Kuznets curve, in my interpretation, also reflects the evolution of urban-rural disparities, which can

have adverse effects on growth. Ultimately, the shortcoming of our procedure is that there is no sharp distinction (in terms of its effects on growth) between those sources of inequality affecting the position on the Kuznets curve and those affecting deviations from it. Nevertheless, the interpretation to be given to our results stands, provided that the position on the Kuznets curve is correlated with the structure of factor returns and deviations from the Kuznets curve are correlated with the distribution of factor endowments.

26. Evoking Leibenstein's X-inefficiency is fully intentional. However, X-inequality should not be taken to mean redundant inequality, which places an economy below an "equity-efficiency frontier." Unlike Leibenstein's X-inefficiency, X-inequality can be negative.

27. The insignificance of this component of inequality should not be surprising since the channels through which its positive effect may operate on growth (rates of factor accumulation) are already included in the regression equation. We will address this issue more fully below.

28. On this subject, see also Sachs and Warner 1995.

29. It is worth noting that both equations are quadratic partly for the same reasons, the interactions between moderately increasing returns to scale and elastic labor supplies at low- and middle-income levels. Indeed, the evolution of factor returns as per capita income changes, which is one factor accounting for the Kuznets curve (eq. 13), is behind the hump-shaped patterns of growth rates (eq. 14). This implies that parameters b_1 and b_2 are not independent of a_1 and a_2.

30. With $\beta < 1$, the negative effect of inequality on growth is large at low levels of inequality and small at high levels. The fact that inequality increases in the intermediate range of incomes would in this case accentuate, rather than moderate, the inverted-U path of the growth rate.

31. Note that the inequality condition 17 may be fulfilled largely as a result of a relatively low g_y at middle-income levels, even though inequality is not particularly high. Such a situation can arise as a result of premature exhaustion of labor surpluses. The resulting growth slowdown is best described, in Kaldor's (1966) terms, as "premature maturity" rather than an inequality trap.

32. As discussed in chapter 1, Quah's (1993) work on transition probabilities estimated over the period 1962–84 finds that both upward and downward mobility is highest among middle-income economies. On the acceleration of growth at middle-income levels, see Kristensen 1974, Chenery and Syrquin 1975, Baumol 1986, Abramovitz 1986, and Baumol and Wolff 1988.

33. See Fajnzylber 1989, 1990, for a pioneer's view on the role of equity in the development experiences of Latin America and East Asia.

Chapter 11

1. See, in particular, Kalecki 1954, reprinted in Kalecki 1976.

2. Kalecki's model is often presented with output in the agricultural sector being fixed so that the price elasticity of supply is assumed to be zero (see

Taylor 1983, 1991; and Basu 1984). I prefer to allow for positive elasticity of the food supply and then explore the implications of this elasticity having a higher or lower value.

3. In the Cobb-Douglas case, for example, $AS = p^{(1-b)/b}S$ and $S = [(p_M/w_M)f(1-b)]^{(1-b)/b}bT$, where $(1-b)$ is the labor share in output.

4. It can be shown, in a more general formulation, that the slope also depends on the elasticity of food demand.

5. If agricultural workers had a positive consumption of manufactures, the higher terms of trade, by increasing employment in agriculture, would tend to increase demand for manufactures by agricultural workers. This effect would tend to offset the decline in employment in manufacturing arising from the lower consumption of manufactures by industrial workers. It would make the schedule flatter, or even positively sloped, depending on the elasticity of the food supply (and thus of agricultural labor demand) to changes in the terms of trade. More generally, the slope of the MM schedule will also depend on the price and income elasticities of food demand. The more elastic food demand is, the smaller the decline in the consumption of manufactures will be, since part of the decline in real wages will now fall upon food demand.

6. Kalecki (1976, 47) goes on to state that "two factors will be involved here: a) the inelastic supply of food leading to a fall in real wages b) the benefit of food price increases accruing not to small proprietors, but to capitalists." He explains the role of this second factor as follows: "[I]f the benefits of higher food prices accrue to landlords, merchants or money lenders, then the reduction in real wages due to the increase in food prices will not have as a counterpart an increased demand for mass consumption goods on the part of the country side; for increased profits will not be spent at all, or will be spent on luxuries." Does this mean that the result depends on the assumption that profits are not spent on M goods? The answer is no, contrary to what Kalecki suggests. A positive propensity to consume out of profits will only make the upward shift of the MM schedule larger than otherwise. The agricultural terms of trade will increase by more, since real wages in terms of food will have to fall by more to compensate for the increased consumption out of profits. But this does not change the fact that the rise in investment leaves industrial employment unaffected. The result depends on the inelastic supply in sector A and the inelasticity of food demand by industrial workers.

7. Noyola 1956 and Sunkel 1958 were the seminal contributions to the Latin American structuralist approach to inflation. See also Cardoso 1981 and Taylor 1983 on structuralist models of inflation. Dutta 1988, Patnaik 1995, and Dutt 1999 provide surveys of the theory of and evidence on the wage-goods constraint.

8. The open economy model with real wage resistance examined later in this chapter explicitly adopts an efficiency wage formulation.

9. For similar formulations, see Cardoso 1981, Taylor 1983, Basu 1984, and Dutt 1990.

10. See Ros 1993b for a review of the literature and different views on the role of conflict and coordination problems in driving wage inflation.

11. This requires that exports be unaffected by changes in I^*. This will be the case as long as L^* is less than the total labor force.

12. If the government attempts to prevent real appreciation through nominal devaluations, this will result in inflation, as will be discussed later.

13. This is true because, with import price elasticity being unity, due to our Cobb-Douglas utility function a positive export price elasticity is enough to fulfill the Marshall-Lerner condition.

14. For interpretations of high-inflation processes along these lines, see Franco 1986, Taylor 1991, and Ros 1993b.

15. See Neary and Roberts 1980 and de Janvry et al. 1991 on peasant household behavior; see Van der Willigen 1986, Taylor 1988, Berthelemy and Morrisson 1989, and Sulemane 1998 on import strangulation and the linkages between manufacturing supply and cash crop production. The present model draws on Berthelemy and Morrisson 1989 and Sulemane 1998.

16. More formally, the reason why the dismantling of price controls on manufacturing goods and real wage flexibility may not reverse the process of decline is that the flex price solution of the model has multiple equilibria due to the presence of increasing returns over a range of M output levels. In the low-level equilibrium, a small urban labor force is fully employed at a low real wage and a high L_M/I ratio. In the high-level equilibrium, a large urban labor force is fully employed at a high real wage and a low L_M/I ratio.

Chapter 12

1. More recently, Barro (1997) has argued that the inclusion of the inflation rate in growth regressions causes the Latin America dummy to become insignificant. As I shall argue later, this result is consistent with the view that the inclusion of the 1980s is critical to the significance of the dummy variables. In the case of sub-Saharan Africa, there is only one variable (the ratio of government consumption to GDP) whose omission causes the dummy to become significant.

2. More generally, one could argue that the hypothesis of limited structural flexibility in growing economies appears reasonable in explaining why they are not growing faster, but it becomes less relevant for stagnating economies that are undergoing considerable structural adjustments at the same time.

3. Contributions to this literature include Bacha 1990; Carneiro and Werneck 1988; Fanelli, Frenkel, and Winograd 1987; Taylor 1991; and Ros 1994b.

4. The assumed adjustment cost function is $V/K = (f/2)(I/K)^2$, where V is the adjustment cost.

5. See Rowthorn 1981, Dutt 1984, Taylor 1985, Bhaduri and Marglin 1990, and, for an earlier discussion, Steindl 1952.

6. The model is thus free from the objection that in the steady state firms' actual capacity utilization may in general not be equal to the desired degree of capacity utilization.

7. The accounting framework is therefore expressed in real terms in two

ways: nominal income and expenditure flows are deflated and financial returns are net of inflation. Real incomes are thus defined as real expenditure plus the change in real financial wealth (see Coutts, Godley, and Gudgin 1984; and Ros 1993a).

8. Under our earlier assumptions on price-setting behavior, the inflation rate is the same regardless of whether it is measured in terms of investment goods prices or the price of domestic sales.

9. Under high inflation, the greater uncertainty about expected real interest rates and exchange rates, especially in the absence of indexation, favors capital flight and, to the extent that foreign assets and domestic investment are substitutes, has a negative effect on private investment. Other reasons for including the inflation rate (with negative effects) among the determinants of private investment are the resource misallocation effects of high inflation associated with the greater price variability and uncertainty about future returns as well as the premature amortization of business sector liabilities. This premature amortization results in an increase in effective financial costs and is a consequence of higher nominal interest rates in the absence of full financial indexation.

10. The debt traps in which the economy may fall as a result are discussed in Ros 1999. Note that in what follows, by neglecting debt dynamics, we ignore the interactions between the interest payment on external debt and the current account deficit.

11. Derivation of equation 10 uses:

$$\Delta H/K = (\Delta H/H)(H/K) = (\Delta H/H)h \quad h = H/K$$

$$\Delta B/K = (\Delta B/B)(B/K) = (\Delta B/B)b \quad b = B/K$$

and

$$\Delta D_G/K = (\Delta D_G/D_G)(D_G/K) = (\Delta D_G/D_G)d_G \quad d_G = D_G/K.$$

12. Equation 10 can also be derived from the definition of the sustainable *primary* deficit. Abstracting from the external debt, the sustainable primary deficit is given by the following expression:

primary deficit $= (g + \pi)h + (g - r_B)b$.

Adding the real interest payments on domestic debt $(r_B b)$ to this sustainable primary deficit and subtracting the inflation tax (πh) yield the sustainable real fiscal deficit $(i_G - s_G$ in our definition):

real deficit $=$ primary deficit $+ r_B b - \pi h = g(h + b)$.

13. Alternatively, if the asset market constraints on government spending are always binding, the economy converges along the $r(g)$ line to the equilibrium rates of profit and accumulation.

14. The treatment of private capital inflows differs formally from the more conventional ones, which specify an explicit function for net capital inflows. The demand for domestic bonds, then, is implicitly determined by the private sector budget constraint. Our treatment also reflects a difference in the approach itself. Foreign assets and domestic investment are close substitutes here: a fall in

private investment will lead to a reduction in net capital inflows, even when interest rate differentials remain unchanged. For many developing countries, this seems more appropriate than the conventional approach for at least one reason: foreign direct investment, which is as procyclical as overall private investment, is an important component of net private capital inflows.

15. If the demand for bonds is not fully inelastic, bond-financed increases in public investment can be made sustainable by increasing the interest rate (and thus the stock demand for bonds, b, and bond seignorage, gb). But this possibility operates within rather narrow limits. First, increases in b will be partly offset by reductions in h, so that the sustainable fiscal deficit will increase by less than bond seignorage. Second, when the real interest rate exceeds the growth rate, the impact of interest payments on the fiscal deficit itself ($r_B \Delta b$) will exceed the gain in bond seignorage ($g \Delta b$), leading to a downward adjustment in public investment (rather than an increase) in order to maintain equilibrium in domestic asset markets. For a discussion of this subject, see Ros 1991.

16. Alternatively, the model can be closed by using the balance of payments identity. Setting the change in international reserves equal to zero, it becomes the equilibrium condition in the foreign exchange market. Using the specification for imports and the relationship between the profit rate and the export ratio implicit in equation 3, we can rewrite the balance of payments equilibrium condition as:

$$\Delta d_P = (\theta \mu - \tilde{d}_G)g + r/\tau(1 - t) + r^* d_G - (1 + a/\tau)\theta v.$$

17. Regressions including the square of the income term were also estimated. The main effect of including this term (which shows a consistently negative sign) was to turn the coefficient on initial income (nonsquared) from negative to positive. I do not reproduce the results here, as they are similar to those reported in chapter 4.

18. Given the recent financial and debt crisis in East Asia, this disappointing performance may also turn out to be a phenomenon predating the late 1990s.

19. The scope for shifting the foreign exchange constraint through a real devaluation is of course a major difference from conventional two-gap models. In the early elasticity-pessimism versions of these models, the locus of (growth and real exchange rates) combinations would be horizontal.

Chapter 13

1. Interestingly, however, Nurkse made use of the parable to explain why the number of nails to be driven determined whether a stone or a hammer technique was called for; the latter involved a more roundabout process of production but was more productive when the number of nails was large (see chap. 4).

2. This point, critical of the neoclassical model, is made by De Long 1997.

3. A threshold level of investments, below which there is no chance of succeeding, seems to be the defining characteristic of the big push argument for Rosenstein-Rodan: "Proceeding 'bit by bit' will not add up in its effects to the

sum total of the single bits. A minimum quantum of investment is a necessary, though not sufficient, condition of success. This, in a nutshell, is the contention of the theory of the big push" (1961, 57). A threshold level of investment, in turn, is a defining characteristic of a model with multiple equilibria.

4. Export conditions appear at two points in the 1943 article. On page 203 it is noted that: "International investment in the nineteenth century was largely self-liquidating, based on exchange of agrarian and industrial products. Nowadays liquidation can no longer be assumed to be 'automatic,' although the problem can be solved if it is properly planned." On page 209, he returns to this question:

> Liquidation will have to planned—i.e. one part of the industries created in Eastern and South-Eastern Europe will have to be export industries. . . . The placing of these exports has to be planned and foreseen in such a way as to minimize the burden of necessary adjustment in the creditor countries. Eastern and South-Eastern Europe will most probably cease to be an exporter of cereals. It will export processed foods and light industrial articles.
>
> International trade in the nineteenth century functioned more or less smoothly because all countries had a high income elasticity of demand for imports. On the higher standard of living in the rich countries of the twentieth century the income elasticity of demand for imports may be lower. There may be only one good for which the income elasticity of demand is high: leisure which does not require imports of material goods. Accordingly, the rich countries may have to accept a part of their share in economic expansion in the form of more leisure.

5. See, for example, Rao 1952 and his warnings against "a rather unintelligent application—not on Keynes's part—of what may be called Keynesian economics to the problems of the underdeveloped countries" (206–7).

6. See also Taylor and Arida's (1988) survey of development theories, which, based on Basu's model, places Rosenstein-Rodan and Nurkse's contributions under the heading "Demand-Driven Models."

7. More explicitly, he noted "the circular relationship in which the decision to invest in large-scale production depended on the size of the market, and the size of the market depended on the decision to invest. Whatever the practical relevance of this theory, it made perfectly good logical sense" (Krugman 1995, 23).

8. The same applies to an open economy version of a model with efficiency wages as long as Kaldorian underemployment exists in the traditional sector.

9. Besides making a low-K intersection more likely, the higher elasticity of labor supply has another consequence. The w curve is flatter in the open economy case. This tends to generate a higher real wage in the high-level equilibrium. In this equilibrium, the M sector is larger than under autarky and wages benefit from the productivity gains associated with the expansion of the M sector as well as from the lower cost of imported S goods. We came across this result in chapter 7.

10. All of this is, incidentally, quite consistent with Rosenstein-Rodan's views: "International trade undoubtedly reduces the size of the minimum push

Notes to Pages 371-73

required, so that not *all* the wage-goods need be produced in the developing country, but it does not eliminate it. . . . International trade does much to reduce the danger of monopolies. It also effectively reduces the size of the minimum quantum of investment. But it does not dispense with the need for a big push" (1961, 63, 65).

11. To facilitate the comparison with the previous case, we assume that the intermediate input is in the nature of a fixed cost. The price of the intermediate good is then independent of output volume in any individual sector, but it falls with the number of sectors that industrialize.

12. "The fact that our authors, other than Allyn Young, seem to lay more emphasis on the 'horizontal' rather than the 'vertical' variant of the balanced-growth doctrine is probably due to the fact that the external economies underlying the former are less frequently discussed in the literature than those underlying the latter. But the 'horizontal' transmission of economies may have been neglected by Marshall and his commentators precisely because, where it exists at all, it is relatively unimportant" (Fleming 1955, 250).

13. Hirschman's (1958) criticism of balanced growth was based mostly on feasibility considerations: "This is, of course, the major bone I have to pick with the balanced growth theory: its application requires huge amounts of precisely those abilities which we have identified as likely to be very limited in supply in underdeveloped countries" (52–53).

References

Abramovitz, M. 1952. Economics of growth. In B. F. Haley, ed., *A Survey of Contemporary Economics*. Homewood, IL: Richard D. Irwin.

Abramovitz, M. 1986. Catching up, forging ahead, and falling behind. *Journal of Economic History* 46:385–406.

Adelman, I., and S. Robinson. 1988. Income distribution and development. In H. Chenery and T. N. Srinivasan, eds., *Handbook of Development Economics,* vol. 2. Amsterdam: Elsevier Science Publishers.

Aghion, P., and P. Howitt. 1998. *Endogenous Growth Theory.* Cambridge: MIT Press.

Agosin, M., and R. Ffrench-Davis. 1993. Trade liberalization and growth: Recent experiences in Latin America. *CEPAL Review* 50 (August): 41–62.

Ahluwalia, M. 1974. Income inequality: Some dimensions of the problem. In H. Chenery et al., eds., *Redistribution with Growth.* New York: Oxford University Press.

Ahluwalia, M. 1976. Inequality, poverty, and development. *Journal of Development Economics* 3:307–42.

Akerlof, G. A., and J. L. Yellen. 1985. A near-rational model of the business cycle, with wage and price inertia. *Quarterly Journal of Economics* 100: S823–38.

Akerlof, G. A., and J. L. Yellen. 1986. *Efficiency Wage Models of the Labor Market.* New York: Cambridge University Press.

Akyuz, Y., and C. Gore. 1996. The investment-profits nexus in East Asian industrialization. *World Development* 24:461–70.

Alesina, A., S. Ozler, N. Roubini, and P. Swagel. 1996. Political instability and economic growth. *Journal of Economic Growth* 1:193–215.

Alesina, A., and R. Perotti. 1994. The political economy of growth: A critical survey of the recent literature. *World Bank Economic Review* 8:351–71.

Alesina, A., and D. Rodrik. 1994. Distributive politics and economic growth. *Quarterly Journal of Economics* 109:465–90.

Amsden, A. E. 1989. *Asia's Next Giant: South Korea and Late Industrialization.* New York: Oxford University Press.

Anand, S., and S. M. R. Kanbur. 1993a. The Kuznets process and the inequality-development relationship. *Journal of Development Economics* 40:25–52.

Anand, S., and S. M. R. Kanbur. 1993b. Inequality and development: A critique. *Journal of Development Economics* 41:19–43.

Arrow, K. J. 1962. The economic implications of learning by doing. *Review of Economic Studies* 29:155–73.

Auty, R. M. 1990. *Resource-Based Industrialization: Sowing the Oil in Eight Developing Countries.* New York: Oxford University Press.

Azariadis, C., and A. Drazen. 1990. Threshold externalities in economic development. *Quarterly Journal of Economics* 105:501–26.

Azariadis, C. 1996. The economics of poverty traps. Part 1: Complete markets. *Journal of Economic Growth* 1:449–86.

Bacha, E. L. 1984. Growth with limited supplies of foreign exchange: A reappraisal of the two-gap model. In M. Syrquin, L. Taylor, and L. Westphal, eds., *Economic Structure and Performance.* Orlando, FL: Academic Press.

Bacha, E. L. 1990. A three-gap model of foreign transfers and the GDP growth rate in developing countries. *Journal of Development Economics* 32:279–96.

Baer, W., and I. Kerstenetzky. 1964. *Inflation and Growth in Latin America.* New Haven: Yale University Press.

Bairam, E. I. 1987. The Verdoorn law, returns to scale, and industrial growth: A review of the literature. *Australian Economic Papers* 26:20–42.

Bardhan, P. 1970. *Economic Growth, Development, and Foreign Trade: A Study in Pure Theory.* New York: Wiley Interscience.

Bardhan, P. 1982. Unequal exchange in the world of Lewis. In M. Gersovitz, C. Diaz-Alejandro, G. Ranis, and M. Rosenzweig, eds., *The Theory and Experience of Economic Development: Essays in Honor of Sir W. Arthur Lewis.* London: George Allen and Unwin.

Barro, R. J. 1990. Government spending in a simple model of endogenous growth. *Journal of Political Economy* 98 (5):103–25.

Barro, R. J. 1991. Economic growth in a cross section of countries. *Quarterly Journal of Economics* 106:407–44.

Barro, R. J. 1997. *Determinants of Economic Growth.* Cambridge: MIT Press.

Barro, R. J., and J. Lee. 1993a. International comparisons of educational attainment. *Journal of Monetary Economics* 32:363–94.

Barro, R. J., and J. Lee. 1993b. Losers and winners in economic growth. *Proceedings of the World Bank Annual Conference on Development Economics, 1993.* Supplement to the *World Bank Economic Review* and the *World Bank Research Observer.*

Barro, R. J., and J. Lee. 1994. Data set of a panel of 138 countries, obtained from nber.org.

Barro, R. J., and X. Sala-i-Martin. 1995. *Economic Growth.* New York: McGraw-Hill.

Basu, K. 1984. *The Less Developed Economy: A Critique of Contemporary Theory.* Oxford: Basil Blackwell.

Basu, K. 1997. *Analytical Development Economics: The Less Developed Economy Revisited.* Cambridge: MIT Press.

Baumol, W. J. 1986. Productivity growth, convergence, and welfare: What the long-run data show. *American Economic Review* 76:1072–86.

Baumol, W. J., S. A. Blackman, and E. W. Wolff. 1989. *Productivity and American Leadership: The Long View.* Cambridge: MIT Press.

Baumol, W. J., and E. W. Wolff. 1988. Productivity, convergence, and welfare: Reply. *American Economic Review* 78:1155–59.

Becker, G., K. Murphy, and R. Tamura. 1990. Human capital, fertility, and growth. *Journal of Political Economy 98* (5):S12–37.

Bénabou, R. 1996. Inequality and growth. In B. S. Bernanke and J. Rotemberg, eds., *NBER Macroeconomics Annual.* Cambridge: MIT Press.

Benhabib, J., and M. M. Spiegel. 1994. The role of human capital in economic development: Evidence from aggregate cross-country data. *Journal of Monetary Economics* 34:143–73.

Bernard, A. B., and C. I. Jones. 1996. Technology and convergence. *Economic Journal* 106:1037–44.

Berthelemy, J. C., and C. Morrisson. 1989. *Agricultural Development in Africa and the Supply of Manufactured Goods.* Paris: OECD.

Berthelemy, J. C., and A. Varoudakis. 1996. Economic growth, convergence clubs, and the role of financial development. *Oxford Economic Papers* 48:300–28.

Bertola, G. 1993. Market structure and income distribution in endogenous growth models. *American Economic Review* 83:1184–99.

Bhaduri, A., and S. Marglin. 1990. Unemployment and the real wage: The economic basis for contesting political ideologies. *Cambridge Journal of Economics* 14:375–93.

Bhagwati, J. N. 1958. Immiserizing growth: A geometrical note. *Review of Economic Studies* 25:201–5.

Bhagwati, J. N. 1985. *Essays on Development Economics.* Vol. 1. Cambridge: MIT Press.

Birdsall, N., D. Ross, and R. Sabot. 1995. Inequality and growth reconsidered: Lessons from East Asia. *World Bank Economic Review* 9:477–508.

Bouillon, C., A. Legovini, and N. Lustig. 1999. Can education explain income inequality in Mexico? Inter-American Development Bank. Mimeo

Bourguignon, F., and C. Morrisson. 1990. Income distribution, development, and foreign trade: A cross-sectional analysis. *European Economic Review* 34:1113–32.

Bowles, S. 1985. The production process in a competitive economy: Walrasian, Marxian, and neo-Hobbesian models. *American Economic Review* 75:16–36.

Cardoso, E. A. 1981. Food supply and inflation. *Journal of Development Economics* 8:269–84.

Carneiro, D., and R. Werneck. 1988. External debt, economic growth, and fiscal adjustment. Texto para Discussao, no. 202, Departamento de Economia, PUC/Rio.

Chenery, H. B., and M. Bruno. 1962. Development alternatives in an open economy: The case of Israel. *Economic Journal* 72:79–103.

Chenery, H. B., and A. M. Strout. 1966. Foreign assistance and economic development. *American Economic Review* 56:679–733.

Chenery, H. B., and M. Syrquin. 1975. *Patterns of Development, 1950–1970.* London: Oxford University Press.

Chenery, H. B., and M. Syrquin. 1986. The semi-industrial countries. In H. B.

Chenery, S. Robinson, and M. Syrquin, eds., *Industrialization and Growth: A Comparative Study.* New York: Oxford University Press for the World Bank.

Ciccone, A., and K. Matsuyama. 1996. Start up costs and pecuniary externalities as barriers to economic development. *Journal of Development Economics* 49:33–60.

Clarke, G. 1995. More evidence on income distribution and growth. *Journal of Development Economics* 47:403–27.

Corden, W. M. 1984. Booming sector and Dutch disease economics: Survey and consolidation. *Oxford Economic Papers* 36:359–80.

Corden, W. M., and J. P. Neary. 1982. Booming sector and de-industrialisation in a small open economy. *Economic Journal* 92:825–48.

Cortés Conde, R. 1985. The export economy of Argentina, 1880–1930. In R. Cortés Conde and S. Hunt, eds., *The Latin American Economies: Growth and the Export Sector, 1880–1930.* London and New York: Macmillan.

Coutts, K., W. Godley, and G. Gudgin. 1984. *Inflation Accounting of Whole Economic Systems.* Cambridge: Department of Applied Economics, University of Cambridge.

Cripps, T. F., and R. J. Tarling. 1973. *Growth in Advanced Capitalist Economies, 1950–1970.* Cambridge: Cambridge University Press.

De Janvry, A., et al. 1991. Peasant household behaviour with missing markets: Some paradoxes explained. *Economic Journal* 101:1400–1417.

De Long, J. B. 1988. Productivity growth, convergence, and welfare: Comment. *American Economic Review* 78:1138–54.

De Long, J. B. 1997. Cross-country variations in national economic growth rates: The role of technology. In J. Fuhrer and J. Sneddon Little, eds., *Technology and Growth.* Boston: Federal Reserve Bank of Boston.

De Long, J. B., and L. H. Summers. 1991. Equipment investment and economic growth. *Quarterly Journal of Economics* 106:445–502.

Deininger, K., and L. Squire. 1996. A new data set measuring income inequality. *World Bank Economic Review* 10:565–91.

Diaz-Alejandro, C. 1984. No less than one hundred years of Argentine economic history. In G. Ranis et al., eds., *Comparative Development Perspectives.* Boulder: Westview.

Diaz-Alejandro, C. 1985. Argentina, Australia, and Brazil before 1929. In D. C. Platt and G. di Tella, eds., *Argentina, Australia, and Canada: Studies in Comparative Development, 1870–1965.* New York: St. Martin's.

Dixit, A. K., and V. D. Norman. 1980. *The Theory of International Trade.* Cambridge: Cambridge University Press.

Dixit, A. K., and J. Stiglitz. 1977. Monopolistic competition and optimum product diversity. *American Economic Review* 72:389–405.

Dollar, D. 1992. Outward-oriented developing economies really do grow more rapidly: Evidence from 95 LDCs, 1976–1985. *Economic Development and Cultural Change* 40:523–44.

Domar, E. 1957. *Essays in the Theory of Economic Growth.* London: Oxford University Press.

Dutt, A. K. 1984. Stagnation, income distribution, and monopoly power. *Cambridge Journal of Economics* 8:25–40.

Dutt, A. K. 1990. *Growth, Distribution, and Uneven Development.* Cambridge: Cambridge University Press.

Dutt, A. K. 1999. Demand and wage-goods constraints in agriculture-industry interaction in less-developed countries: A theoretical analysis. In A. Bose, D. Ray, and A. Sarkar, eds., *Essays in Honor of Mihir Rakshit.* Forthcoming.

Dutta, J. 1988. The wage-goods constraint on a developing economy: Theory and evidence. *Journal of Development Economics* 28 (3):341–63.

Easterly, W. 1994. Economic stagnation, fixed factors, and policy thresholds. *Journal of Monetary Economics* 23:525–57.

Easterly, W., and R. Levine. 1997. Africa's growth tragedy: Policies and ethnic divisions. *Quarterly Journal of Economics* 112 (4): 1203–50.

Edwards, S. 1993. Openness, trade liberalization, and growth in developing countries. *Journal of Economic Literature* 31 (3): 1358–98.

Esteban, J., and D. Ray. 1994. On the measurement of polarization. *Econometrica* 62:819–51.

Ethier, W. J. 1982. National and international returns to scale in the modern theory of international trade. *American Economic Review* 72:389–405.

Fajnzylber, F. 1989. *Industrialización en América Latina: De la "Caja Negra" al "Casillero Vacío."* Cuadernos de la CEPAL. Santiago de Chile: CEPAL.

Fajnzylber, F. 1990. *Unavoidable Industrial Restructuring in Latin America.* Durham and London: Duke University Press.

Fanelli, J. M., R. Frenkel, and C. Winograd. 1987. *"Argentina," Stabilization, and Adjustment Policies and Programmes.* Country Studies, no. 12. Helsinki: WIDER.

Fei, J., and G. Ranis. 1961. A theory of economic development. *American Economic Review* 51:533–65.

Fei, J., and G. Ranis. 1964. *Development of the Labor Surplus Economy.* Homewood, IL.: Irwin.

Feldman, G. A. 1928. K teorii tempov narodnogo dokhoda. *Planovoe Khoziaistvo* 11:146–70. Discussed in E. Domar, *Essays in the Theory of Economic Growth* (London: Oxford University Press, 1957).

Ferreira, F., P. Lanjouw, and M. Neri. 1998. *The Urban Poor in Brazil in 1996: A New Poverty Profile Using PPV, PNAD, and Census Data.* World Bank, Urban Poverty Strategy, background paper.

Fields, G. 1975. Rural-urban migration, urban unemployment and underemployment, and job-search activity in LDCs. *Journal of Development Economics* 2:165–87.

Fields, G., and G. Jakubson. 1994. New evidence on the Kuznets Curve. Cornell University. Mimeo

Findlay, R. 1981. The fundamental determinants of the terms of trade. In S. Grassman and E. Lundberg, eds. *The World Economic Order: Past and Prospects.* New York: Saint Martin's.

Findlay, R., and M. Lundahl. 1994. Natural resources, vent for surplus, and the staples theory. In G. M. Meier, ed., *From Classical Economics to Development Economics*. New York: St. Martin's.

Fishlow, A. 1995. Inequality, poverty, and growth: Where do we stand? In M. Bruno and B. Pleskovic, eds., *Annual World Bank Conference on Development Economics, 1995*. Supplement to the *World Bank Economic Review* and the *World Bank Research Observer*.

Fleming, J. M. 1955. External economies and the doctrine of balanced growth. *Economic Journal* 65:241–56.

Franco, G. 1986. Aspects of the economics of hyperinflations: Theoretical issues and historical studies of four European hyperinflations in the 1920s. Ph.D. diss., Department of Economics, Harvard University.

Frankel, J. A., and D. Romer. 1999. Does trade cause growth? *American Economic Review* 89:379–99.

Furtado, C. 1969. Desarrollo y estancamiento en América Latina: Un enfoque estructuralista. In A. Bianchi, ed., *América Latina: Ensayos de Interpretación Económica*. Santiago: Ed. Universitaria.

Galor, O., and H. Zang. 1993. Fertility, income distribution, and economic growth: Theory and cross country evidence. Brown University. Mimeo.

Galor, O., and J. Zeira. 1993. Income distribution and macroeconomics. *Review of Economic Studies* 60:35–52.

Gelb, A. H. 1988. *Windfall Gains: Blessing or Curse?* New York: Oxford University Press.

Gerschenkron, A. 1962. *Economic Backwardness in Historical Perspective*. Cambridge: Harvard University Press.

Gersovitz, M., ed. 1993. *Selected Economic Writings of W. Arthur Lewis*. New York: New York University Press.

Gomulka, S. 1971. *Inventive Activity, Diffusion, and the Stages of Economic Growth*. Aarhus: Institute of Economics and Aarhus University Press.

Graham, F. 1923. Some aspects of protection further considered. *Quarterly Journal of Economics* 37:199–227.

Griffin, K. 1989. *Alternative Strategies of Economic Development*. London: Macmillan.

Grossman, G. M., and E. Helpman. 1991. *Innovation and Growth in the Global Economy*. Cambridge: MIT Press.

Grossman, G. M., and E. Helpman. 1994. Endogenous innovation in the theory of growth. *Journal of Economic Perspectives* 8:23–44.

Haavelmo, T. 1954. *A Study in the Theory of Economic Evolution*. Amsterdam: North-Holland.

Haberler, G. 1961. Terms of trade and economic development. In H. S. Ellis, ed., *Economic Development for Latin America*. New York: St. Martin's.

Haggard, S., and S. B. Webb. 1993. What do we know about the political economy of economic policy reform? *World Bank Research Observer* 8:143–68.

Hall, R. E. 1988. Intertemporal substitution in consumption. *Journal of Political Economy* 96:339–57.

Hanushek, E. 1992. The trade-off between child quantity and quality. *Journal of Political Economy* 100 (1):84–117.

Harris, J. R., and M. Todaro. 1970. Migration, unemployment, and development: A two-sector analysis. *American Economic Review* 60:126–42.

Harrod, R. F. 1939. An essay on dynamic theory. *Economic Journal* 49:14–33.

Helleiner, G., ed. 1992. *Trade Policy, Industrialization, and Development: New Perspectives.* New York: Oxford University Press.

Heston, A., and R. Summers. 1996. International price and quantity comparisons: Potentials and pitfalls. *American Economic Review* 86 (2):20–24.

Hirschman, A. 1958. *The Strategy of Economic Development.* New Haven: Yale University Press.

Hirschman, A. 1977. A generalized linkage approach to development, with special reference to staples. *Economic Development and Cultural Change* 25:S67–98.

Inada, K. 1963. On a two-sector model of economic growth: Comments and a generalization. *Review of Economic Studies* 30:119–27.

Innis, H. A. 1930. *The Fur Trade in Canada: An Introduction to Canadian Economic History.* Toronto: University of Toronto Press.

Innis, H. A. 1940. *The Cod Fisheries: The History of an International Economy.* Toronto: University of Toronto Press.

Islam, N. 1995. Growth empirics: A panel data approach. *Quarterly Journal of Economics* 110:1127–70.

Jones, L. E., and R. E. Manuelli. 1990. A convex model of equilibrium growth: Theory and policy implications. *Journal of Political Economy* 98:1008–28.

Jones, R. W. 1971. A three-factor model in theory, trade, and history. In J. N. Bhagwati et al., eds., *Trade, Balance of Payments, and Growth: Essays in Honor of C. P. Kindleberger.* Amsterdam: North-Holland.

Jorgenson, D. 1961. The development of a dual economy. *Economic Journal* 71:309–34.

Jorgenson, D. 1967. Surplus agricultural labour and the development of a dual economy. *Oxford Economic Papers* 19:288–312.

Kaldor, N. 1956. Alternative theories of distribution. *Review of Economic Studies* 23:83–100.

Kaldor, N. 1957. A model of economic growth. *Economic Journal* 67:591–624.

Kaldor, N. 1966. *Causes of the Slow Rate of Economic Growth of the United Kingdom.* Cambridge: Cambridge University Press.

Kaldor, N. 1967. *Strategic Factors in Economic Development.* Ithaca: Cornell University. Frank W. Pierce Memorial Lectures, October 1966. Geneva, NY: W. F. Humphrey Press.

Kaldor, N. 1968. Productivity and growth in manufacturing industry: A reply. *Economica* 35:385–91.

Kaldor, N., and J. A. Mirrlees. 1962. A new model of economic growth. *Review of Economic Studies* 29:174–92.

Kalecki, M. 1954. El problema del financiamiento del desarrollo económico. *El Trimestre Económico* 21:381–401.

Kalecki, M. 1976. *Essays on Developing Economies.* Hassocks, UK: Harvester Press.

Keefer, P., and S. Knack. 1997. Polarization, property rights, and the links between inequality and growth. Manuscript.

King, R. G., and R. Levine. 1993. Finance and growth: Schumpeter might be right. *Quarterly Journal of Economics* 108:717–37.

King, R. G., and S. T. Rebelo. 1993. Transitional dynamics and economic growth in the neoclassical model. *American Economic Review* 83:908–31.

Knack, S., and P. Keefer. 1995. Institutions and economic performance: Empirical tests using alternative measures of institutions. IRIS Working Papers, no. 109.

Kravis, I. 1960. International differences in the distribution of income. *Review of Economics and Statistics* 42 (November): 408–16.

Kristensen, T. 1974. *Development in Rich and Poor Countries.* New York: Praeger.

Krugman, P. 1987. The narrow moving band, the Dutch disease, and the competitiveness consequences of Mrs. Thatcher: Notes on trade in the presence of dynamic scale economies. *Journal of Development Economics* 27 (October): 41–55.

Krugman, P. 1992. Toward a counter-counterrevolution in development theory. In *Proceedings of the World Bank Annual Conference on Development Economics, 1992.* Supplement to the *World Bank Economic Review* and the *World Bank Research Observer.*

Krugman, P. 1995. *Development, Geography, and Economic Theory.* Cambridge: MIT Press.

Krugman, P., and L. Taylor. 1978. Contractionary effects of devaluation. *Journal of International Economics* 8:445–56.

Kuznets, S. 1955. Economic growth and income inequality. *American Economic Review* 45:1–28.

Kuznets, S. 1963. Quantitative aspects of the economic growth of nations. Part 8: Distribution of income by size. *Economic Development and Cultural Change* 11 (January): 1–80.

Lane, P., and A. Tornell. 1996. Power, growth, and the voracity effect. *Journal of Economic Growth* 1 (2):213–41.

Leamer, E. 1988. Measures of openness. In R. Baldwin, ed., *Trade Policy Issues and Empirical Analysis.* National Bureau of Economic Research Conference Report Series, Chicago: University of Chicago Press.

Leeson, P. F. 1979. The Lewis model and development theory. *Manchester School of Economic and Social Studies* 66:196–210.

Leibenstein, H. 1957. *Economic Backwardness and Economic Growth.* New York: Wiley.

Leijonhufvud, A. 1968. *On Keynesian Economics and the Economics of Keynes.* New York: Oxford University Press.

Levine, R., and D. Renelt. 1992. A sensitivity analysis of cross-country growth regressions. *American Economic Review* 82:942–63.

Lewis, A. 1954. Economic development with unlimited supplies of labor. *Manchester School of Economic and Social Studies* 28:139–91.

Lewis, A. 1958. Unlimited labor: Further notes. *Manchester School of Economic and Social Studies* 32:1–32.

Lewis, A. 1969. *Aspects of Tropical Trade, 1883–1965.* Stockholm: Almqvist & Wicksell. Wicksell Lectures.

Lewis, A. 1972. Reflections on unlimited labor. In L. E. di Marco, ed., *International Economics and Development (Essays in honour of Raoul Prebisch)*. New York: Academic Press.

Lewis, A. 1976. Development and distribution. In A. Cairncross and M. Puri, eds., *Essays in Honor of Hans Singer*. New York: Holms & Meier.

Lipton, M., and M. Ravaillon. 1995. Poverty and policy. In J. Behrman and T. Srinivasan, eds., *Handbook of Development Economics*. Vol. 3B. Amsterdam: Elsevier.

Little, I. 1982. *Economic Development: Theory, Policy, and International Relations*. New York: Basic Books.

Little, I., T. Scitovsky, and M. Scott. 1970. *Industry and Trade in Some Developing Countries*. London: Oxford University Press.

Londregan, J., and K. Poole. 1990. Poverty, the coup trap, and the seizure of executive power. *World Politics* 42:151–83.

Loury, G. 1981. Intergenerational transfers and the distribution of earnings. *Econometrica* 49:843–67.

Lucas, R. E., Jr. 1988. On the mechanics of economic development. *Journal of Monetary Economics* 22:3–42.

Lucas, R. E., Jr. 1990. Why doesn't capital flow from rich to poor countries? *American Economic Review* 80 (May): 92–96.

Lucas, R. E., Jr. 1993. Making a miracle. *Econometrica* 61:251–72.

Lustig, N. 1980. Underconsumption in Latin American economic thought: Some considerations. *Review of Radical Political Economics* 12:35–43.

Maddison, A. 1982. *Phases of Capitalist Development*. Oxford: Oxford University Press.

Maddison, A. 1991. *Dynamic Forces in Capitalist Development*. Oxford: Oxford University Press.

Maddison, A. 1993. Explaining the economic performance of nations. In W. Baumol, R. Nelson, and E. Wolff, eds., *Convergence of Productivity*. Oxford: Oxford University Press.

Maddison, A. 1995. *Monitoring the World Economy, 1820–1992*. Paris: OECD.

Mahalanobis, P. C. 1995. The approach to operational research to planning in India. *Sankhya: The Indian Journal of Statistics* 16:3–62.

Mankiw, G. 1995. The growth of nations. *Brookings Papers on Economic Activity* 1:275–310.

Mankiw, G., D. Romer, and D. Weil [MRW]. 1992. A contribution to the empirics of economic growth. *Quarterly Journal of Economics* 107:407–37.

Mazumdar, D. 1959. The marginal productivity theory of wages and disguised unemployment. *Review of Economic Studies* 26:190–97.

McCombie, J. S. L. 1983. Kaldor's law in retrospect. *Journal of Post Keynesian Economics* 5:414–29.

McLean, I. W. 1989. Growth in a small open economy: A historical view. In B. Chapman, ed., *Australian Economic Growth*. Melbourne: Macmillan.

Meade, J. E. 1952. External economies and diseconomies in a competitive situation. *Economic Journal* 62:54–67.

Meier, G. M. 1963. *International trade and development*. New York: Harper and Row.

Mill, J. S. 1848. *Principles of Political Economy.* London: J. W. Parker.

Murphy, K., A. Shleifer, and R. Vishny. 1989a. Income distribution, market size, and industrialization. *Quarterly Journal of Economics* 104:537–64.

Murphy, K., A. Shleifer, and R. Vishny. 1989b. Industrialization and the big push. *Journal of Political Economy* 97:1003–26.

Myint, H. 1958. The classical theory of international trade and the underdeveloped countries. *Economic Journal* 68:317–33.

Myrdal, G. 1957. *Economic Theory and Underdeveloped Regions.* London: Duckworth.

Neary, J. P., and K. W. Roberts. 1980. The theory of household behaviour under rationing. *European Economic Review* 13:25–42.

Nelson, R. 1956. A theory of the low level equilibrium trap in underdeveloped economies. *American Economic Review* 46:894–908.

North, D. 1966. *The Economic Growth of the United States, 1790–1860.* New York: Norton.

Noyola, J. F. 1956. El desarrollo económico y la inflación en México y otros países latinoamericanos. *Investigación Económica* 16:603–48.

Nurkse, R. 1952. Some international aspects of the problem of economic development. *American Economic Review* 42 (May): 571–83.

Nurkse, R. 1953. *Problems of Capital Formation in Underdeveloped Countries.* New York: Oxford University Press.

Nurkse, R. 1961. *Patterns of Trade and Development.* New York: Oxford University Press.

OECD. 1992. *OECD Economic Surveys: Mexico.* Paris: OECD.

OECD. 1996. *Historical Statistics.* Paris: OECD.

Olivera, J. 1964. On structural inflation and Latin American structuralism. *Oxford Economic Papers* 16:321–32.

Pack, H. 1994. Endogenous growth theory: Intellectual appeal and empirical shortcomings. *Journal of Economic Perspectives* 8:55–72.

Pasinetti, L. 1981. *Structural Change and Economic Growth.* Cambridge: Cambridge University Press.

Patnaik, P. 1995. Introduction. In P. Patnaik, ed., *Macroeconomics.* New Delhi: Oxford University Press.

Perotti, R. 1993. Fiscal policy, income distribution, and growth. Columbia University, Department of Economics. Mimeo.

Perotti, R. 1996. Growth, income distribution, and democracy: What the data say. *Journal of Economic Growth* 1:149–87.

Persson, T., and G. Tabellini. 1994. Is inequality harmful for growth? Theory and evidence. *American Economic Review* 84:600–621.

Phelps, E. 1995. Comment on Mankiw. *Brookings Papers on Economic Activity* 1:313–20.

Pritchett, L. 1995. *Divergence, Big Time.* Policy Research Working Papers, no. 1522. Washington, DC: World Bank.

Quah, D. T. 1993. Galton's fallacy and tests of the convergence hypothesis. *Scandinavian Journal of Economics* 95:427–43.

Ranis, G. 1995. Another look at the East Asian miracle. *World Bank Economic Review* 9:509–34.

Rao, V. K. R. V. 1952. Investment, income, and the multiplier in an underdeveloped economy. *Indian Economic Review* 1:55–67. Reprinted in A. N. Agarwala and S. P. Singh, eds., *The Economics of Underdevelopment.* Delhi: Oxford University Press, 1958.

Rebelo, S. 1991. Long run policy analysis and long run growth. *Journal of Political Economy* 99:500–521.

Robinson, S. 1976. A note on the U-hypothesis relating income inequality and economic development. *American Economic Review* 66:437–40.

Rodriguez-Clare, A. 1996. The division of labor and economic development. *Journal of Development Economics* 49:3–32.

Rodrik, D. 1994. Getting interventions right: How South Korea and Taiwan grew rich. NBER Working Papers, no. 4964.

Romer, P. M. 1986. Increasing returns and long-run growth. *Journal of Political Economy* 94:1002–37.

Romer, P. M. 1989. Human capital and growth: Theory and evidence. NBER Working Papers, no. 3173.

Romer, P. M. 1990a. Capital, labor, and productivity. *Brookings Papers on Economic Activity* (special issue): 337–420.

Romer, P. M. 1990b. Endogenous technological change. *Journal of Political Economy* 98(2): 71–102.

Romer, P. M. 1991. Increasing returns and new developments in the theory of growth. In W. Barnett, ed., *Equilibrium Theory and Applications: Proceedings of the 6th International Symposium in Economic Theory and Econometrics.* Cambridge: Cambridge University Press.

Romer, P. M. 1994. The origins of endogenous growth. *Journal of Economic Perspectives* 8:3–22.

Romer, P. 1995. Comment on Mankiw. *Brookings Papers on Economic Activity* 1:313–20.

Ros, J. 1986. Trade, growth, and the pattern of specialisation. *Political Economy* 2.55–71.

Ros, J. 1987. Mexico from the oil boom to the debt crisis: An analysis of policy responses to external shocks, 1978–1985. In R. Thorp and L. Whitehead, eds., *Latin American Debt and the Adjustment Crisis.* Oxford: Macmillan.

Ros, J. 1991. La movilidad del capital y la eficacia de la política con una corrida del crédito. *El Trimestre Económico* 58:561–88.

Ros, J. 1992. Capital mobility and policy effectiveness under a credit run: The Mexican economy in the 1980s. In T. Banuri and J. Schor, eds., *Financial Openness and National Autonomy.* New York: Oxford University Press.

Ros, J. 1993a. Aspectos macroeconómicos de la estabilización heterodoxa. In J. Ros, ed., *La Edad de Plomo del Desarrollo Latinoamericano.* Mexico City: Fondo de Cultura Económica.

Ros, J. 1993b. Inflación inercial y conflicto distributivo. In J. Ros, ed., *La Edad de Plomo del Desarrollo Latinoamericano.* Mexico City: Fondo de Cultura Económica.

Ros, J. 1994a. La Economia Mexicana en el largo plazo. Paper presented at the Fundación Barros Sierra Conference on Mexico's Long Term Prospects, Mexico City. Mimeo.

Ros, J. 1994b. Fiscal and foreign exchange constraints on growth. In A. Dutt, ed., *New Directions in Analytical Political Economy.* Aldershot and Brookfield: Edward Elgar.

Ros, J. 1995a. Mercados financieros, flujos de capital y tipo de cambio en México. *Economía Mexicana* 4:5–67.

Ros, J. 1995b. Trade liberalization with real appreciation and slow growth: Sustainability issues in Mexico's trade policy reform. In G. Helleiner, ed., *Manufacturing for Export in the Developing World.* London: Routledge.

Ros, J. 1999. Employment, structural adjustment, and sustainable growth in Mexico. *Journal of Development Studies.* Forthcoming.

Ros, J., and P. Skott. 1998. Dynamic effects of trade liberalization and currency overvaluation under conditions of increasing returns. *Manchester School of Economic and Social Studies* 66(4): 466–89.

Rosenstein-Rodan, P. 1943. Problems of industrialization in Eastern and South-Eastern Europe. *Economic Journal* 53:202–11.

Rosenstein-Rodan, P. 1961. Notes on the theory of the big push. In H. Ellis, ed., *Economic Development for Latin America.* New York: St. Martin's. Proceedings of a Conference held by the IEA.

Rosenstein-Rodan, P. 1984. Natura facit saltum: Analysis of the disequilibrium growth process. In G. Meier and D. Seers, eds., *Pioneers in Development.* New York: Oxford University Press. Published for the World Bank.

Rowthorn, R. 1979. A note on Verdoorn's law. *Economic Journal* 89:131–33.

Rowthorn, R. 1981. Demand, real wages, and economic growth. *Studi Economici* 18:2–53.

Rowthorn, R., and R. Kozul-Wright. 1998. Globalization and economic convergence: An assessment. UNCTAD Discussion Papers, no. 131.

Sachs, J. D., and A. M. Warner. 1995. Natural resource abundance and economic growth. National Bureau of Economic Research Working Papers, no. 5398. NBER.

Sachs, J. D., and A. M. Warner. 1997. Fundamental sources of long-run growth. *American Economic Review* 87 (May): 184–88.

Sala-i-Martin, X. 1997. I just ran two million regressions. *American Economic Review* 87 (May): 178–83.

Samuelson, P. A. 1971. Ohlin was right. *Swedish Journal of Economics* 73:365–84.

Sarkar, P. 1998. The catching-up debate: A statistical investigation. Helen Kellogg Institute for International Studies Working Papers, no. 252. University of Notre Dame.

Schumpeter, J. 1947. *Capitalism, Socialism, and Democracy.* New York: Harper and Brothers.

Scitovsky, T. 1954. Two concepts of external economies. *Journal of Political Economy* 62:143–51.

Sen, A. 1966. Peasants and dualism with or without surplus labor. *Journal of Political Economy* 74:425–50.

Sen, A. 1993. Economic regress: Concepts and features. In *Proceedings of the World Bank Annual Conference on Development Economics 1993.* World

Bank. Supplement to the *World Bank Economic Review* and the *World Bank Research Observer.*

Sheehey, E. J. 1996. The growing gap between rich and poor countries: A proposed explanation. *World Development* 24:1379–84.

Skott, P., and M. Larudee. 1998. Uneven development and the liberalization of trade and capital flows: The case of Mexico. *Cambridge Journal of Economics* 22:277–95.

Skott, P., and J. Ros. 1997. The "big push" in an open economy with non tradable inputs. *Journal of Post Keynesian Economics* 20:149–62.

Smith, A. [1776] 1904. *An Inquiry into the Nature and Causes of the Wealth of Nations.* E. Cannan edition. New York: G. P. Putnam's Sons.

Solberg, C. E. 1985. Land tenure and land settlement: Policy and patterns in the Canadian prairies and the Argentine pampas, 1880–1930. In D. C. Platt and G. di Tella, eds., *Argentina, Australia, and Canada: Studies in Comparative Development, 1870–1965.* New York: St. Martin's.

Solow, R. M. 1956. A contribution to the theory of economic growth. *Quarterly Journal of Economics* 70:65–94.

Solow, R. M. 1979. Another possible source of wage stickiness. *Journal of Macroeconomics* 1:79–82.

Solow, R. M. 1988. *Growth Theory: An Exposition.* Oxford: Oxford University Press.

Solow, R. M. 1994. Perspectives on growth theory. *Journal of Economic Perspectives* 8:45–54.

Spraos, J. 1980. The statistical debate on the net barter terms of trade between primary commodities and manufactures. *Economic Journal* 90:107–28.

Srinivasan, T. N. 1994. Long run growth theories and empirics: Anything new? Paper presented at the Endogenous Growth and Development Conference at the International School of Economic Research, University of Siena, July 3–9, Certosa di Pontignano, Siena, Italy.

Steindl, J. 1952. *Maturity and Stagnation in American Capitalism.* Oxford: Basil Blackwell.

Stewart, F., and E. Ghani. 1992. Externalities, development, and trade. In G. Helleiner, ed., *Trade Policy, Industrialization, and Development.* New York: Oxford University Press.

Stiglitz, J. 1976. The efficiency wage hypothesis, surplus labor, and the distribution of labor in LDCs. *Oxford Economic Papers* 28:185–207.

Stiglitz, J. 1992. Comment on "Toward a Counter-Counterrevolution in Development Theory" by Krugman. In *Proceedings of the World Bank Annual Conference on Development Economics, 1992.* World Bank. Supplement to the *World Bank Economic Review* and the *World Bank Research Observer.*

Stolper, W., and P. Samuelson. 1941. Protection and real wages. *Review of Economic Studies* 9:58–73.

Sulemane, J. 1998. Economic decline: A study with reference to Mozambique. Department of Economics, University of Notre Dame. Mimeo.

Summers, R., and A. Heston. 1984. Improved international comparisons of real product and its composition, 1950–1980. *Review of Income and Wealth* 30:207–62.

Summers, R., and A. Heston. 1988. A new set of international comparisons of real product and price levels estimates for 130 countries, 1950–85. *Review of Income and Wealth* 34:1–26.

Summers, R., and A. Heston. 1991. The Penn World Table (Mark 5): An expanded set of international comparisons, 1950–1988. *Quarterly Journal of Economics* 106:327–68.

Sunkel, O. 1958. La inflación chilena: Un enfoque heterodoxo. *El Trimestre Económico* 25:570–99.

Sunkel, O. 1960. Inflation in Chile: An unorthodox approach. *International Economic Papers* 10:107–31.

Swan, T. W. 1955. Longer-run problems of the balance of payments. In H. W. Arndt and W. M. Corden, eds., *The Australian Economy: A Volume of Readings.* Melbourne: Cheshire.

Syrquin, M. 1986. Productivity growth and factor reallocation. In H. Chenery, S. Robinson, and M. Syrquin, eds., *Industrialization and Growth: A Comparative Study.* New York: Oxford University Press.

Tavares, M. C. y J. Serra. 1971. Más allá del estancamiento: Una discusión sobre el estilo de desarrollo reciente. *El Trimestre Económico* 33:905–50.

Taylor, L. 1983. *Structuralist Macroeconomics: Applicable Models for the Third World.* New York: Basic Books.

Taylor, L. 1985. A stagnationist model of economic growth. *Cambridge Journal of Economics* 9:383–403.

Taylor, L. 1988. *Varieties of Stabilization Experience.* Oxford: Clarendon.

Taylor, L. 1991. *Income Distribution, Inflation, and Growth: Lectures on Structuralist Macroeconomic Theory.* Cambridge: MIT Press.

Taylor, L., and P. Arida. 1988. Long-run income distribution and growth. In H. Chenery and T. Srinivisan, eds., *Handbook of Development Economics.* Vol. 1. Amsterdam: North-Holland.

Taylor, L., and E. L. Bacha. 1976. The unequalizing spiral: A first growth model for Belindia. *Quarterly Journal of Economics* 90:187–219.

Temple, J. 1999. The new growth evidence. *Journal of Economic Literature* 37 (1): 112–56.

Thirlwall, A. P. 1983. A plain man's guide to Kaldor's laws. *Journal of Post Keynesian Economics* 5:345–58.

Todaro, M. P. 1969. A model of labor migration and urban unemployment in less developed countries. *American Economic Review* 59:138–48.

Todaro, M. P. 1994. *Economic Development.* 5th ed. New York: Longman.

Tornell, A., and P. Lane. 1999. The voracity effect. *American Economic Review* 89 (1): 22–46.

UNCTAD. 1994. *Handbook of International Trade and Development Statistics, 1993.* Geneva: United Nations.

UNCTAD. 1997. *Trade and Development Report.* New York and Geneva: United Nations.

UNDP. Various years. *Human Development Report.* New York: Oxford University Press.

United Nations. 1950. *The Economic Development of Latin America and Its Principal Problems.* New York: United Nations.

United Nations. 1976. *Statistical Yearbook, 1975.* New York: United Nations.

Van der Willigen, T. 1986. Cash crop production and the balance of trade in a less developed economy: A model of temporary equilibrium with rationing. *Oxford Economic Papers* 38:424–42.

Verdoorn, P. J. 1949. Fattori che regolano lo sviluppo della produttivita del lavoro [Factors governing the growth of labor productivity]. *L'Industria* 1:3–10.

Viner, J. 1931. Cost curves and supply curves. *Zeitschrift fur Nationalokonomie* 3:23–46. Reprinted in American Economic Association, *Readings in Price Theory.* London: Allen and Unwin.

Wade, R. 1990. *Governing the Market: Economic Theory and the Role of Government in East Asian Industrialization.* Princeton: Princeton University Press.

Wan, H. Y., Jr. 1971. *Economic Growth.* New York: Harcourt Brace Jovanovich.

Watkins, M. H. 1963. A staple theory of economic growth. *Canadian Journal of Economics and Political Science* 29:141–58.

Williamson, J. G. 1991. *Inequality, Poverty, and History.* Cambridge: Basil Blackwell.

Williamson, J. G. 1993. Human capital deepening, inequality, and demographic events along the Asia-Pacific Rim. In N. Ogawa, G. W. Jones, and J. Williamson, eds., *Human Resources in Development along the Asia-Pacific Rim.* Singapore: Oxford University Press.

World Bank. Various issues. *World Development Report.* New York: Oxford University Press.

World Bank. 1999. *World Development Indicators 1999.* CD-ROM. Washington, DC.

You, J-I. 1994. Macroeconomic structure, endogenous technical progress and growth. *Cambridge Journal of Economics* 18:213–33.

Young, A. 1928. Increasing returns and economic progress. *Economic Journal* 38:527–42.

Young, A. 1992. A tale of two cities: Factor accumulation and technical change in Hong Kong and Singapore. In O. J. Blanchard and S. Fischer, eds., *NBER Macroeconomics Annual,* 13–54. London and Cambridge: MIT Press.

Young, A. 1995. The tyranny of numbers: Confronting the statistical realities of the East Asian growth experience. *Quarterly Journal of Economics* 110:641–80.

Index

Abramovitz, M., 16, 129, 379n.11, 390n. 14, 398n. 32
Absolute convergence, 26, 28. *See also* convergence
Activity rate, 22–23, 33, 122
Adelman, I., 266
Africa, 72, 266–68. *See also* sub-Saharan Africa
Aghion, P., 377n. 5, 390n. 16
Agosin, M., 391n. 1
Agricultural surplus, 90–91, 305–6, 311, 383n. 18, 399n. 3
Ahluwalia, M., 283, 396n. 3
Akerlof, G. A., 384n. 29
AK model, 4, 12, 159–61, 163, 168, 171, 359, 361, 378n. 11, 389n. 3, 389n. 11
Akyuz, Y., 382n. 11
Alesina, A., 285–87, 289, 299
Amsden, A., 253
Anand, S., 266, 396n. 12
Argentina, 25–26, 30, 81–83, 226, 234, 284, 286, 351, 356–57, 393nn. 9–12
Arida, P., 7, 403n. 6
Arrow, K., 101–2, 384n. 3, 385n. 10
Asia, 28, 45, 266–68, 287–88, 350. *See also* East Asia
Australia, 18, 226, 234, 379n. 9, 393n. 9, 394n. 16
Auty, R. M., 393n. 8
Azariadis, C., 24, 107, 180

Bacha, E., 314, 397n. 24, 400n. 5
Backward linkages. *See* linkages
Baer, W., 312
Bairam, E. I., 130

Balanced growth, 147, 372–73
Bangladesh, 82–83
Bardhan, P., 391n. 5, 392n. 9
Barro, R., 26, 64, 66, 107, 124, 126, 269, 332, 339–40, 377n. 3, 378n. 3, 380n. 12, 381n. 15, 386nn. 21–22, 389n. 3, 400n. 1
Basu, K., 305, 310, 364, 398n. 2, 399n. 9, 403n. 6
Baumol, W., 28, 119–20, 379n. 11, 386n. 17, 390n. 14, 398n. 32
Becker, G., 397n. 22
Bénabou, R., 269, 286, 288, 395n. 1
Benhabib, J., 380n. 13
Bernard, A. B., 52
Berthelemy, C., 171, 389n. 11, 400n. 15
Bertola, G., 285
Bhaduri, A., 289, 337, 400n. 3
Bhagwati, J., 212, 222, 362–63, 369–70
Big push model, 12, 15, 102–11, 135–40, 147–55, 227, 229–32, 362–66, 369–73. *See also* profitability trap
Birdsall, N., 169–70, 288, 299, 397n. 17
Blackman, S., 386n. 17
Bolivia, 82, 357
Botswana, 25, 28, 379n. 8
Bouillon, C., 396n. 5
Bourguignon, F., 283–84, 294
Bowles, S., 384n. 29
Brazil, 82–83, 286, 351, 356–57, 396n. 5

Cameroon, 82
Canada, 18, 226, 234, 393nn. 9–12